TWENTIETH-CENTURY
LITERATURE READER:
TEXTS AND DEBATES

Twentieth-Century Literature: Texts and Debates

The series comprises:

Aestheticism and Modernism: Debating Twentieth-Century Literature 1900–1960, edited by Richard Danson Brown and Suman Gupta, published by Routledge in association with The Open University.

The Popular and the Canonical: Debating Twentieth-Century Literature 1940–2000, edited by David Johnson, published by Routledge in association with The Open University.

A Twentieth-Century Literature Reader: Texts and Debates, edited by Suman Gupta and David Johnson, published by Routledge in association with The Open University.

A
TWENTIETH-CENTURY
LITERATURE READER:
TEXTS AND DEBATES

edited by

Suman Gupta and David Johnson

Routledge
Taylor & Francis Group

LONDON AND NEW YORK

in association with

The Open
University

First published 2005
by Routledge
2 Park Square, Milton Park, Abingdon, Oxon OX14 4RN

Simultaneously published in the USA and Canada
by Routledge
270 Madison Ave, New York, NY 10016

Routledge is an imprint of the Taylor & Francis Group

Typeset in Garamond Three
by Florence Production Ltd, Stoodleigh, Devon

Printed and bound in Great Britain by
MPG Books Ltd, Bodmin

British Library Cataloguing in Publication Data
A catalogue record for this book is available from the British Library

Library of Congress Cataloging in Publication Data
A catalog record for this book has been requested

ISBN 0–415–35170–7 (hbk)
ISBN 0–415–35171–5 (pbk)

This text forms part of an Open University course
A300 *Twentieth Century Literature: Texts and Debates*. Details of this and other
Open University courses can be obtained from the Course Reservations Centre,
PO Box 724, The Open University, Milton Keynes MK7 6ZS,
United Kingdom: tel +44 (0)1908 653231

For availability of this or other course components,
contact Open University Worldwide Ltd, The Berrill Building, Walton Hall,
Milton Keynes MK7 6AA, United Kingdom:
tel +44 (0)1908 858585, fax +44 (0)1908 858787,
e-mail ouwenq@open.ac.uk

Alternatively, information can be found at The Open University's website:
http://www.open.ac.uk

CONTENTS

ACKNOWLEDGEMENTS

Every effort has been made to obtain permission to reprint all the extracts included. Persons entitled to fees for any extract reprinted here are invited to apply in writing to the publishers. Permission given by the authors and copyright holders for the following extracts is gratefully acknowledged.

2   George Orwell, 'Review of *The Novel Today* by Philip Henderson' from *The Collected Essays, Journalism and Letters of George Orwell, Volume 1: An Age Like This, 1920-1940*, edited by Sonia Orwell and Ian Angus, © 1968 by Sonia Brownwell and renewed 1996 by Mark Hamilton, reprinted by permission of Harcourt, Inc. (© George Orwell, 1936) by permission of Bill Hamilton as the Literary Executor of the Estate of the Late Sonia Brownwell Orwell and Secker & Warburg Ltd.

3   *The Collected Poems of Wilfred Owen* edited by C. Day Lewis, published by Chatto & Windus. Reprinted by permission of The Random House Group Ltd.

4   'Review of an English performance of *The Cherry Orchard*', unsigned notice in *The Times* 30 May 1911. Reprinted by permission of *The Times*/NI Syndication.

5   Beverley Hahn, 'A Note on Translations', pp. ix–xiii in B. Hahn (ed) *Chekhov: A Study of the Major Stories and Plays*, 1977. © Cambridge University Press, reproduced with permission.

6   pp. 167–168 (*c.*500 words) from 'Peasant Benefactor and Chronicler' from *A New Life of Anton Chekhov* by Chekhov translated and edited by Hingley, Ronald (1976). By permission of Oxford University Press.

7   Anatoly Smeliansky, 'Chekhov at the Moscow Art Theatre', pp. 29–40 in Gottlieb and Allain (eds), *The Cambridge Companion to Chekhov*, 2000. © Cambridge University Press, reproduced with permission.

8   Reprinted from Sydney Jane Kaplan, *Katherine Mansfield and the Origins of Modernist Fiction* pp. 114–17. © 1991 by Cornell University Press. Used by permission of the publisher, Cornell University Press.

9   With permission of Macmillan Education for the material from Clare Hanson and Andrew Gurr, *Katherine Mansfield*, 1981, Macmillan.

ACKNOWLEDGEMENTS

11   A. Bennett and N. Royle, 'Pleasure' from *An Introduction to Literature, Criticism and Theory: Key Critical Concepts*, 1995, Prentice Hall. Reprinted by permission of Pearson Education Ltd.

12.1, 12.2, 12.3   Reproduced by permission of the Estate of the late Mrs J. L. Mitchell.

13.2   Compton MacKenzie, 'Four Good Novels. Some Young Authors of Promise'. *Daily Mail*, 13 September 1932. Reprinted by permission of The Society of Authors as the Literary Representative of the Estate of Compton MacKenzie.

13.3   Anonymous review of *Sunset Song: A Novel*. By Lewis Grassic Gibbon, *The Fife Herald and Journal,* 21 September 1932, by permission of *The Fife Herald*; author's reply (to the editor), *The Fife Herald and Journal*, 28 September 1932. © The Estate of the late Mrs J. L. Mitchell.

14.1   Neil M. Gunn, 'Nationalism in Writing: Tradition and Magic in the Work of Lewis Grassic Gibbon', *The Scots Magazine*, October 1938. Reproduced by permission of the Neil Gunn Literary Estate.

14.2   James Barke, 'Lewis Grassic Gibbon', *Left Review*, 2.5, February 1936, pp. 220–5. Reproduced by permission of David Higham Associates.

14.3   Keith Dixon, 'The Gospels According to Saint Bakunin: Lewis Grassic Gibbon and Libertarian Communism', in M. P. McCulloch and S. M. Dunnigan (eds) *A Flame in the Mearns. Lewis Grassic Gibbon: A Centenary Celebration*, 2003, Association for Scottish Literary Studies. Reproduced by permission of ASLS and Keith Dixon.

15   W. H. Auden, 'Introduction' in *The Oxford Book of Light Verse*, Clarendon Press, 1938, © 1938 by W. H. Auden. Reprinted by permission of Curtis Brown, Ltd.

16   Virginia Woolf, 'The Leaning Tower', in *Collected Essays*, vol. 2, The Hogarth Press, 1966, reprinted by permission of The Society of Authors as the Literary Representative of the Estate of Virginia Woolf.

17   Arthur Symons, 'Jules Laforgue' in *The Symbolist Movement in Literature*, Heinemann 1899. Reproduced by permission of the Estate of Arthur Symons.

18.2   Henri Bergson, from *Matter and Memory*, translated by N. M. Paul and W. Scott Palmer, Macmillan, 1911. Reproduced by permission of Zone Books.

19   Wyndham Lewis (ed.), *Blast*, vol. 1. © Wyndham Lewis and the Estate of the late Mrs G. A. Wyndham Lewis by kind permission of the Wyndham Lewis Memorial Trust (a registered charity).

20.1   Excerpts from T. S. Eliot 'Tradition and the Individual Talent' in *Selected Essays*, 1932. Reprinted by permission of the publisher, Faber & Faber Ltd.

20.2   T. E. Hulme, 'Romanticism and Classicism' from *Speculations: Essays on Humanism*, ed. H. Reed, 1924, Routledge & Kegan Paul. Reproduced by permission of the publisher.

21   Excerpts from *The Diary Of Virginia Woolf*, vol. III: 1925–1930 by Virginia Woolf, © 1980 by Quentin Bell and Angelica Garnett, published by Hogarth Press. Reprinted by permission of Harcourt, Inc. and The Random House Group Ltd.

22   Virginia Woolf, 'Mr Bennett and Mrs Brown', in *Collected Essays*, vol. 1, The Hogarth Press, 1966, reprinted by permission of The Society of Authors as the Literary Representative of the Estate of Virginia Woolf.

23   Excerpts from *A Room Of One's Own* by Virginia Woolf, © 1929 by Harcourt, Inc. and renewed 1957 by Leonard Woolf, reprinted by permission of the publisher and The Society of Authors as the Literary Representative of the Estate of Virginia Woolf.

24–26   Excerpts from *Brecht on Theatre* edited and translated by John Willett. Translation © 1964, renewed 1992 by John Willett. Reprinted by permission of Hill and Wang, a division of Farrar, Straus and Giroux, LLC and Methuen Publishing Ltd.

27   Ernst Schumacher, 'The Dialectics of *Galileo*', *TDR: The Drama Review*, vol. 12, issue # 2, 1968. Reprinted by permission of *TDR*.

29   From *Labyrinths with Path of Thunder* by Christopher Okigbo. Reprinted by permission of Harcourt Education.

30   Excerpts from Daphne du Maurier, *The Rebecca Notebook*, published by Victor Gollancz, a division of The Orion Publishing Group. © The Chichester Partnership 1981. Reproduced with permission of the publisher and Curtis Brown Ltd, London on behalf of The Chichester Partnership.

31   Excerpts from Freud: Sigmund Freud © The Institute of Psycho-Analysis and The Hogarth Press for permission to quote from *The Standard Edition of the Complete Psychological Works of Sigmund Freud* translated and edited by James Strachey. Reprinted by permission of The Random House Group Ltd. And from *The Collected Papers, Volume 5* by Sigmund Freud. Edited by James Strachey. Published by Basic Books, Inc. by arrangement with The Hogarth Press, Ltd. And the Institute of Psycho-Analysis, London. Reprinted by permission of Basic Books, a member of Perseus Books, LLC.

32   From *The Last Avant-Garde* by David Lehman, © 1998 by David Lehman. Used by permission of Doubleday, a division of Random House, Inc.

33   From *Collected Poems* by Frank O'Hara, © 1971 by Maureen Granville-Smith, Administratrix of the Estate of Frank O'Hara. Used by permission of Alfred A. Knopf, a division of Random House, Inc.

34   Jim Elledge, *Frank O'Hara: To Be True to A City*. Ann Arbor: The University of Michigan Press, 1990. Reprinted by permission of the publisher.

35   John Storey, 'Mass Culture in America: The Post-War Debate', in *An Introduction to Cultural Theory and Popular Culture*, 3rd edition, Prentice Hall, 2000, reprinted by permission of Pearson Education Limited.

37   Kevin R. McNamara, '*Blade Runner*'s Post-individual Worldspace and Philip K. Dick's *Do Androids Dream of Electric Sheep?*' In *Contemporary Literature* 38.3. © 1997. Reprinted by permission of the University of Wisconsin Press.

38   'Mechanical Mirrors, the Double, and *Do Androids Dream of Electric Sheep?*' pp. 117–32 from *Mind in Motion: The Fiction of Philip K. Dick* by Patricia S. Warrick. © 1987 by the Board of Trustees, Southern Illinois University, reprinted by permission of the publisher.

39   Michael Dunne, 'Dialogism in Manuel Puig's *Kiss of the Spider Woman*', *South Atlantic Review*, 60.2, May 1995. Reproduced by permission of *South Atlantic Review*.

40   Stephanie Merrim, 'Through the Film Darkly: Grade "B" Movies and Dreamwork in *Tres tristes tigres* and *El beso de la mujer araña*', *Modern Language Studies*, 15.4, Fall 1985. Reproduced by permission of *Modern Language Studies*.

41   Samuel Beckett, 'Three Dialogues' from *Disjeda: Miscellaneous Writing and A Dramatic Fragment*, Calder Publications, 1983. Reproduced by permission of the publisher.

42   Hans Bertens, 'Introduction' from *The Idea of the Postmodern: A History*, Routledge, 1995. Reproduced by permission of the publisher.

43   James F. English, 'Winning the Culture Game: Prizes, Awards, and the Rules of Art'. *New Literary History* 33:1 (2002), pp. 113–35. © New Literary History, University of Virginia. Reprinted with permission of The Johns Hopkins University Press.

44   Excerpt from 'Crediting Poetry: The Nobel Lecture' from *Opened Ground: Selected Poems 1966-1996* by Seamus Heaney. © 1998 by Seamus Heaney. Reprinted by permission of Farrar, Straus and Giroux, LLC and Faber & Faber Ltd.

45   Conor Cruise O'Brien, 'A Slow North-East Wind', review of Seamus Heaney's *North* in *The Listener*, 25 September 1975. © Conor Cruise O'Brien, 1975. Reprinted by permission of Greene & Heaton Ltd.

46   Ciaran Carson, 'Escaped from the Massacre? *North* by Seamus Heaney', in *The Honest Ulsterman*, 50, 1975. Reprinted by permission of Ciaran Carson.

47   Pico Iyer, 'The Empire Writes Back', *Time*, 4 February 1993, © 1993 Time Inc. reprinted by permission.

48   Graham Huggan, 'The Post-Colonial Exotic' from *Transition*, 64, © 1994 by the W. E. B. Dubois Institute. Used by permission of Soft Skull Press, Inc.

49   Abdulrazak Gurnah, 'Imagining the Postcolonial Writer', in S. Nasta (ed.) *Reading the 'New' Literatures in a Postcolonial Era*, 2000, The English Association, Essays and Studies. Reproduced by permission of the author and The English Association.

50   Abdulrazak Gurnah, 'An Idea of the Past', *Moving Worlds*, 2.2, 2002. Reproduced by permission of the author.

51.1 Candice Rodd, 'Spirits in Waiting/Booker Nomination; *The Ghost Road* by Pat Barker', *Independent on Sunday*, 10 September 1995. © 1995 *The Independent*.

51.2 Harriet Patterson, 'Trench Trauma and Jungle Ghosts: The Final Part of Pat Barker's War Trilogy Explores a Society with the Lid Off', *The Independent*, 23 September 1995. © 1995 *The Independent*.

52   Lorna Sage, 'Both Sides: *The Ghost Road* by Pat Barker', *London Review of Books*, 5 October, 1995. This article first appeared in the *London Review of Books* and is reproduced with permission. www.lrb.co.uk.

53   Reproduced from *On Histories and Stories* by A. S. Byatt (© A. S. Byatt 2000) published by Chatto & Windus/Vintage. Reprinted by permission of PFD (www.pfd.co.uk) on behalf of A. S. Byatt and by The Random House Group Ltd.

INTRODUCTION

As ever-increasing numbers of people in the twentieth century have engaged with all forms of literature, passionate disagreements, debates and controversies about literary texts and literature in general have emerged. In this Reader, we introduce and reprint a wide variety of materials that convey the intellectual energy and excitement of such debates and controversies, with reference to some of the literary texts that were at the centre of these debates.

A Twentieth-Century Literature Reader: Texts and Debates is the third book in a three-volume series which is designed for the third-level Open University Literature course *Twentieth Century Literature: Texts and Debates*. Several kinds of materials are selected here. The Reader includes material exemplifying and elucidating twentieth-century critical ideas and theoretical positions – 'art for art's sake', art as propaganda, romanticism and classicism, modernism and postmodernism, feminism, Marxism, psychoanalysis, queer theory and postcolonialism, to name but the most obvious examples. In an associated manner, material that helps to place these ideas, positions, schools and movements in their different historical contexts is also included. These creative and critical debates and ideas are not conveyed in an exclusively abstract manner, in terms of general statements and critical commentary. Rather, most of the above material is positioned in relation to specific texts, and the debates surrounding those texts. Extracts of general critical positions are accordingly placed in juxtaposition with material that clarifies the production and reception of the specific texts. For the latter, as regards the production of these texts, sources and influential literary and philosophical precursors are included, and as regards their reception, both immediate responses (reviews, interviews) and more considered critical and theoretical responses (critical essays) are included. All the conventional genres of literature – poetry, fiction, drama – are considered.

This Reader is structured in terms of four major areas of literary debate that have accompanied the production and reception of twentieth-century literary texts. These four debates follow a loosely chronological sequence, and for each debate, there are in turn four exemplary literary works.

1

Part I

WHAT IS LITERATURE FOR?

1 Oscar Wilde, Preface to *The Picture of Dorian Gray* (1891)

Novelist, playwright, poet, critic and conversationalist Oscar Wilde (1854–1900) was the leading proponent and public embodiment of aestheticism in the London of the 1890s. The preface to his novel *The Picture of Dorian Gray* (1891) encapsulates both his radical conception of the purpose of art ('All art is quite useless') and his epigrammatic style.

Wilde, O., 'Preface', in *The Picture of Dorian Gray*, ed. by I. Murray, Oxford World's Classics, Oxford: Oxford University Press, 1974, pp. xxii–xxiv

The artist is the creator of beautiful things.
To reveal art and conceal the artist is art's aim.
The critic is he who can translate into another manner or a new material his impression of beautiful things.
The highest as the lowest form of criticism is a mode of autobiography.
Those who find ugly meanings in beautiful things are corrupt: without being charming. This is a fault.
Those who find beautiful meanings in beautiful things are the cultivated. For these there is hope.
They are the elect to whom beautiful things mean only Beauty.
There is no such thing as a moral or an immoral book.
Books are well written, or badly written. That is all.
The nineteenth century dislike of Realism is the rage of Caliban seeing his own face in a glass.
The nineteenth century dislike of Romanticism is the rage of Caliban not seeing his own face in a glass.

*The moral life of man forms part of the subject-matter of
the artist, but the morality of art consists in the perfect use
of an imperfect medium.*

*No artist desires to prove anything. Even things that are true
can be proved.*

    *No artist has ethical sympathies. An ethical sympathy in
an artist is an unpardonable mannerism of style.*

    *No artist is ever morbid. The artist can express
everything.*

*Thought and language are to the artist instruments of an
art.*

    Vice and virtue are to the artist materials for an art.

*From the point of view of form, the type of all the arts is the art of the
musician. From the point of view of feeling, the actor's craft is the
type.*

    All art is at once surface and symbol.

    Those who go beneath the surface do so at their peril.

    Those who read the symbol do so at their peril.

It is the spectator, and not life, that art really mirrors.

    *Diversity of opinion about a work of art shows that the work
is new, complex, and vital.*

    When critics disagree the artist is in accord with himself.

*We can forgive a man for making a useful thing as long as he
does not admire it. The only excuse for making a useless thing is
that one admires it intensely.*

    All art is quite useless.

OSCAR WILDE

2 George Orwell, Review of *The Novel Today* by Philip Henderson (1936)

George Orwell (the pseudonym of Eric Arthur Blair, 1903–50) was a novelist and critic, who reviewed extensively throughout his writing life. He was a committed Socialist, who fought in support of the Republican government during the Spanish Civil War; he was, however, always critical of Communism and Marxism. This review from 1936 shows Orwell in typically combative mood rubbishing the rarefied claims of aesthetes while also demonstrating his scepticism about theories of Christian apologists and orthodox Marxists.

Orwell, G., Review of *The Novel Today* by Philip Henderson, in *The Collected Essays, Journalism and Letters of George Orwell*, vol. 1: *An Age Like This*, ed. by S. Orwell and I. Angus, Harmondsworth: Penguin, 1970, pp. 288–91

Mr Philip Henderson's book, *The Novel Today*, is a survey of the contemporary novel from a Marxist standpoint. It is not a very good book, in fact it can be described as a weaker version of Mirsky's *Intelligentsia of Great Britain*, written by someone who has got to live in England and cannot afford to insult too many people, but it is of some interest because it raises the question of art and propaganda which now rumbles like a sort of 'noises off' round every critical discussion.

On the last occasion when *Punch* produced a genuinely funny joke, which was only six or seven years ago, it was a picture of an intolerable youth telling his aunt that when he came down from the University he intended to 'write'. 'And what are you going to write about, dear?' his aunt inquires. 'My dear aunt,' the youth replies crushingly, 'one doesn't write *about* anything, one just *writes*.' This was a perfectly justified criticism of current literary cant. At that time, even more than now, art for art's sake was going strong, though the phrase itself had been discarded as ninety-ish; 'art has nothing to do with morality' was the favourite slogan. The artist was conceived as leaping to and fro in a moral, political and economic void, usually in pursuit of something called 'Beauty', which was always one jump ahead. And the critic was supposed to be completely 'impartial', i.e. to deal in abstract aesthetic standards which were completely unaffected by his other prejudices. To admit that you liked or disliked a book because of its moral or religious tendency, even to admit noticing that it *had* a tendency, was too vulgar for words.

This is still the official attitude, but it is in process of being abandoned, and especially by the extremists at the opposite poles of thought, the Communist and the Catholic. Both the Communist and the Catholic usually believe, though unfortunately they do not often say, that abstract aesthetic standards are all bunkum and that a book is only a 'good' book if it preaches the right sermon. To the Communist, good literature means 'proletarian' literature. (Mr Henderson is careful to explain, however, that this does not mean literature written by proletarians; which is just as well, because there isn't any.) In Henri Barbusse's *One Look at Russia*, for instance, it is stated almost in so many words that a novel about 'bourgeois' characters cannot be a good novel. So expressed this is an absurdity, but in some ways it is not a bad position to take up. Any critic who stuck to it consistently would at least do useful work by dragging into the light the (often quite unaesthetic) reasons for which books are liked or disliked. But unfortunately the notion of art for art's sake, though discredited, is too recent to be forgotten, and there is always a temptation to revert to it in moments of difficulty. Hence the frightful intellectual dishonesty which can be observed in nearly all propagandist critics. They are employing a double set of values and dodging

ANTON CHEKHOV, *THE CHERRY ORCHARD*

4 Anon, Review of an English Performance of *The Cherry Orchard* (1911)

This extract is an anonymous (or 'unsigned') review from *The Times* of an English performance of *The Cherry Orchard* in 1911. It gives a flavour of the reaction to the form, but particularly the content, of Chekhov's play. A brief glance at the language indicates that its perspective is dominated by considerations of nationality ('foreigners', and 'alien types'), and it raises the issue of working with a text in translation.

Unsigned notice in *The Times*, in V. Emeljanow (ed.), *Chekhov: The Critical Heritage*, London: Routledge & Kegan Paul, 1981, p. 92

30 May 1911, 13
. . . For anything I see, said Johnson's friend, 'old' Meynell, foreigners are fools. Russians are foreigners, but, even so, it is highly improbable that they are such fools as they seem in the English version of Chekhov's comedy. The fact is, when actors are set to present alien types which they have never seen and which they can only imagine from the necessarily imperfect indications of a translation, they are bound to produce grotesques. Further, who says translation says transvaluation – the relations of the parts are altered, and so the balance of the whole is upset. Though Anton Chekhov's comedy may be a harmonious work of art, presented at home in its own atmosphere before people who know all about, if they do not actually live, the life it depicts, Mrs. Edward Garnett's 'Cherry Orchard' cannot but strike an English audience as something queer, outlandish, even silly. . . . [The characters] all seem children who have never grown up. Genuine comedy and scenes of pure pathos are mixed with knock-about farce.

The players did their best; it was not their fault that the entertainment was not entertaining.

5 Beverly Hahn, A Note on Translations (1977)

This extract, by Beverly Hahn, investigates the issue of translation in more detail, and is much more positive about the challenges of encountering Chekhov's drama as an English speaker. The extract takes the form of a prefatory 'Note on Translations' from her book, *Chekhov: A Study of the Major Stories and Plays*, published in 1977. Comparison of two well-used translations of the play (by Constance Garnett and Elisaveta Fen) concludes her exploration of the process of rendering Chekhov in English.

'A Note on Translations', in B. Hahn, *Chekhov: A Study of the Major Stories and Plays*, Cambridge: Cambridge University Press, 1977, pp. ix–xiii

Any work which attempts to deal with an author writing in a foreign language and in the context of a foreign culture will necessarily discover limitations and difficulties. These are not lessened by the critic's need – as distinct from that of the historian of ideas – to attend at all times to precise stylistic qualities of the writing (as something inseparable from its imaginative 'content') and to the subtleties of nuance which probably escape any but the natives of a culture. I am therefore aware that, in the present work, there are limitations on what I may do in the way of close textual commentary, accepting these as an inevitable disadvantage of a subject too compelling in other respects for me to discard.

However, in Chekhov's case there are some special factors to help mitigate the difficulties. In the first place, Chekhov's art is almost always highly structured, requiring, for a full understanding, a response to the way detail is organized in an overall pattern. Speeches, images and even whole scenes are carefully, and often ironically, juxtaposed against one another, so that one rarely finds any single set of values or single emotion holding sway. These formal properties naturally survive translation intact and are thus available for comment by the non-native critic. Secondly, the prevalence of simile rather than metaphor in the language of the original means that poetic effects themselves are more easily and reliably translatable, and that they too are generally accessible to a reader who is not a Russian-speaker. The 'big white birds' of *Three Sisters*, for example, ultimately take on a broadly metaphoric force, but they are first introduced through simile:

Скажите мне, отчего я сегодня так счастлива? Точно я на парусах, надо мной широкое голубое небо и носятся большие белые птицы.

Tell me, why am I so happy today? *As if* I were sailing, above me
a wide blue sky and big white birds moving about.

Indeed, though they are present here only figuratively, these birds later
become real creatures (invisible from the stage, but nonetheless indicated as
physically flying overhead) whom Masha addresses longingly in Act IV when
Vershinin's departure is imminent:

The migratory birds are already in flight . . . (*looks up*). Swans or
geese . . . my beloved, happy ones.

In nearly every example I can recall, the major images in Chekhov's work
are natural images which are to some extent independent of the figures of
speech which embody them from point to point. Thus, if the precise effect
of one simile (or the less frequent metaphor) is lost in translation, it is likely
that the non-native reader can still feel the composite poetic effect of (say)
the falling snow in 'Misery', the cherry orchard in *The Cherry Orchard* or, in
Three Sisters, Moscow's blossoms, sunlight and warmth. Moreover, even less
central images, like the recurrent water images in 'Easter Eve' or the surreal
imagery of the moonlight shining through the window-bars in 'Ward
No. 6', seem to survive translation more or less intact.

Perhaps most important of all, there exists in English a standard translation of the main body of Chekhov's stories, novellas and plays, completed
by a single translator and therefore preserving a certain uniformity of sensibility: Constance Garnett's translations of prose works, published between
1916 and 1923, and of the major plays, published in the early 1920s.[1]
(At the time of writing, Ronald Hingley's new edition of Chekhov's works,
the 'Oxford Chekhov', is still incomplete. However, I have consulted such
volumes as were available and am grateful for the opportunity of comparison they provided.) The Garnett translations, and especially her translations
of the plays, have hardly, of course, been immune from attack; and the most
recent has come from David Magarshack in his 'Introduction' to his *The Real
Chekhov* (London, 1972). But while it is true that Mrs Garnett does occasionally take liberties with Russian colloquialisms and other idioms, the
question of their 'quaintness' or otherwise seems to me a matter of taste;
and, allowing for the fact that there are probably better translations of the
plays, still the number of Garnett's 'misconceptions' (if we consider her translations overall) seems to me to have been exaggerated. She has, at the least,
a fine ear for English cadence; and since for more than fifty years after
Chekhov's death hers was the only substantial selection of Chekhov's stories

available in English, her *Tales* have themselves attained something of the status of an English classic. For this reason, and although I have consulted the originals at points where definite differences occur between current English translations, the following accounts of works and of the development of Chekhov's art take the Garnett version of him as their basis.

Even so, I do think that a distinctively 'Chekhovian' sensibility emerges through a whole range of English translations of Chekhov's work. In part, this has to do with the structural emphases of which I have already spoken, which I shall attend to subsequently. But as well as this there are consistencies of tone and of manner from one translator to another which emerge despite inevitable differences in the translators' sensibilities. If this is not conspicuously so with the overall narrative tone and stance of the stories, it is largely because their narrative style is a 'neutral' one, without the obvious stylistic formality of (say) Pushkin or even, to some extent, of Lermontov. The narrative does not draw attention to its own 'manner'. But, particularly with the plays, it is surely possible to feel different textures of speech associated with different characters, which a variety of English translators succeed in capturing. Even a non-native reader can feel the differences deriving from the original Russian. For example, take these two speeches from *The Cherry Orchard*, placed side by side and out of context. I quote them first in Russian, from *Вишневый сад* (Letchworth: Bradda Books, 1965):

Епиходов. Я пойду. (*Намыкаемся на смуп, коморый пабаем.*) вот ... (*Как бы морэсесмеуя.*) Вот видите, извините за выражение, какое обстоятельство, между прочим ... Зто просто даже замечательно! (*Ухобцм.*) (р. 17)

Любовь Андреевна (*глябцм в окно на саб*). О, мое детство, чистота моя! В зтой детской я спала, глядела отсюда на сад, счастье просыпалось вместе со мною каждое утро, и тогда он был точно таким, ничто не изменилось. (*Смеемся ом рабосмц.*) Весь, весь белый! О, сад мой! После темной ненастной осени и холодной зимы опять ты молод, полон счастья, ангелы небесные не покинули тебя ... Если бы онять с груди и с плеч моих тяжелый камень, если бы я могла забыть мое црошлое! (р. 28)

Both of the translations which follow (by Constance Garnett in *The Cherry Orchard and Other Plays* (London, 1922) and by Elisaveta Fen in *Chekhov Plays* (Harmondsworth, 1971)) capture the staccato and comically pompous quality of Epihodov's speech on the one hand, and the lyrical but partly sentimental and theatrical quality of Lyubov's address to the orchard on the other:

Garnett:

> EPIHODOV. I am going (*stumbles against a chair, which falls over*). There! (*as though triumphant*). There you see now, excuse the expression, an accident like that among others . . . It's positively remarkable (*goes out*). (p. 5)
>
> LYUBOV (*looking out of the window into the garden*). Oh, my childhood, my innocence! It was in this nursery I used to sleep, from here I looked out into the orchard, happiness waked with me every morning and in those days the orchard was just the same, nothing has changed (*laughs with delight*). All, all white! Oh, my orchard! After the dark gloomy autumn, and the cold winter; you are young again, and full of happiness, the heavenly angels have never left you . . . If I could cast off the burden that weighs on my heart, if I could forget the past! (p. 20)

Fen:

> YEPIHODOV. I'll leave you now. (*Bumps into a chair which falls over.*) You see! (*Triumphantly.*) You can see for yourself what it is, I mean to say . . . so to speak . . . It's simply extraordinary! (*Goes out.*) (p. 335)
>
> LIUBOV ANDRYEEVNA (*looks through the window at the orchard*). Oh, my childhood, my innocent childhood! I used to sleep in this nursery; I used to look on to the orchard from here, and I woke up happy every morning. In those days the orchard was just as it is now, nothing has changed. (*Laughs happily.*) All, all white! Oh, my orchard! After the dark, stormy autumn and the cold winter, you are young and joyous again; the angels have not forsaken you! If only this burden could be taken from me, if only I could forget my past! (pp. 347–8)

Though in this instance the Garnett translation is generally more accurate to the original, surer and more eloquent, both versions manifest in each passage a common impulse derived from the stylistic texture of the original, so that although our valuation of Chekhov's power as a writer (in the local characteristics of the writing) might vary slightly according to whether he were being received through the Garnett version or the Fen, there are, I think, sufficient grounds for confidence about what *kind* of writer he is at any given point. It is also possible to make fairly confident interpretative judgments about the quality of the characters' emotions (even down to its rhythmic manifestations) conveyed through such speech.

It is, at any rate, on such a basis that some elements of my accounts will rest.

Note

1   *The Tales of Tchehov*, 13 vols. (London, 1916–23): I. *The Darling and Other Stories*, 1916. II. *The Duel and Other Stories*, 1916. III. *The Lady with the Dog and Other Stories*, 1917. IV. *The Party and Other Stories*, 1917. V. *The Wife and Other Stories*, 1918. VI. *The Witch and Other Stories*, 1918. VII. *The Bishop and Other Stories*, 1919. VIII. *The Chorus Girl and Other Stories*, 1920. IX. *The Schoolmistress and Other Stories*, 1920. X. *The Horse-Stealers and Other Stories*, 1921. XI. *The Schoolmaster and Other Stories*, 1921. XII. *The Cook's Wedding and Other Stories*, 1922. XIII. *Love and Other Stories*, 1923.

    The Plays of Tchehov, 2 vols. (London, 1922–3; reprinted 1965–70): I. *The Cherry Orchard and Other Plays*, 1922. II. *Three Sisters and Other Plays*, 1923.

    In the present essay, references to the Garnett edition of Chekhov's stories are made in parentheses, by volume and page number only: thus, '(VII.28)' means *'The Bishop and Other Stories*, p. 28'. [. . .]

6 Ronald Hingley, Peasant Benefactor and Chronicler (1976)

This extract is from Ronald Hingley's biography of Chekhov, published in 1976. Though there have been more recent biographical studies of Chekhov (by V. S. Pritchett in 1988 and by Donald Rayfield in 1997 for example), Hingley's text is very readable, and is a source of much relevant contextual information. The extract here is a discussion of the state of the peasantry in Imperial Russia, something that interested Chekhov as a short story writer, as a dramatist and as a doctor.

Hingley, R., 'Peasant Benefactor and Chronicler', in *A New Life of Anton Chekhov*, Oxford: Oxford University Press, 1976, pp. 167–8

The peasants formed the largest and most primitive of the social "estates" among which the citizenry of Imperial Russia was distributed in law. . . . there was no such thing as a Russian citizen pure and simple. There were Russian gentlemen, Russian clerics, Russian merchants; there were Cossacks, there were military persons; there were officials and students; there were townsfolk of various brands. And there were, above all, peasants. One or other of these classifications would be inscribed in the "passport" which, in a country highly bureaucratized by nineteenth-century standards, every travelling citizen was required to carry for identification purposes. That these regulations were—like almost all nineteenth-century Russian regulations—laxly enforced, Chekhov's own case illustrates, since he himself jogged along for years without being assigned to any official estate. But the majority of his new neighbours were registered as peasants. Those of Melikhovo were just a few score among about a hundred million in the country as a whole, for this was by far the largest social category: 81.5 per cent in a population of about 126 million, as recorded in the 1897 census.

After sheer weight of numbers, the peasantry's second most striking characteristic was primitiveness. Of the rural population aged between nine and forty-nine only 22 per cent were recorded by the same census as able to read and write, the proportion of illiterates being particularly high among women. Still more depressing was peasant health. Chekhov himself once informally reckoned village infant mortality as 60 per cent up to the age of five. And he even claimed that not one single healthy woman might be found among the many millions in the villages, in the factories and in the back streets of the towns: a comment horrifying indeed, since it came from so detached and highly qualified an observer. To illiteracy and poor health we must add desperate poverty, overwork and inadequate nourishment. The atmosphere did not encourage a high standard of morality and social virtue. To call the typical Russian peasant a drunken brute who regularly beat his wife and children might be going too far, but certainly violence and bestial cruelty were common features of village life. Too poor to get drunk very often (the Empire's *per capita* consumption of alcohol was surprisingly low), the peasant was liable to become violently intoxicated when vodka did chance to be available in quantity, as on feast days or at weddings. With him an orgy was an orgy. To these unseemly features may be added a deep-seated, all too understandable, hatred and mistrust of landowners and officials. Yet the peasant was still apt to revere the Tsar—conceived as a remote, semi-divine, vaguely benevolent figure. And the peasant also prized Orthodox Church ritual, which brought colour, music, mystery and consolation to the drab, monochrome, mud-surrounded or snow-bound huts of the village. . . .

7 Anatoly Smeliansky, Chekhov at the Moscow Art Theatre (2000)

This extract is an essay by Anatoly Smeliansky, who from 1980 was the Associate Artistic Director of the Moscow Art Theatre. He still held this post in 2000, when the essay was published. Its subject is the changing nature of Chekhov productions at this theatre, and it concentrates particularly on the impact on these productions of political events in Russia. Though this last extract is most obviously related to the question of what literature is for, all four extracts are relevant to the discussion of this question.

Smeliansky, A., 'Chekhov at the Moscow Art Theatre', in V. Gottlieb and P. Allain (eds), *The Cambridge Companion to Chekhov*, Cambridge: Cambridge University Press, 2000, pp. 29–40

Chekhov's relationship with the Moscow Art Theatre is a story in itself, and quite a tangled one at that. It is the story of how Chekhov's theatre came into being and Stanislavsky and Nemirovich-Danchenko's struggle to master the poetics of his drama. It is the story of how even in the dramatist's life-time the Chekhov canon evolved into a theatrical straitjacket from which it became necessary to break free. It is the story of the deep divisions between theatre and dramatist involving the most fundamental questions concerning the art of theatre: the precise genre of Chekhov's plays; his view of character and his attitude towards the whole historical development of Russia itself. In an attempt to console Stanislavsky after Chekhov's death, Nemirovich-Danchenko said: 'We had already lost Chekhov with *The Cherry Orchard*. He would never have written anything else.'[1] This merciless verdict expresses all the tension that existed between Chekhov and the Moscow Art Theatre.

After Chekhov's death, his plays began to be perceived in the light of new theatrical developments. The MAT's productions of Chekhov started to break free, not from Chekhov himself, but rather from the style of the 'theatre of mood' and from the detailed naturalism that had only recently brought fame and success to the young company. A few words should be said about this naturalism, which was to come under attack not only from Meyerhold but from Stanislavsky himself (which was how the two men came together and established the Studio on Povarskaya Street in 1905).

The techniques of the early MAT are well known. The audience of Treplev's play (in *The Seagull*) casually sitting with their backs to the audience; Astrov swatting mosquitoes in *Uncle Vanya*; the evening half-light in the house of the three sisters; the crackling of logs in the stove; the chirping of a cricket; a single candle-flame; the sounds of the fire; hushed, non-actorish voices, the child's abandoned chair on Ranevskaya's estate – all of this combined to create a powerful sense of the flow of life. Hence, the effect of the so-called 'fourth wall'.

The early MAT revitalised the art of acting, made a cult of the pause, the subtext and the constant interaction of characters. There emerged the concept of the ensemble and a psychological style of acting. The productions

Knebel,[7] Nemirovich formulated his directorial interpretation and ideas, aimed at dispelling the MAT's acting clichés. Amongst these was the 'exaggerated and distorted use of the device of "the objective" (the style of intensive interaction with a partner which Stanislavsky had invented at the beginning of the century, as a means of overcoming the practice of directly addressing the audience and ignoring one's on-stage partner, which was habitual in the Imperial theatres). Nemirovich went on to criticise 'a drawn-out tempo' (here, as we have seen, he was in agreement with Stanislavsky); 'talking inaudibly to oneself' (for the sake of poorly understood simplicity) and sentimentalism, instead of lyricism. In opposition to such clichés, Nemirovich-Danchenko proposed new directorial techniques for Chekhov: a clearly defined 'core' for the production i.e. a new 'super-objective' with a fully understood and sustained subtext, 'robustness', poetry, simplicity and *genuine* theatricality.[8]

In achieving his ends, Nemirovich as director proved to be quite a virtuoso. A new poeticised Chekhov emerged, complete with an avenue of birch trees, and with 'the yearning for a better life' as the firm core of the production. But even this directorial masterpiece was subject to the limitations imposed by its time. Nemirovich ruthlessly cut a number of motifs from the play, the result being that its Chekhovian symphonic quality was lost. Thus, in the final scene he shortened the cynical yet infinitely meaningful line of Chebutykin that prefigured the Theatre of the Absurd: 'If only we knew', and Chebutykin's 'Tarara-boom-deay', lines *not* belonging to two different plays but to the one play by Chekhov with his acute perception of the meaning of life, his harshness and restraint – qualities that were to be in such demand after the Second World War and after the death of Stalin, when a new generation of directors would take over.

In the post-war years, the tradition of Chekhov at the MAT became shallow and meaningless. Michael Kedrov's 1947 production of *Uncle Vanya* (assisted by Litovtseva and Sudakov), was an attempt to interpret the play in the optimistic spirit of Socialist Realism. The only redeeming feature of this well-intentioned but wholly imitative production was the splendid performance of Boris Dobronravov in the title role. Devoid of any ensemble work, it was a mono-play, or solo performance, that threw the theatre back to pre-Chekhovian times.

The most popular of the MAT revivals was *The Seagull*. There was attempt to make a jubilee production of the play to mark Chekhov's one hundredth birthday in 1960, directed by Stanitsyn and Rayevsky, but it did not stay long in the repertoire. Boris Livanov's 1968 production, on the other hand, ran for many years even though there were really no new ideas in it. Stanislavsky would have described its style as 'ordinary Chekhov'.

Partly as a riposte to Livanov's romantic and 'ordinary, generalised' Chekhov, *The Seagull* was produced in the late sixties at the Sovremennik (Contemporary) Theatre,[9] which had begun as the MAT studio-theatre, and which remained linked to its origins in a strained and fractious polemical relationship. The director was Oleg Yefremov who shortly afterwards became Artistic Director of the MAT, a post he has now occupied for thirty years. For this reason it is worth taking a closer look at his first serious encounter with Chekhov. In his work on *The Seagull*, Yefremov identified certain cunning qualities in this 'inspired and heretical play'. This play can start a theatre – but it can also finish it off. *The Seagull* marked the end of Yefremov's work with the Sovremennik.

The Seagull at the Sovremennik reflected the situation at the end of the sixties when 'The Thaw'[10] came to an end, and when Soviet tanks entered Prague. Chekhov's text, seemingly completely irrelevant to these events, nonetheless responded to them. The death of 'the common ideal' set the tone for the production. Chekhov's text was flooded with all the mutual recriminations, disappointments and hostilities that had accumulated over the previous years. Yefremov turned the author of *The Seagull* into a lampoonist, bored rigid by intellectual conversation and critical of writers and actors who talk a lot and do nothing. Yefremov imparted to *The Seagull* the ideological confusion and despair that typified the late sixties. People had stopped hearing or listening to each other. All they did was strike attitudes, make scenes and squabble. And dig for worms for fishing from the flowerbed that the designer, Sergei Barkhin, had installed in the middle of the stage.

At the MAT Yefremov avoided Chekhov for nearly seven years. Perhaps he was discouraged by the failure of his *Seagull* at the Sovremennik. He returned to him again in 1976 with *Ivanov*.

The play – about human decay – which had been so out of tune with the 'cheerful' epoch of the early twenties, now proved to be exceptionally appropriate to the 'stagnation' of the 1970s. In the MAT production, this stagnation was polarised by using two basic colours, black and white. Hovering in the 'background' are the uncouth and useless young guests in Act Four, called 'cavemen, troglodytes' by Lebedev, attacked by Sasha in Act Two and described by Lvov as: 'Those wretched people. Vultures, birds of prey. They only come to tear each other to bits.' These and the constant motif of the 'gooseberry jam', combined with Misha Borkin's bumptiousness (performed by Vyacheslav Nevinny) – were all meant to counterpoint the lofty confessional tone in which Innokenty Smoktunovsky[11] performed the title role. The situation, with Ivanov's *apparently* unmotivated depression, suddenly revealed its 'long-term' meaning. Such complete emptiness of the soul, the 'disease' which Chekhov rated worse than syphilis or sexual impotence, was presented by Smoktunovsky with frightening lyrical profundity.

This MAT production followed another *Ivanov*, directed by Mark Zakharov at the Lenkom Theatre, with Yevgeny Leonov in the title role. Instead of presenting a 'Russian Hamlet',[12] Leonov made him just an average intellectual, not *the* Ivanov – but *one* Ivanov, 'the million and first', as Alexander Kugel once described him. What was important was the typicality of this remarkable actor; Leonov's human dimension matched that of everyone in the audience. In contrast, Smoktunovsky performed precisely the 'Russian Hamlet', an extraordinary man, of undoubted strength, but sick from the common disease of the times. His Ivanov suffered and agonised, unable to define a place for himself either in life or in the space of the MAT stage. Significantly, it was the arrangement of the space, designed by David Borovsky, that physically conveyed the nature of the disease, the desperate but unsatisfied desire for fulfilment that Smoktunovsky tried to enact. The designer furnished the actor with a bare stage enclosed by the colonnaded facade of the manor-house, with the autumnal garden casting the sombre shadows of its leafless branches on the walls. Thus Ivanov acted in a space that looked devastated, as though pillaged, where he literally could find no place for himself, or even anything to lean on. At first the actor rejected this spatial solution, fearing that in this play about everyday life he would be left exposed, without support or cover. The director insisted and in the end the protagonist's anguish in the empty yet claustrophobic space powerfully conveyed Chekhov's perception of life, which caused him once to observe that in Western Europe, people die because their space is cramped and suffocating, while in Russia they die because the space is an endless expanse, in which a little man has no way of finding his bearings.[13] 'The land looks at me, like an orphan', Chekhov's character repeatedly says – and Smoktunovsky conveyed this feeling with exceptional inner strength.

[. . .]

In 1980, ten years after his Sovremennik *Seagull* and four years after *Ivanov*, Yefremov returned to *The Seagull*. As we have seen, in the Sovremennik production, the flower-bed with worms had boldly replaced Chekhov's 'enchanted lake', the trees and even the air that Chekhov's characters breathe. And now, ten years on in his life and in that of the MAT; Yefremov took a fresh look at the play. For the first time in his directorial career, he introduced the concept of transcendent nature which alters the scale of human conflicts. The intellectual debates no longer interested the director but gave way to the drama of life itself. In 1970, *The Seagull* was interpreted as a pamphlet; in 1980, the predominant motif was that of reconciliation, understanding and forgiveness.

[. . .]

For the first time since coming together ten years earlier, the MAT company performed as a perceptible ensemble: Lavrova as Arkadina, Vertinskaya as Nina, Smoktunovsky as Dorn, Andrei Popov as Sorin, Myagkov as Treplev, Nevinny as Shamraev, Kindinov as Medvedenko – these were actors capable of understanding the Chekhov that Yefremov was in the process of rediscovering for himself. There was no lack of opportunities to act. In contrast with the Sovremennik production, at the MAT Yefremov wanted to make every character heard. He immersed the 'words, words, words' in the glittering foliage. True, these characters of Chekhov were garrulous, so garrulous that they did not even notice someone dying: in this production, Sorin (Andrei Popov). But despite all the disillusion and loss, the motif of faith amidst decay was gaining strength – the kind of faith that is fed not by love or hatred, but by an understanding of the basic reality of life as an insoluble drama.

[. . .]

In an odd way, Chekhov at the Moscow Art Theatre accompanied not only the profound changes at the theatre itself but in Russia as a whole. *Uncle Vanya* was premiered in February 1985 and on 30 April it was seen by the newly elected General Secretary, Mikhail Gorbachev. He saw a Chekhov who, in his own way, summed up the consequences of a 'constrained' life. The motif of creative patience became central. Yefremov did not attempt to turn Uncle Vanya, with his complaint 'I haven't lived', into a hero. (How could he not have lived when by definition his life was in fact itself life?) As Astrov, Yefremov was embedded in the daily trivialities of existence – and struggled to break out. The MAT stage revolved, revealing the interiors of the house. Astrov took to drink and there was a brief respite when his soul became free – and everything around him was turned upside down. The undistinguished Herr Professor Serebryakov (played by Yevgeni Yevstigneyev) continued to tyrannise his wife and indulge his whims, and *then* the storm broke. And as a consequence the confessions came flooding out. One person was drinking, another was praying, rendered helpless by unrequited love, while yet another was suffering from lack of self-fulfilment. And together, they made up all human life. Levental had placed the house upstage against the background of an autumnal landscape in the style of Levitan.[14] When the stage was plunged into darkness, we suddenly noticed through the mist a faint light suspended above the dewy ground. It was a small window in a house on a distant hill. The light shone dimly in the darkness, but it shone invitingly, showing the way. Such was the end of the performance, premièred on the very eve of changes that were to transform not only Russia but the entire world.

On 7 May 1985, Gorbachev telephoned Yefremov to give his reactions to the production, saying that he had liked Astrov and that he had found Uncle Vanya simply heartrending. Then he said how much there was to do, that they should meet to discuss the problems of theatre, and that in general it was time 'to set the fly-wheel in motion'. Could he have imagined then where that fly-wheel would end up? I happened to be in Yefremov's office during this conversation, and Yefremov seemed to be speaking in his usual manner, making no attempt to flatter his caller. After hanging up, he suddenly wiped the sweat from his brow. Seeing my surprise, he smiled guiltily and paraphrasing Chekhov, said: 'You know, it's hard to squeeze the slave out of yourself.'

A later production of Chekhov at MAT was *Three Sisters*. It opened in February 1997 during the preparations for the MAT centennial. It bore all the signs of an attempt at 'summing up'. It was as though Yefremov was replaying all the main themes of his productions of Chekhov, beginning with the fate of 'home' – and ending with the theme of patience and submission to the merciless cycle of life. This time, Levental located the house of the Prozorov sisters in a kind of cosmic sphere which changed colour four times from the white of spring on Irina's name-day to the 'sombre blue of winter; from the red suggesting the fire to the rusty colour of the autumnal final act. These symbolic changes of colour reflected the rhythm of life that carries the characters from hope to despair. The closing scene of the three sisters bidding farewell to the departing officers was tragically expressive, and choreographed almost like a ballet. The sisters' arms interwove as they tried to hold together in a circle, but some invisible force drove them apart and broke their embrace.

Yefremov learned Chekhov's most important lesson long ago, one that is being experienced acutely by the whole of Russia. He grasped his objectivity, his detachment from any ideology, doctrine or political label. The age of ideologies that crushed human beings is receding. And Chekhov now stands revealed to us in all his strange, disquieting profundity.

In contrast with the 1940 production of *Three Sisters*, Yefremov's 1997 version lacks *any* optimism, any signs of poetic exaltation. The strains of the march as the regiment leaves the town very quickly give way to Chebutykin's nonsense song. But even his 'Tarara-boom-deay' doesn't embrace the entire expanse of life. The full stop in this production is not 'If only we knew', but the dancing image of the vanishing house. This house that has so stubbornly resisted the change of seasons, retreats upstage, dissolving in the darkening autumn landscape. The sombre, threatening music of Scriabin develops and reinforces the mood of departure. It is as though this play, born at the turn of the century has half anticipated the latest turn of events.

In the play Vershinin philosophises that 'in the past', mankind was busy with wars, campaigns, raids and victories, 'but now' it is all gone and there is nothing to fill this vast empty space . . .

At the end of the twentieth century, Russia finds itself again in this 'vast empty space'. We are trying to fill it. At this time of spiritual hiatus, Chekhov is truly a 'constant companion'.

Notes

1 Letter from V. I. Nemirovich-Danchenko to K. S. Stanislavsky, after 26 July 1904, from V. I. Nemirovich-Danchenko, *Selected Letters of V. I. Nemirovich-Danchenko in Two Volumes*, Moscow, 1979, vol. II, p. 378.

2 K. S. Stanislavsky, *Collected Works of Stanislavsky in 8 Volumes*, Moscow, 1974–82., vol. V, p. 134.

3 Letter from K. S. Stanislavsky to V. I. Nemirovich-Danchenko, October 1923, Berlin, from *Collected Works of Stanislavsky*, vol. VIII, p. 29.

4 From a letter by V. I. Nemirovich-Danchenko to Olga Bokzhanskaya on 9 March 1924, from *Selected Letters of V. I. Nemirovich-Danchenko*, vol. II, p. 304.

5 MAT Museum, Archives of V. I. Nemirovich-Danchenko.

6 See *Chronicles of the Life and Works of Stanislavsky in 8 Volumes*, Izdatelstvo VTO, Moscow, 1973, vol. IV.

7 Maria Knebel (1898–1985), actress, director and teacher. Studied at the Studio of Michael Chekhov in 1918, and then at the Fourth Studio of the MAT. In 1924 she became a member of the MAT Company, with whom she played many roles, and worked on many different productions of the MAT, such as *Kremlin Chimes* and *Difficult Years*. In 1950 she left the MAT to work as director of the Central Children's Theatre. She also taught at GITIS (The Russian State Theatre School). . . .

8 Letter from V. I. Nemirovich-Danchenko to Maria Knebel, April 1942. From *Selected Letters of Nemirovich-Danchenko*, vol. II, p. 536.

9 Yefremov worked at the Sovremennik Theatre from 1956 to 1970.

10 'The Thaw' is the term generally used to describe the end of Stalinist terror with Stalin's death in 1953, and the major speech at the 1956 Party Congress by Khrushchev in which he exposed and condemned many of the excesses of Stalinism, and the end of the long winter of Stalin's regime. With the destruction of 'The Prague Spring' in 1968, the period of 'The Thaw' came to an end. 'The Thaw' as a metaphor was first used by Ilya Ehrenburg in his story of that name, published in the magazine *Znamya* in 1954.

11 Innokenty Smoktunovsky is perhaps best known in Western Europe and America for his brilliant performance as Hamlet in Gregori Kozintsev's film of 1965.

12 The theme of 'Hamlet' runs throughout much of nineteenth-century Russian literature, drama and criticism. The use made of Hamlet was of a character incapable of taking any action about anything – whether his own life, or the needs of his society. For a detailed discussion of this major theme, see Ivan Turgenev's essay of 1858, 'Hamlet and Don Quixote'. For another example of Chekhov's (comic) use of the theme other than in *Ivanov*, see the short story 'In Moscow' (1891) or the dramatised version 'A Moscow Hamlet' in *A Chekhov Quartet*, trans. and ed.

by Vera Gottlieb, Amsterdam, 1996. Ivanov has his own point to make about himself as 'Hamlet' in Act Two, Scene VI in *Ivanov* – and about himself as Don Quixote in Act Four, Scene IX.

13 . . . This is an important reiteration of a major theme and perception of Russian life and Russian philosophy, as reflected in literature and drama. . . .

14 Isaac Levitan (1861–1900), landscape painter and friend of Chekhov's artist brother Nikolai. They shared holidays at Babkino, the estate in the countryside of Moscow Province on which the Chekhovs bought a holiday cottage. Levitan's landscape paintings capture the essence of the Russian countryside, the seasons – and country life. It was when out hunting with Levitan that Chekhov may well have got the idea for *The Seagull*. As he wrote in a letter to his publisher Suvorin, on 8 April 1892 from his estate at Melikhovo: 'Last night we went out shooting. He shot a snipe and the bird, wounded in the wing, fell into a puddle. I picked it up: long beak, big black eyes, and beautiful plumage. It looked astonished. What should we do with it? Levitan frowned, closed his eyes, then begged me in a shaky voice, 'My dear friend, hit his head against the gunstock . . .' I said, 'I can't.' He went on shaking, shrugging his shoulders, his head twitching, and begging me; and the snipe went on looking at us in astonishment. I had to agree with Levitan and kill it. One more beautiful delightful creature less, while two idiots went home and sat down to supper.'

THE STORIES OF
KATHERINE MANSFIELD

8 Sydney Janet Kaplan, *Katherine Mansfield and the Origins of Modernist Fiction* (1991)

Kaplan is among the critics who are concerned to establish the importance of Mansfield's contribution to modernism in general. Kaplan sees two major strands of development in literary modernism, a masculine strand represented by figures such as Ford Madox Ford, Ezra Pound and T. S. Eliot and a female strand to which writers such as May Sinclair, Dorothy Richards, Katherine Mansfield and Virginia Woolf belong. Although Mansfield never overtly embraced feminist politics, Kaplan sees feminism as an implied presence throughout her writing. The extract below is from Kaplan's reading of the revision of 'The Aloe' as 'Prelude'. Kaplan emphasises the innovative modernity of Mansfield's 'spatial' representations of her characters' inner lives. She finds evidence, in letters to Virginia Woolf as well as within 'Prelude' itself, that Mansfield was experimenting with techniques for rendering women's psychological experience before her contemporaries. In Kaplan's view, Mansfield's pruning away of narrative explanation concentrates, rather than weakens, the story's critique of gender. She sees 'Prelude' as not only conveying the inner lives of the women in the story but as offering a pessimistic view of the potential roles and futures available for its main character. Her chapter concludes by suggesting that this aspect of 'Prelude' allies it with the *Bildungsroman* (novel of development) genre. Her analysis implies that Mansfield had in mind the deterministic paradigms that engaged so many of the Victorian novelists whose influence is palpable in her stories.

Kaplan, S. J., *Katherine Mansfield and the Origins of Modernist Fiction*, Ithaca and London: Cornell University Press, 1991, pp. 114–17

... *The Aloe* becomes, through its evolution into "Prelude," an awakening into female sexuality. It is also a rejection of male modes, and this strategy is apparent in its all-over structure: its multiplicity, its fluidity, its lack of a central climax, and its many moments of encoded sexual pleasure. What makes "Prelude" so revolutionary as a narrative is its implicit statement that the construction of gender should be the motivating center of the text. The technical innovations are devices to reveal this process of reproduction. Reproduction in several forms dominates the text: in terms of procreation—Linda's pregnancy, the blossoming of the aloe; re-production of gender roles in the games of the children and in Kezia's questioning about sexual differences; and the re-production of bourgeois family life in the interactions of the family members as they respond to the pressures of their "roles." This reproduction assumes the continued dominance of the patriarchal society—the dominance of Stanley as businessman, rule-maker, center of authority—and it occurs in a world of upward mobility—"fleets of aloes," more children, more property. And it relies on the proficiency of the matriarchal center in Mrs. Fairfield. ... But "Prelude" also reveals that a counter-process of resistance and rebellion is always at work within these dynamics. Linda's resistance counters Stanley's demands, but ineffectively. Hers is primarily a negative force: passive resistance. The imaginative powers necessary for active rebellion are not brought into force. She fantasizes escape but cannot envision what shape it should take. Yet the imaginative powers, the talents she will never develop, are also in her daughter Kezia, who shares so many of her mother's internal responses. ...

Three modes of female sexual response are suggested in this story: First, Linda's initial attraction to sexuality (the baby bird in her dream), revulsion when the bird swells, and fear when it turns into a human baby; second, Beryl's fantasies of romance, centered in self-love, narcissism, and envy, a body-consciousness purely visual—specular. The third response is that of Kezia, the child not yet completely gendered, who longs for her grand-mother's arms, to be stroked and to stroke, to experience the tactile pleasures. She is still polymorphous, responsive to a whole range of stimuli. But she already fears any that might overpower her. Her sexuality requires mutuality, not assault.

[. . .]

In "Prelude" we are presented with multiple viewpoints, nearly all those of female characters. Only the short sections from the point of view of the father, Stanley Burnell, allow for the intrusion of the masculine. His consciousness works as counterpoint in a minor key. It strikes me that the story is structured like a female organism (which invariably contains some subordinated masculine characteristics). In working on this story, nearly a decade before Woolf's *Mrs. Dalloway*, Mansfield was already attempting a spatial rendering of a few days in the inner lives of her characters (she was even closer to Woolf's technique in revealing several minds living through *one* day in the later story about the Burnells, "At the Bay").

Remarkable as it is as a piece of experimental fiction, "Prelude" is even more immediately accessible to us as an exploration of feminine consciousness. . . . Mansfield establishes connections, psychic connections that link all of the female characters. The overriding theme of the story is female sexual identity. Linda Burnell, Kezia's mother, strains against her given role and does not want to be a mother. She avoids her children and dreads the sexuality that might lead to the birth of yet another one. She thinks of her husband with a mixture of affection and revulsion: "For all her love and respect and admiration she hated him. And how tender he always was after times like those, how submissive, how thoughtful. . . . There were all her feelings for him, sharp and defined, one as true as the other. And there was this other, this hatred, just as real as the rest" (p. 258).

Linda's ambivalence toward her role is one possible direction for female sexual identity. . . . Linda's unmarried sister Beryl represents another. Her outlet is fantasy; she imagines a lover while she gazes at herself in the mirror for self-gratification. And yet another direction is embodied in the grandmother, who represents the earlier, more traditional generation and totally accepts her role. . . . Kezia adores her grandmother, but Mansfield makes us see that Kezia shares more deeply the fearsome personal isolation and acute imagination of the mother she does not really know very well than the placid, assured rootedness of the grandmother she hugs, strokes, and calls her "Indian brave."

Early in the story Kezia asks the storeman the difference between a ram and a sheep, expressing the central question of her awakening consciousness. The storeman, embarrassed, typically avoids the truth by saying, "well, a ram has horns and runs for you." But Kezia intuitively knows what he means:

> "I don't want to see it frightfully," she said. "I hate rushing animals like dogs and parrots. I often dream that animals rush at me—even camels—and while they are rushing, their heads swell e-enormous." (p. 225)

Kezia's language here is nearly identical to her mother's later in the story when she alludes to her husband with:

> If only he wouldn't jump at her so, and bark so loudly, and watch her with such eager, loving eyes. He was too strong for her; she had always hated things that rush at her, from a child. (p. 258)

Such similar thought patterns establish a psychic connection between mother and daughter deeper than the external aloofness of their behavior with each other. "Prelude" is filled with points of connection like this one: images repeated in new contexts, phrases echoed or parodied by different characters, daydreams merging into waking reality.

Older Freudian readings of "Prelude" often consider how Kezia's response to the killing of the duck relates to castration anxiety. But in terms of feminist revisionary theory, the most noteworthy aspect is that it is the "head" that is cut off. To lose the head—mind, intellect, consciousness—is to participate in women's fate as constructed in masculine definitions of women's position in relation to civilization. Kezia responds with excitement and then with fear. She wants the head put back on. She would like genders to be as interchangeable as the earrings she suddenly notices on Pat's ears—to recognize that one can go back and forth in the costumes of gender, that the roles are as simple as impersonation, that "death" is not permanent and loss can be reversed.

"Prelude" breaks the form of the *bildungsroman* but is a narrative of *bildung* nonetheless. The spatial organization suggests simultaneity, but the typical linear pattern of individual development is rather spread out among the female characters, who tend to represent the central consciousness at various stages of her life: early childhood, late adolescence, young motherhood, and old age. The child, aunt, mother, and grandmother embody the female life cycle. But the inevitability of the continuation of conventional female roles seems implicit in this structuring. The only opening is for Kezia, the child yet unformed, but already containing within herself the inner structure to be unfolded.

9 Clare Hanson and Andrew Gurr,
Katherine Mansfield (1981)

Hanson and Gurr provide a useful brief summary of the modernist development of the 'plotless' short story. Their book as a whole is a valuable account of the melding of realism and symbolism in Mansfield's work. They discuss the plotless story (also termed the 'free' story by critics such as Elizabeth Bowen), as a development alongside the more highly plotted form derived from Gothic fiction. Hanson and Gurr see the plotless story as particularly attuned to the intellectual context of the time of its evolution in the late nineteenth century (the extract below from Walter Pater's *The Renaissance* provides some of this context). They also discuss the importance for modernism of the epiphanic 'blazing moment', which forms the 'focal point' of Mansfield's stories.

Hanson, Clare and Andrew Gurr, *Katherine Mansfield*, London and Basingstoke: Macmillan, 1981, pp. 17–19

Katherine Mansfield and Rudyard Kipling are among the very few writers in English to establish a reputation entirely on the basis of the short story form. It is no accident that they were writing at approximately the same time. The development of the short story in England lagged behind that in America and Russia chiefly because of differences in opportunities for magazine publication. By the 1890s, however, a huge expansion in the numbers of quarterlies and weeklies created the situation described by H. G. Wells:

> The 'nineties was a good and stimulating period for a short story writer . . . No short story of the slightest distinction went for long unrecognised . . . Short stories broke out everywhere.

Two entirely different types of story flourished together at the close of the nineteenth century. First, there was the story with a definite plot, which was the lineal descendant of the Gothic tale; and second, there was the new, 'plotless' story, concentrating on inner mood and impression rather than on external event. The latter was associated especially with *The Yellow Book*, the famous 'little magazine' of the nineties, and with the circle of writers gathered round its publisher John Lane – George Egerton, Ella D'Arcy, Evelyn Sharp and others. The innovatory quality of many of the stories published by these writers, and the contribution that they made to the development of the short story, is now becoming increasingly evident.

The plotless story seems to arise naturally from the intellectual climate of its time. In a world where, as the German philosopher Nietzsche declared, God was dead, and evolutionary theory had produced a sharp sense of man's insignificance in a changing universe, the only alternative seemed to be the retreat within, to the compensating powers of the imagination. With such a retreat came the stress on the significant moment, which would be called 'vision' or 'epiphany' by later writers such as James Joyce – the moment of insight which is outside space and time, vouchsafed only fleetingly to the imagination, but redeeming man's existence in time.

In fiction a shift in time-scale seems to accompany this emphasis on the moment. Throughout the nineteenth century the unit of fiction had been the year – from *Emma* to *The Ambassadors* we can say that this was so. In the late nineteenth and early twentieth century, the unit of fiction became the day. Elizabeth Bowen has written of this, saying that Katherine Mansfield was the first writer to see in the short story 'the ideal reflector of the day'. It is perhaps significant, however, that many other writers began their careers with short story writing in this period – Forster, for example, with the aptly named *The Eternal Moment*, and also D. H. Lawrence, James Joyce, and Virginia Woolf. It can even be suggested that the novels of these writers – Lawrence excepted – are in a sense simply extended short stories. Virginia Woolf's *Mrs Dalloway* is an obvious example, but there is also Joyce's *Ulysses*, originally projected as a story for his collection of stories called *Dubliners*, to be titled 'Mr Hunter's Day'. It is as though the short story is the paradigmatic form of the early twentieth century, best able to express its fragmented and fragmentary sensibility.

Katherine Mansfield certainly saw her kind of story as a quintessentially modern form, a point she makes more than once in her reviews of fiction for *The Athenaeum*. She was also very conscious in her use of epiphany as the focal point of her stories. In one of her reviews she discusses the way in which internal crisis has replaced external crisis of plot in modern fiction, at the same time warning against the loss of all sense of crisis or significance which she detected in the work of some modern novelists:

> Without [the sense of crisis] how are we to appreciate the import-
> ance of one 'spiritual event' rather than another? What is to prevent
> each being unrelated complete in itself – if . . . the gradual unfolding
> in growing, gaining light is not to be followed by one blazing
> moment? . . .

10 Walter Pater, Conclusion to *Studies in the History of the Renaissance* (1873)

Pater's famous Conclusion summarises his aestheticist views and was of great significance to a number of modernist writers. The conclusion conveys Pater's sense of life as consisting of 'unstable, flickering' impressions punctuated by fleeting moments of intense experience. These moments are the best that life can offer us, and can be experienced in the fiercest intensity in art. Hence his infamous declaration of 'the love of art for arts sake . . . for art comes to you professing frankly to give nothing but the highest quality to your moments as they pass, and simply for those moments' sake'. There is obviously no sense of God, or an afterlife in Pater's philosophy. Our 'one chance', of expanding the brief 'interval' of our lives, lies 'in getting as many pulsations as possible into the given time'.

Whilst many modernists sought to reject the elaborate prose style of Victorian prose writers such as Pater, the influence of his work is palpable in their pre-occupation with fragmented experience and their emphasis on epiphanic moments at which a 'single sharp impression' grants us our only experience of reality. Yet such a moment, Pater emphasises, is effectively over before it is felt, 'a single moment, gone while we try to apprehend it'. In the next extract, Bennett and Royle discussed the dissolution of identity as intrinsic to these moments of acute experience, a pattern that Pater called 'that strange perpetual weaving and unweaving of ourselves'. Pater's exhortation to seek experience as an end in itself, 'to burn always' with a 'hard gem-like flame' and to achieve a 'sense of the splendour of our experience and of its awful brevity' operated as a manifesto for the artistic endeavour, and lives, of many who came after him.

Pater, W., 'Conclusion', in *Studies in the History of the Renaissance*, London: Macmillan, 1873, pp. 207–13

Λέγει που Ἡράκλειτος ὅτι πάντα χωρεῖ καὶ οὐδὲν μένει.

To regard all things and principles of things as inconstant modes or fashions has more and more become the tendency of modern thought. Let us begin with that which is without—our physical life. Fix upon it in one of its more exquisite intervals, the moment, for instance, of delicious recoil from the flood of water in summer heat. What is the whole physical life in that moment but a combination of natural elements to which science gives their names? But these elements, phosphorus and lime and delicate fibres, are present not in the human body alone: we detect them in places most remote from it. Our physical life is a perpetual motion of them—the passage of the blood, the wasting and repairing of the lenses of the eye, the modification of the tissues of the brain by every ray of light and sound—processes which science reduces to simpler and more elementary forces. Like the elements of which we are composed, the action of these forces extends beyond us; it rusts iron and ripens corn. Far out on every side of us these elements are broadcast, driven by many forces; and birth and gesture and death and the springing of violets from the grave are but a few out of ten thousand resulting combinations. That clear perpetual outline of face and limb is but an image of ours under which we group them—a design in a web, the actual threads of which pass out beyond it. This at least of flame-like our life has, that it is but the concurrence, renewed from moment to moment, of forces parting sooner or later on their ways.

Or if we begin with the inward world of thought and feeling, the whirlpool is still more rapid, the flame more eager and devouring. There it is no longer the gradual darkening of the eye and fading of colour from the wall,—the movement of the shore side, where the water flows down indeed, though in apparent rest,—but the race of the midstream, a drift of momentary acts of sight and passion and thought. At first sight experience seems to bury us under a flood of external objects, pressing upon us with a sharp importunate reality, calling us out of ourselves in a thousand forms of action. But when reflection begins to act upon those objects they are dissipated under its influence; the cohesive force is suspended like a trick of magic; each object is loosed into a group of impressions,—colour, odour, texture,— in the mind of the observer. And if we continue to dwell on this world, not of objects in the solidity with which language invests them, but of impressions unstable, flickering, inconsistent, which burn and are extinguished with our consciousness of them, it contracts still further; the whole scope of observation is dwarfed to the narrow chamber of the individual mind. Experience, already reduced to a swarm of impressions, is ringed round for each one of us by that thick wall of personality through which no real voice has ever pierced on its way to us, or from us to that which we can only conjecture to be without. Every one of those impressions is the impression of the individual in his isolation, each mind keeping as a solitary prisoner its own dream of a world.

Analysis goes a step further still, and tells us that those impressions of the individual to which, for each one of us, experience dwindles down, are in perpetual flight; that each of them is limited by time, and that as time is infinitely divisible, each of them is infinitely divisible also; all that is actual in it being a single moment, gone while we try to apprehend it, of which it may ever be more truly said that it has ceased to be than that it is. To such a tremulous wisp constantly reforming itself on the stream, to a single sharp impression with a sense in it, a relic more or less fleeting, of such moments gone by, what is *real* in our life fines itself down. It is with the movement, the passage and dissolution of impressions, images, sensations, that analysis leaves off,—that continual vanishing away, that strange perpetual weaving and unweaving of ourselves.

Philosophiren, says Novalis, *ist dephlegmatisiren, vivificiren*. The service of philosophy, and of religion and culture as well, to the human spirit, is to startle it into a sharp and eager observation. Every moment some farm grows perfect in hand or face; some tone on the hills or sea is choicer than the rest; some mood of passion or insight or intellectual excitement is irresistibly real and attractive for us,—for that moment only. Not the fruit of experience, but experience itself is the end. A counted number of pulses only is given to us of a variegated, dramatic life. How may we see in them all that is to be seen in them by the finest senses? How can we pass most swiftly from point to point, and be present always at the focus where the greatest number of vital forces unite in their purest energy?

To burn always with this hard gem-like flame, to maintain this ecstasy, is success in life. Failure is to form habits; for habit is relative to a stereotyped world; meantime it is only the roughness of the eye that makes any two persons, things, situations, seem alike. While all melts under our feet, we may well catch at any exquisite passion, or any contribution to knowledge that seems, by a lifted horizon, to set the spirit free for a moment, or any stirring of the senses, strange dyes, strange flowers, and curious odours, or work of the artist's hands, or the face of one's friend. Not to discriminate every moment some passionate attitude in those about us, and in the brilliance of their gifts some tragic dividing of forces on their ways is, on this short day of frost and sun, to sleep before evening. With this sense of the splendour of our experience and of its awful brevity, gathering all we are into one desperate effort to see and touch, we shall hardly have time to make theories about the things we see and touch. What we have to do is to be for ever curiously testing new opinions and courting new impressions, never acquiescing in a facile orthodoxy of Comte or of Hegel, or of our own. Theories, religious or philosophical ideas, as points of view, instruments of criticism, may help us to gather up what might otherwise pass unregarded by us. *La philosophie, c'est la microscope de la pensée.* The theory, or idea, or system, which requires of us, the sacrifice of any part of this experience, in consideration of some interest into which we cannot enter, or some abstract morality we have not identified with ourselves, or what is only conventional, has no real claim upon us.

One of the most beautiful places in the writings of Rousseau is that in the sixth book of the 'Confessions,' where he describes the awakening in him of the literary sense. An undefinable taint of death had always clung about him, and now in early manhood he believed himself stricken by mortal disease. He asked himself how he might make as much as possible of the interval that remained; and he was not biassed by anything in his previous life when he decided that it must be by intellectual excitement, which he found in the clear, fresh writings of Voltaire. Well, we are all *condamnés*, as Victor Hugo says: *les hommes sont tous condamnés a morte avec des sursis indéfinis*: we have an interval, and then our place knows us no more. Some spend this interval in listlessness, some in high passions, the wisest in art and song. For our one chance is in expanding that interval, in getting as many pulsations as possible into the given time. High passions give one this quickened sense of life, ecstasy and sorrow of love, political or religious enthusiasm, or the 'enthusiasm of humanity.' Only, be sure it is passion, that it does yield you this fruit of a quickened, multiplied consciousness. Of this wisdom, the poetic passion, the desire of beauty, the love of art for art's sake has most; for art comes to you professing frankly to give nothing but the highest quality to your moments as they pass, and simply for those moments' sake.

11 Andrew Bennett and Nicholas Royle, Pleasure (1995)

Bennett and Royle take Mansfield's story 'Bliss' as the basis for an exploration of literature and the idea of pleasure. Their essay on 'Pleasure' forms a chapter within a work that introduces a number of concepts of fundamental importance to the study of literature. They find that Mansfield's story epitomises much of what they want to explore in their analysis of pleasure. Pleasure is as much the effect as the subject of Mansfield's text. Bennett and Royle discuss the ways in which 'Bliss' draws readers into the experiences described in the story, offering them amongst other things the pleasure of reading about 'erotic feelings between people'. Reading 'Bliss' involves the pleasures of 'identification, irony, suspense and social satire'. It also, most importantly, involves pleasure in language. Whilst the story invokes a sense of pleasures that lie beyond language, it does so via the experience of words themselves. Literature, Bennett and Royle suggest 'is about the possibilities of pleasure'. It is 'erotic' in the sense that 'it is always concerned with seducing the reader'. The state into which the reader is seduced can be termed as one of 'disavowal' in which we know that what we are reading is fiction, but that knowledge co-exists with a state of seduction into the 'world of literature' in which we read 'a work of fiction as though it were not only words'.

Bennett and Royle discuss the historical context for the concentration on fleeting moments of pleasure in modernist writing. They single out the Conclusion to Pater's *The Renaissance* (reprinted as the previous extract), as an especially valuable text for understanding the legacy of aestheticism. The Paterian moment, over before it is grasped, implies a constant unravelling of identity as inherent to the moment of pleasure. From here, Bennett and Royle move on to consider the important theories of the French Structuralist critic Roland Barthes, who analysed pleasure as a concept fundamental to literature. Barthes's concept of *jouissance*, or 'bliss' defines an unsettling type of pleasure such as that represented and provoked by Mansfield's 'Bliss'. The dissolution of identity that threatens to follow on the experience of pleasure in Mansfield's story figures the fragmenting, hysterical power of reading itself.

Bennett, A., and Royle, N., 'Pleasure', in *An Introduction to Literature, Criticism and Theory: Key Critical Concepts*, Hemel Hempstead: Prentice Hall, 1995, pp. 187–96

Whether in a seminar or at the pub, often the first thing that gets asked about a book is: Did you enjoy it? . . . We may talk about things we enjoy in a work of literature – the gripping narrative, the appealing characters, the power of the language, the comedy and pathos – but we do not very often talk about the enjoyment itself, about what enjoyment or pleasure *is*. There are at least two reasons for this. In the first place, pleasure, enjoyment, emotional and indeed erotic excitement are extremely difficult, or even impossible, to talk about. Secondly, such pleasures tend to border on the transgressive or taboo. But as we hope to show in the course of this chapter, pleasure is crucial to, and even synonymous with, literature itself. This is not to construe the literary as 'mere' play, as simply hedonistic or self-indulgent. Instead we will seek to describe a sense of pleasure and of literature that may be both disconcerting and subversive.

Take a text that might seem relatively innocuous, a story called 'Bliss' (1920) by the New Zealand writer Katherine Mansfield. 'Bliss' concerns a thirty-year-old woman called Bertha Young and her feelings of extreme pleasure before and during a dinner-party at her home. . . . Bertha is consistently described as feeling a 'fire of bliss' (311) inside her: 'Everything was good – was right. All that happened seemed to fill again her brimming cup of bliss' (311). She is 'as much in love as ever' (308) with her husband, but she has also fallen in love with the beautiful Pearl Fulton: 'she always did fall in love with beautiful women who had something strange about them' (307). Whether it is the lovely appearance of the dinner table or the blossoming pear tree which Bertha takes Pearl to look at from the drawing-room balcony, everything helps to give Bertha the feeling of being (like Keats in 'Ode to a Nightingale') 'too happy' (308). The story ends with an excruciating moment of revelation, however, as Bertha inadvertently discovers that her husband and Pearl Fulton are lovers: unaware that Bertha can see them, the couple exchange intimacies in the hall. Bertha's feelings of bliss are finally, brutally effaced. This is how 'Bliss' begins:

> Although Bertha Young was thirty she still had moments like this when she wanted to run instead of walk, to take dancing steps on and off the pavement, to bowl a hoop, to throw something up in the air and catch it again, or to stand still and laugh at – nothing – at nothing, simply.
>
> What can you do if you are thirty and, turning the corner of your own street, you are overcome, suddenly, by a feeling of bliss – absolute bliss! – as though you'd suddenly swallowed a bright piece of that late afternoon sun and it burned in your bosom, sending

out a little shower of sparks into every particle, into every finger and toe? (305)

Bertha can scarcely contain herself, she is overcome by such a feeling of bliss that she does not know what to do with herself. The passage suggests a number of significant things about the nature of pleasure. First, there is an evocation of laughter. . . . Bertha wants 'to stand still and laugh at – nothing – at nothing, simply'. Laughter, the desire to laugh, is one manifestation of Bertha's feelings of extreme pleasure or 'bliss'. But more precisely laughter is identified with a sense of 'nothing simply'. We may recall here Georges Bataille's remark: '[when I laugh,] I am in fact nothing other than the laughter which takes hold of me' (Bataille 1973, 364). There is, for Bertha, the desire to laugh but a desire for laughter that would be 'at nothing', a sense of laughter as pointless, as itself nothing.

Second, and related to this, there is the sense of bliss (like the force of uncontrollable laughter) as something by which a subject – Bertha Young – is 'overcome'. The subject is no longer in control, but rather is in danger of no longer being a subject. She is in danger of shattering, as if into a 'shower of sparks'. Third, the passage suggests a striking correlation between 'bliss' and the inexpressible. The language of the extract resorts to the metaphorical, figurative and paradoxical (it was '*as though* you'd suddenly swallowed a bright piece of that late afternoon sun') precisely because it would appear that there is no other way of describing this 'feeling of bliss'. This feeling of bliss is like having a foreign body inside you (as if you'd suddenly swallowed a piece of the sun): it's alien to yourself but burning inside you. Fourth, and leading on from this, there is the suggestion that pleasure can be painful at the same time: the burning bosom here might be compared with the 'aching Pleasure' evoked in Keats's 'Ode on Melancholy'.

Finally, and perhaps most crucially, the passage draws the reader into the experience that is being described. It intimates a subtle kind of performative . . ., that is to say we can think about the passage as not only describing something but also *doing something*. Pleasure, up to and perhaps even beyond the extreme form of pleasure to which Bertha gives the name 'bliss', is not just a topic or theme in the text: it also is the text, it is the title of the text and it is a potential effect of reading and interacting with the text. The text draws us into a sense of what Wordsworth refers to when he declares, in *The Prelude*: 'Bliss was it in that dawn to be alive' (Book XI, 108). Through its evocations of the loveliness of the world (a blue dish, a pear tree in blossom), Mansfield's story affirms and calls on us to affirm the inexpressible pleasures of being alive. It also gives us the pleasure of reading about eroticism, about the subtleties of erotic feelings between people. It gives us the pleasures of identification, irony, suspense and social satire. Last but not least, 'Bliss' gives us all of these things in language: the experience of pleasure is an experience of words, a pleasure in words, even as it points towards a sense of pleasure that is inexpressible, beyond words.

The pleasure of reading 'Bliss' starts with the deceptive simplicity of its narrative perspective. We are confronted here with an apparently omniscient or telepathic narrator who is capable of inhabiting the mind, body and feelings of the protagonist. The narrator gives us Bertha Young's thoughts and feelings: she does this not only through a third-person narration ('she still had moments', 'she wanted to run') but also, in the second paragraph of the extract, in the second-person ('you are overcome'). This is unusual – though an important characteristic of Mansfield's work generally and strangely insidious: the 'you', after all, may not finally stop short of *you*, the reader. The subtle, almost imperceptible way in which the text draws us into the experience of what is being described can be illustrated in the very opening words of the story: 'Although Bertha Young was thirty she still had moments like this'. The word 'this' seems to call on the reader to acknowledge or accept something already evident, already presented to her or him. Discreetly, deftly, it brings the reader into the immediate here and now of the experience of bliss.

Another aspect of the pleasure of Mansfield's story has to do with its creation of irony and suspense. The text works through suspense, through the pleasure of suspension and an ominous suspension of pleasure. For while the narrative perspective invites us to identify with Bertha and her feelings of bliss, the text also generates other, more specifically *readerly* kinds of pleasure. Bertha's feelings of 'bliss', for example, are at various moments represented in ironic terms. The reader is given a strong sense that – despite the repeated evocations of the 'fire of bliss', the incredible beauty of the table, the pear tree and so on – Bertha Young may have a rather limited experience of bliss, especially in sexual terms. Near the end of the story we are told that, as people are about to start leaving the party, 'For the first time in her life Bertha Young desired her husband' (314). Bliss in this case seems to have been postponed. The reader takes pleasure, then, in being able to identify with the protagonist but to experience at the same time a sense of ironic detachment. Above all, readerly pleasure is generated by the pervasive sense that something is going to happen, that the narrator knows something (and soon perhaps the reader will know something too) which fundamentally complicates Bertha's feelings of 'bliss'. Bliss, then, seems to involve a state of suspension – for Bertha, for the reader and, differently, for the very structure of narration.

On this basis we can perhaps formulate one or two more general propositions about pleasure and literature. Literature is about the possibilities of pleasure. It is about the idea that readerly pleasure is erotic. Literature is erotic (even if it is not literally concerned with erotic or sexual topics or themes) because it is always concerned with seducing the reader. . . . In particular, a literary text can seduce us through a logic of what Freud calls 'disavowal'. Disavowal involves the situation in which someone knows that such and such is not true but nevertheless thinks, speaks or acts as if it is true. Disavowal involves thinking: 'I know, but still . . .'. The process of disavowal whereby we can be seduced into the world of literature, into fictional worlds, has been neatly phrased by Roland Barthes in his book, *The Pleasure of the Text* (1973): the reader *disavows*, in other words he or she keeps thinking, '*I know these are only words, but all the same* . . .' (Barthes 1990a, 47). The logic of disavowal perhaps offers a more precise way of thinking about how we read works of literature than Coleridge's famous idea of a willing suspension of disbelief: the notion of disavowal more dramatically highlights the contradictoriness of what is going on in the act of reading. . . .

This principle of disavowal – of reading a work of fiction as though it were not only words – permits us to suggest a way of distinguishing between literature and pornography. Both have a capacity for erotic and sexual stimulation but the difference between them could be said to consist in the fact that a literary work does not allow the reader to forget the process by which he or she is being seduced, whereas pornography calls for the abolition if the 'as though' altogether. . . . Katherine Mansfield's 'Bliss' is not likely to be classified as pornography, but it is certainly about erotic and sexual feelings – both in what it tells and in its telling, both in its characters and narrative and in ourselves as readers. More particularly, the story explores some of the limits of pleasure: it dramatizes the ways in which pleasure is concerned with strangeness (the nothingness of laughter), paradox (the inarticulable) and contradiction (disavowal). Fundamental to this is what Mansfield's text suggests about the curious temporality of pleasure. . . . The word 'this' ('moments like this') suggests something immediate, here and now. In fact, the time of 'this' is uncertain and strange: it is as if the present of 'moments like this' is already gone. 'Moments like this' are presented in the past tense in such a way as to suggest that they are already 'moments like that' or 'moments like those'. The ambiguity of the this-ness of 'this' is compounded by multiplicity: Bertha wanted to run, to dance, to bowl a hoop, to throw and catch something, to stand still and laugh. Are these all different moments or are they different ways of figuring one single moment ('moments like this [one]')? The sense of time, in the context of extreme pleasure or 'bliss', seems to involve an undecidable, uncontainable multiplicity. Time cannot contain itself when it comes to bliss.

Katherine Mansfield's special focus on moments of intense feeling belongs to a specific historical context and in particular to the literary and cultural aftermath of late nineteenth-century aestheticism. This is to say that pleasure and bliss can be thought about in historical terms: they are experienced and represented differently at different times. A full-scale account of the aestheticism of such figures as Walter Pater, Oscar Wilde, Algernon Swinburne, Aubrey Beardsley and others need not detain us here. Its principal concerns were with the idea of art for art's sake, beauty as truth, and the appeal of the moment for the moment's sake (there is no past, no future, only ever the present moment). In recent times it is the aesthetes above all who made of pleasure a philosophy, a moral creed, a way of being. At the heart of aestheticism is a focus on the beauty and power of the present moment. . . . The most succinct and eloquent text for an understanding of aestheticism is Walter Pater's Conclusion to his book *The Renaissance* (1873). This Conclusion, only a few pages in length, offers us remarkable insight into the work of many modernist writers.

[. . .]

Pater's unprecedented emphasis on the present moment played a crucial role in the development of aestheticism. . . . It haunts modernist writing in turn – whether in the form of epiphanies (in James Joyce's *A Portrait of the Artist as a Young Man* for example), or of what Virginia Woolf famously refers to as 'moments of being', or of what Mansfield, at the start of 'Bliss', refers to as 'moments like this'. All of these writers in their different ways are concerned with the uncontainable, delirious, ecstatic, inexpressible quality of individual moments, of time as (only) now. It is not simply a question of a *'carpe diem'* ('seize the day') motif in modern literature. Rather, it is a matter of how the present moment resists any attempt to appropriate or 'seize' it. It is a matter of how moments of extreme pleasure (including orgasm) are at the same time moments of loss: such moments involve, indeed, a kind of dissolution and more generally suggest a sense of experience in terms of what Pater calls 'that continual vanishing away, that strange, perpetual weaving and unweaving of ourselves' (196).

In other words, as Mansfield's story suggests, pleasure can be thought about in terms of a subversion of identity. . . . Nor can one say that the kind of thinking and experience that Pater calls for constitutes mere self-indulgence or a contemptible neglect of political and social realities. . . .

Roland Barthes[1] stresses that 'hedonism has been repressed by nearly every philosophy' and he is at pleasurable pains to argue against such repression. The value and originality of his study consists not in the politically suspect project of advocating hedonism in a traditional sense but rather in the critical delineation of the paradoxes of pleasure, specifically in the experience of reading. Barthes offers a sort of critical anatomy of pleasure in reading. In particular, he distinguishes between two sorts of pleasure: pleasure of the 'comfortable' sort and pleasure of a more disturbing and subversive kind. Barthes writes:

> Text of pleasure: the text that contents, fills, grants euphoria; the text that comes from culture and does not break with it, is linked to a *comfortable* practice of reading. Text of bliss: the text that imposes a state of loss, the text that discomforts (perhaps to the point of a certain boredom), unsettles the reader's historical, cultural, psychological assumptions, the consistency of his tastes, values, memories, brings to a crisis his relation with language. (14)

Barthes's book suggests, then, that there are two ways in which we could think about pleasure. One is basically recuperative: it does not break with culture but rather reinforces traditional or comfortable notions of meaning, society, ideology, etc. The other sense of pleasure ('bliss') is more unsettling and strange. No doubt all literary and other cultural texts are susceptible to being read in both of these ways. Barthes' own emphasis, however, falls on 'bliss' ('jouissance' in French). 'Bliss' has to do with the inexpressible: 'pleasure can be expressed in words, bliss cannot' (21). Bliss has to do with a deconstruction of the political: it is thus engaged in 'de-politicizing what is apparently political, and in politicizing what apparently is not' (44). Or as Barthes puts it: 'The text is (should be) that uninhibited person who shows his behind to the *Political Father*' (53). Above all, bliss has to do with the subversion of identity itself. As with the uncontrollable force of laughter or the moment of orgasm, the extreme pleasure of bliss involves a shattering of self, a (momentary) dissolution of identity. The subject is thus 'never anything but a "living contradiction": a split subject, who simultaneously enjoys, through the text, the consistency of his selfhood and its collapse, its fall' (21).

By way of conclusion, we would like to suggest that – while Barthes refers to the reader as 'he' – the 'living contradiction' he describes may be thought about as, in the final analysis, undecidably gendered. Partly what makes Barthes's work unusual and challenging is that it explicitly centres on the importance of 'emotion', defining this as 'a disturbance, a bordering on collapse' (25). For Barthes, we could say, the pleasure of reading inevitably involves 'getting hysterical'. But the collapse of selfhood, the shattering force of bliss which he talks about, is a collapse in which it is no longer clear whether there is a subject, let alone what gender it might belong to. Mansfield's story can also be considered in these terms. Insofar as it is a text about 'women and hysteria', it suggests that 'getting hysterical' (306) is just as much a male as a female tendency. 'Bliss', that is to say, is as much about male hysteria as it is about female hysteria. This is evident, in particular, in Mansfield's characterization of Eddie Warren, the poet who is '(as usual) in a state of acute distress', and whose first words for example provide a hysterical account of his journey to the Youngs':

> 'I have had such a *dreadful* experience with a taxi-man; he was *most* sinister. I couldn't get him to *stop*. The more I knocked and called the *faster* he went. And in the moonlight this *bizarre* figure with the *flattened* head *crouching* over the *lit-tle* wheel . . .' (309)

But it is also evident in Mansfield's characterization of Bertha's husband Harry, who is one moment 'rush[ing] into battle where no battle was' (310) and at others 'extravagantly [i.e. hysterically] cool and collected' (310, 315). More radically, however, 'Bliss' is a story about the condition of 'living contradiction' which Barthes evokes. It suggests that that extreme of pleasure called 'bliss' is the very undoing of identity, including the undoing of gender-identity.

The story concludes with Harry locking up and Bertha recalling Pearl Fulton's final words to her ('Your lovely pear tree!'):

> And then she was gone, with Eddie following, like the black cat following the grey cat.
> 'I'll shut up shop,' said Harry, extravagantly cool and collected.
> 'Your lovely pear tree – pear tree – pear tree!'
> Bertha simply ran over to the long windows.
> 'Oh, what is going to happen now?' she cried.
> But the pear tree was as lovely as ever and as full of flower and as still. (315)

'Bliss' ends with this 'still'. It leaves the question of bliss itself in suspense, inexpressible, unbearable. As Barthes remarks: 'Pleasure's force of *suspension* can never be overstated' (Barthes 1990a, 65). Pleasure remains resistant

45

and enigmatic, like 'literature'. At its most extreme, the pleasure of literature is less to do with the fact that it 'holds a mirror up to nature' and offers a reflection of 'life' and much more to do with an experience of 'living contra-diction' – with what suspends or momentarily shatters our very identity.

Note

1   Roland Barthes, *The Pleasure of the Text*, trans. Richard Miller, Oxford: Blackwell, 1990, p. 57.

LEWIS GRASSIC GIBBON,
SUNSET SONG

Lewis Grassic Gibbon's novel *Sunset Song* has provoked passionate responses ever since its first publication in 1932. Many of these responses have been defined by the different reviewers' strong sense of what literature is for – or at least should be for – and the extracts reprinted below provide a vivid flavour of the variety of ideas and debates inspired by the novel from 1932 to 2003. The first group of extracts, listed under no. 12, is selected from Gibbon's own writings, and include: Extract 12.1, his 1935 'Contribution to The Writers' International Controversy' in which he sets out his ideas on the relation between literature and politics, and the role of the creative writer; Extract 12.2, a passage from a letter he wrote in 1933 to Helen Cruickshank in which he explains in personal terms the political anger that drives his writing, that makes him 'shout too loudly'; and Extract 12.3, a passage from his 1934 essay 'The Antique Scene' in which he protests against the sanitised, official version of Scottish history. The second group of extracts, listed under no. 13, is a selection of reviews of the first edition of *Sunset Song* that were published between September 1932 and April 1933. The controversial reception of *Sunset Song* is conveyed in these reviews, which range from the hostile (Extract 13.3 from the *Fife Herald and Journal*), to the condescending (Extract 13.4 from the *Modern Scot*), to the enthusiastic (Extract 13.1 from the *Aberdeen Bon Accord*, Extract 13.2 from the *Daily Mail* and Extract 13.5 from the *New York Times Book Review*). Also included in Extract 13.3 is Gibbon's own vigorous reaction to the negative review in the *Fife Herald*. The third group of extracts, listed under no. 14, contains four different views of how *Sunset Song* should be interpreted, or more particularly, what *Sunset Song*-as-Literature might be for. The first two extracts – Extract 14.1 by Neil Gunn and Extract 14.2 by James Barke – were both published in the 1930s, and express conflicting views regarding the political allegiances implicit in Gibbon's literary work, with Gunn appealing to a Scottish nationalist interpretation, and Barke to an international Socialist agenda. The final two extracts (both published in 2003) demonstrate *Sunset Song*'s continuing capacity to generate debate, as they provide quite different views of how the novel has been, or indeed might be used: Keith Dixon in Extract 14.3 condemns the appropriation of *Sunset Song* by the conservative Scottish establishment, whereas film director Terence Davies in Extract 14.4 sees the novel as a timeless exploration of 'mysteries of land, home, and family'.

12.1 Lewis Grassic Gibbon, Contribution to The Writers' International Controversy (1935)

Gibbon, L. G., 'Contribution to The Writers' International Controversy', *Left Review*, 1.5, February 1935, pp. 179–80

A great part of the thesis seems to me to propound ideas which are false, and projects which are irrelevant.

It is nonsense to say that modern literature is narrowing in 'content'; there was never in the history of English letters such a variety of books on such a variety of subjects, never such continuous display of fit and excellent technique. One need do no more than glance through an issue of *The Times Literary Supplement* to be convinced of this.

To say that the period 1913 to 1934 is a decadent period is just, if I may say so, Bolshevik blah. Neither in fiction, sociological writing, biography (to take only three departments) was there work done half so well in any Victorian or Edwardian period of equal length.

So-called revolutionary statements on decadence (such as that contained in the resolution) seem to me to be inspired by (a) misapprehension; (b) ignorance; or (c) spite.

It is obvious that such revolutionists imagine that modern fiction means only Aldous Huxley, modern dramas Noel Coward, modern biography the Lytton Stracheyites, and modern history the half-witted Spenglerites.

So much for misapprehension and ignorance. But the spite is also very real. Not only do hordes of those 'revolutionary' writers never read their contemporaries (they wallow instead, and exclusively, in clumsy translations from the Russian and German) but they hate and denigrate those contemporaries with a quite Biblical uncharitableness and malice. With a little bad Marxian patter and the single adjective 'bourgeois' in their vocabularies they proceed (in the literary pages of the *Daily Worker* and like organs) to such spiteful displays of spiteful exhibitionism as warrant the attention of a psycho-analyst. From their own innate second-rateness they hate and despise good work just as they look upon any measure of success accruing to a book (not written by one of their intimate circle) with a moronic envy.

Not all revolutionary writers (I am a revolutionary writer) are cretins. But the influence of such delayed adolescents, still in the grip of wishfulfilment dreams, seems to have predominated in the drawing up of this resolution. Capitalist literature, whether we like it or not, is not in decay; capitalist economics have reached the verge of collapse, which is quite a different matter. Towards the culmination of a civilization the arts, so far from decaying, always reach their greatest efflorescence (the veriest tyro student of the historic process knows this).

That efflorescence is now in being. It is not a decayed and decrepit dinosaur who is the opponent of the real revolutionary writer, but a very healthy and vigorous dragon indeed – so healthy he can still afford to laugh at the revolutionist. If revolutionary writers believe they can meet in fraternal pow-wows and talk the monster to death by calling it 'bourgeois' and 'decadent' they are living in a clown's paradise.

Having said this in criticism, I'll proceed to a little construction:

First, I'm in favour of a union of revolutionary writers. But this union would

(a) Consist only of those who have done work of definite and recognized literary value (from the revolutionary viewpoint). It would consist of professional journalists, novelists, historians, and the like, who before admittance would have to prove their right to admittance.

(b) Exclude that horde of paragraphists, minor reviewers, ghastly poetasters and all the like amateurs who clog up the machinery of the left wing literary movement.

(c) Set its members, as a first task, to drawing up a detailed and unimpassioned analysis of contemporary literature and the various literary movements.

(d) Be a shock brigade of writers, not a P.S.A. sprawl. I hate capitalism; all my books are explicit or implicit propaganda. But because I am a revolutionist I see no reason for gainsaying my own critical judgment – hence this letter!

12.2 Lewis Grassic Gibbon, Letter to Helen Cruickshank (1933)

Gibbon, L. G., Letter to Helen Cruickshank (1933), in W. K. Malcolm, 'Shouting Too Loudly: Leslie Mitchell, Humanism and the Art of Excess', in M. P. McCullough and S. M. Dunnigan (eds), *A Flame in the Mearns. Lewis Grassic Gibbon: A Centenary Celebration*, Glasgow: Association for Scottish Literary Studies, 2003, p. 76

... Yes, horrors do haunt me. That's because I'm in love with humanity. Ancient Greece is never the Parthenon to me: it's a slave being tortured in a dungeon in the Athenian law-courts; Ancient Egypt is never the Pyramids: it's the blood and tears of Goshen; Ancient Scotland is never Mary Queen: it's those serfs they kept chained in the Fifeshire mines a hundred years ago. And so on. And so with the moderns: I am so horrified by all our dirty little cruelties and bestialities that I would feel the lowest kind of skunk if I didn't shout the horror of them from the house-tops. Of course I shout too loudly. But the filthy conspiracy of silence there was in the past! And is coming again in a new guise, called Renaissance, and Objectivity, and National Art and what not. Blithering about Henryson and the Makars (whoever these cretins were) and forgetting the Glasgow slums.

12.3 Lewis Grassic Gibbon, The Antique Scene (1934)

Gibbon, L. G., 'The Antique Scene' (1934), in V. Bold (ed.), *Smeddum: A Lewis Grassic Gibbon Anthology*, Edinburgh: Canongate, 2001, pp. 3–5

The history of Scotland may be divided into the three phases of Colonisation, Civilisation, and Barbarisation. That the last word is a synonym for Anglicisation is no adverse reflection upon the quality of the great English culture. Again and again, in the play of the historic forces, a great civilisation on an alien and lesser has compassed that alien's downfall.

Few things cry so urgently for rewriting as does Scots history, in few aspects of her bastardised culture has Scotland been so ill-served as by her historians. The chatter and gossip of half the salons and drawing-rooms of European intellectualism hang over the antique Scottish scene like a malarial fog through which peer the fictitious faces of heroic Highlanders, hardy Norsemen, lovely Stewart queens, and dashing Jacobite rebels. Those stage-ghosts shamble amid the dimness, and mope and mow in their ancient parts with an idiotic vacuity but a maddening persistence. Modern research along orthodox lines balks from the players, or renames them shyly and retires into footnotes on Kaltwasser.

Yet behind those grimaces of the romanticised or alien imagination a real people once lived and had its being, and hoped and feared and hated, and was greatly uplifted, and loved its children, and knew agony of the patriotic spirit, and was mean and bestial, and generous, and sardonically merciful. Behind the posturings of those poltergeists are the lives of millions of the lowly who wiped the sweats of toil from browned faces and smelt the pour of waters by the Mull of Kintyre and the winds of autumn in the Grampian haughs and the sour, sweet odours of the upland tarns; who tramped in their varying costumes and speeches to the colour and play of the old guild-towns; who made great poetry and sang it; who begat their kind in shame or delight in the begetting; who were much as you or I, human animals bedevilled or uplifted by the play of the forces of civilisation in that remote corner of the Western world which we call Scotland. . . .

13.1 *Aberdeen Bon Accord, Sunset Song.* Striking Story of Mearns Life (1932)

J. F. G., '*Sunset Song.* Striking Story of Mearns Life', *Aberdeen Bon Accord and Northern Chronicle*, 9 September 1932, 4

In "Sunset Song" (Jarrolds, Paternoster Row, London: 7/6), Lewis Grassic Gibbon has produced a very notable first novel. Whether the author is a he or a she is a matter of doubt in the mind of the present writer. It is evident, however, that Lewis Grassic Gibbon – we miss the final "k" in Grassick – is an aboriginal Scot, possibly belonging to Echt, who is familiar with that part of the Mearns in which the scenes of the story are placed, but it is also certain that he – we shall admit the implication of the masculine pseudonym – seems to have lived "furth" of Scotland for some time. Hence probably the reference to "taking the B.A. degree" in Aberdeen, and the holding of an inquest on a suicide; also perhaps the assumption that the terms of a will, which would be quite in accordance with English law, would not have been upset as much as challenged in a Scots Court. Then we have the ascription of the notorious rhyme about the foundation of Laurencekirk to Thomas of Ercildoune, but that, perhaps, is just a sly though not very clearly perceptible stroke of humour.

The "word painting"

These are very minor spots on the sun of what is relatively a great achievement. Though Mr Gibbon – we shall not boggle about the "Mr" – devotes much of his space to word painting, and is sparing in his dialogue, the interest of the story is cumulative and one reads right to the end with ever increasing enthusiasm and admiration. Allusion has been made to the word paintings, but not with derogatory intention. These are the most impressive parts of the book. The late George Warrington Steevens, who was a master in the art, never more successfully conveyed the "atmosphere" of a place or district than Mr Gibbon, who is also equally successful in his character sketches. His peasant farmers, however, are not peculiar to the Mearns; they are common to the whole kingdom, but with the difference that it is only the Scotsman who possesses at once a vicious irresponsible tongue and all the qualities that make a good neighbour.

With the probable exception of Dr. William Alexander's "Johnny Gibb of Gushetneuk," and some of the same writer's tales in "Life Among My Ain Folk," "Sunset Song" is the most realistic story of North-Eastern peasant-farmer life ever written. Mr Gibbon, however, is much more starkly "photographic" in his methods than Dr. Alexander. Many otherwise complaisant readers may think that sex is unduly obtruded, and that some, if not all the characters, are suffering from sex-obsession. Mr Gibbon may reply that the Scottish peasants rightly regard sex as the most important of the essential forces in their nature, and therefore as proper a topic of discussion as their religion or their victuals. The peasants' own defence is that "nothing which is natural can be nasty." Let us leave it at that.

[. . .]

The departing peasant class

This is only a wretchedly incomplete summary of the narrative which has for its "grand finale" the consecration of the Druidic standing stones at the Loch of Kinraddie as a memorial of the parish's fallen sons. These stones and the loch are frequently introduced in the story and almost as memorably as Stonehenge in "Tess of the Durbervilles." Mr Gibbon has devoted much loving care to his study of Chris; and in spite of what the hypercritical world would criticise as too much "intimate revelation" she retains the sympathy and affection of every sound-hearted reader throughout. Some may think that the latter incidents are not quite convincing and have been devised to give Mr Gibbon an opportunity of bringing to his tale an impressive conclusion, but criticism of that sort does not detract materially from the artistic merits of the book. Undoubtedly there are some painful scenes in "Sunset Song," but all of them are developed with a power which reminds one of the "House with the Green Shutters." Others dealing with incidents of domestic life such as the wedding and the barn dance will be admired for their Dutch-like fidelity. Mr Gibbon, as already indicated, has written a classic of Scottish peasant life, which he intends to be taken as the "Sunset Song" of a class that is bound to disappear as a result of the changed conditions caused by the war. The book places the author in the front-rank of present-day writers of fiction.

13.2 *Daily Mail,* Four Good Novels. Some Young Authors of Promise (1932)

Compton MacKenzie, 'Four Good Novels. Some Young Authors of Promise', *Daily Mail*, 13 September 1932, 4

I have no hesitation in saying that *Sunset Song* by Lewis Grassic Gibbon (Jarrolds, 7s 6d) is the richest novel about Scottish life written for many years.

Of yore we learnt our A.B.C. To-day we learn our B.B.C. Mr. Gibbon is the first of our contemporary Scottish writers to use the dialect with such effect that the most fanatical admirer of B.B.C. English and accent will have to admit the impoverishment that English prose has suffered from its failure to absorb and use 'braid Scots.'

Mr. Gibbon has enriched the English novel as surely as Livy enriched Latin history with his Patavinity. There is internal evidence that he had already struggled hard to acquire a mastery of English prose before he ventured to approach his present task. It is experience which has given him the right to experiment, and there is so much in this novel to interest a fellow-craftsman on the side of technique that it is tempting to embark on a long discussion of it.

However, that is not the way to persuade the great majority of novel readers into reading 'Sunset Song'. The mention of technique evokes hideously high-browed bogies, and frightens the average reader into the comfortable security of the technique with which he is familiar. So all I will say is that, in spite of its originality of presentation, 'Sunset Song' is perfectly easy to read – a notable triumph indeed for a new technique.

The language is often coarse and sometimes brutal, and the statement of facts is always unequivocal. Mr. Gibbon can summon Robert Burns as witness for the defence. Indeed the comparison with Burns is constant in the reader's mind, for Tam o'Shanter rides through Mr Gibbon's prose all the time.

The theme is the extinction of the crofter by the conditions of the modern world. I myself am optimistic enough to believe that Mr. Gibbon's epic elegy is premature, and that even yet that rich agricultural life can be restored; but such optimism only makes me more grateful for this superb lament which shows what is in danger of being for ever lost.

13.3 *Fife Herald and Journal*, Review of *Sunset Song: A Novel*. By Lewis Grassic Gibbon (1932)

Anon, 'Review of *Sunset Song: A Novel*. By Lewis Grassic Gibbon', *The Fife Herald and Journal*, 21 September 1932, 2

The 'jacket' of this book says it may mark a new epoch in Scots literature, and Mr Gibbon the founder of a new school. Judging from certain passages in the story, one is forced to conclude that the writer is a Mrs Gibbon. Advertisements in the daily Press quote G. Malcolm Thomson as hailing this novel as "the most important Scottish novel since 'The House with the Green Shutters.'" Before the present reviewer saw this advertisement, he felt that "Sunset Song" was a bad copy of "The House with the Green Shutters," published 30 odd years ago and still to be bought in a popularly priced edition. In "Sunset Song", houses with "green shutters" are mentioned twice. The 30-year-old book was certainly realistic, but it was written by a man who knew many phases of Scotland. He did not write of "inquests" in Scotland and a "B.A." of Aberdeen University as Lewis Grassic Gibbon does; nor did the former writer mix up gigs and motor cars, finishing his tale with the time of the Great War. It is a story of crofter life near Stonehaven; but it is questionable if the author, or authoress, is correct in the description of crofter girls' underclothing of that period. The coarse bits of the book are in italic type, just as a woman underlines her letters. How some of it passed the publishers' censor we cannot fathom. The explanation, possibly, is that he did not understand the Scotch; for the book is Scotch in places. A frequent expression, underlined, is "Damn't to hell." "Feint," meaning little, and "futret" for weasel are always cropping up in the tale, and with "meikie" for "muckle," and some vulgar words, these are about all the Scotch words in this "Scotch" novel. The following is a sample of a Scotch husband's talk to his wife, "Chris.":- "Any (not ony) supper left – unless you're too bloody standoffish even to have (not hae) that? . . . For Christ's sake let a man sit down (not doon)." "Chris" is the heroine, and the "jacket" says she is "one of the loveliest figures in fiction"! In some moods she is not so bad, but the description is far-fetched. The writer of the novel seems to have a spite at English people and Parish Church ministers. Zola's "La Terre" was extremely racy of the soil, and the English translation was banned by the British Law Courts. The "Sunset Song" has none of the artistry of Zola or any other French novelist: it is crude, and no credit to Scotland. We question if a Scotch publisher would have handled it; certainly, no newspaper in this country would print it unaltered as a serial story; and yet Mr Compton

Mackenzie, the present lord rector of Glasgow University, is advertised as saying of "Sunset Song" – "I have no hesitation in saying that it is the richest novel about Scottish life written for many years . . . it is a notable triumph . . . the comparison with Burns is constant in the reader's mind, for Tam o'Shanter rides through Mr Gibbon's prose all the time." The Lord Rector must have skipped the book considerably!

Lewis Grassic Gibbon, '"Sunset Song." Author's Reply (To the Editor)', *The Fife Herald and Journal*, 28 September 1932, 2

Sir, – An agency has sent me a review of my novel, "Sunset Song," which appeared in an issue of your paper dated the 21st September. I would be glad of a little space in which to deal with your reviewer's remarks. Novel reviewers are, of course, entitled to their opinions of a book's artistic merits; they are not, however, entitled either deliberately to misrepresent the contents of a book or to exercise what appears to be (strangely enough) a personal spite against the author.

I. Let me set your reviewer's mind at rest: I am not "Mrs" Gibbon – and, consequently, under no disabilities in dealing with either cads or clowns among the critics.

II. I "mix up gigs and motor cars"? If your reviewer had ridden in both, as I have done, he'd realise there is no "mix-up". Both were, and still are, quite common phenomena on the roads of the Mearns.

III. "The coarse bits of the book are in italic type." This is just a plain lie. Italic type is used throughout the book to represent conversation – and for no other purpose.

IV. The publisher's censors "did not understand the Scotch," otherwise the book would not have been allowed to pass. The book was read in manuscript by three prominent Scotsmen, and passed by them with as much acclaim as it has subsequently received from the entire Press in Scotland and England – excepting your anonymous reviewer.

V. Your reviewer comments sneeringly on the quality of the "Scotch" in which the book is written. His reference to the dialect as "Scotch" proves his own abysmal ignorance of the subject. That apart, however, "Sunset Song" makes no pretence to be written in *Scots* – as is distinctly stated in an introductory note to the book. This again is an example of deliberate distortion on the part of your reviewer.

VI. "The writer seems to have a spite at English people and Parish Church ministers." (a) "Sunset Song" has been reviewed by some thirty Englishmen in the most important periodicals of the country without one of them appearing to note my anti-English bias. (They are capable of appreciating humorous comment.) (b) "The Scots Observer" is the official organ of the Church of Scotland, and very apt to defend it against calumny. On the 15th of this month it devoted a column and a half to an eulogistic review of "Sunset Song", without mention of any anti-Church "spite".

VII. Finally, the suggestion that the Lord Rector of Glasgow University "skipped the book" in spite of passing an authoritative opinion upon it is a piece of petty scoundrelism which, no doubt, your reviewer believes can be practised safely from the refuge of provincial obscurity and a sneaking anonymity. I am, etc.,

L. GRASSIC GIBBON
24 September 1932

13.4 *Modern Scot*, Two Scottish Novels (1932)

Anon, 'Two Scottish Novels. *Poor Tom*. By Edwin Muir. Dent. *Sunset Song*. By Lewis Grassic Gibbon', *The Modern Scot*, 3.3 (October 1932): 250–2

There are several more novelists who are more richly endowed than Mr [Edwin] Muir with the gifts of eye and ear that enable the novelist to gather his material, but who fail to make such good use of it. Such is Lewis Grassic Gibbon, who attempts – like the majority of novelists – to handle a mass of material which would require tremendous gifts to organize into a fully satisfying art-form. The dialogue of *Sunset Song* recaptures admirably the clipped, racy speech of the Mearns; the anecdotes of bed and bothy have the stamp of truth; the characters are lifelike. But the tragedy moves jerkily to its close, with a very big jerk before the magnificent epilogue, and the style is, in the words of one reviewer, "a little . . . hot in the collar." On the first page Mr Gibbon dismays his reader with sentences like this (an attempt to convey historical atmosphere): "And maybe he said a bit prayer by that stone and then he rode into the Mearns, and the story tells no more of his riding, but that at last he rid to Kinraddie, a tormented place, and they told him where the gryphon slept, down there in the den of Kinraddie." And there are many occasions in the book when the reader comes across as serious faults of taste. For all its entertainment value, and its moving account of life on a croft, the reader feels that Mr Gibbon is making his novel, especially the first part, as Mr Shaw says Mr Barrie makes his plays – as a milliner makes a bonnet, by matching and sewing together the materials – not by transmuting his impressions into an art-form. Mr Gibbon's story of

Kinraddie is like the map drawn on the boards of the novel: it has not, in Mr Lubbock's words, "shed its irrelevancy," has not "passed through an imagination." It is readable, and probably the best recent Scottish story of its kind, but it leaves the novel where it was thirty years ago.

13.5 *New York Times Book Review*, A Scotch Novel that is Close to the Soil (1933)

Peter Monro Jack, 'A Scotch Novel That Is Close to the Soil', *The New York Times Book Review*, 2 April 1933, 2

Talk of a Scottish renaissance of literature would be very idle indeed but for the occasional achievement of books like 'Sunset Song.' Although it is a regional novel primarily coming from the heart of agricultural Scotland and exactly abiding by its Scotch quality, it may be read with delight the world over. It recovers the national scene and sense in literature, intermittently lost to antiquarians or lent to the English, and it does this with authentic passion for its material as well as a fine directive power in universalizing the material. To indicate its place we may quote the minister's epigram of the Scot's countryside: fathered by a kailyard and a bonnie brier bush in the lee of a house with green shutters. And naturally Mr. Gibbon is indebted to these separate aspects of Scots life pictured by Barrie, Maclaren and Douglas; but he succumbs neither to Scotch sentiment nor Scotch censoriousness, least of all to Scotch charm. His distinction is the breadth and security of his vision: in short, his truly representative character. [Plot summary]

[. . .]

All of this has been narrated in a style that is itself a part of the village life. The quotations show that Mr. Gibbon writes neither English nor Scotch, but a cunning interplay of both. He uses many words – canty, keek, sumph, scraich, gloaming, gomeril, pleiter – that are in actual use, not rescued (after the fashion of some revivalists) from medieval literature. They have no exact equivalents in English, but their meaning is sufficiently obvious in the context. Even more effectively, he has soaked his English in the Scottish rhythm and turn of phrase so that one seems to be listening to the village itself speaking – the highest reach of naturalism – intimately and informally, with a running commentary in that sly panky censorious deliberation common to the Scotch but difficult to define: not free from malice and suspicion, but perhaps no more than the sharper side of a kindly heart that has to protect itself (people being what they are) from its own kindness. The Scottish farmer lives so completely in this novel that you can hear the tone of his voice.

14.1 Neil M. Gunn, Nationalism in Writing (1938)

Gunn, Neil M., 'Nationalism in Writing: Tradition and Magic in the Work of Lewis Grassic Gibbon', *The Scots Magazine*, 30.1, October 1938, pp. 28–35

It is a basic distinction, and one that may reasonably be taken to indicate Mitchell's own preoccupation with life; on the one hand, the concern of the creative artist; on the other, the concern of the man for the iniquitous condition of the poor, strengthened by knowledge gained from his studies in archaeology and anthropology. Accordingly it might broadly be suggested that when Mitchell is using orthodox English, he is manipulating intellectual rather than blood values, and consequently in the realm of the emotions such English does not move us with a sense of the unconditional magic of life or of that life's being rooted in the breeding soil of tradition.

[. . .]

Yet what a troubling division was in him just there! For he never imaginatively realised this Cosmopolis; he merely accepted it, like Tennyson or Mr H. G. Wells, as something in the nature of "Progress" that is inevitable; and it was inevitable for Mitchell, I feel, not because of any ultimate need for it *in itself*, but because it was for humanity's final good *on the material or economic plane*. When we attain Cosmopolis, economic slavery and physical want will have vanished (though precisely why—as apart from piously—is never explained by any Cosmopolitan). It was not his anthropological studies, his scientific visualisations, if I may use such a phrase, that moved him here so much as his genuine, profoundly sensitive concern for the downtrodden; not that this concern expressed itelf in the natural positive terms of love or kindness or Christian charity, but, characteristically (of himself and of his age), in a hatred of the oppressors—individual and system—that drew from him so often language of scathing directness or of obliterating irony. His sympathy is with "the lowly, the oppressed, the Cheated of the Sunlight, the bitter relics of the savagery of the Industrial Revolution," and he "would welcome the end of Braid Scots and Gaelic, our culture, our history, our nationhood under the heels of a Chinese army of occupation if it would cleanse the Glasgow slums, give a surety of food and play—the elementary right of every human being—to those people of the abyss."

[. . .]

From that economic-ethical standpoint it is impossible to divorce the creative writer. Nor is there any need to, for the dichotomy is apparent only, even if Mitchell does not always appear to have realised as much himself. For to us the fact is that when he came to do his finest creative work he deliberately chose not a language of Cosmopolis, not even orthodox English (which is near enough to cosmopolitan size for all practical purposes), but a particular use and pattern of English applicable to a small part of the small country of Scotland, a regional rhythm—and dying at that!

Not only so, but he (in "Scottish Scene") has a characteristically fierce onslaught on all living Scottish authors writing in English, for him they are not Scottish authors at all, but, at the best, "brilliantly unorthodox Englishmen writing on Scotshire." Quite apart from the "heights of Scots literature," they do not attain even its "pedestrian levels."

From *economic* Cosmopolis to *creative* Nationalism, the turnabout is absolutely complete. And by his own work, it is absolutely justified. From the last ever-widening ring, he has come back in a rush to the heart of the disturbance. His rationalising of this may be faulty. In "Sunset Song," for example, he justly recognises himself as a Scots writer attempting Scots work. But his use of English is similar in kind and creative intention to that of a considerable number of modern Irish writers, whose reputations are worldwide; to what is being produced in America; and possibly to what is being attempted in Scotland, if the mannerism was not always pronounced enough to take his fancy. But if his reasoning is inadequate here, the urge that moved him to it is sound. In a similar way his professed readiness to accept the Chinese army of occupation is sound, though at the same time palpably fantastic, simply because the Scots people, reforming and running their own social system, could cleanse the Glasgow slums without help either from the Chinese or from Cosmopolis. Why a Scot may not consume the surplus he produces until he has got the permission of an Asiatic or Cosmopolist is a mystery that is not going to remain for ever dark. I would have had more faith in Mitchell's Cosmopolis if Mitchell had shown more faith in his own Scotland, and that for the obvious reason that the chance of reforming the world becomes possible only in so far as we show a disposition to reform ourselves. If a Scot is going to help the world towards Socialism, then the place for him is Glasgow or Dundee; if towards Cosmopolis, then still Glasgow or Dundee; if towards some still finer conception, yet again his native heath. . . .

14.2 James Barke, Lewis Grassic Gibbon (1936)

Barke, J., 'Lewis Grassic Gibbon', *Left Review*, 2.5, February 1936, pp. 220–5

It is doubtful if there are more than four Scottish novelists worthy of serious critical consideration. Of the four, Mr. Neil M. Gunn is, perhaps, the greatest, and Lewis Grassic Gibbon the most important, literary artist. This comparison will not seriously be questioned by the student of Scottish literature. Nevertheless an analysis and explanation may help to clarify the present writer's standpoint and prepare the reader for what follows.

Gunn is a Gaelic culture revivalist: and it follows that, philosophically, he is an Idealist. He distils from the Gaelic past something of the quality which he believes to be the dominant racial quality of the Gael: aristocratic, individualist quality. The survival of this quality is all-important to Gunn. Hence his Scottish Nationalist alignment. For Scottish Nationalism is largely inspired by the superior race-theory of the Gael and the "currency" demagogy of Major Douglas. The identity of Gunn's Nationalist ideology with that of the Aryan theoreticians of Hitler Fascism is not so fortuitous as its superficial form and expression might indicate.

Gibbon on the other hand is an internationalist: he looks forward, he is consumed with the vision of Cosmopolis. Philosophically he is a materialist. True, his view of history is distorted by a discredited and unscientific "Diffusionism." But, in the main, he is a materialist. He sees clearly enough that the mode of production in material life determines the general character of the social, political and spiritual processes of life."

The fundamental difference of approach between Gunn and Gibbon is of first importance. Gunn is no more a "pure" idealist than Gibbon is a "pure" materialist. Gunn, having a smaller field of vision than Gibbon, is able to concentrate more intensely on it. The result is that his literary art is on a higher level than Gibbon's. Gunn is, in fact, one of the greatest literary artists writing in the English tongue. Gibbon, having a much wider field of vision and working at much higher pressure than Gunn, is not such a great artist. But because of the breadth of his vision (and since he deals with decisive and fundamental issues) he is a much more important artist than Gunn.

[. . .]

[It is] essential not only to disarm criticism in advance but to make clear the nature and purpose of this criticism of *A Scots Quair*. To the reader unsympathetic or unconcerned with the struggle of the working class, to the critic who does not recognize the class war (far less the class nature of society) and who concerns himself with "art" and "literature" (deprecating, scorning "propaganda") this insistence on the essential class content of *A Scots Quair* may appear irrelevant or even distorted. But there is no irrelevance or distortion. Even a superficial understanding of the content of *A Scots Quair* should reveal its true purpose, nature and significance. All art is propaganda. Gibbon had no illusions about this elementary truth. ("All my books are explicit or implicit propaganda." LEFT REVIEW, February, 1935.) Nor had he any doubt as to the nature of his propaganda. ("I am a revolutionary writer." *Ibid.*)

*   *   *

There remains the task of evaluating *A Scots Quair* with relation to the literature, not only of Scotland, but of Great Britain.

Born and brought up in the Mearns country, Gibbon, early in his life, passed over to the English: that is he became ("like the overwhelming majority of British Islanders") a British citizen. That he loved the country of his birth did not mean that he was a perverted, illogical and reactionary Nationalist. He realized that Scotland and England had become, since the Union (and before it), inseparably welded together in economic and cultural interest: that there was no essential difference between the Scots and the English. He was certainly "much more at home" in London than he would have been in Glasgow, Edinburgh or Aberdeen. Nevertheless there is a Scottish literature that is, a literature dealing with Scottish Life and Character. *A Scots Quair* is probably the greatest Scots novel in Scottish literature. Certainly it is in the first three. (It is possible to place it so accurately: Scottish fiction is not so rich that such a "placing" is unwise or valueless.)

There is an increasing body of commercial fictionists who can (rather arbitrarily no doubt) be labelled Scots. A few of them have been choices or recommendations of various clubs or societies whose function it is to choose fictional soporifics for their members. These fictionists do their job almost as well as their English contemporaries: supply a commercial want; and are no more to be sneered at than other commercial people *as such*. But though the corpus of genuine Scottish literature is almost negligible in quantity, its quality is indisputably high. In the quality of his art, Neil Gunn has little to learn from his English, Welsh or Irish contemporaries. He can stand four square with the best of modern bourgeois art. But Gibbon on the other hand, though he had not shed all his acquired bourgeois characteristics, was, in the main, a revolutionary writer.

The importance and significance of *A Scots Quair* has compelled recognition from many of the bourgeois critics: they have been forced to recognize Gibbon as a literary artist of the highest standing. But if Gibbon stands high in the estimation of the more honest bourgeois critic he stands higher than they know or can know. For *A Scots Quair* is a worthy forerunner of the novel that will dominate the coming literary scene: the novel that will be written by workers for workers, expressing the hopes, ideals and aspirations of workers. And in that day when "proletarian humanism" (to use Gorky's phrase) is victorious, *A Scots Quair* will still be read and Lewis Grassic Gibbon remembered for a magnificent and heroic pioneer achievement.

14.3 Keith Dixon, The Gospels According to Saint Bakunin: Lewis Grassic Gibbon and Libertarian Communism (2003)

Dixon, K., 'The Gospels According to Saint Bakunin: Lewis Grassic Gibbon and Libertarian Communism', in M. P. McCullough and S. M. Dunnigan (eds), *A Flame in the Mearns. Lewis Grassic Gibbon: A Centenary Celebration*, Glasgow: Association for Scottish Literary Studies, 2003, pp. 136–9

The canonisation of Grassic Gibbon

One of the perverse effects of the canonisation of James Leslie Mitchell/Lewis Grassic Gibbon over the last quarter of a century, within Scottish academia, and subsequently within the secondary school curriculum in Scotland, has been a substantial rewriting of his politics, or the erasure of his politics altogether from academic discussion and educational presentation, which of course amounts more or less to the same thing. The process has gone so far that those whom I would like to describe as his natural allies in contemporary Scottish cultural politics are loath to cite him as an influence or inspiration. Now perceived as an icon of the Scottish literary establishment, Lewis Grassic Gibbon has become bad news for Scotland's cultural radicals. When questioned on the subject, James Kelman, for example, has shown a remarkable lack of interest in Grassic Gibbon's work and has seen no point of comparison between his own work and the political and cultural activities of the black sheep of the Mearns, despite evident similarities in their use of voice, for example. Another contemporary Scottish writer, Christopher Brookmyre, who very much shares Grassic Gibbon's un-Calvinist delight in the pleasures of the flesh, goes even further than this in *One Fine Day in the Middle of the Night*, where he has one of his characters describe Gibbon as one of the major culprits in teenage alienation from literature as taught in contemporary Scottish schools. Meeting up with a former school teacher from the 1980s, the character in question, Ali McQuade, provides a retroactive explanation for the unruliness within the English class:

> Christ what did you expect, inflictin' that Grassic Gibbon damage on us? You'd be up on an abuse charge for that these days. [. . .] you could have made it easier on yoursel's. I know it was the curriculum, but I mean, if it was up to you and you were tryin' tae get teenagers interested in books, is that what you'd throw at them? Grassic Gibbon? Teuchter farmyard dreichness?

And yet a glance back at the reactions that Grassic Gibbon's *Sunset Song* provoked in the local Scottish press in 1932 only serves as confirmation of his proximity to today's bad boys (and girls) of the cultural scene. The *Paisley Express* was not alone in condemning Grassic Gibbon's first Scottish novel in terms that should have some contemporary resonance for writers like Kelman or Brookmyre. Have they not also been castigated for 'the un-redeemed close-packed filth, meanness, spite, brutality, lying squalor and stupidity' of their novels?

... [T]here is nothing particularly new about this situation: writers of the past, and particularly politically radical writers of the past have often suffered the same fate, wheedled onto the school and university syllabi, once their literary or political wings (or both) have been conveniently clipped (exit the revolutionary poems of Burns or the bawdy poems of Pushkin). As far as Lewis Grassic Gibbon is concerned, the process began in the 1970s, as the strength of cultural and political nationalism began to grow in Scottish society: the predominantly nationalist and accommodative readings of his work date back to this time. Of course, the academics most directly involved in the process of reappropriation and respectabilisation were more at home, for a variety of reasons which I do not have room to deal with here, with nationalist or nationalist/ruralist readings of Lewis Grassic Gibbon than with exploring his revolutionary stand in both the cultural and political fields. At university level, a handful of academics, in particular in Edinburgh and Glasgow, provided alternative but innocuous readings of Grassic Gibbon which the Scottish Education Department could easily do business with. They were to set the mould in Scottish Grassic Gibbon studies for the next quarter of a century. The Longman Modern Classics edition of *Sunset Song* (1971), aimed at secondary school consumption, with commentary and notes by J.T. Low, is noteworthy in this respect: a monument of understatement and polite suppression, not to mention more straightforward misrepresenta-tion. Thus, in the biographical note on James Leslie Mitchell provided by Low, Mitchell's participation in the Aberdeen Soviet in 1918 becomes an interest 'in economic and social problems and in left-wing politics'; his sacking from his job on the *Scottish Farmer* in Glasgow after it was discov-ered that he'd been fiddling his expense account becomes 'trouble with his editor eventually led to his dismissal'; the crofters of Lewis Grassic Gibbon's Kinraddie who lost their lives during the First World War are described with impeccable Great British political correctness as 'the men who gave their lives for their country (and their way of living)', in flagrant contra-diction of the violent critique of British militarism and of the war hysteria that accompanied the 'Great War' which we find not only in the trilogy but throughout Grassic Gibbon's writing; the final sermon at the end of

Cloud Howe in which the Reverend Colquohoun urges his parishioners to abandon their Christianity, to 'forget the dream of the Christ' and seek out a 'stark, sure creed that will cut like a knife, a surgeon's knife through the doubt and disease' – a creed, communism, that the young Ewan Tavendale is to embody in *Grey Granite*, becomes an 'elegy or requiem by Colquohoun' by means of which 'Grassic Gibbon is placing the theme of this Scottish story in a universal context'. Above all, Low takes up the academically well-worn 'Chris Caledonia' theme to claim that the central character of the trilogy 'is seen to be an allegorical figure who personifies the history of Scotland and the Scot, and perhaps more generally the relationship between Woman and the Land'. It seems to have escaped the author of this presentation that Lewis Grassic Gibbon did not share this 'organic' vision of Scottish history and well knew there was no such thing as 'the Scot', but Scottish rulers and ruled, masters and servants, bosses and workers.

Nevertheless, conveniently shorn of his subversive potentialities, hung, drawn and quartered by academic bad faith, transformed miraculously into the nationalist he never had been, Lewis Grassic Gibbon was, by the mid-1970s seen fit to enter the pantheon of ScotLit.

14.4 Terence Davies, Earth Mother (2003)

Davies, T., 'Earth Mother', *Guardian*, Media Supplement, 18 August 2003, p. 15

It is 30 years ago now, when the Sunday night serial on BBC1 went out in ancient black and white. *Sunset Song* by Lewis Grassic Gibbon was one of them, and its grandeur has stayed with me.

It is a dark and brooding novel about the Scottish peasantry, about the land in general and one family – the Guthries – in particular. They are subsistence farmers extracting a meagre living from the earth. It is a novel about the power and cruelty of both family and nature, about the enduring presence of the land and the courage of the human spirit in the face of hardship.

Against this background – but of equal stature – is the story of the daughter of the family, Chris Guthrie, and her evolution from schoolgirl to wife to mother to widow then finally becoming a symbol for Scotland itself.

The novel is both symbolic and rhapsodic. It is a work of epic intimacy set before, during and after the Great War. Yet it is delicate. A filigree of the music of the seasons together with the more modest music of pipes and accordion, played at weddings with the Scottish voices singing the melancholy airs of the old times – The Flowers of the Forest and Auld Robin

– songs to pull the heartstrings, to make you remember the long-dead, making you wish for the longed-for happiness which we all need, content and secure in the knowledge that we will never die, for we are young and in our prime.

But time is cruel and so is the land which gives life its harsh beauty, as well as its moments of epiphany beside the lamp or in the firelight at gloaming. The song is yours and mine, of all who feel and have suffered or been happy. It is the song heard with quiet courage in the face of death. Or life.

But Chris has a deeper insight, an innate wisdom. Chris sings the song of the earth for humanity, a rhapsody for us all as she charts the eternal cycle of birth, marriage and death, as the song explores the timeless mysteries of land, home and family – this last one being the greatest mystery of all. For the family contains all our greatest ecstasies and all our cherished terrors.

The book is suffused with a lyrical melancholy, a quiet threnody for the mystery of life . . . for life is a mystery contained within an enigma. How can we bear time or subdue nature? We cannot. We can only endure.

At the end of the work a remembrance parade and service is held in an attempt to heal all suffering. At the end of this great work, time and the land endure beyond war, beyond human suffering, even beyond life itself.

It is a story that deserves to be told. It is a film that has to be made.

THE POETRY
OF THE 1930S

15 W. H. Auden, Introduction to *The Oxford Book of Light Verse* (1938)

W. H. Auden (1907–1974) came to prominence during the 1930s; he was widely seen as being the most significant poet writing in English since T. S. Eliot. His Introduction to *The Oxford Book of Light Verse* (1938) exemplifies his approach to literary history. Drawing on a Marxist reading of history, he argues that the Industrial Revolution marks a decisive break between poets and their readers – before this point, they shared a common understanding of the purpose of poetry; after it, poets lapsed into obscurantism. Auden implies that it may be possible in the future to reconnect poets and readers after large-scale social change.

Auden, W. H., 'Introduction to *The Oxford Book of Light Verse*', in W. H. Auden: *Prose and Travel Books in Prose and Verse*, vol. 1: *1926–1938*, ed. by E. Mendelson, London: Faber & Faber, 1996, pp. 430–6

I

Behind the work of any creative artist there are three principal wishes: the wish to make something; the wish to perceive something, either in the external world of sense or the internal world of feeling; and the wish to communicate these perceptions to others. Those who have no interest in or talent for making something, i.e. no skill in a particular artistic medium, do not become artists; they dine out, they gossip at street corners, they hold forth in cafés. Those who have no interest in communication do not become artists either; they become mystics or madmen.

There is no biological or mathematical law which would lead us to suppose that the quantity of innate artistic talent varies very greatly from generation to generation. The major genius may be a rare phenomenon but no art is the creation solely of geniuses, rising in sudden isolation like craters from

66

a level plain; least of all literature, whose medium is language—the medium of ordinary social intercourse.

If, then, we are to understand the changes that do in fact take place, why in the history of poetry there should be periods of great fertility, and others comparatively barren, why both the subject-matter and the manner should vary so widely, why poetry should sometimes be easy to understand, and sometimes very obscure, we must look elsewhere than to the idiosyncrasies of the individual poets themselves.

The wish to make something, always perhaps the greatest conscious pre-occupation of the artist himself, is a constant, independent of time. The things that do change are his medium, his attitude to the spoken and written word, the kind of things he is interested in or capable of perceiving, and the kind of audience with whom he wants to communicate. He wants to tell the truth, and he wants to amuse his friends, and what kind of truth he tells and what kind of friends he has depend partly on the state of society as a whole and partly on the kind of life which he, as an artist, leads.

When the things in which the poet is interested, the things which he sees about him, are much the same as those of his audience, and that audience is a fairly general one, he will not be conscious of himself as an unusual person, and his language will be straightforward and close to ordinary speech. When, on the other hand, his interests and perceptions are not readily accept-able to society, or his audience is a highly specialised one, perhaps of fellow poets, he will be acutely aware of himself as the poet, and his method of expression may depart very widely from the normal social language.

In the first case his poetry will be "light" in the sense in which it is used in this anthology. Three kinds of poetry have been included:

(1) Poetry written for performance, to be spoken or sung before an audi-ence [e.g. Folk-songs, the poems of Tom Moore].
(2) Poetry intended to be read, but having for its subject-matter the everyday social life of its period or the experiences of the poet as an ordinary human being [e.g. the poems of Chaucer, Pope, Byron].
(3) Such nonsense poetry as, through its properties and technique, has a general appeal [Nursery rhymes, the poems of Edward Lear].[1]

Light verse can be serious. It has only come to mean *vers de société*, trio-lets, smoke-room limericks, because, under the social conditions which produce the Romantic Revival, and which have persisted, more or less, ever since, it has been only in trivial matters that poets have felt in sufficient intimacy with their audience to be able to forget themselves and their singing-robes.

II

But this has not always been so. Till the Elizabethans, all poetry was light in this sense. It might be very dull at times, but it was light.

As long as society was united in its religious faith and its view of the universe, as long as the way in which people lived changed slowly, audience and artists alike tended to have much the same interests and to see much the same things.

It is not until the great social and ideological upheavals of the sixteenth and seventeenth centuries that difficult poetry appears, some of Shakespeare, Donne, Milton, and others. The example of these poets should warn us against condemning poetry because it is difficult. Lightness is a great virtue, but light verse tends to be conventional, to accept the attitudes of the society in which it is written. The more homogeneous a society, the closer the artist is to the everyday life of his time, the easier it is for him to communicate what he perceives, but the harder for him to see honestly and truthfully, unbiased by the conventional responses of his time. The more unstable a society, and the more detached from it the artist, the clearer he can see, but the harder it is for him to convey it to others. In the greatest periods of English Literature, as in the Elizabethan period, the tension was at its strongest. The artist was still sufficiently rooted in the life of his age to feel in common with his audience, and at the same time society was in a sufficient state of flux for the age-long beliefs and attitudes to be no longer compulsive on the artist's vision.

[. . .]

The Restoration marks a return both to a more settled society and to a more secure position for the artist under aristocratic patronage. His social status rose. When Dryden in his "Essay on the Dramatic Poetry of the Last Age" ascribes the superiority in correctness of language of the new dramatists to their greater opportunities of contact with genteel society, he is stating something which had great consequences for English Poetry. With a settled and valued place in society, not only minor poets, but the greatest, like Dryden and Pope, were able to express themselves in an easy manner, to use the speaking-voice, and to use as their properties the images of their everyday, i.e. social, life.

Their poetry has its limits, because the society of which they were a part was a limited part of the community, the leisured class, but within these limits, certain that the aim of poetry was to please, and certain of whom they had to please, they moved with freedom and intelligence.

This ease continued until the Romantic Revival which coincided with the beginning of the Industrial Revolution. From a predominantly agricultural country, where the towns were small and more important as places for social intercourse than as wealth-producing centres, England became a country of large manufacturing towns, too big for the individual to know anybody else except those employed in the same occupation. The divisions between classes became sharper and more numerous. At the same time there was a great increase in national wealth, and an increase in the reading public. With the increase in wealth appeared a new class who had independent incomes from dividends, and whose lives felt neither the economic pressure of the wage-earner nor the burden of responsibility of the landlord. The patronage system broke down, and the artist had either to write for the general public, whose condition was well described by Wordsworth in his preface to the *Lyrical Ballads*,

> A multitude of causes, unknown to former times, are now acting with a combined force to blunt the discriminating powers of the mind, and, unfitting it for all voluntary exertion, to reduce it to a state of almost savage torpor. The most effective of these causes are the great national events which are daily taking place, and the increasing accumulation of men in cities, where the uniformity of their occupations produces a craving for extraordinary incident, which the rapid communication of intelligence hourly gratifies;

or if he had an artistic conscience he could starve, unless he was lucky enough to have independent means.

As the old social community broke up, artists were driven to the examination of their own feelings and to the company of other artists. They became introspective, obscure, and highbrow.

[. . .]

Isolated in an amorphous society with no real communal ties, bewildered by its complexity, horrified by its ugliness and power, and uncertain of an audience, they turned away from the life of their time to the contemplation of their own emotions and the creation of imaginary worlds—Wordsworth to Nature, Keats and Mallarmé to a world of pure poetry,[2] Shelley to a future Golden Age, Baudelaire and Hölderlin to a past,

> . . . ces epoques nues
> Dont Phoebus se plaisait à dorer les statues,

the Pre-Raphaelites to the Middle Ages. Instead of the poet regarding himself as an entertainer, he becomes the prophet, "the unacknowledged legislator of the world," or the Dandy who sits in the café, "proud that he is less base than the passers-by, saying to himself as he contemplates the smoke of his cigar: 'What does it matter to me what becomes of my perceptions?'"

This is not, of course, to condemn the Romantic poets, but to explain why they wrote the kind of poetry they did, why their best work is personal, intense, often difficult, and generally rather gloomy.

The release from social pressure was, at first, extremely stimulating. The private world was a relatively unexplored field, and the technical discoveries made were as great as those being made in industry. But the feeling of excitement was followed by a feeling of loss. For if it is true that the closer bound the artist is to his community the harder it is for him to see with a detached vision, it is also true that when he is too isolated, though he may see clearly enough what he does see, that dwindles in quantity and importance. He "knows more and more about less and less."

It is significant that so many of these poets either died young like Keats, or went mad like Hölderlin, or ceased producing good work like Wordsworth, or gave up writing altogether like Rimbaud. "I must ask forgiveness for having fed myself on lies, and let us go . . . . One must be absolutely modern." For the private world is fascinating, but it is exhaustible. Without a secure place in society, without an intimate relation between himself and his audience, without, in fact, those conditions which make for Light Verse, the poet finds it difficult to grow beyond a certain point.

[. . .]

IV

The nineteenth century saw the development of a new kind of light poetry, poetry for children and nonsense poetry. The breakdown of the old village or small-town community left the family as the only real social unit, and the parent-child relationship as the only real social bond. The writing of nonsense poetry which appeals to the Unconscious, and of poetry for children, who live in a world before self-consciousness, was an attempt to find a world where the divisions of class, sex, occupation did not operate, and the great Victorian masters of this kind of poetry, Lewis Carroll and Edward Lear, were as successful in their day as Mr Walt Disney has been in ours. The conditions under which folk-poetry is made ensure that it shall keep its lightness or disappear, but the changing social conditions are reflected in its history by a degeneration both in technique and in treatment. The Border ballad could be tragic; the music-hall song cannot. Directness and ease of expression has been kept, but at the cost of excluding both emotional subtlety and beauty of diction. Only in America, under the conditions of frontier expansion and prospecting and railway development, have the last hundred years been able to produce a folk-poetry which can equal similar productions of pre-industrial Europe, and in America, too, this period is ending.

The problem for the modern poet, as for every one else to-day, is how to find or form a genuine community, in which each has his valued place and can feel at home. The old pre-industrial community and culture are gone and cannot be brought back. Nor is it desirable that they should be. They were too unjust, too squalid, and too custom-bound. Virtues which were once nursed unconsciously by the forces of nature must now be recovered and fostered by a deliberate effort of the will and the intelligence. In the future, societies will not grow of themselves. They will either be made consciously or decay. A democracy in which each citizen is as fully conscious and capable of making a rational choice, as in the past has been possible only for the wealthier few, is the only kind of society which in the future is likely to survive for long.

In such a society, and in such alone, will it be possible for the poet, without sacrificing any of his subtleties of sensibility or his integrity, to write poetry which is simple, clear, and gay.

For poetry which is at the same time light and adult can only be written in a society which is both integrated and free.

Notes

1 A few pieces, e.g. Blake's *Auguries of Innocence* and Melville s *Billy in the Darbies* do not really fall into any of these categories, but their technique is derived so directly from the Popular style that it seemed proper to include them. When Blake, for instance, deserts the proverbial manner of the *Auguries* for the eccentric manner of the Prophetic Books, he ceases to write 'light verse'.

2 Mr Stephen Spender, in his essay on Keats in *From Anne to Victoria*, has analysed the gulf between the world of the poems and the world of the letters. Keats's abandonment of 'Hyperion' with the remark that there were too many Miltonic inversions in it, is a sign that he was becoming aware of this gulf. When the subject-matter of poetry ceases to be the social life of man, it tends to dispense with the social uses of language grammar, and word-order, a tendency which Mallarmé carried to its logical conclusion.

Browning is an interesting case of a poet who was intensely interested in the world about him and in a less socially specialized period might well have been the 'easiest' poet of his generation, instead of the most 'difficult.'

71

16 Virginia Woolf, The Leaning Tower[1] (1940)

The novelist and critic Virginia Woolf (1882–1941) belonged to the previous literary generation from Auden. Like other members of the Bloomsbury Group, she believed in the value of art and argued that literature should not support specific ideological positions. In 'The Leaning Tower', she provides a metaphorical account of the education and attitudes of nineteenth- and early twentieth-century writers, which she contrasts with the very different outlook of writers like MacNeice and Spender. Though not precisely an aesthete, Woolf advances a traditional understanding of poetry as a Wordsworthian art 'We listen to . . . when we are alone'.

Woolf, V., 'The Leaning Tower', in *Collected Essays*, vol. 2, London: The Hogarth Press, 1966, pp. 162–76

A writer is a person who sits at a desk and keeps his eye fixed, as intently as he can, upon a certain object—that figure of speech may help to keep us steady on our path if we look at it for a moment. He is an artist who sits with a sheet of paper in front of him trying to copy what he sees. What is his object—his model? Nothing so simple as a painter's model; it is not a bowl of flowers, a naked figure, or a dish of apples and onions. Even the simplest story deals with more than one person, with more than one time. Characters begin young; they grow old; they move from scene to scene, from place to place. A writer has to keep his eye upon a model that moves, that changes, upon an object that is not one object but innumerable objects. Two words alone cover all that a writer looks at—they are, human life.

Let us look at the writer next. What do we see—only a person who sits with a pen in his hand in front of a sheet of paper? That tells us little or nothing. And we know very little. Considering how much we talk about writers, how much they talk about themselves, it is odd how little we know about them. Why are they so common sometimes; then so rare? Why do they sometimes write nothing but masterpieces, then nothing but trash? And why should a family, like the Shelleys, like the Keatses, like the Brontës, suddenly burst into flame and bring to birth Shelley, Keats, and the Brontës? What are the conditions that bring about that explosion? There is no answer—naturally. Since we have not yet discovered the germ of influenza, how should we yet have discovered the germ of genius? We know even less about the mind than about the body. We have less evidence. It is less than two hundred years since people took an interest in themselves; Boswell was almost the first writer who thought that a man's life was worth writing a book about. Until we have more facts, more biographies, more autobiographies, we cannot know much about ordinary people, let alone about extraordinary people. Thus at present we have only theories about writers—a great many theories, but they all differ. The politician says that a writer is the product of the society in which he lives, as a screw is the product of a screw machine; the artist, that a writer is a heavenly apparition that slides across the sky, grazes the earth, and vanishes. To the psychologists a writer is an oyster; feed him on gritty facts, irritate him with ugliness, and by way of compensation, as they call it, he will produce a pearl. The genealogists say that certain stocks, certain families, breed writers as fig trees breed figs—Dryden, Swift, and Pope they tell us were all cousins. This proves that we are in the dark about writers; anybody can make a theory; the germ of a theory is almost always the wish to prove what the theorist wishes to believe.

[. . .]

If we want to risk a theory, we can say that peace and prosperity were influences that gave the nineteenth-century writers a family likeness. They had leisure; they had security; life was not going to change; they themselves were not going to change. They could look; and look away. They could forget; and then—in their books—remember. Those then are some of the conditions that brought about a certain family likeness, in spite of the great individual differences, among the nineteenth-century writers. The nineteenth century ended; but the same conditions went on. They lasted, roughly speaking, till the year 1914. Even in 1914 we can still see the writer sitting as he sat all through the nineteenth century looking at human life; and that human life is still divided into classes; he still looks most intently at the class from which he himself springs; the classes are still so settled that he has almost forgotten that there are classes; and he is still so secure himself that he is almost unconscious of his own position and of its security. He believes that he is looking at the whole of life; and will always so look at it. That is not altogether a fancy picture. Many of those writers are still alive. Sometimes they describe their own position as young men, beginning to write, just before August 1914. How did you learn your art? one can ask them. At College they say—by reading; by listening; by talking.

[. . .]

But before we go on with the story of what happened after 1914, let us look more closely for a moment, not at the writer himself, nor at his model; but at his chair. A chair is a very important part of a writer's outfit. It is the chair that gives him his attitude towards his model; that decides what he sees of human life; that profoundly affects his power of telling us what he sees. By his chair we mean his upbringing, his education. It is a fact, not a theory, that all writers from Chaucer to the present day, with so few exceptions that one hand can count them, have sat upon the same kind of chair—a raised chair. They have all come from the middle class; they have had good, at least expensive, educations. They have all been raised above the mass of people upon a tower of stucco—that is their middle-class birth; and of gold—that is their expensive education. That was true of all the nineteenth-century writers, save Dickens; it was true of all the 1914 writers, save D. H. Lawrence. Let us run through what are called 'representative names': G. K. Chesterton; T. S. Eliot; Belloc; Lytton Strachey; Somerset Maugham; Hugh Walpole; Wilfred Owen; Rupert Brooke; J. E. Flecker; E. M. Forster; Aldous Huxley; G. M. Trevelyan; O. and S. Sitwell; Middleton Murry. Those are some of them; and all, with the exception of D. H. Lawrence, came of the middle class, and were educated at public schools and universities. There is another fact, equally indisputable: the books that they wrote were among the best books written between 1910 and 1925. Now let us ask, is there any connexion between those facts? Is there a connexion between the excellence of their work land the fact that they came of families rich enough to send them to public schools and universities?

Must we not decide, greatly though those writers differ, and shallow as we admit our knowledge of influences to be, that there must be a connexion between their education and their work? It cannot be a mere chance that this minute class of educated people has produced so much that is good as writing; and that the vast mass of people without education has produced so little that is good. It is a fact, however. Take away all that the working class has given to English literature and that literature would scarcely suffer; take away all that the educated class has given, and English literature would scarcely exist. Education must then play a very important part in a writer's work.

[. . .]

That seems so obvious that it is astonishing how little stress has been laid upon the writer's education. It is perhaps because a writer's education is so much less definite than other educations. Reading, listening, talking, travel, leisure—many different things it seems are mixed together. Life and books must be shaken and taken in the right proportions. A boy brought up alone in a library turns into a bookworm; brought up alone in the fields he turns into an earthworm. To breed the kind of butterfly a writer is you must let him sun himself for three or four years at Oxford or Cambridge—so it seems. However it is done, it is there that it is done—there that he is taught his art. And he has to be taught his art.

[. . .]

He had been taught it by about eleven years of education—at private schools, public schools, and universities. He sits upon a tower raised above the rest of us; a tower built first on his parents' station, then on his parents' gold. It is a tower of the utmost importance; it decides his angle of vision; it affects his power of communication.

All through the nineteenth century, down to August 1914, that tower was a steady tower. The writer was scarcely conscious either of his high station or of his limited vision. Many of them had sympathy, great sympathy, with other classes; they wished to help the working class to enjoy the advantages of the tower class; but they did not wish to destroy the tower, or to descend from it—rather to make it accessible to all. Nor had the model, human life, changed essentially since Trollope looked at it, since Hardy looked at it: and Henry James, in 1914, was still looking at it. Further, the tower itself held firm beneath the writer during all the most impressionable years, when he was learning his art, and receiving all those complex influences and instructions that are summed up by the word education. These were conditions that influenced their work profoundly. For when the crash came in 1914 all those young men, who were to be the representative writers of their time, had their past, their education, safe behind them, safe within them. They had known security; they had the memory of a peaceful boyhood, the knowledge of a settled civilization. Even though the war cut into their lives, and ended some of them, they wrote, and still write, as if the tower were firm beneath them. In one word, they are aristocrats; the unconscious inheritors of a great tradition. Put a page of their writing under the magnifying-glass and you will see, far away in the distance, the Greeks, the Romans; coming nearer, the Elizabethans; coming nearer still, Dryden, Swift, Voltaire, Jane Austen, Dickens, Henry James. Each, however much he differs individually from the others, is a man of education; a man who has learnt his art.

From that group let us pass to the next—to the group which began to write about 1925 and, it may be, came to an end as a group in 1939. If you read current literary journalism you will be able to rattle off a string of names—Day Lewis, Auden, Spender, Isherwood, Louis MacNeice and so on. They adhere much more closely than the names of their predecessors. But at first sight there seems little difference, in station, in education. Mr. Auden in a poem written to Mr. Isherwood says: Behind us we have stucco suburbs and expensive educations. They are tower dwellers like their predecessors, the sons of well-to-do parents, who could afford to send them to public schools and universities. But what a difference in the tower itself, in what they saw from the tower! When they looked at human life what did they see? Everywhere change; everywhere revolution. In Germany, in Russia, in Italy, in Spain, all the old hedges were being rooted up; all the old towers were being thrown to the ground. Other hedges were being planted; other towers were being raised. There was communism in one country; in another fascism. The whole of civilization, of society, was changing. There was, it is true, neither war nor revolution in England itself. All those writers had time to write many books before 1939. But even in England towers that were built of gold and stucco were no longer steady towers. They were leaning towers. The books were written under the influence of change, under the threat of war. That perhaps is why the names adhere so closely; there was one influence that affected them all and made them, more than their predecessors, into groups. And that influence, let us remember, may well have excluded from that string of names the poets whom posterity will value most highly, either because they could not fall into step, as leaders or as followers, or because the influence was adverse to poetry, and until that influence relaxed, they could not write. But the tendency that makes it possible for us to group the names of these writers together, and gives their work a common likeness, was the tendency of the tower they sat on—the tower of middle-class birth and expensive education—to lean.

Let us imagine, to bring this home to us, that we are actually upon a leaning tower and note our sensations. Let us see whether they correspond to the tendencies we observe in those poems, plays, and novels. Directly we feel that a tower leans we become acutely conscious that we are upon a tower. All those writers too are acutely tower conscious; conscious of their middle-class birth; of their expensive educations. Then when we come to the top of the tower how strange the view looks—not altogether upside down, but slanting, sidelong. That too is characteristic of the leaning-tower writers; they do not look any class straight in the face; they look either up, or down, or sidelong. There is no class so settled that they can explore it unconsciously. That perhaps is why they create no characters. Then what do we feel next, raised in imagination on top of the tower? First discomfort; next self-pity for that discomfort; which pity soon turns to anger—to anger against the builder, against society, for making us uncomfortable. Those too seem to be tendencies of the leaning-tower writers. Discomfort; pity for themselves; anger against society. And yet—here is another tendency—how can you altogether abuse a society that is giving you, after all, a very fine view and some sort of security? You cannot abuse that society whole-heartedly while you continue to profit by that society. And so very naturally you abuse society in the person of some retired admiral or spinster or armament manufacturer; and by abusing them hope to escape whipping yourself. The bleat of the scapegoat sounds loud in their work, and the whimper of the schoolboy crying 'Please, Sir, it was the other fellow, not me'. Anger; pity; scapegoat beating; excuse finding—these are all very natural tendencies; if we were in their position we should tend to do the same. But we are not in their position; we have not had eleven years of expensive education. We have only been climbing an imaginary tower. We can cease to imagine. We can come down.

But they cannot. They cannot throw away their education; they cannot throw away their upbringing. Eleven years at school and college have been stamped upon them indelibly. And then, to their credit but to their confusion, the leaning tower not only leant in the thirties, but it leant more and more to the left. Do you remember what Mr. MacCarthy said about his own group at the university in 1914? 'We were not very much interested in politics . . . philosophy was more interesting to use than public causes'? That shows that his tower leant neither to the right not to the left. But in 1930 it was impossible—if you were young, sensitive, imaginative—not to be interested in politics; not to find public causes of much more pressing interest than philosophy. In 1930 young men at college were forced to be aware of what was happening in Russia; in Germany; in Italy; in Spain. They could not go on discussing aesthetic emotions and personal relations. They could not confine their reading to the poets; they had to read the politicians. They read Marx. They became communists; they became anti-fascists. The tower they realized was founded upon injustice and tyranny; it was wrong for a small class to possess an education that other people paid for; wrong to stand upon the gold that a bourgeois father had made from his bourgeois profession. It was wrong; yet how could they make it right? Their education could not be thrown away; as for their capital—did Dickens, did Tolstoy ever throw away their capital? Did D. H. Lawrence, a miner's son, continue to live like a miner? No; for it is death for a writer to throw away his capital; to be forced to earn his living in a mine or a factory. And thus, trapped by their education, pinned down by their capital, they remained on top of their leaning tower, and their state of mind as we see it reflected in their poems and plays and novels is full of discord and bitterness, full of confusion and of compromise.

These tendencies are better illustrated by quotation than by analysis. There is a poem by one of those writers, Louis MacNeice, called *Autumn Journal*. It is dated March 1939. It is feeble as poetry, but interesting as autobiography. He begins of course with a snipe at the scapegoat—the bourgeois, middle-class family from which he sprang. The retired admirals, the retired generals, and the spinster lady have breakfasted off bacon and eggs served on a silver dish, he tells us. He sketches that family as if it were already a little remote and more than a little ridiculous. But they could afford to send him to Marlborough and then to Merton, Oxford. This is what he learnt at Oxford:

We learned that a gentleman never misplaces his accents,
That nobody knows how to speak, much less how to write
English who has not hob-nobbed with the great-grandparents
     of English.

Besides that he learnt at Oxford Latin and Greek; and philosophy, logic, and metaphysics:

Oxford [he says] crowded the mantelpiece with gods—
Scaliger, Heinsius, Dindorf, Bentley, Wilamowitz.

It was at Oxford that the tower began to lean. He felt that he was living under a system—

That gives the few at fancy prices their fancy lives
While ninety-nine in the hundred who never attend the banquet
Must wash the grease of ages off the knives.

But at the same time, an Oxford education had made him fastidious:

It is so hard to imagine
A world where the many would have their chance without
A fall in the standard of intellectual living
And nothing left that the highbrow cares about.

At Oxford he got his honours degree; and that degree—in humane letters—put him in the way of a 'cushy job'—seven hundred a year, to be precise, and several rooms of his own.

If it were not for Lit. Hum. I might be climbing
A ladder with a hod,
And seven hundred a year
Will pay the rent and the gas and the phone and the grocer—

And yet, again, doubts break in; the 'cushy job' of teaching more Latin and Greek to more undergraduates does not satisfy him—

. . . the so-called humane studies
May lead to cushy jobs
But leave the men who land them spiritually bankrupt,
Intellectual snobs.

And what is worse, that education and that 'cushy job' cut one off, he complains, from the common life of one's kind.

> All that I would like to be is human, having a share
> In a civilized, articulate and well-adjusted
> Community where the mind is given its due
> But the body is not distrusted.

Therefore in order to bring about that well-adjusted community he must turn from literature to politics, remembering, he says,

> Remembering that those who by their habit
> Hate politics, can no longer keep their private
> Values unless they open the public gate
> To a better political system.

So, in one way or another, he takes part in politics, and finally he ends:

> What is it we want really?
> For what end and how?
> If it is something feasible, obtainable,
> Let us dream it now,
> And pray for a possible land
> Not of sleep-walkers, not of angry puppets,
> But where both heart and brain can understand
> The movements of our fellows,
> Where life is a choice of instruments and none
> Is debarred his natural music . . .
> Where the individual, no longer squandered
> In self-assertion, works with the rest . . .

Those quotations give a fair description of the influences that have told upon the leaning-tower group. Others could easily be discovered. The influence of the films explains the lack of transitions in their work and the violently opposed contrasts. The influence of poets like Mr. Yeats and Mr. Eliot explains the obscurity. They took over from the elder poets a technique which, after many years of experiment, those poets used skilfully, and used it clumsily and often inappropriately. But we have time only to point to the most obvious influences; and these can be summed up as Leaning Tower Influences. If you think of them, that is, as people trapped on a leaning tower from which they cannot descend, much that is puzzling in their work is easier to understand. It explains the violence of their attack upon bourgeois society and also its half-heartedness. They are profiting by a society which they abuse. They are flogging a dead or dying horse because a living horse, if flogged, would kick them off its back. It explains the destructiveness of their work; and also its emptiness. They can destroy bourgeois society, in part at least; but what have they put in its place? How can a writer who has no first-hand experience of a towerless, of a classless society create that society? Yet as Mr. MacNeice bears witness, they feel compelled to preach, if not by their living, at least by their writing, the creation of a society in which everyone is equal and everyone is free. It explains the pedagogic, the didactic, the loud-speaker strain that dominates their poetry. They must teach; they must preach. Everything is a duty—even love. Listen to Mr. Day Lewis ingerminating love. 'Mr. Spender', he says, 'speaking from the living unit of himself and his friends appeals for the contraction of the social group to a size at which human contact may again be established and demands the destruction of all impediments to love. Listen.' And we listen to this:

We have come at last to a country
Where light, like shine from snow, strikes all faces.
Here you may wonder
How it was that works, money; interest, building could ever
Hide the palpable and obvious love of man for man.

We listen to oratory, not poetry. It is necessary, in order to feel the emotion of those lines, that other people should be listening too. We are in a group, in a class-room as we listen.
Listen now to Wordsworth:

Lover had he known in huts where poor men dwell,
His daily teachers had been woods and ruts,
The silence that is in the starry sky,
The sleep that is among the lonely hills.

We listen to that when we are alone. We remember that in solitude. Is that the difference between politician's poetry and poet's poetry? We listen to the one in company; to the other when we are alone? But the poet in the thirties was forced to be a politician. That explains why the artist in the thirties was forced to be a scapegoat. If politics were 'real', the ivory tower was an escape from 'reality'. That explains the curious, bastard language in which so much of this leaning-tower prose and poetry is written. It is not the rich speech of the aristocrat: it is not the racy speech of the peasant.

It is betwixt and between. The poet is a dweller in two worlds, one dying, the other struggling to be born. And so we come to what is perhaps the most marked tendency of leaning-tower literature—the desire to be whole; to be human. 'All that I would like to be is human'—that cry rings through their books—the longing to be closer to their kind, to write the common speech of their kind, to share the emotions of their kind, no longer to be isolated and exalted in solitary state upon their tower, but to be down on the ground with the mass of human kind.

These then, briefly and from a certain angle, are some of the tendencies of the modern writer who is seated upon a leaning tower. No other generation has been exposed to them. It may be that none has had such an appallingly difficult task. Who can wonder if they have been incapable of giving us great poems, great plays, great novels? They had nothing settled to look at; nothing peaceful to remember; nothing certain to come. During all the most impressionable years of their lives they were stung into consciousness—into self-consciousness, into class-consciousness, into the consciousness of things changing, of things falling, of death perhaps about to come. There was no tranquility in which they could recollect. The inner mind was paralysed because the surface mind was always hard at work.

Yet if they have lacked the creative power of the poet and the novelist, the power—does it come from a fusion of the two minds, the upper and the under?

[. . .]

The leaning-tower writer has had the courage, at any rate, to throw that little box of toys out of the window. He has had the courage to tell the truth, the unpleasant truth, about himself.

[. . .]

That is the first step towards telling the truth about other people. By analysing themselves honestly, with help from Dr. Freud, these writers have done a great deal to free us from nineteenth-century suppressions. The writers of the next generation may inherit from them a whole state of mind, a mind no longer crippled, evasive, divided. They may inherit that unconsciousness which, as we guessed—it is only a guess—at the beginning of this paper, is necessary if writers are to get beneath the surface, and to write something that people remember when they are alone. For that great gift of unconsciousness the next generation will have to thank the creative and honest egotism of the leaning-tower group.

Note

1   A paper read to the Workers' Educational Association, Brighton, May 1940.

Part II

CONTENDING
MODERNISMS

T. S. ELIOT, *PRUFROCK AND OTHER OBSERVATIONS*

17 Arthur Symons, Jules Laforgue (1899)

The late nineteenth-century French language poets who are usually thought of as symbolist had a substantial influence on modernist early twentieth-century English language poetry by, among others, W. B. Yeats (1865–1939), Ezra Pound (1885–1972), Wallace Stevens (1879–1955) and T. S. Eliot (1888–1965). Briefly, the symbolist poets attempted to express an inner, deeper and eternal reality by using symbols, a condensed syntax, and free verse, to a large extent to counter what they regarded as the ephemeral and trivial qualities of conventional poetry. To English language readers, the work of the symbolist poets was first introduced by poet and critic Arthur Symons (1865–1945) in his book *The Symbolist Movement in Literature* (1899). In this he discussed the poetry of Gérard de Nerval (1808–55), Villiers de l'Isle Adam (1840–89), Arthur Rimbaud (1854–91), Paul Verlaine (1844–96), Jules Laforgue (1860–87) and Stéphane Mallarmé (1842–98) as the main representatives of French symbolist poetry. It is difficult to convey the distinguishing features of symbolist poetry in descriptive terms; perhaps the best way to get a sense of this is through the experience of reading the poetry and attending to the ideas of the poets. After a brief and impressionistic introduction, this is what Symons tried to do through selective quotation and contextualised commentary. The chapter on Jules Laforgue is given below as a typical instance of Symons's introduction to symbolist poets, and is of particular interest because of the enormous impact Laforgue had on T. S. Eliot's early *Prufrock* poems (initially through the medium of Symons's book).

Symons, A., 'Jules Laforgue', in *The Symbolist Movement in Literature*, London: Heinemann, 1899, pp. 103–14

Jules Laforgue was born at Montevideo, of Breton parents, August 20, 1860. He died in Paris in 1887, two days before his twenty-seventh birthday. From

1880 to 1886 he had been reader to the Empress Augusta at Berlin. He married only a few months before his death. *D'allures?* says M. Gustave Kahn, *fort correctes, de hauts gibus, des cravates sobres, des vestons anglais, des pardessus clergymans, et de par les nécessités, un parapluie immuablement placé sous le bras.* His portraits show us a clean-shaved, reticent face, betraying little. With such a personality anecdotes have but small chance of appropriating those details by which expansive natures express themselves to the world. We know nothing about Laforgue which his work is not better able to tell us. The whole of that work is contained in two small volumes, one of prose, the *Moraliltés Légendaires*, the other of verse, *Les Complaintes, L'Imitation de Notre-Dame la Lune*, and a few other pieces, all published during the last three years of his life.

The prose and verse of Laforgue, scrupulously correct, but with a new manner of correctness, owe more than any one has realised to the half-unconscious prose and verse of Rimbaud. Verse and prose are alike a kind of travesty, making subtle use of colloquialism, slang, neologism, technical terms, for their allusive, their factitious, their reflected meanings, with which one can play, very seriously. The verse is alert, troubled, swaying, deliberately uncertain, hating rhetoric so piously that it prefers, and finds its piquancy in, the ridiculously obvious. It is really *vers libre*, but at the same time correct verse, before *vers libre* had been invented. And it carries, as far as that theory has ever been carried, the theory which demands an instantaneous notation (Whistler, let us say) of the figure or landscape which one has been accustomed to define with such rigorous exactitude. Verse, always elegant, is broken up into a kind of mockery of prose.

> Encore un de met pierrots mort;
> Mort d'un chronique orphelinisme;
> C'était un cœur plein de dandysme
> Lunaire, en un drôle de corps;

he will say to us, with a familiarity of manner, as of one talking languidly, in a low voice, the lips always teased into a slightly bitter smile; and he will pass suddenly into the ironical lilt of

> Hotel garni
> De l'infini,
>
> Sphinx et Jaconde
> Des défunts mondes;

and from that into this solemn and smiling end of one of his last poems, his own epitaph, if you will:

Il prit froid l'autre automne,
S'étant attardi vers les peines des cors,
Sur la fin d'un beau jour.
Oh! ce fut pour vos cors, et ce fut pour l'automne,
Qu'il nous montra qu' "on meurt d'amour!"
On ne le verra plus aux fêtes nationales,
S'enfermer dans l'Histoire et tirer les verrous,
Il vint trop tard, il est reparti sans scandale;
O vous qui m'écoutez, rentrez chacun chez vous.

The old cadences, the old eloquence, the ingenuous seriousness of poetry, are all banished, on a theory as self-denying as that which permitted Degas to dispense with recognisable beauty in his figures. Here, if ever, is modern verse, verse which dispenses with so many of the privileges of poetry, for an ideal quite of its own. It is, after all, a very self-conscious ideal, becoming artificial through its extreme naturalness; for in poetry it is not "natural" to say things quite so much in the manner of the moment, with however ironical an intention.

The prose of the Moralités Legendaires is perhaps even more of a discovery. Finding its origin, as I have pointed out, in the experimental prose of Rimbaud, it carries that manner to a singular perfection. Disarticulated, abstract, mathematically lyrical, it gives expression, in its icy ecstasy, to a very subtle criticism of the universe, with a surprising irony of cosmical vision. We learn from books of mediæval magic that the embraces of the devil are of a coldness so intense that it may be called, by an allowable figure of speech, fiery. Everything may be as strongly its opposite as itself; and that is why this balanced, chill, colloquial style of Laforgue has, in the paradox of its intensity, the essential heat of the most obviously emotional prose. The prose is more patient than the verse, with its more compassionate laughter at universal experience. It can laugh as seriously, as profoundly, as in that graveyard monologue of Hamlet, Laforgue's Hamlet, who, Maeterlinck ventures to say, "is at moments more Hamlet than the Hamlet of Shakespeare." Let me translate a few sentences from it.

"Perhaps I have still twenty or thirty years to live, and I shall pass that way, like the others. Like the others? O Totality, the misery of being there no longer! Ah! I would like to set out to-morrow, and search all through the world for the most adamantine processes of embalming. They, too, were, the little people of History, learning to read, trimming their nails, lighting the dirty lamp every evening, in love, gluttonous, vain, fond of compliments, hand-shakes, and kisses, living on bell-tower gossip, saying, 'What sort of weather shall we have to-morrow? Winter has really come. . . . We have had no plums this year.' Ah! everything is good, if it would not come to an end. And thou, Silence, pardon the Earth; the little madcap hardly knows what she is doing; on the day of the great summing-up of consciousness before the Ideal, she will be labelled with a pitiful *idem* in the column of the miniature evolutions of the Unique Evolution, in the column of negligeable quantities . . . To die! Evidently, one dies without knowing it, as, every night, one enters upon sleep. One has no consciousness of the passing of the last lucid thought into sleep, into swooning, into death. Evidently. But to be no more, to be here no more, to be ours no more! Not even to be able, any more, to press against one's human heart, some idle afternoon, the ancient sadness contained in one little chord on the piano!"

In these always "lunar" parodies, *Salomé*, *Lohengrin*, *Fils de Parsifal*, *Persée et Andromède*, each a kind of metaphysical myth, he realises that *la créature va hardiment à être cérébrale, anti-naturelle*, and he has invented these fantastic puppets with an almost Japanese art of spiritual dislocation. They are, in part, a way of taking one's revenge upon science, by an ironical borrowing of its very terms, which dance in his prose and verse, derisively, at the end of a string.

In his acceptance of the fragility of things as actually a principle of art, Laforgue is a sort of transformed Watteau, showing his disdain for the world which fascinates him, in quite a different way. He has constructed his own world, lunar and actual, speaking slang and astronomy, with a constant disengaging of the visionary aspect, under which frivolity becomes an escape from the arrogance of a still more temporary mode of being, the world as it appears to the sober majority. He is terribly conscious of daily life, cannot omit, mentally, a single hour of the day; and his flight to the moon is in sheer desperation. He sees what he calls *l'Inconscient* in every gesture, but he cannot see it without these gestures. And he sees, not only as an imposition, but as a conquest, the possibilities for art which come from the sickly modern being, with his clothes, his nerves: the mere fact that he flowers from the soil of his epoch.

It is an art of the nerves, this art of Laforgue, and it is what all art would tend towards if we followed our nerves on all their journeys. There is in it all the restlessness of modern life, the haste to escape from whatever weighs too heavily on the liberty of the moment, that capricious liberty which demands only room enough to hurry itself weary. It is distressingly conscious of the unhappiness of mortality, but it plays, somewhat uneasily, at a disdainful indifference. And it is out of these elements of caprice, fear, contempt, linked together by an embracing laughter, that it makes its existence.

Il n'y a pas de type, il y a la vie, Laforgue replies to those who come to him with classical ideals. *Votre idéal est bien vite magnifiquement submergé*, in life itself, which should form its own art, an art deliberately ephemeral, with the attaching pathos of passing things. There is a great pity at the root of this art of Laforgue: self-pity, which extends, with the artistic sympathy, through mere clearness of vision, across the world. His laughter, which Maeterlinck has defined so admirably as "the laughter of the soul," is the laughter of Pierrot, more than half a sob, and shaken out of him with a deplorable gesture of the thin arms, thrown wide. He is a metaphysical Pierrot, *Pierrot lunaire*, and it is of abstract notions, the whole science of the unconscious, that he makes his showman's patter. As it is part of his manner not to distinguish between irony and pity, or even belief, we need not attempt to do so. Heine should teach us to understand at least so much of a poet who could not otherwise resemble him less. In Laforgue, sentiment is squeezed out of the world before one begins to play at ball with it.

And so, of the two, he is the more hopeless. He has invented a new manner of being René or Werther: an inflexible politeness towards man, woman, and destiny. He composes love-poems hat in hand, and smiles with an exasperating tolerance before all the transformations of the eternal feminine. He is very conscious of death, but his *blague* of death is, above all things, gentlemanly. He will not permit himself, at any moment, the luxury of dropping the mask: not at any moment.

Read this *Autre Complainte de Lord Pierrot*, with the singular pity of its cruelty, before such an imagined dropping of the mask:

> Celle qui doit me mettre au courant de la Femme!
>   Nous lui dirons d'abord, de mon air le moins froid:
> "La somme des angles d'un triangle, chère âme,
>   Est égale à deux droits."
>
> Et si ce cri lui part: "Dieu de Dieu que je t'aime!"
>   —"Dieu reconnaîtra les siens." Ou piquée au vif:
> —"Mes claviers ont du cœur, tu sera mon seul thème."
>   Moi: "Tout est relatif."
>
> De tous ses yeux, alors! se sentant trop banale:
>   "Ah! tu ne m'aime pas; tant d'autres sont jaloux!"
> Et moi, d'un œil qui vers l'Inconscient s'emballe:
>   "Merci, pas mal; et vous?"

"Jouons au plus fidèle!"—A quoi bon, ô Nature!
    "Autant à qui perd gagne." Alors, autre couplet:
—"Ah! tu te lasseras le premier, j'en suis sûre."
    —"Après vous, s'il vous plait."

Enfin, si, par un soir, elle meurt dans mes livres,
    Douce; feignant de n'en pas croire encor mes yeux,
J'aurai un: "Ah ça, mais, nous avions De Quoi vivre!
    C'était donc sérieux?"

And yet one realises, if one but reads him attentively enough, how much
suffering and despair, and resignation to what is, after all, the inevitable,
are hidden away under this disguise, and also why this disguise is possible.
Laforgue died at twenty-seven: he had been a dying man all his life, and his
work has the fatal evasiveness of those who shrink from remembering the
one thing which they are unable to forget. Coming as he does after Rimbaud,
turning the divination of the other into theories, into achieved results, he
is the eternally grown up, mature to the point of self-negation, as the other
is the eternal *enfant terrible*. He thinks intensely about life, seeing what is
automatic, pathetically ludicrous in it, almost as one might who has no part
in the comedy. He has the double advantage, for his art, of being condemned
to death, and of being, in the admirable phrase of Villiers, "one of those
who come into the world with a ray of moonlight in their brains."

18.1 Henri Bergson, *Creative Evolution* (1907)

French philosopher Henri Bergson (1859–1941) is primarily remembered for his
attempts to bring developments in biology to bear on his theory of consciousness. In an age which was particularly absorbed in understanding the concept of time (developments in the natural sciences had undermined traditional
ideas regarding both the linearity of time and the extent to which the past can
be charted), Bergson's metaphysical notion of 'duration' – as a constant flow
of moments that underlies evolution and consciousness, which cannot be
measured in the ordinary sense of clock time – was enormously influential.
This extract from his *L'Évolution créatice* (1907) [*Creative Evolution*, 1911] and
the next from *Matière et mémoire* (1896) [*Matter and Memory*, 1908] focus on
some elements of his ideas of the 'present' and 'duration'. Such ideas had a
particular influence on T. S. Eliot's early *Prufrock* poems – Eliot had attended
Bergson's lectures in 1911 at the Collège de France, Paris. Bergson's ideas

also influenced the literary works of writers like Marcel Proust (1871–1922), Paul Valery (1871–1945), and Charles Peguy (1873–1914).

Bergson, H., *Creative Evolution*, trans. by A. Mitchell, London: Macmillan, 1911, pp. 1–3

The evolution of life—mechanism and teleology

The existence of which we are most assured and which we know best is unquestionably our own, for of every other object we have notions which may be considered external and superficial, whereas, of ourselves, our perception is internal and profound. What, then, do we find? In this privileged case, what is the precise meaning of the word "exist"? Let us recall here briefly the conclusions of an earlier work.

I find, first of all, that I pass from state to state. I am warm or cold, I am merry or sad, I work or I do nothing, I look at what is around me or I think of something else. Sensations, feelings, volitions, ideas—such are the changes into which my existence is divided and which colour it in turns. I change, then, without ceasing. But this is not saying enough. Change is far more radical than we are at first inclined to suppose.

For I speak of each of my states as if it formed a block and were a separate whole. I say indeed that I change, but the change seems to me to reside in the passage from one state to the next: of each state, taken separately, I am apt to think that it remains the same during all the time that it prevails. Nevertheless, a slight effort of attention would reveal to me that there is no feeling, no idea, no volition which is not undergoing change every moment: if a mental state ceased to vary, its duration would cease to flow. Let us take the most stable of internal states, the visual perception of a motionless external object. The object may remain the same. I may look at it from the same side, at the same angle, in the same light; nevertheless the vision I now have of it differs from that which I have just had, even if only because the one is an instant older than the other. My memory is there, which conveys something of the past into the present. My mental state, as it advances on the road of time, is continually swelling with the duration which it accumulates: it goes on increasing—rolling upon itself, as a snowball on the snow. Still more is this the case with states more deeply internal, such as sensations, feelings, desires, etc., which do not correspond, like a simple visual perception, to an unvarying external object. But it is expedient to disregard this uninterrupted change, and to notice it only when it becomes sufficient to impress a new attitude on the body, a new direction on the attention. Then, and then only, we find that our state has changed.

91

The truth is that we change without ceasing, and that the state itself is nothing but change.

This amounts to saying that there is no essential difference between passing from one state to another and persisting in the same state. If the state which "remains the same" is more varied than we think, on the other hand the passing from one state to another resembles, more than we imagine, a single state being prolonged; the transition is continuous. But, just because we close our eyes to the unceasing variation of every psychical state, we are obliged, when the change has become so considerable as to force itself on our attention, to speak as if a new state were placed alongside the previous one. Of this new state we assume that it remains unvarying in its turn, and so on endlessly. The apparent discontinuity of the psychical life is then due to our attention being fixed on it by a series of separate acts: actually there is only a gentle slope; but in following the broken line of our acts of attention, we think we perceive separate steps. True, our psychic life is full of the unforeseen. A thousand incidents arise, which seem to be cut off from those which precede them, and to be disconnected from those which follow. Discontinuous though they appear, however, in point of fact they stand out against the continuity of a background on which they are designed, and to which indeed they owe the intervals that separate them; they are the beats of the drum which break forth here and there in the symphony. Our attention fixes on them because they interest it more, but each of them is borne by the fluid mass of our whole psychical existence. Each is only the best illuminated point of a moving zone which comprises all that we feel or think or will—all, in short, that we are at any given moment. It is this entire zone which in reality makes up our state. Now, states thus defined cannot be regarded as distinct elements. They continue each other in an endless flow. . . .

18.2 Henri Bergson, *Matter and Memory* (1896)

Bergson, H., *Matter and Memory*, trans. by N. M. Paul and W. Scott Palmer, London: Macmillan, 1911, pp. 176–8, 225–6

. . . What is, for me, the present moment? The essence of time is that it goes by; time already gone by is the past, and we call the present the instant in which it goes by. But there can be no question here of a mathematical instant. No doubt there is an ideal present—a pure conception, the in-divisible limit which separates past from future. But the real, concrete, live present—that of which I speak when I speak of my present perception— that present necessarily occupies a duration. Where then is this duration placed? Is it on the hither or on the further side of the mathematical point which I determine ideally when I think of the present instant? Quite evidently, it is both on this side and on that; and what I call 'my present' has one foot in my past and another in my future. In my past, first, because 'the moment in which I am speaking is already far from me'; in my future, next, because this moment is impending over the future: it is to the future that I am tending, and could I fix this indivisible present, this infinitesimal element of the curve of time, it is the direction of the future that it would indicate. The psychical state, then, that I call 'my present,' must be both a perception of the immediate past and a determination of the immediate future. Now the immediate past, in so far as it is perceived, is, as we shall see, sensation, since every sensation translates a very long succession of elementary vibrations; and the immediate future, in so far as it is being determined, is action or movement. My present, then, is both sensation and movement; and, since my present forms an undivided whole, then the move-ment must be linked with the sensation, must prolong it in action. Whence I conclude that my present consists in a joint system of sensations and move-ments. My present is, in its essence, sensori-motor.

This is to say that my present consists in the consciousness that I have of my body. Having extension in space, my body experiences sensations and at the same time executes movements. Sensations and movements being localized at determined points of this extended body, there can only be, at a given moment, a single system of movements and sensations. That is why my present appears to me to be a thing absolutely determined, and contrasting with my past. Situated between the matter which influences it and that on which it has influence, my body is a centre of action, the place where the impressions received choose intelligently the path they will follow to transform themselves into movements accomplished. Thus it indeed repre-sents the actual state of my becoming, that part of my duration which is in process of growth. More generally, in that continuity of becoming which is reality itself, the present moment is constituted by the quasi-instantaneous section effected by our perception in the flowing mass; and this section is precisely that which we call the material world. Our body occupies its centre; it is, in this material world; that part of which we directly feel the flux; in its actual state the actuality of our present lies. If matter, so far as extended in space, is to be defined (as we believe it must) as a present which is always beginning again, inversely, our present is the very materiality of our exist-ence, that is to say, a system of sensations and movements, and nothing else. And this system is determined, unique for each moment of duration, just because sensations and movements occupy space, and because there cannot be in the same place several things at the same time.

[. . .]

We have supposed that the mind travels unceasingly over the interval comprised between its two extreme limits, the plane of action and the plane of dream. Let us suppose that we have to make a decision. Collecting, organizing the totality of its experience in what we call its character, the mind causes it to converge upon actions in which we shall afterwards find, together with the past which is their matter, the unforeseen form which is stamped upon them by personality; but the action is not able to become real unless it succeeds in encasing itself in the actual situation, that is to say, in that particular assemblage of circumstances which is due to the particular position of the body in time and space. Let us suppose, now, that we have to do a piece of intellectual work, to form a conception, to extract a more or less general idea from the multiplicity of our recollections. A wide margin is left to fancy on the one hand, to logical discernment on the other; but, if the idea is to live, it must touch present reality on some side; that is to say, it must be able, from step to step, and by progressive diminutions or contractions of itself, to be more or less acted by the body at the same time as it is thought by the mind. Our body, with the sensations which it receives on the one hand and the movements which it is capable of executing on the other, is then, that which fixes our mind, and gives it ballast and poise. The activity of the mind goes far beyond the mass of accumulated memories, as this mass of memories itself is infinitely more than the sensations and movement of the present hour; but these sensations and these movements condition what we may term our *attention to life*, and that is why everything depends on their cohesion in the normal work of the mind, as in a pyramid which should stand upon its apex.

19 Wyndham Lewis, The *Blast* Manifesto (1914)

The Manifesto in the first volume of the journal *Blast* (20 June 1914), edited by artist, novelist and critic Wyndham Lewis (1882–1957) with enthusiastic support from Ezra Pound (1885–1972), was intended as a philosophical statement of Vorticism – which they regarded as a movement in English art. In art Vorticists were seen as adhering to an abstract style, with a strong focal point and a spiralling effect that could draw the viewer in. In fact, it is debatable whether any artist (including Lewis) adhered rigorously to such stylistic strictures, or followed its philosophical ambitions strictly; insofar as it was a movement it was dominated overwhelmingly by the personality of Lewis and the energy of Pound. The two volumes of *Blast* (the second volume appeared in July 1915) did however cause a stir, partly by bringing together some impressive modernist artwork and literature, and partly because of the rousing, irreverential, *avant garde* spirit in which its Manifesto and critical statements were written and the journal presented (both in content and design). Apart from Lewis and Pound, signatories of the Manifesto included the poet Richard Aldington (1892–1962) and the sculptor Henri Gaudier-Brzeska (1891–1915).

Lewis, W. (ed.) ([1914] 1981) *Blast*, vol. 1, Santa Barbara: Black Sparrow, pp. 30–1, 40–3

Manifesto

I

1 Beyond Action and Reaction we would establish ourselves.
2 We start from opposite statements of a chosen world. Set up violent structure of adolescent clearness between two extremes.
3 We discharge ourselves on both sides.
4 We fight first on one side, then on the other, but always for the SAME cause, which is neither side or both sides and ours.
5 Mercenaries were always the best troops.
6 We are Primitive Mercenaries in the Modern World.
7 Our <u>Cause</u> Is NO-MAN'S.
8 We set Humour at Humour's throat.
  Stir up Civil War among peaceful apes.
9 We only want Humour if it has fought like Tragedy.
10 We only want Tragedy if it can clench its side-muscles like hands on it's belly, and bring to the surface a laugh like a bomb.

VII

1 Once this consciousness towards the new possibilities of expression in present life has come, however, it will be more the legitimate property of Englishmen than of any other people in Europe.
2 It should also, as it is by origin theirs, inspire them more forcibly and directly.
3 They are the inventors of this bareness and hardness, and should be the great enemies of Romance.

4 The Romance peoples will always be, at bottom, its defenders.

5 The Latins are at present, for instance, in their "discovery" of sport, their Futuristic gush over machines, aeroplanes, etc., the most romantic and sentimental "moderns" to be found.

6 It is only the second-rate people in France or Italy who are thorough revolutionaries.

7 In England, on the other hand, there is no vulgarity in revolt.

8 Or, rather, there is no revolt, it is the normal state.

9 So often rebels of the North and the South are diametrically opposed species.

10 The nearest thing in England to a great traditional French artist, is a great revolutionary English one.

Signatures for Manifesto

R. Aldington
Arbuthnot
L. Atkinson
Gaudier Brzeska
J. Dismorr
C. Hamilton
E. Pound
W. Roberts
H. Sanders
E. Wadsworth
Wyndham Lewis

20.1 T. S. Eliot, Tradition and the Individual Talent (1919)

One of the interesting features of some of the best-known self-styled modernist writers in English – particularly T. S. Eliot (1888–1965), but also to some extent Ezra Pound (1885–1972), Wyndham Lewis (1882–1957), Richard Aldington (1892–1962) and others – was that they combined their stylistic daring and formal innovations with rather conservative aesthetic and ideological views (including a defining regard for 'tradition' and 'classicism'). The influence of T. E. Hulme's (1887–1917) views, some of which are conveyed in the next extract below from his essay on 'Romanticism and Classicism' (1913–14, published posthumously in the 1924 collection *Speculations*, ed. Herbert Read) has a role to play in this. For literary modernists Hulme's influence was largely exercised through a close relationship with Ezra Pound. Briefly, Hulme argues here for a return to a disciplined classicism to succeed what he regarded as the sentimental excesses of romanticism.

T. S. Eliot's essay, 'Tradition and the Individual Talent' (1919, included in *The Sacred Wood*, 1920), is possibly the single most influential document for this variety of modernism. In this he argues that it is important for poets to be in touch with tradition to come to grips with the contemporary world, and promotes artistic impersonality in a classicist spirit. The essay has been used extensively both as a key to Eliot's own poetry and thinking, and as representing the modernist *zeitgeist* of the post-First World War period.

Eliot, T. S., 'Tradition and the Individual Talent', in *Selected Essays*, London: Faber & Faber, 1932, pp. 13–22

I

In English writing we seldom speak of tradition, though we occasionally apply its name in deploring its absence. We cannot refer to 'the tradition' or to 'a tradition'; at most, we employ the adjective in saying that the poetry of So-and-so is 'traditional' or even 'too traditional'. Seldom, perhaps, does the word appear except in a phrase of censure. If otherwise, it is vaguely approbative, with the implication, as to the work approved, of some pleasing archaeological reconstruction. You can hardly make the word agreeable to English ears without this comfortable reference to the reassuring science of archaeology.

Certainly the word is not likely to appear in our appreciations of living or dead writers. Every nation, every race, has not only its own creative, but its own critical turn of mind; and is even more oblivious of the shortcomings and limitations of its critical habits than of those of its creative genius. We know, or think we know, from the enormous mass of critical writing that has appeared in the French language the critical method or habit of the French, we only conclude (we are such unconscious people) that the French are 'more critical' than we, and sometimes even plume ourselves a little with the fact, as if the French were the less spontaneous. Perhaps they are, but we might remind ourselves that criticism is as inevitable as breathing, and that we should be none the worse for articulating what passes in our minds when we read a book and feel an emotion about it, for criticizing our own minds in their work of criticism. One of the facts that might come to light in this process is our tendency to insist, when we praise a poet, upon those aspects of his work in which he least resembles anyone else. In these aspects or parts of his work we pretend to find what is individual, what is the peculiar essence of the man. We dwell with satisfaction upon the poet's difference from his predecessors, especially his immediate predecessors; we endeavour to find something that can be isolated in order to be enjoyed. Whereas if we approach a poet without this prejudice we shall often find that not only the best, but the most individual parts of his work may be those in which the dead poets, his ancestors, assert their immortality most vigorously. And I do not mean the impressionable period of adolescence, but the period of full maturity.

Yet if the only form of tradition, of handing down, consisted in following the ways of the immediate generation before us in a blind or timid adherence to its successes, 'tradition' should positively be discouraged. We have seen many such simple currents soon lost in the sand; and novelty is better than repetition. Tradition is a matter of much wider significance. It cannot be inherited, and if you want it you must obtain it by great labour. It involves, in the first place, the historical sense, which we may call nearly indispensable to anyone who would continue to be a poet beyond his twenty-fifth year; and the historical sense involves a perception, not only of the pastness of the past, but of its presence; the historical sense compels a man to write not merely with his own generation in his bones, but with a feeling that the whole of the literature of Europe from Homer and within it the whole of the literature of his own country has a simultaneous existence and composes a simultaneous order. This historical sense, which is a sense of the timeless as well as of the temporal and of the timeless and of the temporal together, is what makes a writer traditional. And it is at the same time what makes a writer most acutely conscious of his place in time, of his own contemporaneity.

No poet, no artist of any art, has his complete meaning alone. His significance, his appreciation is the appreciation of his relation to the dead poets and artists. You cannot value him alone; you must set him, for contrast and comparison, among the dead. I mean this as a principle of aesthetic, not merely historical, criticism. The necessity that he shall conform, that he shall cohere, is not onesided; what happens when a new work of art is created is something that happens simultaneously to all the works of art which preceded it. The existing monuments form an ideal order among themselves, which is modified by the introduction of the new (the really new) work of art among them. The existing order is complete before the new work arrives; for order to persist after the supervention of novelty, the *whole* existing order must be, if ever so slightly, altered; and so the relations, proportions, values of each work of art toward the whole are readjusted; and this is conformity between the old and the new. Whoever has approved this idea of order, of the form of European, of English literature will not find it preposterous that the past should be altered by the present as much as the present is directed by the past. And the poet who is aware of this will be aware of great difficulties and responsibilities.

In a peculiar sense he will be aware also that he must inevitably be judged by the standards of the past. I say judged, not amputated, by them; not judged to be as good as, or worse or better than, the dead; and certainly not judged by the canons of dead critics. It is a judgment, a comparison, in which two things are measured by each other. To conform merely would be for the new work not really to conform at all; it would not be new, and would therefore not be a work of art. And we do not quite say that the new is more valuable because it fits in; but its fitting in is a test of its value— a test, it is true, which can only be slowly and cautiously applied, for we are none of us infallible judges of conformity. We say: it appears to conform, and is perhaps individual, or it appears individual, and may conform; but we are hardly likely to find that it is one and not the other.

To proceed to a more intelligible exposition of the relation of the poet to the past: he can neither take the past as a lump, an indiscriminate bolus, nor can he form himself wholly on one or two private admirations, nor can he form himself wholly upon one preferred period. The first course is inadmissible, the second is an important experience of youth, and the third is a pleasant and highly desirable supplement. The poet must be very conscious of the main current, which does not at all flow invariably through the most distinguished reputations. He must be quite aware of the obvious fact that art never improves, but that the material of art is never quite the same. He must be aware that the mind of Europe—the mind of his own country— a mind which he learns in time to be much more important than his own private mind—is a mind which changes, and that this change is a development which abandons nothing *en route*, which does not superannuate either Shakespeare, or Homer, or the rock drawing of the Magdalenian draughtsmen. That this development, refinement perhaps, complication certainly, is not, from the point of view of the artist, any improvement. Perhaps not even an improvement from the point of view of the psychologist or not to the extent which we imagine; perhaps only in the end based upon a complication in economics and machinery. But the difference between the present and the past is that the conscious present is an awareness of the past in a way and to an extent which the past's awareness of itself cannot show.

Someone said: 'The dead writers are remote from us because we *know* so much more than they did'. Precisely, and they are that which we know.

I am alive to a usual objection to what is clearly part of my programme for the *métier* of poetry. The objection is that the doctrine requires a ridiculous amount of erudition (pedantry), a claim which can be rejected by appeal to the lives of poets in any pantheon. It will even be affirmed that much learning deadens or perverts poetic sensibility. While, however, we persist in believing that a poet ought to know as much as will not encroach upon his necessary receptivity and necessary laziness, it is not desirable to confine knowledge to whatever can be put into a useful shape for examinations, drawing-rooms, or the still more pretentious modes of publicity. Some can absorb knowledge, the more tardy must sweat for it. Shakespeare acquired more essential history from Plutarch than most men could from the whole British Museum. What is to be insisted upon is that the poet must develop or procure the consciousness of the past and that he should continue to develop this consciousness throughout his career.

What happens is a continual surrender of himself as he is at the moment to something which is more valuable. The progress of an artist is a continual self-sacrifice, a continual extinction of personality.

There remains to define this process of depersonalization and its relation to the sense of tradition. It is in this depersonalization that art may be said to approach the condition of science. I therefore invite you to consider, as a suggestive analogy, the action which takes place when a bit of finely filiated platinum is introduced into a chamber containing oxygen and sulphur dioxide.

II

Honest criticism and sensitive appreciation is directed not upon the poet but upon the poetry. If we attend to the confused cries of the newspaper critics and the susurrus of popular repetition that follows, we shall hear the names of poets in great numbers; if we seek not Blue-book knowledge but the enjoyment of poetry, and ask for a poem, we shall seldom find it. I have tried to point out the importance of the relation of the poem to other poems by other authors, and suggested the conception of poetry as a living whole of all the poetry that has ever been written. The other aspect of this Impersonal theory of poetry is the relation of the poem to its author. And I hinted, by an analogy, that the mind of the mature poet differs from that of the immature one not precisely in any valuation of 'personality', not being necessarily more interesting, or having 'more to say', but rather by being a more finely perfected medium in which special, or very varied, feelings are at liberty to enter into new combinations.

The analogy was that of the catalyst. When the two gases previously mentioned are mixed in the presence of a filament of platinum, they form sulphurous acid. This combination takes place only if the platinum is present; nevertheless the newly formed acid contains no trace of platinum, and the platinum itself is apparently unaffected: has remained inert, neutral, and unchanged. The mind of the poet is the shred of platinum. It may partly or exclusively operate upon the experience of the man himself; but, the more perfect the artist, the more completely separate in him will be the man who suffers and the mind which creates; the more perfectly will the mind digest and transmute the passions which are its material.

The experience, you will notice, the elements which enter the presence of the transforming catalyst, are of two kinds: emotions and feelings. The effect of a work of art upon the person who enjoys it is an experience different in kind from any experience not of art. It may be formed out of one emotion, or may be a combination of several; and various feelings, inhering for the writer in particular words or phrases or images, may be added to compose the final result. Or great poetry may be made without the direct use of any emotion whatever: composed out of feelings solely. Canto XV of the *Inferno* (Brunetto Latini) is a working up of the emotion evident in the situation; but the effect, though single as that of any work of art, is obtained by considerable complexity of detail. The last quatrain gives an image, a feeling attaching to an image, which 'came', which did not develop simply out of what precedes, but which was probably in suspension in the poet's mind until the proper combination arrived for it to add itself to. The poet's mind is in fact a receptacle for seizing and storing up numberless feelings, phrases, images, which remain there until all the particles which can unite to form a new compound are present together.

If you compare several representative passages of the greatest poetry you see how great is the variety of types of combination, and also how completely any semi-ethical criterion of 'sublimity' misses the mark. For it is not the 'greatness', the intensity, of the emotions, the components, but the intensity of the artistic process, the pressure, so to speak, under which the fusion takes place, that counts. The episode of Paolo and Francesca employs a definite emotion, but the intensity of the poetry is something quite different from whatever intensity in the supposed experience it may give the impression of. It is no more intense, furthermore, than Canto XXVI, the voyage of Ulysses, which has not the direct dependence upon an emotion. Great variety is possible in the process of transmutation of emotion: the murder of Agamemnon, or the agony of Othello, gives an artistic effect apparently closer to a possible original than the scenes from Dante. In the *Agamemnon*, the artistic emotion approximates to the emotion of an actual spectator; in *Othello* to the emotion of the protagonist himself. But the difference between art and the event is always absolute; the combination which is the murder of Agamemnon is probably as complex as that which is the voyage of Ulysses. In either case there has been a fusion of elements. The ode of Keats contains a number of feelings which have nothing particular to do with the nightingale, but which the nightingale, partly perhaps because of its attractive name, and partly because of its reputation, served to bring together.

The point of view which I am struggling to attack is perhaps related to the metaphysical theory of the substantial unity of the soul: for my meaning is, that the poet has, not a 'personality' to express, but a particular medium, which is only a medium and not a personality, in which impressions and experiences combine in peculiar and unexpected ways. Impressions and experiences which are important for the man may take no place in the poetry, and those which become important in the poetry may play quite a negligible part in the man, the personality.

I will quote a passage which is unfamiliar enough to be regarded with fresh attention in the light—or darkness—of these observations:

> And now methinks I could e'en chide myself
> For doating on her beauty, though her death
> Shall be revenged after no common action.
> Does the silkworm expend her yellow labours
> For thee? For thee does she undo herself?
> Are lordships sold to maintain ladyships
> For the poor benefit of a bewildering minute?
> Why does yon fellow falsify highways,
> And put his life between the judge's lips,
> To refine such a thing—keeps horse and men
> To beat their valours for her? . . .

In this passage (as is evident if it is taken in its context) there is a combination of positive and negative emotions: an intensely strong attraction toward beauty and an equally intense fascination by the ugliness which is contrasted with it and which destroys it. This balance of contrasted emotion is in the dramatic situation to which the speech is pertinent, but that situation alone is inadequate to it. This is, so to speak, the structural emotion, provided by the drama. But the whole effect, the dominant tone, is due to the fact that a number of floating feelings, having an affinity to this emotion by no means superficially evident, have combined with it to give us a new art emotion.

It is not in his personal emotions, the emotions provoked by particular events in his life, that the poet is in any way remarkable or interesting. His particular emotions may be simple, or crude, or flat. The emotion in his poetry will, be a very complex thing, but not with the complexity of the emotions of people who have very complex or unusual emotions in life.

One error, in fact, of eccentricity in poetry is to seek for new human emotions to express; and in this search for novelty in the wrong place it discovers the perverse. The business of the poet is not to find new emotions, but to use the ordinary ones and, in working them up into poetry, to express feelings which are not in actual emotions at all. And emotions which he has never experienced will serve his turn as well as those familiar to him. Consequently, we must believe that 'emotion recollected in tranquillity' is an inexact formula. For it is neither emotion, nor recollection, nor, without distortion of meaning, tranquillity. It is a concentration, and a new thing resulting from the concentration, of a very great number of experiences which to the practical and active person would not seem to be experiences at all; it is a concentration which does not happen consciously or of deliberation. These experiences are not 'recollected', and they finally unite in an atmosphere which is 'tranquil' only in that it is a passive attending upon the event. Of course this is not quite the whole story. There is a great deal, in the writing of poetry, which must be conscious and deliberate. In fact, the bad poet is usually unconscious where he ought to be conscious, and conscious where he ought to be unconscious. Both errors tend to make him 'personal'. Poetry is not a turning loose of emotion, but an escape from emotion; it is not the expression of personality, but an escape from personality. But, of course, only those who have personality and emotions know what it means to want to escape from these things.

III

ὁ δὲ νοῦς ἴσως θειότερόν τι καὶ ἀπαθές ἐστιν.

This essay proposes to halt at the frontier of metaphysics or mysticism, and confine itself to such practical conclusions as can be applied by the responsible person interested in poetry. To divert interest from the poet to the poetry is a laudable aim: for it would conduce to a juster estimation of actual poetry, good and bad. There are many people who appreciate the expression of sincere emotion in verse, and there is a smaller number of people who can appreciate technical excellence. But very few know when there is an expression of *significant* emotion, emotion which has its life in the poem and not in the history of the poet. The emotion of art is impersonal. And the poet cannot reach this impersonality without surrendering himself wholly to the work to be done. And he is not likely to know what is to be done unless be lives in what is not merely the present, but the present moment of the past, unless he is conscious, not of what is dead, but of what is already living.

20.2 T. E. Hulme, Romanticism and
Classicism (1924)

Hulme, T. E., 'Romanticism and Classicism, in *Speculations: Essays on Humanism and the Philosophy of Art*, ed. by H. Reed, London: Routledge & Kegan Paul, 1924, pp. 113–14, 116–22

I want to maintain that after a hundred years of romanticism, we are in for a classical revival, and that the particular weapon of this new classical spirit, when it works in verse, will be fancy. And in this I imply the superiority of fancy—not superior generally or absolutely, for that would be obvious nonsense, but superior in the sense that we use the word good in empirical ethics—good for something, superior for something. I shall have to prove then two things, first that a classical revival is coming, and, secondly, for its particular purposes, fancy will be superior to imagination.

So banal have the terms Imagination and Fancy become that we imagine they must have always been in the language. Their history as two differing terms in the vocabulary of criticism is comparatively short. Originally, of course, they both mean the same thing; they first began to be differentiated by the German writers on æsthetics in the eighteenth century.

I know that in using the words "classic" and "romantic" I am doing a dangerous thing. They represent five or six different kinds of antitheses, and while I may be using them in one sense you may be interpreting them in another. In this present connection I am using them in a perfectly precise and limited sense. I ought really to have coined a couple of new words, but I prefer to use the ones I have used, as I then conform to the practice of the group of polemical writers who make most use of them at the present day, and have almost succeeded in making them political catchwords. I mean Maurras, Lasserre and all the group connected with *L'Action Française*.

[. . .]

Here is the root of all romanticism: that man, the individual, is an infinite reservoir of possibilities; and if you can so rearrange society by the destruction of oppressive order then these possibilities will have a chance and you will get Progress.

One can define the classical quite clearly as the exact opposite to this. Man is an extraordinarily fixed and limited animal whose nature is absolutely constant. It is only by tradition and organisation that anything decent can be got out of him.

This view was a little shaken at the time of Darwin. You remember his particular hypothesis, that new species came into existence by the cumulative effect of small variations—this seems to admit the possibility of future

104

progress. But at the present day the contrary hypothesis makes headway in the shape of De Vries's mutation theory, that each new species comes into existence, not gradually by the accumulation of small steps, but suddenly in a jump, a kind of sport, and that once in existence it remains absolutely fixed. This enables me to keep the classical view with an appearance of scientific backing.

Put shortly, these are the two views, then. One, that man is intrinsically good, spoilt by circumstance; and the other that he is intrinsically limited, but disciplined by order and tradition to something fairly decent. To the one party man's nature is like a well, to the other like a bucket. The view which regards man as a well, a reservoir full of possibilities, I call the romantic; the one which regards him as a very finite and fixed creature, I call the classical.

[. . .]

I must now shirk the difficulty of saying exactly what I mean by romantic and classical in verse. I can only say that it means the result of these two attitudes towards the cosmos, towards man, in so far as it gets reflected in verse. The romantic, because he thinks man infinite, must always be talking about the infinite; and as there is always the bitter contrast between what you think you ought to be able to do and what man actually can, it always tends, in its later stages at any rate, to be gloomy.

[. . .]

What I mean by classical in verse, then, is this. That even in the most imaginative flights there is always a holding back, a reservation. The classical poet never forgets this finiteness, this limit of man. He remembers always that he is mixed up with earth. He may jump, but he always returns back; he never flies away into the circumambient gas.

You might say if you wished that the whole of the romantic attitude seems to crystallise in verse round metaphors of flight. Hugo is always flying, flying over abysses, flying up into the eternal gases. The word infinite in every other line.

In the classical attitude you never seem to swing right along to the infinite nothing. If you say an extravagant thing which does exceed the limits inside which you know man to be fastened, yet there is always conveyed in some way at the end an impression of yourself standing outside it, and not quite believing it, or consciously putting it forward as a flourish. You never go blindly into an atmosphere more than the truth, an atmosphere too rarefied for man to breathe for long. You are always faithful to the conception of a limit. It is a question of pitch; in romantic verse you move at a certain pitch of rhetoric which you know, man being what he is, to be a little high-falutin. The kind of thing you get in Hugo or Swinburne. In the coming classical reaction that will feel just wrong. For an example of the opposite thing, a verse written in the proper classical spirit, I can take the song from Cymbeline beginning with "Fear no more the heat of the sun." I am just using this as a parable. I don't quite mean what I say here. Take the last two lines:

"Golden lads and girls all must,
Like chimney sweepers come to dust."

Now, no romantic would have ever written that. Indeed, so ingrained is romanticism, so objectionable is this to it, that people have asserted that these were not part of the original song.

Apart from the pun, the thing that I think quite classical is the word lad. Your modern romantic could never write that. He would have to write golden youth, and take up the thing at least a couple of notes in pitch.

I want now to give the reasons which make me think, that we are nearing the end of the romantic movement.

The first lies in the nature of any convention or tradition in art. A particular convention or attitude in art has a strict analogy to the phenomena of organic life. It grows old and decays. It has a definite period of life and must die. All the possible tunes get played on it and then it is exhausted; moreover its best period is its youngest. Take the case of the extraordinary efflorescence of verse in the Elizabethan period. All kinds of reasons have been given for this—the discovery of the new world and all the rest of it. There is a much simpler one. A new medium had been given them to play with—namely, blank verse, it was new and so it was easy to play new tunes on it.

The same law holds in other arts. All the masters of painting are born into the world at a time when the particular tradition from which they start is imperfect. The Florentine tradition was just short of full ripeness when Raphael came to Florence, the Bellinesque was still young when Titian was born in Venice. Landscape was still a toy or an appanage of figure-painting when Turner and Constable arose to reveal its independent power. When Turner and Constable had done with landscape they left little or nothing for their successors to do on the same lines. Each field of artistic activity is exhausted by the first great artist who gathers a full harvest from it.

This period of exhaustion seems to me to have been reached in romanticism. We shall not get any new efflorescence of verse until we get a new technique, a new convention, to turn ourselves loose in.

VIRGINIA WOOLF,
ORLANDO

21 Virginia Woolf, *The Diary of Virginia Woolf* (1927–8)

Woolf kept a diary throughout her life, detailing miscellaneously her varied social engagements, her various illnesses, her affairs and friendships and the germination and progress of her writing. The following extracts from her diary of September 1927 through to May 1928 relate to the composition of her experimental novel *Orlando*, from the first thought of 'a most amusing book', 'truthful but fantastic' with her then lover Vita Sackville-West appearing as 'Orlando', through to sending the completed manuscript to press. Her remarks make it clear to what extent *Orlando* was conceived easily and excitingly as a joke, a holiday and as something of an illicit pleasure because so unserious. Her entries also suggest to what extent *Orlando* in its inception was both an escape from the straight history of fiction she was supposed to have been writing 'that intolerable dull Fiction' and a displacement of it. The diary also shows Woolf endeavouring to finish *Orlando* at the same time as conceiving the lecture entitled 'Women and Fiction' to be given in Cambridge, which would subsequently be expanded and published in 1929 as *A Room of One's Own*. The juxtaposition prompts the thought that the two texts, despite their very different modes, share many of Woolf's current preoccupations about gender and writing. Touchingly, the diary makes it clear, too, not just the headiness of writing but the physical and mental struggle, hampered by doubts, headache, fatigue and the sense – at the age of 46 – of time pressing.

Woolf, V., *The Diary of Virginia Woolf*, vol. 3: *1925–1930*, ed. by A. O. Bell, London: The Hogarth Press, pp. 156–85 passim

Tuesday 20 September 1927[1]

One of these days . . . I shall sketch here, like a grand historical picture, the outlines of all my friends. I was thinking of this in bed last night, & for some reason I thought I would begin with a sketch of Gerald Brenan. There may be something in this idea. It might be a way of writing the memoirs of one's own times during peoples lifetimes. It might be a most amusing book. The question is how to do it. Vita [Sackville-West] should be a young nobleman. There should be Lytton. & it should be truthful; but fantastic. Roger [Fry]. Duncan [Grant]. Clive [Bell]. Adrian [Stephen]. Their lives should be related. But I can think of more books than I shall ever be able to write. How many little stories come into my head!

Wednesday 5 October

If my pen allowed, I should now try to make out a work table, having done my last article for the Tribune, & now being free again. And instantly the usual exciting devices enter my mind: a biography beginning in the year 1500 & continuing to the present day, called Orlando: Vita; only with a change about from one sex to another. I think, for a treat, I shall let myself dash this in for a week, while   [*text ends*]

The Woolfs returned to London on Thursday 6 October.

Saturday 22 October

This is a book, I think I have said before, which I write after tea. [. . .]

"I shall let myself dash this in for a week"—I have done nothing, nothing, nothing else for a fortnight; & am launched somewhat furtively but with all the more passion upon Orlando: A Biography. It is to be 'a small book, & written by Christmas. I thought I could combine it with *Fiction*, but once the mind gets hot it cant stop; I walk making up phrases; sit, contriving scenes; am in short in the thick of the greatest rapture known to me; from which I have kept myself since last February, or earlier. Talk of planning a book, or waiting for an idea! This one came in a rush; I said to pacify myself, being bored & stale with criticism & faced with that intolerable dull Fiction, "You shall write a page of a story for treat: you shall stop sharp at 11.30 & then go on with the Romantics". I had very little idea what the story was to be about. But the relief of turning my mind that way about was such that I felt happier than for months; as if put in the sun, or laid on cushions; & after two days entirely gave up my time chart & abandoned myself to the pure delight of this farce: which I enjoy as much as I've ever enjoyed anything; & have written myself into half a headache & had to come to a halt, like a tired horse, & take a little sleeping draught last night: which made our breakfast fiery. I did not finish my egg. I am writing Orlando half in a mock style very clear & plain, so that people will understand every word. But the balance between truth & fantasy must be careful. It is based on Vita, Violet Trefusis, Lord Lascelles, Knole &c.[2]

Sunday 20 November

I will now snatch a moment from what Morgan calls 'life' to enter a hurried note. My notes have been few; life a cascade, a glissade, a torrent: all together. I think on the whole this *is* our happiest autumn. So much work, & success now, & life on easy terms: heaven knows what. My morning rushes, pell mell, from 10 to 1. I write so quick I can't get it typed before lunch. This I suppose is the main backbone of my autumn—*Orlando*. Never do I feel this except for a morning or two, writing criticism. Today I began the third chapter. Do I learn anything? Too much of a joke perhaps for that; yet I like these plain sentences; & the externality of it for a change. It is too thin of course; splashed over the canvas; but I shall cover the ground by Jan. 7th (I say) & then re-write.

Tuesday 20 December

I am still writing the 3rd Chap. of Orlando. I have had of course to give up the fancy of finishing by February & printing this spring. It is drawing out longer than I meant. I have just been thinking over the scene when O. meets a girl (Nell) in the Park & goes with her, to a neat room in Gerrard Street. There she will disclose herself. They will talk. This will lead to a diversion or two about women's love. This will bring in O.'s night life; & her clients (thats the word). Then she will see Dr Johnson, & perhaps write (I want somehow to quote it) To all you Ladies.[3] So I shall get some effect of years passing; & then there will be a description of the lights of the 18th Century burning; & the clouds of the 19th Century rising. Then on to the 19th. But I have not considered this. I want to write it all over hastily, & so keep unity of tone, which in this book is very important. It has to be half laughing, half serious: with great splashes of exaggeration.
[. . .]
How extraordinarily unwilled by me but potent in its own right by the way Orlando was! as if it shoved everything aside to come into existence. Yet I see looking back just now to March that it is almost exactly in spirit, though not in actual facts, the book I planned then as an escapade; the spirit to be satiric, the structure wild. Precisely.
Yes, I repeat, a very happy, a singularly happy autumn.

Saturday 11 February

I am so cold I can hardly hold the pen. The futility of it all—so I broke off; & have indeed been feeling that rather persistently, or perhaps I should have written here. Hardy & Meredith together sent me torpid to bed with headache. I know the feeling now, when I can't spin a sentence, & sit mumbling & turning; & nothing flits by my brain which is as a blank window. So I shut my studio door, & go to bed, stuffing my ears with rubber; & there I lie a day or two. And what leagues I travel in the time! Such 'sensations' spread over my spine & head directly I give them the chance; such an exaggerated tiredness; such anguishes & despairs; & heavenly relief & rest; & then misery again. Never was anyone so tossed up & down by the body as I am, I think. But it is over: & put away; & Lord Sackville is dead & lies at Withyam, & I passed Knole with Vita yesterday & had to look away from the vast masterless house, without a flag. This is what she minds most. When she left the house behind the old cart horses, she went for ever, she said, after complete rule for three days.[4]

For some reason, I am hacking rather listlessly at the last chapter of Orlando, which was to have been the best. Always always the last chapter slips out of my hands. One gets bored. One whips oneself up. I still hope for a fresh wind, & dont very much bother, except that I miss the fun, which was so tremendously lively all October, November & December. I have my doubts if it is not empty; & too fantastic to write at such length.

Saturday 18 February

[. . .]

My mind is woolgathering about Women & Fiction, which I am to read at Newnham in May. The mind is the most capricious of insects—flitting fluttering. I had thought to write the quickest most brilliant pages in Orlando yesterday—not a drop came, all, forsooth, for the usual physical reasons, which declared themselves today. It is the oddest feeling: as if a finger stopped the flow of the ideas in the brain: it is unsealed, & the blood rushes all over the place. Again, instead of writing O. I've been racing up & down the whole field of my lecture. And tomorrow, alas, we motor; for I must get back into the book—which has brightened the last few days satisfactorily. Not that my sensations in writing are an infallible guide.

[. . .]

I doubt that I shall ever write another novel after O. I shall invent a new name for them.

Sunday 18 March

I have lost my writing board; an excuse for the anaemic state of this book. Indeed I only write now, in between letters to say that Orlando was finished

yesterday as the clock struck one. Anyhow the canvas is covered. There will
be three months of close work needed, imperatively, before it can be printed;
for I have scrambled & splashed, & the canvas shows through in a thousand
places. But it is a serene, accomplished feeling, to write, even provisionally,
The End, & we go off on Saturday, with my mind appeased.

I have written this book quicker than any; & it is all a joke; & yet gay
& quick reading I think; a writers holiday. I feel more & more sure that I
will never write a novel again. Little bits of rhyme come in.

Thursday 22 March

There are the last pages at the end of Orlando, & it is twenty five minutes
to one; & I have written everything I have to write, & on Saturday we go
abroad.

Yes its done—Orlando—begun on 8th October, as a joke; & now rather
too long for my liking. It may fall between stools, be too long for a joke,
& too frivolous for a serious book.

Thursday 31 May

[. . .]

The sun is out again; I have half forgotten Orlando already, since
L.[eonard] has read it & it has half passed out of my possession. I think it
lacks the sort hammering I should have given it if I had taken longer: is
too freakish & unequal. Very brilliant now & then. As for the effect of the
whole, that I cant judge. Not, I think 'important' among my works. L. says
a satire.

[. . .]

L. takes Orlando more seriously than I had expected. Thinks it in some
ways better than The Lighthouse;[5] about more interesting things, & with
more attachment to life, & larger. The truth is I expect I began it as a joke,
& went on with it seriously. Hence it lacks some unity. He says it is very
original. Anyhow I'm glad to be quit this time of writing 'a novel'; & hope
never to be accused of it again. Now I want to write some very closely
reasoned criticism; book on fiction; an essay of some sort (but not Tolstoy
for the Times). Dr Burney's evening party I think for Desmond. And then?
I feel anxious to keep the hatch down: not to let too many projects come
in. Something abstract poetic next time—I dont know. I rather like the idea
of these Biographies of living people. Ottoline [Morrell] suggests herself—
but no. And I must tear up all that manuscript, & write a great many notes
& adventure out into the world—as I shall do tomorrow, when I go to have
my ears pierced with Vita [Sackville-West].

Notes

1 VW has misdated this entry 'Tuesday Sept. 18th'.

2 Violet Trefusis, *née* Keppel (1894–1972), with whom Vita, often disguised as a man, had had a passionate and dramatic love affair between 1918–21 (see Nigel Nicolson, *Portrait of a Marriage*, 1973). Henry, Viscount Lascelles (1882–1974), who married the Princess Royal in 1922 and was to succeed his father as 6th Earl of Harewood in 1929, had courted Vita before she engaged herself to Harold Nicolson in 1913. Sasha the Russian Princess and the Archduchess Harriet in *Orlando* were based upon what VW learned of these two from Vita.

3 'To all you Ladies' was written in 1665 by Vita's ancestor Charles Sackville, Earl of Dorset. VW does not quote it in *Orlando*.

4 Vita's father, the 3rd Baron Sackville, died at Knole on 28 January, aged sixty; he was buried, as the Sackvilles have been since the fourteenth century, in the family chapel at Withyham Church, his coffin drawn thither by carthorses. Since he had no son, his tides and estates passed to his brother Charles.

5 *To the Lighthouse*, Woolf's most recent novel, had been published in 1927.

22 Virginia Woolf, Mr Bennett and Mrs Brown (1924)

This essay takes as its subject the state of modem fiction. In expressing dissatisfaction with the late Edwardian social realists Wells, Bennett and Galsworthy, Woolf elaborates an early and important manifesto describing the practices, priorities and subject-matter of a modernist fiction, exemplified by her own work, and that of T. S. Eliot, James Joyce, E. M. Forster, D. H. Lawrence and Lytton Strachey. Characteristically, Woolf structures her consideration of the Edwardian writers within a whimsical narrative of a train journey from Richmond to Waterloo in which she witnesses an enigmatic conversation between a Mr Bennett and a Mrs Brown. From fleshing out this conversation into fully-realised plot and characters, Woolf moves on to consider various fictional techniques for realising Mrs Brown, imagining Mr Bennett travelling cheek by jowl with the elusive and elderly Mrs Brown, trying by unsuccessful interrogation to capture her in fiction. Woolf's central and consciously exaggerated contention is that 'in or about December, 1910, human character changed' and with it all human relationships between the sexes and between the classes. As a result, this profound change mandates a change in the nature of fiction, its conventional investigative practices and stylistic strategies. Woolf describes this change as 'the sound of breaking and falling, crashing and destruction' and characterises her literary age – the age of the modernists – as 'a season of failures and fragments' which will lead to 'one of the great ages of English literature'.

Woolf, V., 'Mr Bennett and Mrs Brown', in *Collected Essays*, vol. 1, London: The Hogarth Press, 1966, pp. 319–37

It seems to me possible, perhaps desirable, that I may be the only person in this room who has committed the folly of writing, trying to write, or failing to write, a novel. And when I asked myself, as your invitation to speak to you about modern fiction made me ask myself, what demon whispered in my ear and urged me to my doom, a little figure rose before me—the figure of a man, or of a woman, who said, 'My name is Brown. Catch me if you can.'

Most novelists have the same experience. Some Brown, Smith, or Jones comes before them and says in the most seductive and charming way in the world, 'Come and catch me if you can.' And so, led on by this will-o'-the-wisp, they flounder through volume after volume, spending the best years of their lives in the pursuit, and receiving for the most part very little cash in exchange. Few catch the phantom; most have to be content with a scrap of her dress or a wisp of her hair.

My belief that men and women write novels because they are lured on to create some character which has thus imposed itself upon them has the sanction of Mr. Arnold Bennett. In an article from which I will quote he says, 'The foundation of good fiction is character-creating and nothing else. . . . Style counts; plot counts; originality of outlook counts. But none of these counts anything like so much as the convincingness of the characters. If the characters are real the novel will have a chance; if they are not, oblivion will be its portion. . . .' And he goes on to draw the conclusion that we have no young novelists of first-rate importance at the present moment, because they are unable to create characters that are real, true, and convincing.

These are the questions that I want with greater boldness than discretion to discuss tonight. I want to make out what we mean when we talk about 'character' in fiction; to say something about the question of reality which Mr. Bennett raises; and to suggest some reasons why the younger novelists fail to create characters, if, as Mr. Bennett asserts, it is true that fail they, do. This will lead me, I am well aware, to make some very sweeping and some very vague assertions. For the question is an extremely difficult one. Think how little we know about character—think how little we know about art. But, to make a clearance before I begin, I will suggest that we range Edwardians and Georgians into two camps; Mr. Wells, Mr. Bennett, and Mr. Galsworthy I will call the Edwardians; Mr. Forster, Mr. Lawrence, Mr. Strachey, Mr. Joyce, and Mr. Eliot I will call the Georgians. And if I speak in the first person, with intolerable egotism, I will ask you to excuse me. I do not want to attribute to the world at large the opinions of one solitary, ill-informed, and misguided individual.

My first assertion is one that I think you will grant—that everyone in this room is a judge of character. Indeed it would be impossible to live for a year without disaster unless one practised character-reading and had some skill in the art. Our marriages, our friendships depend on it; our business largely depends on it; every day questions arise which can only be solved by its help. And now I will hazard a second assertion, which is more disputable perhaps, to the effect that in or about December, 1910, human character changed.

I am not saying that one went out, as one might into a garden, and there saw that a rose had flowered, or that a hen had laid an egg. The change was not sudden and definite like that. But, a change there was, nevertheless; and, since one must be arbitrary, let us date it about the year 1910. The first signs of it are recorded in the books of Samuel Butler, in *The Way of All Flesh* in particular; the plays of Bernard Shaw continue to record it. In life one can see the change, if I may use a homely illustration, in the character of one's cook. The Victorian cook lived like a leviathan in the lower depths, formidable, silent, obscure, inscrutable; the Georgian cook is a creature of sunshine and fresh air; in and out of the drawing-room, now to borrow the *Daily Herald* now to ask advice about a hat. Do you ask for more solemn instances of the power of the human race to change? Read the *Agamemnon*, and see whether, in process of time, your sympathies are not almost entirely with Clytemnestra. Or consider the married life of the Carlyles and bewail the waste, the futility, for him and for her, of the horrible domestic tradition which made it seemly for a woman of genius to spend her time chasing beetles, scouring saucepans, instead of writing books. All human relations have shifted—those between masters and servants, husbands and wives, parents and children. And when human relations change there is at the same time a change in religion, conduct, politics, and literature. Let us agree to place one of these changes about the year 1910.

[. . .]

I let my Mrs. Brown slip through my fingers. I have told you nothing whatever about her. But that is partly the great Edwardians' fault. I asked them—they are my elders and betters—How shall I begin to describe this woman's character? And they said: 'Begin by saying that her father kept a shop in Harrogate. Ascertain the rent. Ascertain the wages of shop assistants in the year 1878. Discover what her mother died of. Describe cancer. Describe calico. Describe—' But I cried: 'Stop! Stop!' And I regret to say that I threw that ugly, that clumsy, that incongruous tool out of the window, for I knew that if I began describing the cancer and the calico, my Mrs. Brown, that vision to which I cling though I know no way of imparting it to you, would have been dulled and tarnished and vanished for ever.

That is what I mean by saying that the Edwardian tools are the wrong ones for us to use. They have laid an enormous stress upon the fabric of things. They have given us a house in the hope that we may be able to deduce the human beings who live there. To give them their due, they have made that house much better worth living in. But if you hold that novels are in the first place about people, and only in the second about the houses they live in, that is the wrong way to set about it. Therefore, you see, the Georgian writer had to begin by throwing away the method that was in use at the moment. He was left alone there facing Mrs. Brown without any method of conveying her to the reader. But that is inaccurate. A writer is never alone. There is always the public with him—if not on the same seat, at least in the compartment next door. Now the public is a strange travelling companion. In England it is a very suggestible and docile creature, which, once you get it to attend, will believe implicitly what it is told for a certain number of years.

[. . .]

Here is the British public sitting by the writer's side and saying in its vast and unanimous way: 'Old women have houses. They have fathers. They have incomes. They have servants. They have hot-water bottles. That is how we know that they are old women. Mr. Wells and Mr. Bennett and Mr. Galsworthy have always taught us that this is the way to recognize them. But now with your Mrs. Brown—how are we to believe in her? We do not even know whether her villa was called Albert or Balmoral; what she paid for her gloves; or whether her mother died of cancer or of consumption. How can she be alive? No; she is a mere figment of your imagination.'

And old women of course ought to be made of freehold villas and copyhold estates, not of imagination.

The Georgian novelist, therefore, was in an awkward predicament. There was Mrs. Brown protesting that she was different, quite different, from what people made out, and luring the novelist to her rescue by the most fascinating if fleeting glimpse of her charms; there were the Edwardians handing out tools appropriate to house building and house breaking; and there was the British Public asseverating that they must see the hot-water bottle first.

[. . .]

Such, I think, was the predicament in which, the young Georgians found themselves about the year 1910. Many of them—I am thinking of Mr. Forster and Mr. Lawrence in particular—spoilt their early work because, instead of throwing away those tools, they tried to use them. They tried to compromise. They tried to combine their own direct sense of the oddity and significance of some character with Mr. Galsworthy's knowledge of the Factory Acts, and Mr. Bennett's knowledge of the Five Towns. They tried it, but they had too keen, too overpowering a sense of Mrs. Brown and her peculiarities to go on trying it much longer. Something had to be done.

At whatever cost to life, limb, and damage to valuable property Mrs. Brown must be rescued, expressed, and set in her high relations to the world before the train stopped and she disappeared for ever. And so the smashing and the crashing began. Thus it is that we hear all round us, in poems and novels and biographies, even in newspaper articles and essays, the sound of breaking and falling, crashing and destruction. It is the prevailing sound of the Georgian age—rather a melancholy one if you think what melodious days there have been in the past, if you think of Shakespeare and Milton and Keats or even of Jane Austen and Thackeray and Dickens; if you think of the language, and the heights to which it can soar when free, and see the same eagle captive, bald, and croaking.

In view of these facts—with these sounds in my ears and these fancies in my brain—I am not going to deny that Mr. Bennett has some reason when he complains that our Georgian writers are unable to make us believe that our characters are real. I am forced to agree that they do not pour out three immortal masterpieces with Victorian regularity every autumn. But, instead of being gloomy, I am sanguine. For this state of things is, I think, inevitable whenever from hoar old age or callow youth the convention ceases to be a means of communication between writer and reader, and becomes instead an obstacle and an impediment. At the present moment we are suffering, not from decay, but from having no code of manners which writers and readers accept as a prelude to the more exciting intercourse of friendship. The literary convention of the time is so artificial—you have to talk about the weather and nothing but the weather throughout the entire visit—that, naturally, the feeble are tempted to outrage, and the strong are led to destroy the very foundations and rules of literary society. Signs of this are every-where apparent. Grammar is violated; syntax disintegrated; as a boy staying with an aunt for the week-end rolls in the geranium bed out of sheer desperation as the solemnities of the sabbath wear on. The more adult writers do not, of course, indulge in such wanton exhibitions of spleen. Their sincerity is desperate, and their courage tremendous; it is only that they do not know which to use, a fork or their fingers. Thus, if you read Mr. Joyce and Mr. Eliot you will be struck by the indecency of the one, and the obscu-rity of the other. Mr. Joyce's indecency in *Ulysses* seems to me the conscious and calculated indecency of a desperate man who feels that in order to breathe he must break the windows. At moments, when the window is broken, he is magnificent. But what a waste of energy! And, after all, how dull inde-cency is, when it is not the overflowing of a superabundant energy or savagery, but the determined and public-spirited act of a man who needs fresh air! Again, with the obscurity of Mr. Eliot. I think that Mr. Eliot has written some of the loveliest single lines in modern poetry. But how intolerant he is of the old usages and politenesses of society—respect for the weak, consideration for the dull! As I sun myself upon the intense and ravishing beauty of one of his lines, and reflect that I must make a dizzy and dangerous leap to the next, and so on from line to line, like an acrobat flying precariously from bar to bar, I cry out, I confess, for the old decorums, and envy the indolence of my ancestors who, instead of spinning madly through mid-air, dreamt quietly in the shade with a book. Again, in Mr. Strachey's books, *Eminent Victorians* and *Queen Victoria*, the effort and strain of writing against the grain and current of the times is visible too. It is much less visible, of course, for not only is he dealing with facts, which are stubborn things, but he has fabricated, chiefly from eighteenth-century material, a very discreet code of manners of his own, which allows him to sit at the table with the highest in the land and to say a great many things under cover of that exquisite apparel which, had they gone naked, would have been chased by the men-servants from the room. Still, if you compare *Eminent Victorians* with some of Lord Macaulay's essays, though you will feel that Lord Macaulay is always wrong, and Mr. Strachey always right, you will also feel a body, a sweep, a richness in Lord Macaulay's essays which show that his age was behind him; all his strength went straight into his work; none was used for purposes of concealment or of conversion. But Mr. Strachey has had to open our eyes before he made us see; he has had to search out and sew together a very artful manner of speech; and the effort, beautifully though it is concealed, has robbed his work of some of the force that should have gone into it, and limited his scope.

For these reasons, then, we must reconcile ourselves to a season of failures and fragments. We must reflect that where so much strength is spent on finding a way of telling the truth, the truth itself is bound to reach us in rather an exhausted and chaotic condition. Ulysses, Queen Victoria, Mr. Prufrock—to give Mrs. Brown some of the names she has made famous lately—is a little pale and dishevelled by the time her rescuers reach her. And it is the sound of their axes that we hear—a vigorous and stimulating sound in my ears—unless of course you wish to sleep, when, in the bounty of his concern, Providence has provided a host of writers anxious and able to satisfy your needs.

Thus I have tried, at tedious length, I fear, to answer some of the questions which I began by asking. I have given an account of some of the difficulties which in my view beset the Georgian writer in all his forms. I have sought to excuse him. May I end by venturing to remind you of the duties and responsibilities that are yours as partners in this business of writing books, as companions in the railway carriage, as fellow travellers with Mrs. Brown? For she is just as visible to you who remain silent as to us who tell stories about her. In the course of your daily life this past week you have had far stranger and more interesting experiences than the one I have tried to describe. You have overheard scraps of talk that filled you with amazement. You have gone to bed at night bewildered by the complexity of your feelings. In one day thousands of ideas have coursed through your brains; thousands of emotions have met, collided, and disappeared in astonishing disorder. Nevertheless, you allow the writers to palm off upon you a version of all this, an image of Mrs. Brown, which has no likeness to that surprising apparition whatsoever. In your modesty you seem to consider that writers are of different blood and bone from yourselves; that they know more of Mrs. Brown than you do. Never was there a more fatal mistake. It is this division between reader and writer, this humility on your part, these professional airs and graces on ours, that corrupt and emasculate the books which should be the healthy offspring of a close and equal alliance between us. Hence spring those sleek, smooth novels, those portentous and ridiculous biographies, that milk and watery criticism, those poems melodiously celebrating the innocence of roses and sheep which pass so plausibly for literature at the present time.

Your part is to insist that writers shall come down off their plinths and pedestals, and describe beautifully if possible, truthfully at any rate, our Mrs. Brown. You should insist that she is an old lady of unlimited capacity and infinite variety; capable of appearing in any place; wearing any dress; saying anything and doing heaven knows what. But the things she says and the things she does and her eyes and her nose and her speech and her silence have an overwhelming fascination, for she is, of course, the spirit we live by, life itself.

But do not expect just at present a complete and satisfactory presentment of her. Tolerate the spasmodic, the obscure, the fragmentary, the failure. Your help is invoked in a good cause. For I will make one final and surpassingly rash prediction—we are trembling on the verge of one of the great ages of English literature. But it can only be reached if we are determined never, never to desert Mrs. Brown.

23 Virginia Woolf, *A Room of One's Own* (1929)

A Room of One's Own originated as a lecture given on 'women and fiction' in Cambridge at Newnham to an all-female audience in the autumn of 1928, and was subsequently expanded and published in 1929. In its entirety it is an exploration of the history of women's writing and the psychological, social, financial and other conditions that have up until the present largely thwarted the production of great women's writing. It is one of the most important texts for feminist literary theory and history, setting out a dazzling range of speculations and hypotheses about the nature of women and the nature of their writing. It is utopian in its belief that women's writing is finally finding its own language in the modern era.

The brief extracts provided here are designed to provide a sidelight onto issues of gender and writing also raised in Woolf's novel *Orlando*; in many ways the two can be seen as companion-pieces, in that both provide stories of the coming of age of the woman writer within a largely masculine tradition. The first extract (I) is the celebrated story of the imaginary Judith Shakespeare, sister to the playwright, designed to illustrate the social impossibility of a Renaissance middle-class woman following a literary career. The second (II) deals with the psychological difficulties of becoming a woman writer in the nineteenth century without a female tradition, stylistics or genre to draw upon – the assumption being that the inherited male tradition – with the possible exception of the novel – would 'be unsuited for a woman's use'. The third extract (III) is that which describes an imaginary modern novel by a woman – concentrating upon the unfamiliarity and indecorum of the 'broken' style and of the crypto-lesbian subject matter. The last extract (IV) introduces Woolf's speculations as to whether the woman writer is crippled by her outsider status and whether she must aspire to 'the androgynous mind' to produce her best work. Read against this text, the double-sexed Orlando is a fictive and optimistic realisation of this speculation – a modern Judith Shakespeare.

Woolf, V., *A Room of One's Own*, San Diego, New York and London: Harcourt Brace Jovanovich, 1929, pp. 48–52, 79–80, 83–6, 100–2, 108–9

I

. . . I thought of that old gentleman, who is dead now, but was a bishop, I think, who declared that it was impossible for any woman, past, present, or to come, to have: the genius of Shakespeare. He wrote to the papers about it. He also told a lady who applied to him for information that cats do not as a matter of fact go to heaven, though they have, he added, souls of a sort. How much thinking those old gentlemen used to save one! How the borders of ignorance shrank back at their approach! Cats do not go to heaven. Women cannot write the plays of Shakespeare.

Be that as it may, I could not help thinking, as I looked at the works of Shakespeare on the shelf, that the bishop was right at least in this; it would have been impossible, completely and entirely, for any woman to have written the plays of Shakespeare in the age of Shakespeare. Let me imagine, since facts are so hard to come by, what would have happened had Shakespeare had a wonderfully gifted sister, called Judith, let us say. Shakespeare himself went, very probably—his mother was an heiress—to the grammar school, where he may have learnt Latin—Ovid, Virgil and Horace—and the elements of grammar and logic. He was, it is well known, a wild boy who poached rabbits, perhaps shot a deer, and had, rather sooner than he should have done, to marry a woman in the neighbourhood, who bore him a child rather quicker than was right. That escapade sent him to seek his fortune in London. He had, it seemed, a taste for the theatre; he began by holding horses at the stage door. Very soon he got work in the theatre, became a successful actor, and lived at the hub of the universe, meeting everybody, knowing everybody, practicing his art on the boards, exercising his wits in the streets, and even getting access to the palace of the queen. Meanwhile his extraordinarily gifted sister, let us suppose, remained at home. She was as adventurous, as imaginative, as agog to see the world as he was. But she was not sent to school. She had no chance of learning grammar and logic, let alone of reading Horace and Virgil. She picked up a book now and then, one of her brother's perhaps, and read a few, pages. But then her parents came in and told her to mend the stockings or mind the stew and not moon about with books and papers. They would have spoken sharply but kindly, for they were substantial people who knew the conditions of life for a woman and loved their daughter—indeed, more likely than not she was the apple of her father's eye. Perhaps she scribbled some pages up in an apple loft on the sly, but was careful to hide them or set fire to them. Soon, however, before she was out of her teens, she was to be betrothed to the son of a neighbouring wool-stapler. She cried out that marriage was hateful to her, and for that she was severely beaten by her father. Then he ceased to scold her. He begged her instead not to hurt him, not to shame him in this matter of her marriage. He would give her a chain of beads or a fine petticoat, he said; and there were tears in his eyes. How could she disobey him? How could she break his heart? The force of her own gift alone drove her to it. She made up a small parcel of her belongings, let herself down by a rope one summer's night and took the road to London. She was not seventeen. The birds that sang in the hedge were not more musical than she was. She had the quickest fancy, a gift like her brother's, for the tune of words. Like him, she had a taste for the theatre. She stood at the stage door; she wanted to act, she said. Men laughed in her face, The manager—a fat, loose-lipped man—guffawed. He bellowed something about poodles dancing and women acting—no woman, he said, could possibly be an actress. He hinted—you can imagine what. She could get no training in her craft. Could she even seek her dinner in a tavern or roam the streets at midnight? Yet her genius was for fiction and lusted to feed abundantly upon the lives of men and women and the study of their ways. At last—for she was very young, oddly like Shakespeare the poet in her face, with the same grey eyes and rounded brows—at last Nick Greene the actor-manager took pity on her; she found herself with child by that gentleman and so—who shall measure the heat and violence of the poet's heart when caught and tangled in a woman's body?—killed herself one winter's night and lies buried at some cross-roads where the omnibuses now stop outside the Elephant and Castle.

That, more or less, is how the, story would run, I think, if a woman in Shakespeare's day had had Shakespeare's genius. But for my part, I agree with the deceased bishop, if such he was—it is unthinkable that any woman in Shakespeare's day should have had Shakespeare's genius. For genius like Shakespeare's is not born among labouring, uneducated, servile people. 'It was not born in England among the Saxons and the Britons. It is not born today among the working classes. How, then, could it have been born among women whose work began, according to Professor Trevelyan, almost before they were out of the nursery, who were forced to it by their parents and held to it by all the power of law and custom? Yet genius of a sort must have existed among women as it must have existed among the working classes. Now and again an Emily Brontë or a Robert Burns blazes out and proves its presence. But certainly it never got itself on to paper. When, however, one reads of a witch being ducked, of a woman possessed by devils, of a wise woman selling herbs, or even of a very remarkable man who had a mother, then I think we are on the track of a lost novelist, a suppressed poet, of some mute and inglorious Jane Austen, some Emily Brontë who dashed her brains out on the moor or mopped and mowed about the highways crazed with the torture that her gift had put her to. Indeed, I would venture to guess that Anon, who wrote so many poems without signing them, was often a woman. It was a woman Edward Fitzgerald, I think, suggested who made the ballads and the folk-songs, crooning them to her children, beguiling her spinning with them, or the length of the winter's night.

This may be true or it may be false—who can say?—but what is true in it, so it seemed to me, reviewing the story of Shakespeare's sister as I had made it, is that any woman born with a great gift in the sixteenth century would certainly have gone crazed, shot herself, or ended her days in some lonely cottage outside the village, half witch, half wizard, feared and mocked at. For it needs little skill in psychology to be sure that a highly gifted girl who had tried to use her gift for poetry would have been so thwarted and hindered by other people, so tortured and pulled asunder by her own contrary instincts, that she must have lost her health and sanity to a certainty.

No girl could have walked to London and stood at a stage door and forced her way into the presence of actor-managers without doing herself a violence and suffering an anguish which may have been irrational—for chastity may be a fetish invented by certain societies for unknown reasons—but were none the less inevitable. Chastity had then, it has even now, a religious import-ance in a woman's life, and has so wrapped itself round with nerves and instincts that to cut it free and bring it to the light of day demands courage of the rarest. To have lived a free life in London in the sixteenth century would have meant for a woman who was poet and playwright a nervous stress and dilemma which might well have killed her. Had she survived, whatever she had written would have been twisted and deformed, issuing from a strained and morbid imagination. And undoubtedly, I thought, looking at the shelf where there are no plays by women, her work would have gone unsigned.

[. . .]

II

But whatever effect discouragement and criticism had upon their writing—and I believe that they had a very great effect—that was unimportant com-pared with the other difficulty which faced them (I was still considering those early nineteenth-century novelists) when they came to set their thoughts on paper—that is that they had no tradition behind them, or one so short and partial that it was of little help. For we think back through our mothers if we are women. It is useless to go to the great men writers for help, however much one may go to them for pleasure. Lamb, Browne, Thackeray, Newman, Sterne, Dickens, De Quincey—whoever it may be—never helped a woman yet, though she may have learnt a few tricks off them and adapted them to her use. The weight, the pace, the stride of a man's mind are too unlike her own for her to lift anything substantial from him successfully. The ape is too distant to be sedulous. Perhaps the first thing she would find, setting pen to paper, was that there was no common sentence ready for her use. All the great novelists like Thackeray and Dickens and Balzac have written a natural prose, swift but not slovenly, expressive but not precious, taking their own tint without ceasing to be common property. They have based it on the sentence that was current at the time. The sentence that was current at the beginning of the nineteenth century ran something like this perhaps: "The grandeur of their works was an argument with them, not to stop short, but to proceed. They could have no higher excitement or satisfaction than in the exercise of their art and endless generations of truth and beauty. Success prompts to exer-tion; and habit facilitates success." That is a man's sentence; behind it one can see Johnson, Gibbon and the rest. It was a sentence that was unsuited for a woman's use. Charlotte Brontë, with all her splendid gift for prose, stumbled and fell with that clumsy weapon in her hands. George Eliot committed atrocities with it that beggar description. Jane Austen looked at it and laughed at it and devised a perfectly natural, shapely sentence proper for her own use and never departed from it. Thus, with less genius for writing than Charlotte Brontë, she got infinitely more said. Indeed, since freedom and fullness of expression are of the essence of the art, such a lack of tradition, such a scarcity and inadequacy of tools, must have told enormously upon the writing of women. Moreover, a book is not made of sentences laid end to end, but of sentences built, if an image helps, into arcades or domes. And this shape too has been made by men out of their own needs for their own uses. There is no reason to think that the form of the epic or of the poetic play suits a woman any more than the sentence suits her. But all the older forms of literature were hardened and set by the time she became a writer. The novel alone was young enough to be soft in her hands—another reason, perhaps, why she wrote novels. Yet who shall say that even now "the novel" (I give it inverted commas to mark my sense of the words' inadequacy), who shall say that even this most pliable of all forms is rightly shaped for her use? No doubt we shall find her knocking that into shape for herself when she has the free use of her limbs; and providing some new vehicle, not necessarily in verse, for the poetry in her. For it is the poetry that is still denied outlet. And I went on to ponder how a woman nowadays would write a poetic tragedy in five acts—would she use verse—would she not use prose rather?

[. . .]

III

I had come at last, in the course of this rambling, to the shelves which hold books by the living; by women and by men; for there are almost as many books written by women now as by men. Or if that is not yet quite true, if the male is still the voluble sex, it is certainly true that women no longer write novels solely. There are Jane Harrison's books on Greek archaeology; Vernon Lee's books on aesthetics; Gertrude Bell's books on Persia. There are books on all sorts of subjects which a generation ago no woman could have touched. There are poems and plays and criticism; there are histories and biographies, books of travel and books of scholarship and research; there are even a few philosophies and books about science and economics. And though novels predominate, novels themselves may very well have changed from association with books of a different feather. The natural simplicity, the epic age of women's writing, may have gone. Reading and criticism may have given her a wider range, a greater subtlety. The impulse towards autobiography may be spent. She may be beginning to use writing as an art, not as a method of self-expression. Among these new novels one might find an answer to several such questions.

I took down one of them at random. It stood at the very end of the shelf, was called *Life's Adventure*, or some such title, by Mary Carmichael, and was published in this very month of October. It seems to be her first book, I said to myself, but one must read it as if it were the last volume in a fairly long series, continuing all those other books that I have been glancing at— Lady Winchilsea's poems and Aphra Behn's plays and the novels of the four great novelists. For books continue each other, in spite of our habit of judging them separately. And I must also consider her—this unknown woman—as the descendant of all those other women whose circumstances I have been glancing at and see what she inherits of their characteristics and restrictions. So, with a sigh, because novels so often provide an anodyne and not an antidote, glide one into torpid slumbers instead of rousing one with a burning brand, I settled down with a notebook and a pencil to make what I could of Mary Carmichael's first novel, *Life's Adventure*.

To begin with, I ran my eye up and down the page. I am going to get the hang of her sentences first, I said, before I load my memory with blue eyes and brown and the relationship that there may be between Chloe and Roger. There will be time for that when I have decided whether she has a pen in her hand or a pickaxe. So I tried a sentence or two on my tongue. Soon it was obvious that something was not quite in order. The smooth gliding of sentence after sentence was interrupted. Something tore, something scratched; a single word here and there flashed its torch in my eyes. She was "unhanding" herself as they say in the old plays. She is like a person striking a match that will not light, I thought. But why, I asked her as if she were present, are Jane Austen's sentences not of the right shape for you? Must they all be scrapped because Emma and Mr. Woodhouse are dead? Alas, I sighed, that it should be so. For while Jane Austen breaks from melody to melody as Mozart from song to song, to read this writing was like being out at sea in an open boat. Up one went, down one sank. This terseness, this short-windedness, might mean that she was afraid of something; afraid of being called "sentimental" perhaps; or she remembers that women's writing has been called flowery and so provides a superfluity of thorns; but until I have read a scene with some care, I cannot be sure whether she is being herself or some one else. At any rate, she does not lower one's vitality, I thought, reading more carefully. But she is heaping up too many facts. She will not be able to use half of them in a book of this size. (It was about half the length of *Jane Eyre*.) However, by some means or other she succeeded in getting us all—Roger, Chloe, Olivia, Tony and Mr. Bigham—

in a canoe up the river. Wait a moment, I said, leaning back in my chair, I must consider the whole thing more carefully before I go any further.

I am almost sure, I said to myself, that Mary Carmichael is playing a trick on us. For I feel as one feels on a switchback railway when the car, instead of sinking, as one has been led to expect, swerves up again. Mary is tampering with the expected sequence. First she broke the sentence; now she has broken the sequence. Very well, she has every right to do both these things if she does them not for the sake of breaking, but for the sake of creating. Which of the two it is I cannot be sure until she has faced herself with a situation. I will give her every liberty, I said, to choose what that situation shall be; she shall make it of tin cans and old kettles if she likes; but she must convince me that she believes it to be a situation; and then when she has made it she must face it. She must jump. And, determined to do my duty by her as reader if she would do her duty by me as writer, I turned the page and read . . . I am sorry to break off so abruptly. Are there no men present? Do you promise me that behind that red curtain over there the figure of Sir Chartres Biron is not concealed? We are all women, you assure me? Then I may tell you that the very next words I read were these— "Chloe liked Olivia . . ." Do not start. Do not blush. Let us admit in the privacy of our own society that these things sometimes happen. Sometimes women do like women.

"Chloe liked Olivia," I read. And then it struck me how immense a change was there. Chloe liked Olivia perhaps for the first time in literature.

[. . .]

IV

At this moment, as so often happens in London, there was a complete lull and suspension of traffic. Nothing came down the street; nobody passed. A single leaf detached itself from the plane tree at the end of the street, and in that pause and suspension fell. Somehow it was like a signal falling, a signal pointing to a force in things which one had overlooked. It seemed to point to a river, which flowed past, invisibly, round the corner, down the street, and took people and eddied them along, as the stream at Oxbridge had taken the undergraduate in his boat and the dead leaves. Now it was bringing from one side of the street to the other diagonally a girl in patent leather boots, and then a young man in a maroon overcoat; it was also bringing a taxi-cab; and it brought all three together at a point directly beneath my window; where the taxi stopped; and the girl and the young man stopped; and they got into the taxi; and then the cab glided off as if it were swept on by the current elsewhere.

The sight was ordinary enough; what was strange was the rhythmical order with which my imagination had invested it; and the fact that the ordinary sight of two people getting into a cab had the power to communicate something of their own seeming satisfaction. The sight of two people coming down the street and meeting at the corner seems to ease the mind of some strain, I thought, watching the taxi turn and make off. Perhaps to think, as I had been thinking these two days, of one sex as distinct from the other is an effort. It interferes with the unity of the mind. Now that effort had ceased and that unity had been restored by seeing two people come together and get into a taxi-cab. The mind is certainly a very mysterious organ, I reflected, drawing my head in from the window, about which nothing whatever is known, though we depend upon it so completely. Why do I feel that there are severances and oppositions in the mind, as there are strains from obvious causes on the body? What does one mean by "the unity of the mind," I pondered, for clearly the mind has so great a power of concentrating at any point at any moment that it seems to have no single state of being. It can separate itself from the people in the street, for example, and think of itself as apart from them, at an upper window looking down on them. Or it can think with other people spontaneously, as, for instance, in a crowd waiting to hear some piece of news read out. It can think back through its fathers or through its mothers, as I have said that a woman writing thinks back through her mothers. Again if one is a woman one is often surprised by a sudden splitting off of consciousness, say in walking down Whitehall, when from being the natural inheritor of that civilisation, she becomes, on the contrary, outside of it, alien and critical. Clearly the mind is always altering its focus, and bringing the world into different perspectives. But some of these states of mind seem, even if adopted spontaneously, to be less comfortable than others. In order to keep oneself continuing in them one is unconsciously holding something back, and gradually the repression becomes an effort. But there may be some state of mind in which one could continue without effort because nothing is required to be held back. And this perhaps, I thought, coming in from the window, is one of them. For certainly when I saw the couple get into the taxi-cab the mind felt as if, after being divided, it had come together again in a natural fusion. The obvious reason would be that it is natural for the sexes to co-operate. One has a profound, if irrational, instinct in favour of the theory that the union of man and woman makes for the greatest satisfaction, the most complete happiness. But the sight of the two people getting into the taxi and the satisfaction it gave me made me also ask whether there are two sexes in the mind corresponding to the two sexes in the body, and whether they also require to be united in order to get complete satisfaction and happiness. And I went on amateurishly to sketch a plan of the soul so that in each of us two powers preside, one male, one female; and in the man's brain, the man predominates over the woman, and in the woman's brain, the woman predominates over the man. The normal and comfortable state of being is that when the two live in harmony together, spiritually co-operating. If one is a man, still the woman part of the brain must have effect; and a woman also must have intercourse with the man in her. Coleridge perhaps meant this when he said that a great mind is androgynous. It is when this fusion takes place that the mind is fully fertilised and uses all its faculties. Perhaps a mind that is purely masculine cannot create, any more than a mind that is purely feminine, I thought.

[. . .]

[T]he very first sentence that I would write here, I said, crossing over to the writing-table and taking up the page headed Women and Fiction, is that it is fatal for any one who writes to think of their sex. It is fatal to be a man or woman pure and simple; one must be woman-manly or man-womanly. It is fatal for a woman to lay the least stress on any grievance; to plead even with justice any cause; in any way to speak consciously as a woman. And fatal is no figure of speech; for anything written with that conscious bias is doomed to death. It ceases to be fertilised. Brilliant and effective, powerful and masterly, as it may appear for a day or two, it must wither at nightfall; it cannot grow in the minds of others. Some collaboration has to take place in the mind between the woman and the man before the act of creation can be accomplished. Some marriage of opposites has to be consummated. The whole of the mind must lie wide open if we are to get the sense that the writer is communicating his experience with perfect fullness. There must be freedom and there must be peace. Not a wheel must grate, not a light glimmer. The curtains must be close drawn. The writer, I thought, once his experience is over, must lie back and let his mind celebrate its nuptials in darkness. He must not look or question what is being done. Rather, he must pluck the petals from a rose or watch the swans float calmly down the river. And I saw again the current which took the boat and the undergraduate and the dead leaves; and the taxi took the man and the woman, I thought, seeing them come together across the street, and the current swept them away, I thought, hearing far off the roar of London's traffic, into that tremendous stream.

BERTOLT BRECHT,
LIFE OF GALILEO

The playwright Bertolt Brecht (1898–1965) was from early in his career a conscious and influential commentator upon and theoriser about his own work; it was part of what made him 'modernist'; it was also the result of his overriding urge to link aesthetic and political or social considerations. Brecht's theory of theatre was built upon – while aiming radically to depart from – Aristotle's, as his choice of title for the work summing-up his views makes plain: 'Ein kleines Organon für das Theater' ('A Short Organum for the Theatre'), the word 'organon' a deliberate echo of Aristotle's treatises on reasoning, the *Organon* or instrument. The 'radical transformation' of contemporary theatre that he sought involved technical effects that he defined in different ways over time, including crucially 'epic', 'alienation' and 'gest', all of which are developed in the extracts that follow: an article from the literary pages of the *Frankfurter Zeitung* in 1927 justifying his 'new school' of play-writing; an essay on 'alienation' in acting prompted by a performance by the Chinese actor Mei Lanfang's company in Moscow in spring 1935; and a series of extracts from the *Organum* (first written in 1948), touching particularly upon his play *Galileo*. The concluding extract, from an essay (published in 1968), by the Marxist critic and Brecht authority Ernst Schumacher, argues that Brecht went on to develop a more 'contradictory' or 'dialectical' rather than 'epic' kind of theatre from the early 1950s onwards, as demonstrated by *Galileo*.

24 Bertolt Brecht, The Epic Theatre and its Difficulties (1927)

Brecht, B., 'The Epic Theatre and its Difficulties', in J. Willet (ed. and trans.), *Brecht on Theatre: The Development of Aesthetic*, London: Methuen, 1974, pp. 22–3

Any theatre that makes a serious attempt to stage one of the new plays risks being radically transformed. What the audience sees in fact is a battle between theatre and play, an almost academic operation where, in so far as it takes any interest in the process of renovating the theatre, all it has to do is observe whether the theatre emerges as victor or vanquished from this murderous clash. (Roughly speaking, the theatre can only emerge victorious over the play if it manages to avoid the risk of the play's transforming it completely – as at present it nearly always succeeds in doing.) It is not the play's effect on the audience but its effect on the theatre that is decisive at this moment.

This situation will continue until our theatres have worked out the style of production that our plays need and encourage. It won't be an adequate answer if theatres invent some kind of special style for them, in the same way as the so-called Munich Shakespearean stage was invented, which could only be used for Shakespeare. It has to be a style that can lend new force to a whole section of the theatrical repertoire which is still capable of life today.

It is understood that the *radical transformation of the theatre* can't be the result of some artistic whim. It has simply to correspond to the whole radical transformation of the mentality of our time. The symptoms of this trans-formation are familiar enough, and so far they have been seen as symptoms of disease. There is some justification for this, for of course what one sees first of all are the signs of decline in whatever is *old*. But it would be wrong to see these phenomena, so-called *Amerikanismus* for instance, as anything but unhealthy changes stimulated by the operation of really new mental influences on our culture's aged body. And it would be wrong too to treat these new ideas as if they were not ideas and not mental phenomena at all, and to try to build up the theatre against them as a kind of bastion of the mind. On the contrary it is precisely theatre, art and literature which have to form the 'ideological superstructure' for a solid, practical rearrangement of our age's way of life.

In its works the new school of play-writing lays down that the *epic theatre* is the theatrical style of our time. To expound the principles of the epic theatre in a few catch-phrases is not possible. They still mostly need to be worked out in detail, and include representation by the actor, stage tech-nique, dramaturgy, stage music, use of the film, and so on. The essential point of the epic theatre is perhaps that it appeals less to the feelings than to the spectator's reason. Instead of sharing an experience the spectator must come to grips with things. At the same time it would be quite wrong to try and deny emotion to this kind of theatre. It would be much the same thing as trying to deny emotion to modern science.

25 Bertolt Brecht, Alienation Effects in Chinese Acting (1935)

Brecht, B., 'Alienation Effects in Chinese Acting', in J. Willet (ed. and trans.), *Brecht On Theatre: The Development of Aesthetic*, London: Methuen, 1974, pp. 93–9

The Western actor does all he can to bring his spectator into the closest proximity to the events and the character he has to portray. To this end he persuades him to identify himself with him (the actor) and uses every energy to convert himself as completely as possible into a different type, that of the character in question. If this complete conversion succeeds then his art has been more or less expended. Once he has become the bank-clerk, doctor or general concerned he will need no more art than any of these people need 'in real life'.

This complete conversion operation is extremely exhausting. Stanislavsky puts forward a series of means – a complete system – by which what he calls 'creative mood' can repeatedly be manufactured afresh at every performance. For the actor cannot usually manage to feel for very long on end that he really is the other person; he soon gets exhausted and begins just to copy various superficialities of the other person's speech and hearing, whereupon the effect on the public drops off alarmingly. This is certainly due to the fact that the other person has been created by an 'intuitive' and accordingly murky process which takes place in the subconscious. The subconscious is not at all responsive to guidance; it has as it were a bad memory.

These problems are unknown to the Chinese performer, for he rejects complete conversion. He limits himself from the start to simply quoting the character played. But with what art he does this! He only needs a minimum of illusion. What he has to show is worth seeing even for a man in his right mind. What Western actor of the old sort (apart from one or two comedians) could demonstrate the elements of his art like the Chinese actor Mei Lan-fang, without special lighting and wearing a 'dinner jacket in an ordinary room full of specialists? It would be like the magician at a fair giving away his tricks, so that nobody ever wanted to see the act again. He would just be showing how to disguise oneself; the hypnotism would vanish and all that would be left would be a few pounds of ill-blended imitation, a quickly-mixed product for selling in the dark to hurried customers. Of course no Western actor would stage such a demonstration. What about the sanctity of Art? The mysteries of metamorphosis? To the Westerner what matters is that his actions should be unconscious; otherwise they would be degraded. By comparison with Asiatic acting our own art still seems hopelessly parsonical. None the less it is becoming increasingly difficult for our actors to bring off the mystery of complete conversion; their subconscious's memory is getting weaker and weaker, and it is almost impossible to extract the truth from the uncensored intuitions of any member of our class society even when the man is a genius.

For the actor it is difficult and taxing to conjure up particular inner moods or emotions night after night; it is simpler to exhibit the outer signs which accompany these emotions and identify them. In this case, however, there is not the same automatic transfer of emotions to the spectator, the same emotional infection. The alienation effect intervenes, not in the form of absence of emotion, but in the form of emotions which need not correspond to those of the character portrayed. On seeing worry the spectator may feel a sensation of joy; on seeing anger, one of disgust. When we speak of exhibiting the outer signs of emotion we do not mean such an exhibition and such a choice of signs that the emotional transference does in fact take place because the actor has managed to infect himself with the emotions portrayed, by exhibiting the outer signs; thus, by letting his voice rise, holding his breath and tightening his neck muscles so that the blood shoots to his head, the actor can easily conjure up a rage. In such a case of course the effect does not occur. But it does occur if the actor at a particular point unexpectedly shows a completely white face, which he has produced mechanically by holding his face in his hands with some white make-up on them. If the actor at the same time displays an apparently composed character, then his terror at this point (as a result of this message, or that discovery) will give rise to an alienation effect. Acting like this is healthier and in our view less unworthy of a thinking being; it demands a considerable knowledge of humanity and worldly wisdom, and a keen eye for what is socially important. In this case too there is of course a creative process at work; but it is a higher one, because it is raised to the conscious level.

The alienation effect does not in any way demand an unnatural way of acting. It has nothing whatever to do with ordinary stylization. On the contrary, the achievement of an A-effect absolutely depends on lightness and naturalness of performance. But when the actor checks the truth of his performance (a necessary operation, which Stanislavsky is much concerned with in his system) he is not just thrown back on his 'natural sensibilities', but can always be corrected by a comparison with reality (is that how an angry man really speaks? is that how an offended man sits down?) and so from outside, by other people. He acts in such a way that nearly every sentence could be followed by a verdict of the audience and practically every gesture is submitted for the public's approval.

The Chinese performer is in no trance. He can be interrupted at any moment. He won't have to 'come round'. After an interruption he will go on with his exposition from that point. We are not disturbing him at the 'mystic moment of creation'; when he steps on to the stage before us the process of creation is already over. He does not mind if the setting is changed around him as he plays. Busy hands quite openly pass him what he needs for his performance. When Mei Lan-fang was playing a death scene a spectator sitting next me exclaimed with astonishment at one of his gestures. One or two people sitting in front of us turned round indignantly and sshhh'd. They behaved as if they were present at the real death of a real girl. Possibly their attitude would have been all right for a European production, but for a Chinese it was unspeakably ridiculous. In their case the A-effect had misfired.

It is not entirely easy to realize that the Chinese actor's A-effect is a transportable piece of technique: a conception that can be prised loose from the Chinese theatre. We see this theatre as uncommonly precious, its portrayal of human passions as schematized, its idea of society as rigid and wrongheaded; at first sight this superb art seems to offer nothing applicable to a realistic and revolutionary theatre. Against that, the motives and objects of the A-effect strike us as odd and suspicious.

When one sees the Chinese acting it is at first very hard to discount the feeling of estrangement which they produce in us as Europeans. One has to be able to imagine them achieving an A-effect among their Chinese spectators too. What is still harder is that one must accept the fact that when the Chinese performer conjures up an impression of mystery he seems uninterested in disclosing a mystery to us. He makes his own mystery from the mysteries of nature (especially human nature): he allows nobody to examine how he produces the natural phenomenon, nor does nature allow him to understand as he produces it. We have here the artistic counterpart of a primitive technology, a rudimentary science. The Chinese performer gets his A-effect by association with magic. 'How it's done' remains hidden; knowledge is a matter of knowing the tricks and is in the hands of a few men who guard it jealously and profit from their secrets. And yet there is already an attempt here to interfere with the course of nature; the capacity to do so leads to questioning; and the future explorer, with his anxiety to make nature's course intelligible, controllable and down-to-earth, will always start by adopting a standpoint from which it seems mysterious, incomprehensible and beyond control. He will take up the attitude of somebody wondering, will apply the A-effect. Nobody can be a mathematician who takes it for granted that 'two and two makes four'; nor is anybody one who fails to understand it. The man who first looked with astonishment at a swinging lantern and instead of taking it for granted found it highly remarkable that it should swing, and swing in that particular way rather than any other, was brought close to understanding the phenomenon by this observation, and so to mastering it. Nor must it simply be exclaimed that the attitude here proposed is all right for science but not for art. Why shouldn't art try, by its *own* means of course, to further the great social task of mastering life?

In point of fact the only people who can profitably study a piece of technique like Chinese acting's A-effect are those who need such a technique for quite definite social purposes.

The experiments conducted by the modern German theatre led to a wholly independent development of the A-effect. So far Asiatic acting has exerted no influence.

The A-effect was achieved in the German epic theatre not only by the actor, but also by the music (choruses, songs) and the setting (placards, film etc.). It was principally designed to historicize the incidents portrayed. By this is meant the following:

The bourgeois theatre emphasized the timelessness of its objects. Its representation of people is bound by the alleged 'eternally human'. Its story is arranged in such a way as to create 'universal' situations that allow Man with a capital M to express himself: man of every period and every colour. All its incidents are just one enormous cue, and this cue is followed by the 'eternal' response: the inevitable, usual, natural, purely human response. An example: a black man falls in love in the same way as a white man; the story forces him to react with the same expression as the white man (in theory this formula works as well the other way round); and with that the sphere of art is attained. The cue can take account of what is special, different; the response is shared, there is no element of difference in it. This notion may allow that such a thing as history exists, but it is none the less unhistorical. A few circumstances vary, the environments are altered, but Man remains unchanged. History applies to the environment, not to Man. The environment is remarkably unimportant, is treated simply as a pretext; it is a variable quantity and something remarkably inhuman; it exists in fact apart from Man, confronting him as a coherent whole, whereas he is a fixed quantity, eternally unchanged. The idea of man as a function of the environment and the environment as a function of man, i.e. the breaking up of the environment into relationships between men, corresponds to a new way of thinking, the historical way. Rather than be sidetracked into the philosophy of history, let us give an example. Suppose the following is to be shown on the stage: a girl leaves home in order to take a job in a fair-sized city (Piscator's *American Tragedy*). For the bourgeois theatre this is an insignificant affair, clearly the beginning of a story; it is what one has to have been told in order to understand what comes after, or to be keyed up for it. The actor's imagination will hardly be greatly fired by it. In a sense the incident is universal: girls take jobs (in the case in question one can be keyed up to see what in particular is going to happen to her). Only in one way is it particular: this girl goes away (if she had remained what comes after would not have happened). The fact that her family lets her go is not the object of the inquiry; it is understandable (the motives are understandable). But for the historicizing theatre everything is different. The theatre concentrates entirely on whatever in this perfectly everyday event is remarkable, particular and demanding inquiry. What! A family letting one of its members leave the nest to earn her future living independently and without help? Is she up to it? Will what she has learnt here as a member of the family help her to earn her living? Can't families keep a grip on their children any longer? Have they become (or remained) a burden? Is it like that with every family? Was it always like that? Is this the way of the world, something that can't be affected? The fruit falls off the tree when ripe: does this sentence apply here? Do children always make themselves independent? Did they do so in every age? If so, and if it's something biological, does it always happen in the same way, for the same reasons and with the same results? These are the questions (or a few of them) that the actors must answer if they want to show the incident as a unique, historical one: if they want to demonstrate a custom which leads to conclusions about the entire structure of a society at a particular (transient) time. But how is such an incident to be represented if its historic character is to be brought out? How can the confusion of our unfortunate epoch be striking? When the mother, in between warnings and moral injunctions, packs her daughter's case – a very small one – how is the following to be shown: So many injunctions and so few clothes? Moral injunctions for a lifetime and bread for five hours? How is the actress to speak the mother's sentence as she hands over such a very small case – 'There, I guess that ought to do you' – in such way that it is understood as a historic dictum? This can only be achieved if the A-effect is brought out. The actress must not make the sentence her own affair, she must hand it over for criticism, she must help us to understand its causes and protest. The effect can only be got by long training. In the New York Yiddish Theatre, a highly progressive theatre, I saw a play by S. Ornitz showing the rise of an East Side boy to be a big crooked attorney. The theatre could not perform the play. And yet there were scenes like this in it: the young attorney sits in the street outside his house giving cheap legal advice. A young woman arrives and complains that her leg has been hurt in a traffic accident. But the case has been bungled and her compensation has not yet been paid. In desperation she points to her leg and says: 'It's started to heal up.' Working without the A-effect, the theatre was unable to make use of this exceptional scene to show the horror of a bloody epoch. Few people in the audience noticed it;

hardly anyone who reads this will remember that cry. The actress spoke the cry as if it were something perfectly natural. But it is exactly this – the fact that this poor creature finds such a complaint natural – that she should have reported to the public like a horrified messenger returning from the lowest of all hells. To that end she would of course have needed a special technique which would have allowed her to underline the historical aspect of a specific social condition. Only the A-effect makes this possible. Without it all she can do is to observe how she is not forced to go over entirely into the character on the stage.

In setting up new artistic principles and working out new methods of representation we must start with the compelling demands of a changing epoch; the necessity and the possibility of remodelling society loom ahead. All incidents between men must be noted, and everything must be seen from a social point of view. Among other effects that a new theatre will need for its social criticism and its historical reporting of completed transformations is the A-effect.

26 Bertolt Brecht, A Short Organum for the Theatre (1948)

Brecht, B., 'A Short Organum for the Theatre', in J. Willet (ed. and trans.), *Brecht on Theatre: The Development of Aesthetic*, London: Methuen, 1974, pp. 192, 198–201, 203

The old A-effects quite remove the object represented from the spectator's grasp, turning it into something that cannot be altered; the new are not odd in themselves, though the unscientific eye stamps anything strange as odd. The new alienations are only designed to free socially-conditioned phenomena from that stamp of familiarity which protects them against our grasp today.

44

For it seems impossible to alter what has long not been altered. We are always coming on things that are too obvious for us to bother to understand them. What men experience among themselves they think of as 'the' human experience. A child, living in a world of old men, learns how things work there. He knows the run of things before he can walk. If anyone is bold enough to want something further, he only wants to have it as an exception. Even if he realizes that the arrangements made for him by 'Providence' are only what has been provided by society he is bound to see society, that vast collection of beings like himself, as a whole that is greater than the sum of its parts and therefore not in any way to be influenced. Moreover, he would be used to things that could not be influenced; and who mistrusts what he is used to? To transform himself from general passive acceptance to a corresponding state of suspicious inquiry he would need to develop that detached eye with which the great Galileo observed a swinging chandelier. He was amazed by this pendulum motion, as if he had not expected it and could not understand its occurring, and this enabled him to come on the rules by which it was governed. Here is the outlook, disconcerting but fruitful, which the theatre must provoke with its representations of human social life. It must amaze its public, and this can be achieved by a technique of alienating the familiar.

[. . .]

61

The realm of attitudes adopted by the characters towards one another is what we call the realm of gest. Physical attitude, tone of voice and facial expression are all determined by a social gest: the characters are cursing, flattering, instructing one another, and so on. The attitudes which people adopt towards one another include even those attitudes which would appear to be quite private, such as the utterances of physical pain in an illness, or of religious faith. These expressions of a gest are usually highly complicated and contradictory, so that they cannot be rendered by any single word and the actor must take care that in giving his image the necessary emphasis he does not lose anything, but emphasizes the entire complex.

62

The actor masters his character by paying critical attention to its manifold utterances, as also to those of his counterparts and of all the other characters involved.

63

Let us get down to the problem of gestic content by running through the opening scenes of a fairly modern play, my own *Life of Galileo*. Since we wish at the same time to find out what light the different utterances cast on one another we will assume that it is not our first introduction to the play. It begins with the man of forty-six having his morning wash, broken by occasional browsing in books and by a lesson on the solar system for Andrea Sarti, a small boy. To play this, surely you have got to know that we shall be ending with the man of seventy-eight having his supper, just after he has said good-bye for ever to the same pupil? He is then more terribly altered than this passage of time could possibly have brought about. He wolfs his food with unrestrained greed, no other idea in his head; he has rid himself of his educational mission in shameful circumstances, as though it were a burden: he, who once drank his morning milk without a care, greedy to teach the boy. But does he really drink it without care? Isn't the pleasure of drinking and washing one with the pleasure which he takes in the new ideas? Don't forget: he thinks out of self-indulgence. . . . Is that good or bad? I would advise you to represent it as good, since on this point you will find nothing in the whole play to harm society, and more especially because you yourself are, I hope, a gallant child of the scientific age. But take careful note: many horrible things will happen in this connection. The fact that the man who here acclaims the new age will be forced at the end to beg this age to disown him as contemptible, even to dispossess him; all this will be relevant. As for the lesson, you may like to decide whether the man's heart is so full that his mouth is overflowing, so that he has to talk to anybody about it, even a child, or whether the child has first to draw the knowledge out of him, by knowing him and showing interest. Again, there may be two of them who cannot restrain themselves, the one from asking, the other from giving the answer: a bond of this sort would be interesting, for one day it is going to be rudely snapped. Of course you will want the demonstration of the earth's rotation round the sun to be conducted quickly, since it is given for nothing, and now the wealthy unknown pupil appears, lending the scholar's time a monetary value. He shows no interest, but he has to be served; Galileo lacks resources, and so he will stand between the wealthy pupil and the intelligent one, and sigh as he makes his choice. There is little that he can teach his new student, so he learns from him instead; he hears of the telescope which has been invented in Holland: in his own way he gets something out of the disturbance of his morning's work. The Rector of the university arrives. Galileo's application for an increase in salary has been turned down; the university is reluctant to pay so much for the theories of physics as for those of theology; it wishes him, who after all is operating on a generally-accepted low level of scholarship, to produce something useful here and now. You will see from the way in which he offers his thesis that he is used to being refused and corrected. The Rector reminds him that the Republic guarantees freedom of research even if she doesn't pay; he replies that he cannot make much of this freedom if he lacks the leisure which good payment permits. Here you should not find his impatience too peremptory, or his poverty will not be given due weight. For shortly after that you find him having ideas which need some explanation: the prophet of a new age of scientific truth considers how he can swindle some money out of the Republic by offering her the telescope as his own invention. All he sees in the new invention, you will be surprised to hear, is a few scudi, and he examines it simply with a view to annexing it himself. But if you move on to the second scene you will find that while he is selling the invention to the Venetian Signoria with a speech that disgraces him by its falsehoods he has already almost forgotten the money, because he has realized that the instrument has not only military but astronomical significance. The article which he has been blackmailed – let us call it that – into producing proves to have great qualities for the very research which he had to break off in order to produce it. If during the ceremony, as he complacently accepts the undeserved honours paid him, he outlines to his learned friend the marvellous discoveries in view – don't overlook the theatrical way in which he does this – you will find in him a far more profound excitement than the thought of monetary gain called forth. Perhaps, looked at in this way, his charlatanry does not mean much, but it still shows how determined this man is to take the easy course, and to apply his reason in a base as well as a noble manner. A more significant test awaits him, and does not every capitulation bring the next one nearer?

64

Splitting such material into one gest after another, the actor masters his character by first mastering the 'story'. It is only after walking all round the entire episode that he can, as it were by a single leap, seize and fix his character, complete with all its individual features. Once he has done his best to let himself be amazed by the inconsistencies in its various attitudes, knowing that he will in turn have to make them amaze the audience, then the story as a whole gives him a chance to pull the inconsistencies together; for the story, being a limited episode, has a specific sense, i.e. only gratifies a specific fraction of all the interests that could arise.

65

Everything hangs on the 'story'; it is the heart of the theatrical performance. For it is what happens *between* people that provides them with all the material that they can discuss, criticize, alter. Even if the particular person represented by the actor has ultimately to fit into more than just the one episode, it is mainly because the episode will be all the more striking if it reaches fulfilment in a particular person. The 'story' is the theatre's great operation, the complete fitting together of all the gestic incidents, embracing the communications and impulses that must now go to make up the audience's entertainment.

66

Each single incident has its basic gest: *Richard Gloster courts his victim's widow. The child's true mother is found by means of a chalk circle. God has a bet with the Devil for Dr Faustus's soul. Woyzeck buys a cheap knife in order to do his wife in,* etc. The grouping of the characters on the stage and the movements of the groups must be such that the necessary beauty is attained above all by the elegance with which the material conveying that gest is set out and laid bare to the understanding of the audience.

67

As we cannot invite the audience to fling itself into the story as if it were a river and let itself be carried vaguely hither and thither, the individual episodes have to be knotted together in such a way that the knots are easily noticed. The episodes must not succeed one another indistinguishably but must give us a chance to interpose our judgment. (If it were above all the obscurity of the original interrelations that interested us, then just this circumstance would have to be sufficiently alienated.) The parts of the story have to be carefully set off one against another by giving each its own structure as a play within the play. To this end it is best to agree to use titles like those in the preceding paragraph. The titles must include the social point, saying at the same time something about the kind of portrayal wanted, i.e. should copy the tone of a chronicle or a ballad or a newspaper or a morality. For instance, a simple way of alienating something is that normally applied to customs and moral principles. A visit, the treatment of an enemy, a lovers' meeting, agreements about politics or business, can be portrayed as if they were simply illustrations of general principles valid for the place in question. Shown thus, the particular and unrepeatable incident acquires a disconcerting look, because it appears as something general, something that has become a principle. As soon as we ask whether in fact it should have become such, or what about it should have done so, we are alienating the incident. The poetic approach to history can be studied in the so-called panoramas at sideshows in fairs. As alienation likewise means a kind of fame certain incidents can just be represented as famous, as though they had for a long while been common knowledge and care must be taken not to offer the least obstacle to their further transmission. In short: there are many conceivable ways of telling a story, some of them known and some still to be discovered.

[. . .]

71

It emphasizes the general gest of showing, which always underlies that which is being shown, when the audience is musically addressed by means of songs. Because of this the actors ought not to 'drop into' song, but should clearly mark it off from the rest of the text; and this is best reinforced by a few theatrical methods such as changing the lighting or inserting a title. For its part, the music must strongly resist the smooth incorporation which is generally expected of it and turns it into an unthinking slavey. Music does not 'accompany' except in the form of comment. It cannot simply 'express itself' by discharging the emotions with which the incidents of the play have filled it. Thus Eisler, e.g. helped admirably in the knotting of the incidents when in the carnival scene of *Galileo* he set the masked procession of the guilds to a triumphant and threatening music which showed what a revolutionary twist the lower orders had given to the scholar's astronomical theories. Similarly in *The Caucasian Chalk Circle* the singer, by using a chilly and unemotional way of singing to describe the servant-girl's rescue of the child as it is mimed on the stage, makes evident the terror of a period in which motherly instincts can become a suicidal weakness. Thus music can make its point in a number of ways and with full independence, and can react in its own manner to the subjects dealt with; at the same time it can also quite simply help to lend variety to the entertainment.

27 Ernst Schumacher, The Dialectics of *Galileo* (2000)

Schumacher, E., 'The Dialectics of *Galileo*' in C. Martin and H. Biol (eds), *Brecht Sourcebook*, London: Routledge, 2000, pp. 113–23

In the early 1950s, Brecht wanted to change from "epic" theatre to "dialectical" theatre. The latter was to keep the "narrative element" of the former, but had a distinct aim: ". . . *deliberately* to develop features – dialectical vestiges – from earlier forms of theatre and make them enjoyable" (*Schriften zum Theatre*, vol. 7, p. 316). "Developmental laws" were to be worked out by means of "the dialectic of the classical writers of socialism, so that we could perceive and enjoy the alterability of the world." To this end, it would be necessary to make perceptible the "imperceptible contradictions" in all things, people, processes. Alienation techniques were to be used to depict the "contradictions and development of human co-existence," and to make dialectic "a source of learning and enjoyment."

[. . .]

Brecht regarded *Galileo* as a play with "restricted" alienation effects, but its extremely powerful dialectic shaped its internal structure, the arrangement and interrelation of the scenes, the characterization, and the language.

[. . .]

In *Galileo*, there are the antitheses of: scene 2, in which Galileo demonstrates his telescope to the Venetian Senate and is highly honored by the very men who make it impossible for him to engage in research, and scene 4, in which Galileo encounters disbelief and contempt at the very court on which he had set his hopes as a research scientist; the scene in which the Jesuits declare Galileo's theories to be correct and the scene in which the Inquisition puts the Copernican doctrine on the Index; the scene showing how Galileo's teachings spread among the common people and the (next) scene, which tells how Galileo is abandoned by the Grand Duke, on whom he relied more than on the common people. Antithesis also determines the internal composition of the scenes, and is complemented by their language. For example, the "reversal" scene in which Galileo decides to take up his research again, and the scene in which he recants.

[. . .]

The theorem that a new age has dawned is integrated into the dramatic action as thesis/antithesis/synthesis. The new age seems agile and nimble, the old age shuffles along. And yet how weak the new age turns out to be! But the plot advances, the new age manages to survive. The discoveries have been made, the new knowledge remains, the old view of the universe will never again appear unshakeable. Reason is given a chance. Galileo seeks reason in the common people. By denying reason, he damages its chances. But even he ultimately realizes that reason is only just starting out and not ending.

[. . .]

The mardi gras of 1632 is a counterpart to the carnival in Bellarmin's home in 1666. But in the earlier scene, the aristocracy is amusing itself; in the later, the common people. The enjoyment is diametric. First the Inquisition refers to Galileo's support by the north Italian cities, then Vanni does — but the ultimate reversal is latent in both comments.

In the same manner the link between the first and the next-to-last scene is strengthened by events whose very similarity makes their dissimilarity apparent, as well as their intimate connection. In the opening scene, it is morning, the dawn of not only a new day but a new era, and in Galileo's room the bed is being made. In the penultimate scene, it is the evening not just of a day but of a life and its ideals, and the bed is being prepared for the night. In the first scene Galileo "sings" an "aria" to the new age. In the later scene he laboriously expresses his conviction that the new age has begun even if it looks like the old. But the theme recurs: at the end Andrea assures us that we are actually only at the beginning.

In the opening scene, Andrea is taught a lesson about nature; in the penultimate scene, a lesson on society. The teacher is the same man, yet totally different each time. The pupil has become a different person and yet remained the same.

In the second scene, Virginia asks Galileo what the night before was like. He answers, "It was bright." In the next-to-last scene, Galileo asks Virginia what the night is like. He receives the same reply. The first time, "bright" refers to nature; the second time, not only to "nature" but to the nature of mankind and history.

Thus symmetry proves crucial, an integral part of the dialectic in the composition. It is much more significant than ending each scene with a statement or an event alluding to the next scene – a practice that *Galileo* shares with many other Aristotelian and non-Aristotelian dramas.

Scene 13 (Galileo's recantation) shows how Brecht used images that require the spectator to compare a present event with earlier ones. Brecht doesn't bother with a sensational trial scene. Instead of letting us watch what would have been an extremely illustrative act of recantation – in church before an ecclesiastical hierarchy – he shows the event in terms of the play's basic "gesture," the scientist's responsibility to society, relating this to the internal action of the play rather than to external history. After showing, in the ninth scene, how Galileo's decision to resume research in forbidden areas affected his students, Brecht demonstrates the effect of Galileo's recantation on them. He presents substance rather than accident.

This scene (like the ninth, to which it refers) is on two levels: in the foreground, Virginia praying for her father's salvation; in the middle-ground, the students filled with anxiety about their master's actions. The characters all act "according to the circumstances" which have molded them. Virginia has concentrated on saving her father's soul from eternal damnation. Andrea is equally passionate about adjuring his idol and ideal. The Little Monk sustains himself with beautiful logic and the logic of beauty, the things that so greatly impressed him about his master. And Federzoni stands among them, hopeful but worried, and a realist at the very moment the others so blatantly give in to their emotions. The scene shows the students' relationship to their teacher (an important component of the plot), confronts the scientist with his daughter, and demonstrates the different meanings of the event for the various characters.

To heighten the dramatic tension, Brecht slows the tempo in two ways. First, he brings on stage the man who announces Galileo's imminent recantation and thereby precipitates Andrea's open avowal of his belief in Copernicus. Next, the author lets the fifth hour pass with no sign of recantation, so that all the students, not just an enthusiastic Andrea, say a prayer of thanksgiving for the birth of the age of knowledge. These retardations are followed by the peripetia: the tolling of bells and the public reading of the recantation formula. But the meaning, drawn from constant variations on the basic constellation – the relationship between Galileo and his pupils – would be incomplete if it were not for the dramatic confrontation between the teacher, changed beyond recognition, and the pupils, who obviously can't understand him. Now the scene reveals its true sense, shedding light on the basic problem of the play. A "final word" seems to have been spoken: "Unhappy the land that needs a hero." Yet it is final only for this scene, not for the total structure, though the scene itself can be understood only in terms of the end, whose meaning it unravels. Its power comes from the dialectical reversals, which are an image of the growth and reversals of play *in toto*. The scene is essential to clarify the theme of the scientist's responsibility in the use of knowledge for or against society.

A form of dialectic also determines *Galileo*'s characterization; it is manifested as a relation in each person between the individual and the typical.

[. . .]

Galileo's behavior reproduces – in counterpoint, as it were – the dialectical growth of the other characters. The enthusiasm of the adult Galileo is repeated in the boy Andrea's passionate adherence to the new cause. Galileo's genius is reflected in the young initiate's intellectual maturation. Andrea's character, however, is an alternative to Galileo's, rather than simply alternating with it. Through following his master, he demonstrates consequences. Although much younger than Galileo, he seems older. Led along, he seems led astray. The result of his devotion: the prototype of a scientist prone to any recantation, denial, refusal, obedience – to whom Galileo's behavior seems natural, rather than dubious, as long as it is a contribution to science. Andrea is not only willing to learn but becomes learnèd as well. Yet while everyone else in *Galileo* should be seen and judged in terms of the end of the play, Andrea is to be judged in terms of his future. So he has at once the rosy bloom of youth and the grayness of old age: intellectual irresponsibility towards mankind. We see corrupt innocence, ruined hope, unfulfilled promise. "Welcome to the gutter, fellow scientist and traitor!" echoes terrifyingly within us. At the end, Andrea adds another line, but we know even this isn't the end of the stanza, whose cynical meaning is clear. "We are actually only at the beginning," he says reassuringly at the close of the play. For better *and* for worse. Galileo sees himself as a dead tree, but Andrea, the "green wood," is not free of rot. We can no more follow Andrea, who has once been led astray, unconditionally than we can follow Galileo: instead, we must find better ways of our own.

Virginia is a further example. This character is based on, but quite different from, a historical model. Her primary function is to demonstrate that the conflict between a new science and an old faith, or – speaking more generally – between social progress and reaction, penetrates the personal and family sphere. Galileo must exist for the whole world, not just for his daughter. He has to ferret out and develop intelligence everywhere; only his daughter's mind is an exception. He accepts the responsibility of being her father and provider but not her intellectual parent. From the beginning, he entrusts her to the Church. Instead of letting her look through the telescope he brushes her aside, saying it is not a toy. His daughter enters the Church to return as a totally different person. Science was her pass into society: Galileo let her circulate as one of his works. She promptly ran into the arms of the Cardinal Inquisitor: the weapon reversed. The unaroused intellect aroused; the misunderstood daughter understood; the girl who was asked nothing asked a great deal. The useless daughter from a good home becomes a useful daughter to the Church.

She still believes that she will marry, and she believes it for eight years, but at the crucial moment she remains for Galileo what she was: a person of secondary importance. Once, she was to be married off as quickly as possible, but now she's left in the lurch. The maiden becomes an old maid. And then she becomes, in effect, a nun. Her only objection to her father's captivity is that she can't be his sole custodian. She is both housekeeper and spiritual advisor to him, supplementing his physical diet with a spiritual one, countering fleshly desires with food for the soul. To the dictates of the two new sciences, she opposes the commands of the old faith, parrying Galileo's logic with theo-logic. She wards off his penitence with the reiteration of charges. She confronts the malice of his ambiguities with the unequivocalness of malicious kindness. She replies to his irony with patience and indulgence. She was once a means to an end for him, and now the situation is reversed. The powerful man is now in her power. The cold that science once brought into their relationship is outdone by the coldness of Christian life.

Never having taught Virginia knowledge, or even tried to teach her, Galileo now cannot be wise. He can only be sly, but his slyness won't save him from damnation and is useless against her condemnation. His hell is terrible not because he has thrown away his own intellectual gift but because he hasn't developed his daughter's – and her own rigidity shows that her life is merely the survival of a destroyed existence.

Ludovico's characterization is also dialectical, although he functions primarily as a type. If he *is* an individual, then it is only despite, not because of, his class. Virginia could have been a different person, but not he. His presence is determined by what he represents, his diction by his class idiocy, his individuality by the rigidity of his caste. Although a man of the world, he is unable to cross the boundaries of his world. He has an expanded horizon – seen from a tower on his estate. When science is accepted by both Court and Church, the scientist's daughter is desirable and eligible for marriage. But the anti-Copernican decree warns him against hasty consequences. It is the father and not the daughter who must endure a period of probation; the daughter need not swear that she is pure, but the future father-in-law must promise to put an end to his impure research. The phases of Venus may have nothing to do with the daughter's behind, but they are intimately connected with the father's appearance. Ludovico may be a scientific layman and a blockhead, but he knows as much as Galileo about the connection between heaven and earth and heaven on earth, and while the Little Monk thinks about the internal agitations of the peasants, Ludovico thinks about the external ones. He has had too much experience with the dynamics of social forces not to realize that the proof of astral motion can be political dynamite. He knows he is right because Galileo grows nasty while Ludovico sticks to the point, remaining discreet and arguing well. When Galileo, losing his temper, goes so far as to threaten to write his works in the Florentine vernacular so that the masses can read them, Ludovico is convinced that this man will always remain a "slave to his passions." Marrying Galileo's daughter could easily jeopardize one's family and social position, so he breaks the engagement.

But although Ludovico in this sense embodies forethought, Galileo incarnates afterthought. And that makes all the difference. Galileo may speculate correctly, but Ludovico calculates correctly. Galileo can act cold but not remain cold. Ludovico, however, can be cool, and turn icy. He is able to remain objective, while Galileo *is* an object lesson, a cause. Ludovico's profile is sharply hewn because it is so impersonal. Galileo carries out functions, but Ludovico is functionalized: a proper manor-lord.

The iron-founder Vanni resembles Ludovico in the way his characterization is placed within a sharply defined social role. Vanni's part in the play is extremely important; without him the Galileo "case" would not be understandable in the way Brecht wished it to be, i.e., as an act of treason against society. But this functionalizes Vanni's role, like Ludovico's. Vanni represents the bourgeoisie of those times. Despite the great respect he, as a layman, has for the scientist, he considers himself on the same level because he is struggling for the same goal: liberation from dependence on feudal power and narrowmindness. He assumes that Galileo can distinguish between friend and foe, and identifies himself as Galileo's friend. He joins the struggle as an economic force that the Grand Duke must take into consideration, for Florence is wedged between the Papal State and the northern Italian city states; she cannot survive without the latter. Galileo's fate hangs in the balance – then he goes over to the Princes and Popes. Vanni has no choice but to leave, regretful but upright, just as he entered. Galileo, who believed he would somehow be able to get out of it as an individual, continues his bootlicking; yet, despite all his writhing and wriggling, he finds no way out.

Of all the characters representing the Church, the Little Monk is the most dialectical: not only a priest but an astronomer. He sees with his own two eyes that Galileo's teachings are right, yet he dare not see this because it is contrary to the Supreme Truth he has been taught. He cannot acknowledge the new knowledge because the consequences will be terrible for the simple people whose misery he is acquainted with and who – in his opinion – so as to endure their misery, need faith in a divine providence underlying the social order. His confusion is great because the contradiction is great. The Little Monk believes that the decree necessarily contains a higher wisdom, but the things he has viewed on heaven and earth, on the moon and in the Campagna, have been so convincing that he cannot take the decree for granted, as do other believers. His passionate craving to unravel the truth from all contradictions is irresistible; it drives him to attempt Galileo's "conversion," and yet forces him to listen to the scientist's arguments, although they not only tear away the scar tissue that religion has spread over the wound in his soul, but enlarge and deepen the injury. The Little Monk confirms Galileo's faith in the gentle power of reason. His actions show that in the long run it will do rulers no good to regimentize thought, influence the minds of their subjects, or enroll as party members the very people they oppress. The chasm between ideology and reality will deepen and widen. Appealed to, called upon, awoken, the "Little Monks" will bring about the victory of reason. Yet at the end of the play he has abandoned research and rests in peace in the church.

Similarly dialectical characterizations can be easily demonstrated for all the figures in the play, and in their language. The dialogue is marked by vivid imagery: the "prosaic," the penetration of new ideology and new "objective" relations on the basis of new conditions of production, is trans-posed into metaphor. The parabolic diction of the Bible is used verbatim in

146

many ways, because of the very nature of the subject matter; but metaphors create the specific nature of the language, and are used by each character according to his social class and function. As for dialectics, our main concern here, the dialogue is remarkably antithetical, not only in a thesis-and-reply pattern which at times becomes stichomythic, but within individual speeches and lines. Opposing views are transcended and dissolved through gnomic maxims, contradictions resolved by "dictums" in which logic and image form a graspable unity. In this constant creation and transcendence of antitheses, a part is played by the association of images and concepts, and occasionally by the evocative use of alliteration. The syntax throughout, in coordinate and subordinate clauses, is used to develop crucial contrasts.

For example: The curator describes the "slavery under whose whip science sighs in many places." "They've cut their whips out of old leather folios. You don't have to know how the stone falls, you have to know what Aristotle writes about it. Eyes are only for reading. Why bother with new laws of falling bodies, if only the laws of genuflection are important?" The Little Monk explains the agony his parents would suffer if the new concept of the universe turned out to be right: "There will be no meaning in their misery. Hunger will simply mean not having eaten, rather than being a test of strength. Hard work will simply be bending and lugging, and not be a virtue." Galileo's reply to him emphasizes a whole series of contradictions: The Campagna peasants are paying for the war fought in Spain and Germany by the mild Lord Jesus' deputy – and why does the pope place the earth in the center of the universe? "So that Saint Peter's throne may stand at the center of the earth?" He goes on:

> If your parents were prosperous and happy, they might develop the virtues of happiness and prosperity. Today the virtues of exhaustion are caused by the exhausted land. For that my new water pumps could work more wonder than their ridiculous superhuman efforts. Be fruitful and multiply: for the fields are barren and war is decimating you! Should I lie to your people?

Finally Galileo sums up: "I can see your people's divine patience, but where is their divine wrath?"

This method of extracting truth from antitheses is also reflected in Galileo's entire approach to research. Thus, before starting to investigate sunspots, he says:

> My intention is not to prove that I was right but to find out *whether* I was right. "Abandon hope all ye who enter – an observation."

Before assuming these phenomena are spots, which would suit us, let us first set about proving that they are not – fishtails . . . In fact, we will approach this observing of the sun with the firm determination to prove that the earth stands still, and only if hopelessly defeated in this pious undertaking can we allow ourselves to wonder if we may not have been right all the time: the earth revolves.

"Unhappy is the land that breeds no hero."/"Unhappy is the land that needs a hero." Galileo is trapped in a contradiction of principles from which he cannot extricate himself. At his last meeting with Andrea he says that he has taught knowledge by denying the truth – Brecht drew the truth from contradictions, through the play's murderous analysis. Galileo's "final words" signify initial knowledge: "Scientists cannot remain scientists if they deny themselves to the masses; the powers of nature cannot be fully developed if mankind does not know how to develop its own powers; machines, meant to bring relief to man, may merely bring new hardships; progress may merely progress away from humanity."

The essence of drama is conflict; conflict depends on the existence of antitheses; antitheses are an essential structural element in the dramatic. *Galileo* is antithetical in its parts and its entirety, and these antitheses are in turn transcended through the dialectical nature of its relationships, characters, and language; yet the transcendences themselves are ephemeral. As I pointed out in the beginning, Brecht toward the end of his life came out in favor of a "dialectical theatre," of which *Galileo*, written long before the theory – is a demonstration, not only in its technique but in its aesthetic essence. It is the "merely" narrative and "purely" demonstrative structure, as well as the appropriately "calm" production of this play, that allows us to grasp and enjoy dialectics in the theatre.

THE POETRY OF
CHRISTOPHER OKIGBO

28 Chinweizu, Onwuchekwa Jemie
and Ihechukwu Madubuike, *Towards the*
Decolonization of African Literature
(1980)

This extract is taken from *Toward the Decolonization of African Literature* (originally published in Nigeria in 1980 by Fourth Dimension and in the UK by Routledge & Kegan Paul in 1985). Written by three Nigerian critics, Chinweizu, Onwuchekwa Jemie and Ihechukwu Madubuike (nicknamed the Troika by Wole Soyinka), the work was intended to be a stinging critique of some of the more recent developments in contemporary African literature and criticism. African writing was, at that time, making a major impact on international literature in English, and many of the leading figures (mostly from Nigeria) were gaining international reputations for their work. Yet Chinweizu, Jemie and Madubuike saw in this simply the perpetuation of Western aesthetic and critical models in Africa by Africans themselves, and as such 'Western imperialism has maintained its hegemony over . . . the literary arts of contemporary Africa'. The work castigates African writers and critics for valorising Western literary and linguistic models over traditional oral forms expressed in African languages. Reproduced below is a part of their lengthy critique of Christopher Okigbo.

Chinweizu, Onwuchekwa Jemie and Ihechukwu Madubuike, *Towards the Decolonization of African Literature: African Fiction and Poetry and their Critics*, London: KPI, 1985, pp. 188–92

Traditional African poetry speaks a public language. Some of our obscurantist poets may retort by pointing to the existence of cult poetry and religious incantations, which, in traditional society, were intelligible, not to the general public, but only to initiates of secret societies and the priesthoods. True.

There was such poetry. But the initiates were the public for such poetry. Such poetry had a limited audience, but was certainly not privatist, was certainly not coded in language intelligible to their composers alone. Besides, such poetry was only a small part of the traditional repertory. If our privatists of today claim that they are descendants of that small tradition, we must ask them: of what cult are you the priesthood? Of what secret rites are your poems the incantations? And if, indeed, your poems are cultic utterances aimed at initiates, why publish and distribute them to the general public? Why not circulate them among initiates only?

As we said before, traditional African poetry speaks a public language. The following invocation and praise of Alajire, a god of suffering, comes from Soyinka's own Yoruba tradition:

> Alajire, we ask you to be patient,
> you are very quick-tempered,
> and we worship you for it.
> We ask you to be moderate,
> you are wildly extravagant
> and we pray to you for it.
> We ask you not to be jealous,
> you are madly jealous,
> and we love you for it.
> Alajire, you have a strange kind of pity:
> will you swallow my head,
> while you are licking away the tears from my face?
> Alajire, you frighten me,
> when you fall gently, like a tired leaf.
> Do not covet the beauty
> on the faces of dead children.
> Alajire, I am lost in the forest,
> but every wrong way I take,
> can become the right way towards your wisdom.
>   (Beier 1970: 30)

In nineteen lucid lines this poem communicates the nexus of feelings that bind the worshipper to the god. A sense of the worshipper's terror at the god's unpredictable nature comes through clearly. The worshipper has to flatter the god's vices, love his jealousy, and distrust his pity. Even the god's gentleness carries an umbra of fear. But the worshipper is never unaware of the possibility of attaining wisdom. Thus, at the end of the poem the reader understands something of the nature of this god and has shared in the experience of worshipping him.

Among the Igbo poets the situation is much the same. Their attempts to revive traditional religious poetry have been equally unsuccessful. For example, Okigbo opens "Heavensgate" with an invocation to Mother Idoto, an African water goddess. But most of the poem is preoccupied with Catholic liturgy and jargon — in fact, the whole framework of the poem is Christian and Catholic, with snippets of traditional African ritual thrown in. Some may want to view this as a case of syncretism, as a fusion of Christianity and African religions. But one can charge Okigbo with insincerity in his approach to African religion. For instance, the opening invocation, supposedly traditional African, is in fact Christian in language and spirit. With a few minor adjustments in vocabulary, one can convert this invocation into a Christian prayer:

OKIGBO ORIGINAL	ADJUSTED (CHRISTIAN)
Before you, Mother Idoto naked I stand; before your watery presence a prodigal	Before you, Father Almighty, contrite I stand, before your divine presence, a pilgrim,
leaning on an oilbean lost in your legend. . . .	waiting at your altar; lost in awe. . . .

But one cannot by similar substitutions convert an authentic traditional invocation into a Christian prayer:

ORIGINAL (AFRICAN)	ADJUSTED (CHRISTIAN)
Prayer to Ekwensu	Prayer to the Devil
Ekwensu we place our hands on you . . . (Beier 1967: 16)	Devil we place our hands on you . . .

Can a Christian say prayers to the devil, that exiled incarnation of evil, and risk damnation from his jealous God? But in an African pantheon, good gods are thanked, difficult ones are appeased, bad ones are bribed, and so on. Again, witness the following:

ORIGINAL (AFRICAN)
Prayer to the Dead Father

My father
I am giving these yams to
   you,
when you are reborn
may you be a farmer of many
   yams.

           (Beier 1967: 17)

ADJUSTED (CHRISTIAN)
Prayer to Saint Peter

O Saint Peter, Fisher of Men,
   Keeper of the Gates of
   heaven
I bring these biscuits to you
when you are reborn
may you be a baker of
   delicious biscuits.

The trouble with this adjustment is of course that the belief in reincarnation which undergirds "Prayer to the Dead Father" is outside of Christian doctrine. If Okigbo had, at that stage of his career, had the humility of a votary and wanted to learn how to properly invoke a divine or ancestral spirit, he could have listened to the village elders or priests whose invocations would have run something like the "Prayer to the Dead Father," translated from the Igbo original:

My father
I am giving these yams to you
when you are reborn
may you be a farmer of many yams.
My father
I am killing this goat for you
When you are reborn
may it be as my own son.
My father
I have brought this dog to you
When you are reborn
slay not your children
and may they not slay you.
May you kill none by accident
but may you kill your enemies with intent.
My father
I am sacrificing this cock to you
when you are reborn
may your *ikenga* stand straight.
As you are now in the spirit world
avert all evil from us.

Let your son who is succeeding you
look after his family
as you did before him.

(Beier 1967: 17)

But having first invoked an indigenous goddess in supposed reverence, even if in the language and spirit of a foreign religion, Okigbo then proceeds to refer to her representatives as "idols," using deprecatory Christian terminology. To reverence the gods and then deprecate their representatives at the altar! — you can't do that!

Worse still, Okigbo desecrates the sacred palm groves with his "cannons," and claims his Messiah ("Lumen mundi . . .") will come there "after the argument in heaven" to receive from penitents "vegetable offerings/ with five/ fingers of chalk." What incongruous nonsense! What sacrilege for the penitents to enact indigenous rituals to propitiate an alien god!

All in all, "Heavensgate" is a dressed-up Christian ritual — and therefore the invocation of an indigenous deity is patently insincere. If you choose to write Christian religious propaganda, do so, but leave our gods alone! It is bad enough for Christianity to have displaced our gods from the consciousness of our elite. It is worse for a seeming revivalist to address our gods as if they were Christian gods or in the Christian manner. The net effect would be to absorb our pantheon into the assembly of lesser Christian godlings, and this is cultural suicide. It should be the other way around Christianity should be domesticated and absorbed into our existing indigenous religious systems – and it is being domesticated among the Cherubim and Seraphim sect and other such non-elite adapters of Christianity.

29 Christopher Okigbo, Introduction to *Labyrinths with Path of Thunder* (1971)

Christopher Okigbo wrote the majority of his poems between 1956 and 1966. His writings appeared in the literary magazines *Black Orpheus* and *Transition*, and he won the poetry prize at the Festival of Negro Arts in Dakar, Senegal in 1966, which he refused to accept. Okigbo was working on a major project before his death, which was thought to be an exploration of the 'poetic process', but the manuscript was lost in the turmoil of civil war. The poems published later as *Labyrinths with Path of Thunder* (1971) appeared originally through African presses as *Heavensgate* (1962), *Silences* (1963 and 1965), *Distances* (1964) and *Limits* (1964). *Path of Thunder*, which marked a new, more politically-orientated direction in his writing, was published posthumously in 1968 and

153

included alongside *Labyrinths* in 1971. In this Introduction, Okigbo explains some of the background to his poems, and gives a vivid sense of the range of influences on his work.

Okigbo, C., 'Introduction', in *Labyrinths with Path of Thunder*, London: Heinemann, 1971, pp. xi–xiv

Although these poems were written and published separately, they are, in fact, organically related.

Heavensgate was originally conceived as an Easter sequence. It later grew into a ceremony of innocence, something like a mass, an offering to Idoto, the village stream of which I drank, in which I washed, as a child; the celebrant, a personage like Orpheus, is about to begin a journey. Cleansing involves total nakedness, a complete self-surrender to the water spirit that nurtures all creation. The various sections of the poem, therefore, present this celebrant at various stations of his cross.

Limits and *Distances* are man's outer and inner worlds projected – the phenomenal and the imaginative, not in terms of their separateness but of their relationship – an attempt to reconcile the universal opposites of life and death in a live–die proposition: one is the other and either is both.

'Siren Limits' presents a protagonist in pursuit of the white elephant. In his progression to a sacred waterfront he falls victim to his own demonic obsession, becomes disembodied or loses his second self. 'Fragments out of the deluge' renders in retrospect certain details of the protagonist and of his milieu – the collective rape of innocence and profanation of the mysteries, in atonement for which he has had to suffer immolation. (*Limits* was written at the end of a journey of several centuries from Nsukka to Yola in pursuit of what turned out to be an illusion.)

Distances is, on the other hand, a poem of homecoming, but of homecoming in its spiritual and psychic aspect. The quest broken off after 'Siren Limits' is resumed, this time in the unconscious. The self that suffers, that experiences, ultimately finds fulfilment in a form of psychic union with the supreme spirit that is both destructive and creative. The process is one of sensual anaesthesia, of total liberation from all physical and emotional tension; the end result, a state of aesthetic grace. (*Distances* was written after my first experience of surgery under general anaesthesia.)

Between *Limits* and *Distances* an interval, *Silences*, is provided, in which two groups of mourners explore the possibilities of poetic metaphor in an attempt to elicit the music to which all imperishable cries must aspire. Both parts of *Silences* were inspired by the events of the day: *Lament of the Silent*

Sisters, by the Western Nigeria Crisis of 1962, and the death of Patrice Lumumba; *Lament of the Drums*, by the imprisonment of Obafemj Awolowo, and the tragic death of his eldest son.

The 'Silent Sisters' are, however, sometimes like the drowning Franciscan nuns of Hopkins' The Wreck of the Deutschland, sometimes like the 'Sirenes' of Debussy's *Nocturne* – two dissonant dreams associated in the dominant motif 'NO in thunder' (from one of Melville's letters to Hawthorne). This motif is developed by a series of related airs from sources as diverse as Malcolm Cowley, Raja Ratnam, Stephane Mallarmé, Rabindranath Tagore, Garçia Lorca and the yet unpublished Peter Thomas – airs which enable the 'Silent Sisters' to evoke, quite often by calling wolf; consonant tunes in life and letters. Section I, for instance, erects an illusion, a storm-tossed ship at mid-sea. The image of drowning virgins, and the dream of ultimate martyrdom are, however, also present. The illusion is enlarged by the motif of carrion-comfort (from one of Hopkins' poems). Section II develops this latter motif in the image of flies and splintered flames gloating over a carrion. The chorus breaks into a 'swan song' in Section III; and in the alternation (Section IV) between the Crier and the Chorus the sea herself, hidden face of the dream, is celebrated in her many colours. In Section V the main actors in the events of the day become almost recognizable in the opening couplets. The problem 'How does one say NO in thunder' is then finally resolved in silence. For the ultimate answer is to be sought only in terms of each poet's response to his medium.

The long-drums are, on the other hand, the spirits of the ancestors, the dead. They begin their lament by invoking the elements which make them up, and imploring evil forces to stay away from the rostrum. In Section II, the drums enter their theme song. They are coming out of their place of confinement, 'soot chamber', 'cinerary tower' (1st strophe), not to rejoice but to lament (2nd strophe). They are like urgent telegrams which are dispatched only when tragic events happen (3rd strophe). 'Babylonian capture', 'martyrdom' and 'chaliced vintage' suggest that someone might have been betrayed by his disciples (5th strophe). The alternation (in Section III) between the horns of elephant tusks (the italicised passages) and the drums establishes an identity between the personage of Section II, and Palinurus, the helmsman of Aeneas' ship during his legendary voyage to Italy. In Section IV, the drums return to their theme song, weary and exhausted from the long excursion of Section III. After a few limbering-up passages (1st, 2nd and 3rd strophes) a treble drum takes a six-phrase solo (4th strophe). A six-phrase response by the mother-of-drums (5th strophe) leads on to the re-entry of the horns in a variation on Ishthar's lament for Tammuz (Section V). Here the theme of the poem is no longer suggested but stated; the personages of the earlier sections together become fused with that of Tammuz, and consequently with the movement of the seasons.

Labyrinths is thus a fable of man's perennial quest for fulfilment. (The title may suggest Minos' legendary palace at Cnossus, but the double headed axe is as much a symbol of sovereignty in traditional Ibo society as in Crete. Besides, the long and tortuous passage to the shrine of the 'long-juju' of the Aro Ibos may perhaps, best be described as a labyrinth.) Inevitably, several presences haunt the complex of rooms and ante-rooms, of halls and corridors that lead to the palace of the White Goddess, and in which a country visitor might easily lose his way. Nevertheless, a poet-protagonist is assumed throughout; a personage, however, much larger than Orpheus; one with a load of destiny on his head, rather like Gilgainesh, like Aeneas, like the hero of Melville's *Moby Dick*, like the Fisher King of Eliot's *Waste Land*; a personage for whom the progression through 'Heavensgate' through 'Limits' through 'Distances' is like telling the beads of a rosary; except that the beads are neither stone nor agate but globules of anguish strung together on memory.

Every work of this kind is necessarily a cry of anguish — of the root extending its branches of coral, of corals extending their roots into each living hour; the swell of the silent sea the great heaving dream at its highest, the thunder of splitting pods — the tears scatter, take root, the cotyledons broken, burgeon into laughter of leaf; or else rot into vital hidden roles in the nitrogen cycle. The present dream clamoured to be born a cadenced cry: silence to appease the fever of flight beyond the iron gate.

Christopher Okigbo

Ibadan
October 1965

Part III

VARIETIES OF THE POPULAR

DAPHNE DU MAURIER, *REBECCA*

30 Daphne du Maurier, The House of Secrets (1946)

In this essay, du Maurier locates the principal inspiration for her bestseller *Rebecca* (1938) within the long history of her obsession with the house that stands behind one of the headlands to the west of Fowey, Cornwall. Menabilly eventually became her home in 1943 for some twenty years. Its exterior and grounds had already served as the model for Manderley. This extract is not included here as a source for *Rebecca* (because it was written eight years after the publication of the novel in 1938, and clearly derives from its opening). However, it is suggestive that du Maurier located the house at the centre of her fiction in this way and striking that she invests so much in the 'personality' of the house and so poignantly regrets its decay and death. It is included here as one of *Rebecca*'s most important 'intertexts', and in part responsible for the invention of 'Daphne du Maurier country'. It newly roots the novel within a verifiable local setting – Fowey and its surroundings – and it sets up a sensibility shared by du Maurier and her narrator as explicitly touristic. In so doing, it solicits subsequent tourism.

du Maurier, D., 'The House of Secrets', in *The Rebecca Notebook and Other Memories*, London: Victor Gollancz, 1981, pp. 130–5

It was an afternoon in late autumn, the first time I tried to find the house. October, November, the month escapes me. But in the west country autumn can make herself a witch, and place a spell upon the walker. The trees were golden brown, the hydrangeas had massive heads still blue and untouched by flecks of wistful grey, and I would set forth at three of an afternoon with foolish notions of August still in my head. "I will strike inland," I thought, "and come back by way of the cliffs, and the sun will yet be high, or at worst touching the horizon beyond the western hills."

Of course, I was still a newcomer to the district, a summer visitor, whose people had but lately bought the old "Swiss Cottage", as the locals called it, a name which, to us, had horrid associations with an underground railway in the Finchley Road at home.

We were not yet rooted. We were new folk from London. We walked as tourists walked, seeing what should be seen. So my sister and I, poring over an old guidebook, first came upon the name of Menabilly. What description the guidebook gave I cannot now remember, except that the house had been first built in the reign of Queen Elizabeth, that the grounds and woods had been in the last century famous for their beauty, and that the property had never changed hands from the time it came into being, but had passed down, in the male line, to the present owner. Three miles from the harbour, easy enough to find; but what about keepers and gardeners, chauffeurs and barking dogs? My sister was not such an inveterate trespasser as I. We asked advice. "You'll find no dogs at Menabilly, nor any keepers either," we were told, "the house is all shut up. The owner lives in Devon. But you'll have trouble in getting there. The drive is nearly three miles long, and overgrown."

I for one was not to be deterred. The autumn colours had me bewitched before the start. So we set forth, Angela more reluctant, with a panting pekinese held by a leash. We came to the lodge at four turnings, as we had been told, and opened the creaking iron gates with the flash courage and appearance of bluff common to the trespasser. The lodge was deserted. No one peered at us from the windows. We slunk away down the drive, and were soon hidden by the trees. Is it really nigh on twenty years since I first walked that hidden drive and saw the beech trees, like the arches of a great cathedral, form a canopy above my head? I remember we did not talk, or if we did we talked in whispers. That was the first effect the woods had upon both of us.

The drive twisted and turned in a way that I described many years afterwards, when sitting at a desk in Alexandria and looking out upon a hard glazed sky and dusty palm trees; but on that first autumnal afternoon, when the drive was new to us, it had the magic quality of a place hitherto untrodden, unexplored. I was Scott in the Antarctic. I was Cortez in Mexico.

[. . .]

The trees grew taller and the shrubs more menacing. Yet still the drive led on, and never a house at the end of it. Suddenly Angela said, "It's after four . . . and the sun's gone." The pekinese watched her, pink tongue lolling. And then he stared into the bushes, pricking his ears at nothing. The first owl hooted . . .

"I don't like it," said Angela firmly. "Let's go home."

"But the house," I said with longing, "we haven't seen the house."

She hesitated, and I dragged her on. But in an instant the day was gone from us. The drive was a muddied path, leading nowhere, and the shrubs, green no longer but a shrouding black, turned to fantastic shapes and sizes. There was not one owl now, but twenty. And through the dark trees, with a pale grin upon his face, came the first glimmer of the livid hunter's moon.

I knew then that I was beaten. For that night only.

"All right," I said grudgingly, "we'll find the house another time."

And, following the moon's light, we struck through the trees and came out upon the hillside. In the distance below us stretched the sea. Behind us the woods and the valley through which we had come. But nowhere was there a sign of any house. Nowhere at all.

"Perhaps," I thought to myself, "it is a house of secrets, and has no wish to be disturbed." But I knew I should not rest until I had found it.

If I remember rightly the weather broke after that day, and the autumn rains were upon us. Driving rain, day after day. And we, not yet become acclimatized to Cornish wind and weather, packed up and returned to London for the winter. But I did not forget the woods of Menabilly, or the house that waited. . . .

We came back again to Cornwall in the spring, and I was seized with a fever for fishing. I would be out in a boat most days, with a line in the water, and it did not matter much what came on the end of it, whether it would be seaweed or a dead crab, as long as I could sit on the thwart of a boat and hold a line and watch the sea. The boatman sculled off the little bay called Pridmouth, and as I looked at the land beyond, and saw the massive trees climbing from the valley to the hill, the shape of it all seemed familiar.

"What's up there, in the trees?" I said.

"That's Menabilly," came the answer, "but you can't see the house from the shore. It's away up yonder. I've never been there myself." I felt a bite on my line at that moment and said no more. But the lure of Menabilly was upon me once again.

Next morning I did a thing I had never done before, nor ever did again, except once in the desert, where to see sunrise is the peak of all experience. In short, I rose at 5:00 a.m. I pulled across the harbour in my pram, walked through the sleeping town, and climbed out upon the cliffs just as the sun himself climbed out on Pont Hill behind me. The sea was glass. The air was soft and misty warm. And the only other creature out of bed was a fisherman, hauling crab pots at the harbour mouth. It gave me a fine feeling of conceit, to be up before the world. My feet in sand shoes seemed like wings. I came down to Pridmouth Bay, passing the solitary cottage by the lake, and, opening a small gate hard by, I saw a narrow path leading to the woods. Now, at last, I had the day before me, and no owls, no moon, no shadows could turn me back.

I followed the path to the summit of the hill and then, emerging from the woods, turned left, and found myself upon a high grass walk, with all the bay stretched out below me and the Gribben head beyond.

I paused, stung by the beauty of that first pink glow of sunrise on the water, but the path led on, and I would not be deterred. Then I saw them for the first time—the scarlet rhododendrons. Massive and high they reared above my head, shielding the entrance to a long smooth lawn. I was hard upon it now, the place I sought. Some instinct made me crouch upon my belly and crawl softly to the wet grass at the foot of the shrubs. The morning mist was lifting, and the sun was coming up above the trees even as the moon had done last autumn. This time there was no owl, but blackbird, thrush and robin greeting the summer day.

I edged my way on to the lawn, and there she stood. My house of secrets. My elusive Menabilly . . .

The windows were shuttered fast, white and barred. Ivy covered the grey walls and threw tendrils round the windows. The house, like the world, was sleeping too. But later, when the sun was high, there would come no wreath of smoke from the chimneys. The shutters would not be thrown back, or the doors unfastened. No voices would sound within those darkened rooms. Menabily would sleep on, like the sleeping beauty of the fairy tale, until someone should come to wake her.

I watched her awhile in silence, and then became emboldened, and walked across the lawn and stood beneath the windows. The scarlet rhododendrons encircled her lawns, to south, to east, to west. Behind her, to the north, were the tall trees and the deep woods.

[. . .]

[S]he had a grace and charm that made me hers upon the instant. She was, or so it seemed to me, bathed in a strange mystery. She held a secret— not one, not two, but many—that she withheld from many people but would give to one who loved her well.

As I sat on the edge of the lawn and stared at her I felt as many romantic, foolish people have felt about the Sphinx. Here was a block of stone, even as the desert Sphinx, made by man for his own purpose—yet she had a personality that was hers alone, without the touch of human hand. One family only had lived within her walls. One family who had given her life. They had been born there, they had loved, they had quarrelled, they had suffered, they had died. And out of these emotions she had woven a personality for herself, she had become what their thoughts and their desires had made her.

And now the story was ended. She lay there in her last sleep. Nothing remained for her but to decay and die. . . .

I cannot recollect, now, how long I lay and stared at her. It was past noon, perhaps, when I came back to the living world. I was empty and light-headed, with no breakfast inside me. But the house possessed me from that day, even as a mistress holds her lover. . . .

31 Sigmund Freud, Female Sexuality (1931)

Sigmund Freud (1856–1939) completed this late paper in 1931. It contains some of his most elaborated thinking upon the development of female sexuality from infancy to adulthood. The extract that is included here cannot replicate the detail and subtlety of his argument in full, but is designed to provide the bare bones of the narrative that Freud constructs. He describes the development of male sexuality (emphasising its psychological rather than merely physical dimension) and compares it with that of female sexuality. Even this brief selection is suggestive when read in conjunction with *Rebecca*. The narrator's obsessional and imaginary relationship with the simultaneously desired and hated *Rebecca*, for example, seems uncannily close to Freud's description of the girl's relationship with her mother, desired, loathed, disparaged and repressed. Equally, Freud's remarks about the ways in which adult women may marry a man as a substitute for their father, but replicate their covertly aggressive and hostile relationship with their mother in that marriage seems reminiscent of the narrator's troubled relationship with Maxim, haunted as it is by the narrator's fantasy Rebecca. Viewed through a Freudian lens, *Rebecca* appears a complicated psychological study of anxieties and hostilities inherent within adult female sexuality, possibly accounting for its well-attested ability to continue to 'haunt' its popular female readership.

Freud, S., 'Female Sexuality', in *On Sexuality: Three Essays on the Theory of Sexuality and Other Works*, ed. by J. Strachey, Penguin Freud Library, vol. 7, Harmondsworth: Penguin, 1991, pp. 371–8, 380–3

I

During the phase of the normal Oedipus complex we find the child tenderly attached to the parent of the opposite sex, while its relation to the parent of its own sex is predominantly hostile. In the case of a boy there is no difficulty in explaining this. His first love-object was his mother. She remains so; and, with the strengthening of his erotic desires and his deeper insight into the relations between his father and mother, the former is bound to become his rival. With the small girl it is different. Her first object, too, was her mother. How does she find her way to her father? How, when and why does she detach herself from her mother?

[. . .]

But it now seems to us that there is a second change of the same sort which is no less characteristic and important for the development of the female: the exchange of her original object – her mother – for her father.

[. . .]

It is well known that there are many women who have a strong attachment to their father . . . where the woman's attachment to her father was particularly intense, analysis showed that it had been preceded by a phase of exclusive attachment to her mother which had been equally intense and passionate. Except for the change of her love-object, the second phase had scarcely added any new feature to her erotic life. Her primary relation to her mother had been built up in a very rich and many-sided manner. The second fact taught me that the *duration* of this attachment had also been greatly underestimated. In several cases it lasted until well into the fourth year – in one case into the fifth year – so that it covered by far the longer part of the period of early sexual efflorescence. Indeed, we had to reckon with the possibility that a number of women remain arrested in their original attachment to their mother and never achieve a true change-over towards men. This being so, the pre-Oedipus phase in women gains an importance which we have not attributed to it hitherto.

[. . .]

Our insight into this early, pre-Oedipus, phase in girls comes to us as a surprise, like the discovery, in another field, of the Minoan–Mycenaean civilization behind the civilization of Greece.

Everything in the sphere of this first attachment to the mother seemed to me so difficult to grasp in analysis – so grey with age and shadowy and almost impossible to revivify – that it was as if it had succumbed to an especially inexorable repression. But perhaps I gained this impression because the women who were in analysis with me were able to cling to the very attachment to the father in which they hat taken refuge from the early phase that was in question.

[. . .]

I shall . . . confine myself to reporting the most general findings and shall give only a few examples of the new ideas which I have arrived at. Among these is a suspicion that this phase of attachment to the mother is especially intimately related to the aetiology of hysteria, which is not surprising when we reflect that both the phase and the neurosis are characteristically feminine, and further, that in this dependence on the mother we have the germ of later paranoia in women. For this germ appears to be the prising, yet regular, fear of being killed (? devoured) by the mother. It is plausible to assume that this fear corresponds to a hostility which develops in the child towards her mother in consequence of the manifold restrictions imposed by the latter in the course of training and bodily care.

[. . .]

First of all, there can be no doubt that the bisexuality, which is present, as we believe, in the innate disposition of human beings comes to the fore much more clearly in women than in men.

[. . .]

In the case of a male, his mother becomes his first love-object as a result of her feeding him and looking after him, and she remains so until she is replaced by someone who resembles her or is derived from her. A female's first object, too, must be her mother: the primary conditions for a choice of object are, of course, the same for all children. But at the end of her development, her father – a man – should have become her new love-object. In other words, to the change in her own sex there must correspond a change in the sex of her object. The new problems that now require investigating are in what way this change takes place, how radically or how incompletely it is carried out, and what the different possibilities are which present themselves in the course of this development.

We have already learned, too, that there is yet another difference between the sexes, which relates to the Oedipus complex.

[. . .]

It is only in the male child that we find the fateful combination of love for the one parent and simultaneous hatred for the other as a rival. In his case it is the discovery of the possibility of castration, as proved by the sight of the female genitals, which forces on him the transformation of his Oedipus complex, and which leads to the creation of his super-ego and thus initiates all the processes that are designed to make the individual find a place in the cultural community. After the paternal agency has been internalized and become a super-ego, the next task is to detach the latter from the figures of whom it was originally the psychical representative. In this remarkable course of development it is precisely the baby's narcissistic interest in his genitals – his interest in preserving his penis – which is turned round into a curtailing of his infantile sexuality.

165

One thing that is left over in men from the influence of the Oedipus complex is a certain amount of disparagement in their attitude towards women, whom they regard as being castrated. In extreme cases this gives rise to an inhibition in their choice of object, and, if it is supported by organic factors, to exclusive homosexuality.

Quite different are the effects of the castration complex in the female. She acknowledges the fact of her castration, and with it, too, the superiority of the male and her own inferiority; but she rebels against this unwelcome state of affairs. From this divided attitude three lines of development open up. The first leads to a general revulsion from sexuality. The little girl, frightened by the comparison with boys, grows dissatisfied with her clitoris, and gives up her phallic activity and with it her sexuality in general as well as a good part of her masculinity in other fields. The second line leads her to cling with defiant self-assertiveness to her threatened masculinity. To an incredibly late age she clings to the hope of getting a penis some time. That hope becomes her life's aim; and the phantasy of being a man in spite of everything often persists as a formative factor over long periods. This 'masculinity complex' in women can also result in a manifest homosexual choice of object. Only if her development follows the third, very circuitous, path does she reach the final normal female attitude, in which she takes her father as her object and so finds her way to the feminine form of the Oedipus complex. Thus in women the Oedipus complex is the end result of a fairly lengthy development. It is not destroyed, but created, by the influence of castration; it escapes the strongly hostile influences which, in the male, have a destructive effect on it, and indeed it is all too often not surmounted by the female at all. For this reason, too, the cultural consequences of its break-up are smaller and of less importance in her. We should probably not be wrong in saying that it is this difference in the reciprocal relation between the Oedipus and the castration complex which gives its special stamp to the character of females as social beings.

We see, then, that the phase of exclusive attachment to the mother, which may be called the *pre-Oedipus* phase, possesses a far greater importance in women than it can have in men. Many phenomena of female sexual life which were not properly understood before can be fully explained by reference to this phase. Long ago, for instance, we noticed that many women who have chosen their husband on the model of their father, or have put him in their father's place, nevertheless repeat towards him, in their married life, their bad relations with their mother. The husband of such a woman was meant to be the inheritor of her relation to her father, but in reality he became the inheritor of her relation to her mother. This is easily explained as an obvious case of regression. Her relation to her mother was the original one, and her attachment to her father was built up on it, and now, in marriage, . . . the original relation emerges from repression. For the main content of her development to womanhood lay in the carrying over of her affective object attachments from her mother to her father.

With many women we have the impression that their years of maturity are occupied by a struggle with their husband, just as their youth was spent in a struggle with their mother. In the light of the previous discussions we shall conclude that their hostile attitude to their mother is not a consequence of the rivalry implicit in the Oedipus complex, but originates from the preceding phase and has merely been reinforced and exploited in the Oedipus situation. And actual analytic examination confirms this view. Our interest must be directed to the mechanisms that are at work in her turning away from the mother who was an object so intensely and exclusively loved.

[. . .]

When the little girl discovers her own deficiency, from seeing a male genital, it is only with hesitation and reluctance that she accepts the unwelcome knowledge. As we have seen, she clings obstinately to the expectation of one day having a genital of the same kind too, and her wish for it survives long after her hope has expired. The child invariably regards castration in the first instance as a misfortune peculiar to herself; only later does she realize that it extends to certain other children and lastly to certain grown-ups. When she comes to understand the general nature of this characteristic, it follows that femaleness – and with it, of course, her mother – suffers a great depreciation in her eyes.

[. . .]

However this may be, at the end of this first phase of attachment to the mother, there emerges, as the girl's strongest motive for turning away from her, the reproach that her mother did not give her a proper penis – that is to say, brought her into the world as a female.

[. . .]

When we survey the whole range of motives for turning away from the mother which analysis brings to light – that she failed to provide the little girl with the only proper genital, that she did not feed her sufficiently, that she compelled her to share her mother's love with others, that she never fulfilled all the girl's expectations of love, and, finally, that she first aroused her sexual activity and then forbade it – all these motives seem nevertheless insufficient to justify the girl's final hostility. Some of them follow inevitably from the nature of infantile sexuality; others appear like rationalizations devised later to account for the uncomprehended change in feeling. Perhaps the real fact is that the attachment to the mother is bound to perish, precisely because it was the first and was so intense.

[...]

We shall conclude, then, that the little girl's intense attachment to her mother is strongly ambivalent, and that it is in consequence precisely of this ambivalence that (with the assistance of the other factors we ... have adduced) her attachment is forced away from her mother. ...

THE POETRY OF
FRANK O'HARA AND
ALLEN GINSBERG

32 David Lehman, *The Last Avant-Garde* (1999)

This extract provides a context for understanding what exactly it was that Frank O'Hara and Allen Ginsberg were doing that was new and experimental in American poetry. Lehman explains the role and influence of the New Criticism that supported an academic approach to poetry, and describes the 'anti-academic' counter-view. One of the main distinctions between the two is a disregard for formal technical devices and literary tradition among the anti-academic poets. While many (like O'Hara and Ginsberg) were fully conscious of the weight of poetic convention, they tended to look elsewhere *as well* for inspiration: to blues and jazz music, for instance. Lehman makes useful comparisons between poetry of the Beats and the New York School, while the extract ends with a description of 'orthodox' poetry in the 1950s.

Lehman, D., *The Last Avant-Garde: The Making of the New York School of Poets*, New York: Anchor Books, 1999, pp. 332–5, 337

The New Criticism was committed to the idea that poetry at its most compelling honored complexity, difficulty, ambiguity, and paradox as cardinal virtues. "An ambiguity in ordinary speech means something very pronounced, and as a rule witty or deceitful," William Empson wrote in *Seven Types of Ambiguity*, a central text in the evolution of the New Criticism. He proposed to use *ambiguity* "in an extended sense" embracing "any verbal nuance, however slight, which gives room for alternative reactions to the same piece of language." The examples of textual ambiguity Empson offers imply a scale of values in which multiple meanings enrich the experience of poetry and intellectual complication is preferable to direct statement. As Cleanth Brooks overstated the case in *The Well-Wrought Urn*, "the language of poetry is the language of paradox," and the touchstone by which modern poetry was to be judged was the "well-wrought urn" of John Donne's "The Canonization," from which the poem's lovers will rise from their ashes in the manner of the legendary phoenix bird. The urn "is the poem itself," Brooks wrote, containing Truth and Beauty as did Keats's Grecian urn.

By the canons of the New Criticism, the metaphysical poems of the seventeenth century—poems such as Donne's "The Canonization," Andrew Marvell's "To His Coy Mistress," and George Herbert's "The Sacrifice"— were interpretatively richer than the poems of subsequent centuries. Not that the New Critics' preference for metaphysical poetry was absolute. It was possible to apply New Critical methods to a Romantic poem as seemingly remote from the ideals of paradox and ambiguity as Coleridge's "Dejection: An Ode," in which that poet contemplates the decay of his creative powers, the loss of his "joy." Joy, Coleridge writes in a crucial passage in the ode, "is the spirit and the power, / Which wedding Nature to us gives in dower / A new Earth and new Heaven." The first impression of these lines is that Joy is the parent, Nature the spouse, of the poet. A New Critic could point out, however, that the syntax allows for a different interpretation, according to which Nature is the parent who weds us to Joy. This double sense of Nature is in fact implicit throughout Coleridge's poem, in which it is deliberately left unclear whether Joy, the agency of the imagination, is something external to humanity or is innately present in the human being. I cite this one example to suggest that New Critical methods do have a considerable sphere of application and do render much of the poetry of the past accessible to a modern sensibility. Unfortunately, however, the immediate effect of the New Criticism on practicing poets was not altogether salutary. Robert Lowell is a prime example. As the critic Joseph Epstein put it, "In his early poems, written as if for New Critical analysis, Lowell supplied enough ambiguity to plaster Mona Lisa's smile permanently on the *punim* of William Empson." But the poetic idiom seems worn out, the syntax clotted, the diction artificially inflated.

The conflict between academic and antiacademic poetry that broke out in America in the late 1950s took the form of a ballyhooed battle of influential anthologies. In 1957, *The New Poets of Britain and America* was published. It was jointly edited by Donald Hall, Robert Pack, and Louis Simpson, and it boasted an introduction by Robert Frost. Devoted to poets under the age of forty, the book defined the academic canon of the day. Among the poets included were Donald Davie, Thom Gunn, Geoffrey Hill, and Philip Larkin from Britain, and Anthony Hecht, Donald Justice, Robert Lowell, James Merrill, W. S. Merwin, Howard Nemerov, Adrienne Rich, May Swenson, Richard Wilbur, and James Wright from the United States.

Formal elegance, technical prowess, and literary wit were the virtues on prominent display. The academic cast of the undertaking was implicit from the start. "As I often say a thousand, two thousand, colleges, town and gown together in the little town they make, give us the best audiences for poetry ever had in all this world," Frost wrote in his introduction.

Three years after the appearance of *The New Poets*, Donald Allen's *The New American Poetry* delivered the counterestablishment's counterpunch. Allen's anthology accommodated the exclusions, at least some of them. It embraced the wild beasts of American poetry, which Allen divided into five rough categories: the Beats (such as Allen Ginsberg, Gregory Corso, Jack Kerouac), the Black Mountain poets (Charles Olson, Robert Duncan, Robert Creeley, Denise Levertov), the poets of the San Francisco Renaissance (Lawrence Ferlinghetti, Philip Lamantia), the New York poets (Ashbery, Koch, O'Hara, Schuyler, Barbara Guest), and assorted others who did not fit easily into a ready-made category (LeRoi Jones, Gary Snyder, Philip Whalen, John Wieners). It was a diverse gathering with, Allen observed, 'tone, common characteristic: a total rejection of all those qualities typical of academic verse." The poems didn't rhyme, didn't scan; it wasn't a literary tradition they appealed to but the traditions of the blues, jazz, East Asian mysticism, Judaic chant, and French Surrealism. The poets were, Allen argued, following in the footsteps of Ezra Pound and William Carlos Williams toward the making of poetry in the spoken American idiom. "These poets have already created their own tradition, their own press, and their public," Allen wrote. "They are our avant-garde, the true continuers of the modern movement in American poetry."

The inclusion of Ashbery, Koch, O'Hara, Schuyler and Barbara Guest in this counterestablishment context cemented their reputations as literary outsiders. To the extent that you are known by the company you keep, the anthology situated the New York poets squarely on the side of protest. What did the poets in Donald Allen's anthology have in common? "I thought the common element was interest in [William Carlos] Williams and the vernacular and idiom," Allen Ginsberg remarked in a recorded conversation with Kenneth Koch. "That's what Frank [O'Hara] said, and that's what was the common element between the Beat school, the Projected Verse people, Black Mountain and the New York school and the Northwest's Snyder and Whalen. Everybody had some reference to the transformation of the diction and the rhythms into vernacular rhythms and/or spoken cadences and idiomatic diction."

[. . .]

The influence of Donald Allen's anthology on poets coming of age in the 1960s was tremendous. For them it was clear enough what the Beat poets and the New York School had in common. The two groups formed, as Ginsberg put it, "a united front against the academic poets to promote a vernacular revolution in American poetry beginning with spoken idiom against academic official complicated metaphor that has a logical structure derived from the study of Dante." Here was poetry of a certain intelligence that you didn't need a graduate degree to understand and enjoy. It was wild, rough, and definitely on the side of Walt Whitman in the perennial *Partisan Review* symposia pitting Whitman in the streets versus Henry James in the library as rival exemplars of the literary life. The book had Allen Ginsberg acting stoned in the "neon fruit supermarket," where Whitman lurked amid the bananas and the tomatoes, "poking among the meats in the refrigerator and eyeing the grocery boys." Here, too, were the opening parts of "Howl" and most of "Kaddish," Ginsberg's elegy for his mother, poems that took Whitman's long verse line and fitted it to the "vernacular revolution" ("the voices in the ceiling shrieking out her ugly early lays for 30 years"). . . .

33 Frank O'Hara, Personism: A Manifesto (1961)

O'Hara's mock-manifesto 'Personism' derives from contemporary debates about the nature of poetry. The tone is deliberately comic and irreverent but for all that his purpose is serious: he aimed to puncture the pretension he felt surrounded American poetry at the time. O'Hara argues for a poetic voice that is spontaneous, colloquial and personal. He has no interest in conscious use of stylistic devices, urging instead that 'you should go with your nerve', which is, unsurprisingly, what he does in his own work. This short but complete essay illustrates one poet's response to the notion that poetry is the preserve of a cultural elite. It is useful to read in conjunction with the extract from David Lehman's *The Last Avant-Garde*.

O'Hara, F., 'Personism: A Manifesto', in *The Collected Poems of Frank O'Hara*, ed. by D. Allen, Berkley, Los Angeles and London: University of California Press, 1995, pp. 498–9.

Everything is in the poems, but at the risk of sounding like the poor wealthy man's Allen Ginsberg I will write to you because I just heard that one of my fellow poets thinks that a poem of mine that can't be got at one reading is because I was confused too. Now, come on. I don't believe in god, so I don't have to make elaborately sounded structures. I hate Vachel Lindsay, always have; I don't even like rhythm, assonance, all that stuff. You just go on your nerve. If someone's chasing you down the street with a knife you just run, you don't turn around and shout "Give it up! I was a track star for Mineola Prep."

That's for the writing poems part. As for their reception, suppose you're in love and someone's mistreating (*mal aimé*) you, you don't say, "Hey, you can't hurt me this way, I care!" you just let all the different bodies fall where they may, and they always do may after a few months. But that's not why you fell in love in the first place, just to hang onto life, so you have to take your chances and try to avoid being logical. Pain always produces logic, which is very bad for you.

I'm not saying that I don't have practically the most lofty ideas of anyone writing today, but what difference does that make? They're just ideas. The only good thing about it is that when I get lofty enough I've stopped thinking and that's when refreshment arrives.

But how can you really care if anybody gets it, or gets what it means, or if it improves them. Improves them for what? For death? Why hurry them along? Too many poets act like a middle-aged mother trying to get her kids to eat too much cooked meat, and potatoes with drippings (tears). I don't give a damn whether they eat or not. Forced feeding leads to excessive thinness (effete). Nobody should experience anything they don't need to, if they don't need poetry bully for them. I like the movies too. And after all, only Whitman and Crane and Williams, of the American poets, are better than the movies. As for measure and other technical apparatus, that's just common sense: if you're going to buy a pair of pants you want them to be tight enough so everyone will want to go to bed with you. There's nothing metaphysical about it. Unless, of course, you flatter yourself into thinking that what you're experiencing is "yearning."

Abstraction in poetry, which Allen [Ginsberg] recently commented on in *It Is*, is intriguing. I think it appears mostly in the minute particulars where decision is necessary. Abstraction (in poetry, not in painting) involves personal removal by the poet. For instance, the decision involved in the choice between "the nostalgia *of* the infinite" and "the nostalgia *for* the infinite" defines an attitude towards degree of abstraction. The nostalgia *of* the infinite representing the greater degree of abstraction, removal, and negative capability (as in Keats and Mallarmé). Personism, a movement which I recently founded and which nobody knows about, interests me a great deal, being so totally opposed to this kind of abstract removal that it is verging on a true abstraction for the first time, really, in the history of poetry. Personism is to Wallace Stevens what *la poésie pure* was to Béranger. Personism has nothing to do with philosophy, it's all art. It does not have to do with personality or intimacy, far from it! But to give you a vague idea, one of its minimal aspects is to address itself to one person (other than the poet himself), thus evoking overtones of love without destroying love's life-giving vulgarity, and sustaining the poet's feelings towards the poem while preventing love from distracting him into feeling about the person. That's part of Personism. It was founded by me after lunch with LeRoi Jones on August 27, 1959, a day in which I was in love with someone (not Roi, by the way, a blond). I went back to work and wrote a poem for this person. While I was writing it I was realizing that if I wanted to I could use the telephone instead of writing the poem, and so Personism was born. It's a very exciting movement which will undoubtedly have lots of adherents. It puts the poem squarely between the poet and the person, Lucky Pierre style, and the poem is correspondingly gratified. The poem is at last between two persons instead of two pages: In all modesty, I confess that it may be the death of literature as we know it. While I have certain regrets, I am still glad I got there before Alain Robbe-Grillet did. Poetry being quicker and surer than prose, it is only just that poetry finished literature off. For a time people thought that Artaud was going to accomplish this, but actually, for all their magnificence, his polemical writings are not more outside literature than Bear Mountain is outside New York State. His relation is no more astounding than Dubuffet's to painting.

What can we expect of Personism? (This is getting good, isn't it?) Everything, but we won't get it. It is too new, too vital a movement to promise anything. But it, like Africa, is on the way. The recent propagandists for technique on the one hand, and for content on the other, had better watch out.

34 Jim Elledge, Never Argue with the Movies: Love and the Cinema in the Poetry of Frank O'Hara (1990)

In this essay, Elledge offers a general survey of the importance of the cinema in O'Hara's poetry, and goes on to offer detailed readings of particular poems. This extract includes his discussion of 'Ave Maria' and 'Fantasy'. 'Ave Maria' is about the experience of going to the cinema, while 'Fantasy' relies on the adventure movie *Northern Pursuit* (1943). The extract shows different ways in which O'Hara values popular culture and absorbs it into his work.

Elledge, J., 'Never Argue with the Movies: Love and the Cinema in the Poetry of Frank O'Hara', in *Frank O'Hara: To Be True to a City*, Ann Arbor: University of Michigan Press, 1990, pp. 350–2, 355–7

No poetry has been more influenced by the movies than Frank O'Hara's. Many critics have noted that O'Hara employed cinematic technique throughout his work, pointing out, as Marjorie Perloff has, that his images "move, dissolve, cut into something else, fade in or out" as scenes in films do.[1] Others, such as James Breslin, view O'Hara's consciousness as "moving, taking in things . . . with the speed and precision of a movie camera."[2] However, O'Hara's use of film goes beyond technique *per se*.

In his long poem "Ode to Michael Goldberg ('s Birth and Other Births)," O'Hara recalls his initial meeting with the silver screen one "sweet-smelling summer" of his youth,[3] and in "To the Film Industry in Crisis" (pp. 232–33), he admits that it is not haut culture—neither "lean quarterlies and swarthy periodicals," "experimental theatre," nor "promenading Grand Opera"—that is important to his life. Rather, in a half-humorous, half-serious apostrophe to the silver screen of his youth, he confesses, "Motion Picture Industry, / it's you I love!"

Fifty-four poems in O'Hara's *Collected Poems* rely on film in varying degrees. Some only allude swiftly and pointedly to scenes or plots, quote snatches of dialogue, or mention actors. Others refer to specific films or make offhand comments about movies in general, which often simply lend poems verisimilitude. In a substantial number of poems, however, O'Hara incorporated film in central, if not primary, roles, illustrating or fortifying major points or suggesting themes, especially about love. The films O'Hara relies upon are decidedly romantic, presenting a fantasy of how love triumphs over any trial and how lovers thus gain a virtual paradise on earth. While such a paradise is, in O'Hara's view, impossible in actuality, it may exist for each of us in our fantasies. In his film-oriented poems, such as "Ave Maria," "Four Little Elegies," and "Fantasy," the homosexual O'Hara ironically chose a decidedly heterosexual medium by which to investigate love, focusing on its transitory nature and on our desire, even need, to believe in the possibility of its permanence, while knowing better.

"Ave Maria" (*CP*, pp. 371–72) opens with humorous advice, one of O'Hara's best wisecracks: "Mothers of America / let your kids go to the movies!" O'Hara's humor continues throughout the poem as he reveals two distinct possibilities of love facing the "kids" if their mothers take O'Hara's advice. The first, romance (or fantasy), is represented by the film played on the movie screen. Because it is a filmed version of love, thus able to be rerun and experienced over and over exactly as the first time, it is permanent. The second, actual (or sexual) love, is what occurs off-screen, and because it is actual, it is temporary, experienced differently each time. O'Hara gives two reasons for his advice: because "the soul / . . . grows in darkness, embossed by [the] silvery images" film offers and because the theater may give "the little tykes" the actual opportunity to meet someone with whom to have "their first sexual experience." O'Hara identifies the potential sexual partner not as another teenager, but as someone older, "a pleasant stranger whose apartment is in the Heaven on Earth Bldg / near the Williamsburg Bridge."

O'Hara does not present the potential sexual relationship of adult and child negatively, but humorously, and views it as a means for the child's maturation. The teen whom the stranger approaches will discover an important fact of actual love, preparing him for adulthood: love is never free but exacts a price. The child, as O'Hara, tongue in cheek, puts it, "will know where candy bars come from / and *gratuitous* bags of popcorn" (italics added)—not simply from the lobby candy counter, but from the stranger whose seemingly free gifts of candy and popcorn are actually barter for the child's "first sexual experience."

O'Hara never insists on the adult–child union but offers it only as a possibility. In fact, the poem continues with an alternative: "if nobody does pick them up in the movies / they won't know the difference / . . . / and they'll have been truly entertained either way." If no actual love is found at the movies, then the romantic variety is still available to "the little tykes" on the screen, where boy meets girl, boy loses girl, boy wins girl back, and together they live happily ever after. Such love also offers the "tykes" a context in which "the soul / . . . grows." Not realistic, as is the relationship "with a pleasant stranger," it offers them an ideal, one that is perhaps unattainable, one to experience perhaps only vicariously, but one which offers a model, if nothing else, by which to measure any future, actual love.

For O'Hara, then, film is itself reason enough to attend and anything gained above and beyond its "silvery images," such as love "with a pleasant stranger," is "sheer gravy." In the poem's coy conclusion, O'Hara lists the alternative faced by mothers who do not allow their "little tykes" to "go to the movies": "don't blame me if you won't take this advice / and the family breaks up / and your children grow old and blind in front of a TV set / seeing / movies you wouldn't let them see when they were young."

[. . .]

In "Ave Maria," O'Hara was a film buff offering advice; in "Four Little Elegies" he was film director/writer/producer, but in "Fantasy" (*CP*, p. 488), O'Hara is "*actor*." At home, O'Hara drifts in and out of reality, in turn speaking to an ailing Allen Ginsberg, who never responds to him, and fantasizing himself into a role in the 1943 anti-Nazi romance/adventure film *Northern Pursuit*. The film contains a romance between Royal Mounted Policeman Steve Wagner (Errol Flynn) and Laura McBain (Julie Bishop) interrupted, and very nearly destroyed, by the evil Nazi flier/spy Hugo von Keller (Helmut Dantine). The hero triumphs, of course, and he and his beloved live happily ever after in a "glamorous country" Warner Brothers constructed.

"Fantasy" opens with O'Hara perched on a window sill, claiming to Ginsberg that he likes "the music of Adolph / Deutsch . . . / better than Max Steiner's," who wrote the *Northern Pursuit* score. As O'Hara begins to expound on its "Helmut Dantine theme," the window drops on his hand, pain sending him into his film role:

> Errol
> Flynn was skiing by. Down
>   down down went the grim
> grey submarine under the "cold" ice.
>   Helmut was
> safely ashore, on the ice.

O'Hara fantasizes being a character a second time after yelling to Ginsberg, "Allen come out of the bathroom / and take it," referring to a concoction of "two aspirins a vitamin C tablet and some baking soda" O'Hara has mixed for Ginsberg and calls "practically an / Alka / Seltzer." The second experience triggering O'Hara's flight into fantasy is unsavory, although not painful to him—Ginsberg's unidentified illness. His fantasy recounts hardships O'Hara faces in *Northern Pursuit*, but filtered through his pop/camp sensibility, they are more reminiscent of Marx Brothers slapstick than Errol Flynn romance/adventure:

> I think someone put butter on my skis instead
> of wax.
>   Ouch. The leanto is falling over in the
> firs, and there is another fatter spy here. They
> didn't tell me they sent
>   him. Well, that takes care
> of him, boy were those huskies hungry.

In this scene, O'Hara is decidedly not the film's hero, but perhaps a side-kick who, despite himself, rises to heroic proportion. Although O'Hara is unsteady on his skis, he is able to take care of the "fatter spy" on his own while Flynn is, presumably, taking care of Dantine. In the process he helps Flynn guarantee "that Canada," and by extension all of the Western Hemisphere, "will remain / free. Just free, that's all. . . ."

Between the two fantasies, however, O'Hara expounds on film as art. He suggests that its "silvery images" and "glamorous country" provide audiences with "dreams ... incredible / fantasies," and he asserts, "The main thing" for film to do "is to tell a story. / It is almost / very important." The story is the ideal, the romance, the fantasy—what holds viewers' attention, keeps them paying "a quarter" for admission, and enables them to recall at will the film in time of need. The "dreams" and "fantasies" film incites are the added attraction of the movies, which for "little tykes" and adults alike is "sheer gravy."

Film, then, provides us with the possibility for an ideal or perfect situation which, in O'Hara, is always related to love. Without it, ideal love is possible only "in / the heavens" and life is simply an uninterrupted continuum of pain. It also provides us with a means by which, ironically, we learn about reality, from which we receive solace for actual pain, and which is, if nothing else, simply entertaining. Film, in O'Hara's vision of the world, is the authority by which we may attempt to live our lives, similar in that respect to the "starched nurse," the "Catholic Church," and the "American Legion" mentioned in "To the Film Industry in Crisis" which, in one way or another, also teach, console, or even entertain. However, it is the "glorious Silver Screen, tragic Technicolor, amorous Cinemascope, / stretching Vistavision and startling Stereophonic Sound"—in short, film—which O'Hara loves because film is perfect, and because it is perfect, and life not, O'Hara concludes "Fantasy" as he had opened "Ave Maria," offering advice which we, always "the little tykes" no matter what our age, would do well to accept: "never argue with the movies."

Notes

1 Marjorie G. Perloff, 'New Thresholds, Old Anatomies: Contemporary Poetry and the Limits of Exegesis,' *Iowa Review*, 5 (1974), 97.

2 James Breslin, 'The Contradictions of Frank O'Hara,' *American Poetry Review*, November/December 1983, p. 7.

3 Frank O'Hara, 'Ode to Michael Goldberg ('s Birth and Other Births),' in *Collected Poems*, ed. Donald Allen (New York: Knopf, 1971), pp. 290–8. All poems by O'Hara quoted in this essay may be found in this edition, which will be cited hereafter as *CP* and followed by relevant page numbers.

35 John Storey, Mass Culture in America: The Post-War Debate (2000)

This extract from John Storey's book, *Cultural Theory and Popular Culture*, provides an overview of academic debates about the nature and role of popular culture in American in the 1950s. It is particularly relevant to the material on Frank O'Hara, a poet entirely comfortable in the new capitalist-consumerist society but who is equally happy with high culture. Evidence of both appears in his work with no concessions to readers' knowledge of classical music, art history, or the cinema. Allen Ginsberg's position is different: capitalism is anathema to him. However, his poetry is spontaneous and experimental, like O'Hara's, and he did a great deal to popularise the genre among the younger generation.

Storey, J., 'Mass Culture in America: The Post-War Debate', in *Cultural Theory and Popular Culture: An Introduction*, London: Prentice Hall, 2000 (3rd edn), pp. 28–33

In the first fifteen or so years following the end of the Second World War, American intellectuals engaged in a debate about so-called mass culture. Andrew Ross sees 'mass' as 'one of the key terms that governs the official distinction between American/UnAmerican'. He argues that, 'The history behind this official distinction is in many ways the history of the formation of the modern national culture.' Following the Second World War, America experienced the temporary success of a cultural and political consensus – supposedly based on liberalism, pluralism and classlessness. Until its collapse in the agitation for black civil rights, the formation of the counterculture, the opposition to America's war in Vietnam, the women's liberation movement, and the campaign for gay and lesbian rights, it was a consensus dependent to a large extent on the cultural authority of American intellectuals. As Ross points out, 'For perhaps the first time in American history, intellectuals, as a social grouping, had the opportunity to recognize themselves as national agents of cultural, moral, and political leadership.' This newly found significance was in part due to 'the intense and quite public, debate about "mass culture" that occupied intellectuals for almost fifteen years, until the late fifties'. Ross spends most of his time relating the debate to the Cold War ideology of 'containment': the need to maintain a healthy body politic both within (from the dangers of cultural impoverishment) and without (from the dangers of Soviet communism). He identifies three positions in the debate:

1. An aesthetic–liberal position which bemoans the fact that given the choice the majority of the population choose so-called second- and

third-rate cultural texts and practices in preference to the texts and practices of high culture;

2. The corporate–liberal or progressive–evolutionist position which claims that popular culture serves a benign function of socializing people into the pleasures of consumption in the new capitalist–consumerist society;

3. The radical or socialist position which views mass culture as a form of, or means to, social control.

As the 1950s wore on, the debate became increasingly dominated by the first two positions. This reflected in part the growing McCarthyite pressure to renounce anything resembling a socialist analysis.

Given limited space, I will focus only on the debate about the health of the body politic within. In order to understand the debate one publication is essential reading, the anthology *Mass Culture: The Popular Arts in America*, published in 1957. Reading the many contributions, one quickly gets a sense of the parameters of the debate – what is at stake in the debate, and who are the principal participants. Bernard Rosenberg (co-editor with David Manning White) argues that the material wealth and well-being of American society are being undermined by the dehumanizing effects of mass culture. His greatest anxiety is that, 'At worst, mass culture threatens not merely to cretinize our taste, but to brutalize our senses while paving the way to totalitarianism.' He claims that mass culture is not American by nature, or by example, nor is it the inevitable culture of democracy. Mass culture, according to Rosenberg, is nowhere more widespread than in the Soviet Union. Its author is not capitalism, but technology. Therefore America cannot be held responsible for its emergence or for its persistence. White makes a similar point but for a different purpose. 'The critics of mass culture', White observes, 'take an exceedingly dim view of contemporary American society.' His defence of American (mass) culture is to compare it with aspects of the popular culture of the past. He maintains that critics romanticize the past in order to castigate the present. He condemns those 'who discuss American culture as if they were holding a dead vermin in their hands', and yet forget the sadistic and brutal reality of animal baiting that was the everyday culture in which Shakespeare's plays first appeared. His point is that every period in history has produced 'men who preyed upon the ignorance and insecurities of the largest part of the populace . . . and therefore we need not be so shocked that such men exist today'. The second part of his defence consists of cataloguing the extent to which high culture flourishes in America: for example, Shakespeare on TV, record figures for book borrowing from libraries, a successful tour by the Sadler's Wells ballet, the fact that more people attend classical music events than attend baseball games, the increasing number of symphony orchestras.

A key figure in the debate is Dwight Macdonald. In a very influential essay, 'A theory of mass culture', he attacks mass culture on a number of fronts. First of all, mass culture undermines the vitality of high culture. It is a parasitic culture; feeding on high culture, while offering nothing in return.

> Folk art grew from below. It was a spontaneous, autochthonous expression of the people, shaped by themselves, pretty much without the benefit of High Culture, to suit their own needs. Mass Culture is imposed from above. It is fabricated by technicians hired by businessmen; its audience are passive consumers, their participation limited to the choice between buying and not buying. The Lords of kitsch, in short, exploit the cultural needs of the masses in order to make a profit and/or to maintain their class-rule . . . in Communist countries, only the second purpose obtains. Folk art was the people's own institution, their private little garden walled off from the great formal park of their masters' High Culture. But Mass Culture breaks down the wall, integrating the masses into a debased form of High Culture and thus becoming an instrument of political domination.

Like other contributors to the debate, Macdonald is quick to deny the claim that America is the land of mass culture: 'the fact is that the U.S.S.R. is even more a land of Mass Culture than is the U.S.A.' This fact, he claims, is often missed by critics who focus only on the 'form' of mass culture in the Soviet Union. But it is mass culture (not folk culture: the expression of the people; nor high culture: the expression of the individual artist); and it differs from American mass culture in that 'its quality is even lower', and in that 'it exploits rather than satisfies the cultural needs of the masses . . . for political rather than commercial reasons'. In spite of its superiority to Soviet mass culture, American mass culture still represents a problem ('acute in the United States'): 'The eruption of the masses onto the political stage [produced] . . . disastrous cultural results.' This problem has been compounded by the absence of 'a clearly defined cultural elite'. If one existed, the masses could have mass culture and the elite could have high culture. However, without a cultural elite, America is under threat from a Gresham's Law of culture: the bad will drive out the good; the result will be not just a homogeneous culture but a 'homogenized culture . . . that threatens to engulf everything in its spreading ooze', dispersing the cream from the top and turning the American people into infantile masses. His conclusions are pessimistic to say the least: 'far from Mass Culture getting better, we will be lucky if it doesn't get worse'.

The analysis changes again as we move from the disillusioned ex-Trotskyism of Macdonald to the optimistic liberalism of Gilbert Seldes. Although Seldes shares some of Macdonald's distaste for mass culture, he blames the producers of mass culture for underestimating the cultural tastes of the American public. Ernest van den Haag suggests that in some ways this is inevitable; it is in the nature of mass production:

> The mass produced article need not aim low, but it must aim at an average of tastes. In satisfying all (or at least many) individual tastes in some respects, it violates each in other respects. For there are so far no average persons having average tastes. Averages are but statistical composites. A mass produced article, while reflecting nearly everybody's taste to some extent, is unlikely to embody anybody's taste fully. This is one source of the sense of violation which is rationalized vaguely in theories about deliberate debasement of taste.

He also suggests another reason: the temptations offered by mass culture to high culture. Two factors must be particularly tempting: (1) the financial rewards of mass culture, and (2) the potentially enormous audience. He uses Dante as an illustration. Although Dante may have suffered religious and political pressures, he was not tempted to shape his work to make it appeal to an average of tastes. Had he been 'tempted to write for *Sports Illustrated*' or had he been asked 'to condense his work for *Reader's Digest*' or had he been given a contract 'to adapt it for the movies', would he have been able to maintain his aesthetic and moral standards? Dante was fortunate; his talent was never really tempted to stray from the true path of creativity: 'there were no alternatives to being as good a writer as his talent permitted'.

It is not so much that mass taste has deteriorated; van den Haag argues, but that mass taste has become more important to the cultural producers in Western societies. Like White, he notes the plurality of cultural texts and practices consumed in America. However, he also notes the way in which high culture and folk culture are absorbed into mass culture, and are consequently consumed as mass culture: 'it is not new nor disastrous that few people read classics. It is new that so many people misread them.' He cannot help in the end declaring that mass culture is a drug which 'lessens people's capacity to experience life itself'. Mass culture is ultimately a sign of impoverishment. It marks the de-individualization of life; an endless search after what Freud calls 'substitute gratifications' (Freud is referring to all art, and not just popular culture); what Leavis refers to as 'substitute living'. The trouble with substitute gratifications, according to the mass culture critique, is that they shut out 'real gratifications'. This leads van den Haag to suggest that the consumption of mass culture is a form of repression; the empty texts and practices of mass culture are consumed to fill an emptiness within, which grows ever more empty the more the empty texts and practices of mass culture are consumed. The operation of this cycle of repression makes it increasingly impossible to experience 'real gratification'. The result is a nightmare in which the cultural 'masturbator' or the 'addict' of mass culture is trapped in a cycle of non-fulfilment, moving aimlessly between boredom and distraction:

> Though the bored person hungers for things to happen to him, the disheartening fact is that when they do he empties them of the very meaning he unconsciously yearns for by using them as distractions. In popular culture even the second coming would become just another 'barren' thrill to be watched on television till Milton Berle comes on.

Van den Haag differs from the 'cultural nostalgics', who use romanticized versions of the past to condemn the present, in his uncertainty about the past. He knows that 'popular culture impoverishes life without leading to contentment. But whether "the mass of men" felt better or worse without mass production techniques of which popular culture is an ineluctable part, we shall never know.' Edward Shils has none of van den Haag's uncertainty. Moreover, he knows that when van den Haag says that industry has impoverished life he is talking nonsense:

> The present pleasures of the working and lower middle class are not worthy of profound aesthetic, moral or intellectual esteem but they are surely not inferior to the villainous things which gave pleasure to their European ancestors from the Middle Ages to the nineteenth century.

Shils rejects completely

> the utterly erroneous idea that the twentieth century is a period of severe intellectual deterioration and that this alleged deterioration is a product of a mass culture. . . . Indeed, it would be far more

correct to assert that mass culture is now less damaging to the lower classes than the dismal and harsh existence of earlier centuries had ever been.

As far as Shils can see the problem is not mass culture, but the response of intellectuals to mass culture. In similar fashion, D. W. Brogan, whilst in agreement with much of Macdonald's argument, remains more optimistic. He believes that Macdonald in being 'so grimly critical of the present America, is too kind to the past in America and to the past and present in Europe'. In this way, Macdonald's pessimism about the present is only sustained by his overly optimistic view of the past. In short, he 'exaggerates . . . the bad eminence of the United States'.

In 'The middle against both ends', Leslie Fiedler, unlike most other contributors to the debate, claims that mass culture

> is a peculiarly American phenomenon. . . . I do not mean . . . that it is found only in the United States, but that wherever it is found, it comes first from us, and is still to be discovered in fully developed form only among us. Our experience along these lines is, in this sense, a preview for the rest of the world of what must follow the inevitable dissolution of the older aristocratic cultures.

For Fiedler, mass culture is popular culture which 'refuses to know its place'. As he explains,

> contemporary vulgar culture is brutal and disturbing: the quasi spontaneous expression of the uprooted and culturally dispossessed inhabitants of anonymous cities, contriving mythologies which reduce to manageable form the threat of science, the horror of unlimited war, the general spread of corruption in a world where the social bases of old loyalties and heroisms have long been destroyed.

Fiedler poses the question: What is wrong with American mass culture? He knows that for some critics, at home and abroad; the fact that it is American is enough reason to condemn it. But, for Fiedler, the inevitability of the American experience makes the argument meaningless; that is, unless those who support the argument are also against industrialization, mass education and democracy. He sees America 'in the midst of a strange two-front class war'. In the centre is 'the genteel middling mind', at the top is 'the ironical-aristocratic sensibility', and at the bottom is 'the brutal-populist mentality'. The attack on popular culture is a symptom of timidity and an expression of conformity in matters of culture: 'the fear of the vulgar is the obverse of the fear of excellence, and both are aspects of the fear of difference: symptoms of a drive for conformity on the level of the timid, sentimental, mindless-bodiless genteel'. The genteel-middling mind wants cultural equality on its own terms. This is not the Leavisite demand for cultural deference, but an insistence on an end to cultural difference. Therefore, Fiedler sees American mass culture as hierarchical and pluralist, rather than homogenized and levelling. Moreover, he celebrates it as such.

Shils suggests a similar model – American culture is divided into three cultural 'classes', each embodying different versions of the cultural: '"superior" or "refined" culture' at the top, '"mediocre" culture' in the middle, and '"brutal" culture' at the bottom. Mass society has changed the cultural map, reducing the significance of 'superior or refined culture', and increasing the importance of both 'mediocre' and 'brutal'. However, Shils does not see this as a totally negative development: 'It is an indication of a crude aesthetic awakening in classes which previously accepted what was handed down to them or who had practically no aesthetic expression and reception.' Like Fiedler, Shils does not shy away from the claim that America is the home of mass culture. He calls America 'that most massive of all mass societies'. But he remains optimistic: 'As a matter of fact, the vitality, the individuality, which may rehabilitate our intellectual public will probably be the fruits of the liberation of powers and possibilities inherent in mass societies.' As Ross suggests, in Fiedler's essay, and in the work of other writers in the 1950s and early 1960s,

> the concept of 'class' makes a conditional return after its years in the intellectual wilderness. This time, however, class analysis returns not to draw attention to conflicts and contradictions, as had been the case in the thirties, but rather to serve a hegemonic moment in which a consensus was being established about the non antagonistic coexistence of different political conceptions of the world. Cultural classes could exist as long as they kept themselves to themselves.

Cultural choice and consumption become both the sign of class belonging and the mark of class difference. However, instead of class antagonism, there is only plurality of consumer choice within a general consensus of the dangers within and the dangers without. In short, the debate about mass culture had become the terrain on which to construct the Cold War ideology of containment. After all, as Melvin Tumin points out, 'America and Americans have available to them the resources, both of mind and matter, to build and support the finest culture the world has ever known.' The fact that this has

185

not yet occurred does not dismay Tumin; for him it simply prompts the question: How do we make it happen? For the answer, he looks to American intellectuals, who 'never before have . . . been so well placed in situations where they can function as intellectuals', and through the debate on mass culture, to take the lead in helping to build the finest *popular culture* the world has ever known.

PHILIP K. DICK,
DO ANDROIDS DREAM OF
ELECTRIC SHEEP?

36 Darko Suvin, Cognition and Estrangement (1979)

Darko Suvin was born in the former Yugoslavia in 1932 but taught at McGill University in Montreal, Canada, from 1968. As well as being a Brecht scholar, Suvin was the first significant *theorist* of science fiction and one of the founders of the journal *Science Fiction Studies*, which first appeared in 1973. 'Cognition and Estrangement' originally appeared in *College English* and *Foundation: The Review of Science Fiction*. This extract is taken from the version in his book *Metamorphoses of Science Fiction* (1979). The book outlines a theoretical approach to science fiction but focuses largely on texts which are not part of the generic or pulp science fiction tradition – he is often discussing what would now be called proto-science fiction from prior to the twentieth century, including Thomas More, Francis Bacon, Jonathan Swift, Jules Verne and H. G. Wells. In part the extract attempts to isolate proto-science fiction and science fiction from the wider literary uses of fantasy and the imagination. Suvin's definition of science fiction as a literature of cognitive estrangement is still used and debated by critics and theorists.

Suvin, D., 'Cognition and Estrangement', in *Metamorphoses of Science Fiction*, New Haven: Yale University Press, 1979, pp. 3–5, 5–7, 7–8, 9–10, 14–15

1 Science fiction as fiction (estrangement)

1.1. The importance of science fiction (SF) in our time is on the increase. First, there are strong indications that its popularity in the leading industrial nations (United States, USSR, United Kingdom, Japan) has risen sharply over the last 100 years, despite all the local and short-range fluctuations. SF has particularly affected such key strata or groups of modem society as college graduates, young writers, and the avant-garde of general readers appreciative of new sets of values. This is a significant cultural effect which goes beyond any merely quantitative census. Second, if one takes the minimal generic difference of SF the presence of a narrative novum (the dramatis personae and/or their context) significantly different from what is the norm in "naturalistic" or empiricist fiction, it will be found that SF has an interesting and close kinship with other literary subgenres that flourished at different times and places of literary history: the classical and medieval "fortunate island" story, the "fabulous voyage" story from antiquity on, the Renaissance and Baroque "utopia" and "planetary novel," the Enlightenment "state [political] novel," the modem "anticipation" and "anti-utopia." Moreover, although SF shares with myth, fantasy, fairy tale, and pastoral an opposition to naturalistic or empiricist literary genres, it differs very significantly in approach and social function from such adjoining non-naturalistic or metaempirical genres. Both these complementary aspects, the sociological and the methodological, are being vigorously debated by writers and critics in several countries, evidence of lively interest in a genre that should undergo scholarly discussion too.

In this chapter, I will argue for an understanding of SF as the *literature of cognitive estrangement*. This definition seems to possess the unique advantage of rendering justice to a literary tradition which is coherent through the ages and within itself, yet distinct from nonfictional utopianism, from naturalistic literature, and from other nonnaturalistic fiction. It thus makes it possible to lay the basis for a coherent poetics of SF.

1.2. I want to begin by postulating a spectrum or spread of literary subject matter which extends from the ideal extreme of exact recreation of the author's empirical environment[1] to exclusive interest in a strange newness, a *novum*. From the 18th to the 20th centuries, the literary mainstream of our civilization has been nearer to the first of these two extremes. However, at the beginnings of a literature, the concern with a domestication of the amazing is very strong. Early tale-tellers relate amazing voyages into the next valley, where they found dog-headed people, also good rock salt which could be stolen or at the worst bartered for. Their stories are a syncretic travelogue and *voyage imaginaire*, daydream and intelligence report. This implies a curiosity about the unknown beyond the next mountain range (sea, ocean, solar system), where the thrill of knowledge joined the thrill of adventure.

From Iambulus and Euhemerus through the classical utopia to Verne's island of Captain Nemo and Wells's island of Dr. Moreau, an island in the far-off ocean is the paradigm of the aesthetically most satisfying goal of the

SF voyage. This is particularly true if we subsume under this the planetary island in the aether ocean – usually the Moon – which we encounter from Lucian through Cyrano to Swift's mini-Moon of Laputa, and on into the nineteenth century. Yet the parallel paradigm of the valley, "over the range" (the subtitle of Butler's SF novel *Erewhon*) which shuts it in as a wall, is perhaps as revealing. It recurs almost as frequently, from the earliest folk-tales about the sparkling valley of Terrestrial Paradise and the dark valley of the Dead, both already in *Gilgamesh*. Eden is the mythological localization of utopian longing, just as Wells's valley in "The Country of the Blind" is still within the liberating tradition which contends that the world is not necessarily the way our present empirical valley happens to be, and that whoever thinks his valley is the world is blind. Whether island or valley, whether in space or (from the industrial and bourgeois revolutions on) in time, the new framework is correlative to the new inhabitants. The aliens – utopians, monsters, or simply differing strangers – are a mirror to man just as the differing country is a mirror for his world. But the mirror is not only a reflecting one, it is also a transforming one, virgin womb and alchemical dynamo: the mirror is a crucible.

[. . .]

1.3 The approach to the imaginary locality, or localized day-dream, practiced by the genre of SF is a supposedly factual one. Columbus's (technically or genologically nonfictional) letter on the Eden he glimpsed beyond the Orinoco mouth, and Swift's (technically nonfactual) voyage to Laputa, Balnibarbi, Glubbdubbdrib, Luggnagg, "and Japan" represent two extremes in the constant intermingling of imaginary and empirical possibilities. Thus SF takes off from a fictional ("literary") hypothesis and develops it with totalizing ("scientific") rigor – the specific difference between Columbus and Swift is smaller than their generic proximity. The effect of such factual reporting of fictions is one of confronting a set normative system – a Ptolemaic-type closed world picture – with a point of view or look implying a new set of: norms; in literary theory this is known as the attitude of *estrangement*. This concept was first developed on non-naturalistic texts by the Russian Formalists ("ostranenie," Viktor Shklovsky) and most successfully underpinned by an anthropological and historical approach in the work of Bertolt Brecht, who wanted to write "plays for a scientific age." While working on a play about the prototypical scientist, Galileo, he defined this attitude ("Verfremdungseffekt") in his *Short Organon for the Theatre*: "A representation which estranges is one which allows us to recognize its subject, but at the same time makes it seem unfamiliar." And further: for somebody to see all normal happenings in a dubious light, "he would need to develop that detached eye with which the great Galileo observed a swinging chandelier. He was amazed by that pendulum motion as if he had not expected it and could not understand its occurring, and this enabled him to come at the rules by which it was governed." Thus, the look of estrangement is both cognitive and creative; and as Brecht goes on to say, "one cannot simply exclaim that such an attitude pertains to science, but not to art. Why should not art, in its own way, try to serve the great social task of mastering Life?"[2] (Later, Brecht would note that it might be time to stop speaking in terms of masters and servants altogether.)

In SF the attitude of estrangement – used by Brecht in a different way, within a still predominantly "realistic" context – has grown into the *formal framework* of the genre.

2 Science fiction as cognition (critique and science)

[. . .]

2.2. *SF is, then, a literary genre whose necessary and sufficient conditions are the presence and interaction of estrangement and cognition, and whose main formal device is an imaginative framework alternative to the author's empirical environment.*

Estrangement differentiates SF from the "realistic" literary mainstream extending from the eighteenth century into the twentieth. Cognition differentiates it not only from myth, but also from the folk (fairy) tale and the fantasy. *The folktale* also doubts the laws of the author's empirical world, but it escapes out of its horizons and into a closed collateral world indifferent to cognitive possibilities. It does not use imagination as a means of understanding the tendencies latent in reality, but as an end sufficient unto itself and cut off from the real contingencies. The stock folktale accessory, such as the flying carpet, evades the empirical law of physical gravity – as the hero evades social gravity – by imagining its opposite. This wish-fulfilling element is its strength and its weakness, for it never pretends that a carpet could be expected to fly – that a humble third son could be expected to become king – while there is gravity. It simply posits another world beside yours where some carpets do, magically, fly, and some paupers do, magically, become princes, and into which you cross purely by an act of faith and fancy. Anything is possible in a folktale, because a folktale is manifestly impossible. Furthermore, the lower-class genre of folktale was from the seventeenth-eighteenth centuries on transformed into the more compensatory, and often simplistic, individualist fairy tale. Therefore, SF

190

retrogressing into fairy tale (for example, "space opera" with a hero-princess-monster triangle in astronautic costume) is committing creative suicide.

[. . .]

2.4. Claiming a Galilean estrangement for SF does not at all mean committing it to scientific vulgarization or even technological prognostication, which it was engaged in at various times (Verne, the United States in the 1920s and 30s, USSR under Stalinism). The needful and meritorious task of popularization can be a useful element of SF works at a juvenile level. But even the *roman scientifique*, such as Verne's *From the Earth to the Moon* – or the surface level of Wells's *Invisible Man* – though a legitimate SF form, is a lower stage in its development. It is very popular with audiences just approaching SF, such as the juvenile, because it introduces into the old empirical context only *one* easily digestible new technological variable (Moon missile, or rays which lower the refractive index of organic matter).[3] The euphoria provoked by this approach is real but limited, better suited to the short story and a new audience. It evaporates much quicker as positivistic natural science loses prestige in the humanistic sphere after the world wars (compare Nemo's *Nautilus* as against the United States Navy's atomic submarine of the same name), and surges back with prestigious peacetime applications in new methodologies (astronautics, cybernetics).

[. . .]

2.5. After such delimitations, it is perhaps possible at least to indicate some differentiations within the concept of "cognitiveness" or "cognition." As used here, this term implies not only a reflecting *of* but also *on* reality. It implies a creative approach tending toward a dynamic transformation rather than toward a static mirroring of the author's environment. Such typical SF methodology – from Lucian, More, Rabelais, Cyrano, and Swift to Wells, London, Zamyatin, and writers of the last decades – is a critical one, often satirical, combining a belief in the potentialities of reason with methodical doubt in the most significant cases. The kinship of this cognitive critique with the philosophical fundaments of modern science is evident.

3 The world of the science fiction genre
(concept and some functions)

3.0. As a full-fledged literary genre, SF has its own repertory of functions, conventions, and devices. Many of them are highly interesting and might prove very revealing for literary history and theory in general.

[. . .]

4 For a poetics of science fiction (anticipation)

4.1. The above sketch should, no doubt, be supplemented by a sociological analysis of the "inner environment" of SF, exiled since the beginning of the twentieth century into a reservation or ghetto which was protective and is now constrictive, cutting off new developments from healthy competition and the highest critical standards. Such a sociological discussion would enable us to point out the important differences between the highest reaches of the genre, glanced at here in order to define functions and standards of SF, and its debilitating average.[4]

4.2. If the whole above argumentation is found acceptable, it will be possible to supplement it also by a survey of forms and subgenres. Along with some which recur in an updated form – such as the utopia and fabulous voyage – the anticipation, the superman story, the artificial intelligence story (robots, androids, and so on), time-travel, catastrophe, the meeting with aliens, and others, would have to be analyzed. The various forms and subgenres of SF could then be checked for their relationships to other literary genres, to each other, and to various sciences. For example, the utopias are – whatever else they may be – clearly sociological fictions or social-science-fiction, whereas modern SF is analogous to modern polycentric cosmology, uniting time and space in Einsteinian worlds with different but covariant dimensions and time scales. Significant modern SF, with deeper and more lasting sources of enjoyment, also presupposes more complex and wider cognitions: it discusses primarily the political, psychological, and anthropological *use and effect of knowledge, of philosophy of science*, and the becoming of failure of new realities as a result of it. The consistency of extrapolation, precision of analogy, and width of reference in such a cognitive discussion turn into aesthetic factors. . . . Once the elastic criteria of literary structuring have been met, *a cognitive – in most cases strictly scientific element – becomes a measure of aesthetic quality, of the specific pleasure to be sought in SF*. In other words, the cognitive nucleus of the plot codetermines the fictional estrangement itself.

Notes

1   A benefit of discussing the seemingly peripheral subject of 'science fiction' is that one has to go back to first principles, one cannot really assume them as given. One must ask, for example, what is literature? Usually, when discussing literature one determines what it says (its subject matter) and how it says what it says (the approach to its themes). If we are talking about literature in the sense of significant works possessing certain minimal aesthetic qualities rather than in the sociological sense of everything that gets published at a certain time or in the

ideological sense of all the writings on certain themes, this principle can more precisely be formulated as a double question. First, epistemologically, what possibility for aesthetic qualities is offered by different thematic fields ('subjects')? The answer given by the aesthetics prevalent at the moment is: an absolutely equal possibility. With this answer the question is booted out of the field of aesthetics and into the lap of ideologists, who pick it up by our default and proceed to bungle it. Second, historically, how has such a possibility in fact been used? Once one begins with such considerations, one comes quickly up against the rather unclear concept of *realism* (not the prose literary movement in the nineteenth century but a metahistorical stylistic principle), since this genre is often pigeonholed as nonrealistic. I would not object but would heartily welcome such labels if one had first persuasively defined what is 'real' and what is 'reality.' True, this genre raises basic philosophical issues, but it is perhaps not necessary to face them in an initial approach. Therefore I shall here substitute for 'reality' (whose existence independent of any observer or group of observers I do not at all doubt, in fact) the concept of 'the author's empirical environment,' which seems as immediately clear as any.

2   Viktor Shklovsky, 'Iskusstvo kak priem,' in *Sborniki po teorii poeticheskogo iazyka*, 2 (Petrograd, 1917). In the translation 'Art as Technique,' in Lee T. Lemon and Marion J. Reis, eds, *Russian Formalist Criticism* (Lincoln, NE, 1965), *ostranenie* is rendered somewhat clumsily as 'defamiliarization.' See also Victor Erlich's classical survey, *Russian Formalism* (The Hague, 1955).

Bertolt Brecht, 'Kleines Organon fur das Theater,' in his *Gesammelte Werke*, 16 (Frankfurt, 1973), translated in John Willett, ed., *Brecht On Theatre* (New York, 1964). My quotations are from pp. 192 and 196 of this translation, but I have changed Mr. Willett's translation of *Verfremdung* as 'alienation' into my 'estrangement,' since 'alienation' evokes incorrect, indeed opposite, connotations: estrangement was for Brecht an approach militating directly against social and cognitive alienation. See Ernst Bloch, '*Ent-fremdung, Verfremdung*: Alienation, Estrangement,' in Erika Munk, ed., *Brecht* (New York, 1972).

3   Note the functional difference from the anti-gravity metal in Wells's *First Men in the Moon*, which is an introductory or 'plausibility-validating' device and not the be-all of a much richer novel. . . .

4   A first approach to the sociology of SF may be found in the special issue of *Science-Fiction Studies*, November 1977, edited and with an introduction by me.

37   Kevin R. McNamara, *Blade Runner*'s Post-Individual Worldspace and Philip K. Dick's *Do Androids Dream of Electric Sheep?* (1997)

Kevin R. McNamara's article, '*Blade Runner*'s Post-Individual Worldspace and Philip K. Dick's *Do Androids Dream of Electric Sheep?*' appeared in *Contemporary Literature* 38 (1997), and focuses largely on racial and racist elements in the film *Blade Runner*, as well as offering this brief comment on the novelistic source. In this reading, the novel features a struggle between a white patriarchal male, paranoid about his potency, and both racialised and gendered others.

McNamara, K. R., '*Blade Runner*'s Post-Individual Worldspace', *Contemporary Literature*, 38.3, 1997, pp. 432–3, 436–7

The dehumanizing power of racism was in fact a key factor in the novel's genesis. Dick recalled that when he began *Do Androids Dream of Electric Sheep?* he had been reading the unpublished records of Gestapo officers in the library at Berkeley (Sammon 23). Indeed the novel opens with a powerful, ironic condemnation of the American legacy of racism: a television commercial offers androids free of charge: "Either as body servants or tireless field hands," to all home buyers in one developer's off-world suburb, which "duplicates the halcyon days of pre-Civil War Southern states!" [16] A form of Euro-colonialist wish fulfillment, the image of colonization: these lands *are* uninhabited wilds; the subject "peoples" *are* not quite human, and they *are* best suited for physical labor. Yet like Thomas Jefferson's *Notes on the State of Virginia*, which discusses slavery's effects on manners among white masters without questioning black, "natural" inferiority (138–40), the novel never really disputes the difference in nature between human and android on which Deckard's return to his "self" depends. Instead, it holds out the hope that we can unplug from the mediated mass-world and, "by listening to our dreams, become fully human" (Mackey 92).

The bio-logic of scientific racism was outlined as early as 1892 by Joseph Le Conte, president of the American Society for the Advancement of Science, professor of natural history at the University of California, and a one-time slave owner. Le Conte proposed that the "intellectual and moral capital" of each "race" is passed on as part of its genetic inheritance (366). Through the device of a graph allegedly representing the narrow limits within which race mixing might be genetically safe (370), Le Conte sought to vindicate "race-prejudice or race-repulsion" as "an instinct necessary to preserve the blood purity of the higher race" (365). Blood purity is equally crucial to identifying the masters in *Androids*. Blood tests measure genetic damage and separate "regular" men and women from the "specials" who, as a result of fallout-induced disease, cannot "reproduce within the tolerances [of genetic normalcy] set by law" [8]. An android, if shot, may "burst and parts of it [fly]" [189], or its "brain box. . . . bl[o]w into pieces" [79], but it will not bleed. [. . .] Blood is also the objective correlative of the empathy excited by the state religion, Mercerism, which is practiced as one caresses the handles of an empathy box while projective identifying with the film image of old Wilbur Mercer, who moves on an endless, uncertain quest [19–20]. By some unexplained transference, cuts Mercer suffers when struck by rock are manifest on the bodies of communicants [22–23, 148]; the flow of blood cites both the crucifixion and Shylock's protest of his own humanity.

[. . .]

The sterile android's threat to women is never established, but it need not be; the danger of rape is a projection that institutes the sexual desire of dominant males as normative and authorizes male violence as a way of maintaining possession of women. What we do see through the novel is that the one object of collective veneration bigger than Mercer is the phallus: Deckard is cocooned in one, his "speedy beefed-up hovercar" [72, 75]. Others dangle from his belt – pistols, laser tubes, and especially the Ajax model Lead Codpiece that he wears to protect his masculinity and also his humanity, which would be compromised if he were no longer capable of "reproduc[ing] within the tolerances set by law" [8]. The symbolic potency of the codpiece is remarked early by a willful Iran, Deckard's wife, who derides an advertisement for the codpiece (in an outburst of penis envy?) as "that awful commercial . . ., the one I hate" [5].

By the novel's end, however, harmony between Rick and Iran has been restored. If she once had refused to dial a 594 on her mood organ ("pleased acknowledgment of husband's superior wisdom" [7]), and he once had wished he had "gotten rid of her" because "nothing penetrates" her anymore ([81]; himself included?), at his final homecoming Iran declares herself "damn glad" that he has returned "home where [he] ought to be" [208]. He retires for some "[l]ong deserved peace" without first dialing a 670 on his own Penfield [209]. As Rick and Iran finally abandon the media apparatus, authentic emotion, and unmediated reality along with it, appears headed for a comeback. It seems likely that they will have sex again and maybe even have children. Most importantly, these final events occur in "real time", as expression of their authentic biological and emotional needs. The novel thereby humanizes Deckard at the same time that it reinstates traditional gender roles.

38 Patricia S. Warrick, Mechanical Mirrors, the Double, and *Do Androids Dream of Electric Sheep?* (1987)

Patricia S. Warrick is Professor of English at the University of Wisconsin, Fox Valley, and has written on cybernetics and artificial intelligence as well as co-editing a number of fiction anthologies. The extract is taken from *Mind in Motion: The Fiction of Philip K. Dick* (1987). In the chapter she has already outlined two themes: the transformation of landscape by the atom bomb and technology, and the universal principle of entropy or decay, before moving onto a third: the problem of evil, especially as the main protagonist of the novel (who should be read as the hero) is effectively a state-sponsored assassin and one of his targets, the android opera singer Luba Luft (who is one of the enemies), questions his morality. Warrick also discusses the structure of the novel, noting that the characters tend to be paired off, with one acting as a double for or mirror of another. This is particularly striking in the paralleled narrative threads of Rick Deckard and J. R. Isidore's respective days.

Warrick, P. S., 'Mechanical Mirrors, the Double, and *Do Androids Dream of Electric Sheep?*', in *Mind in Motion: The Fiction of Philip K. Dick*, Carbondale and Edwardsville: Southern Illinois University Press, 1987, pp. 122–4, 124–9

How can we justify killing, even when it is done with the approval of the law, as in the case of Rick Deckard? The creative good that opposes the destructive is metaphored by the repairman or the artist – a single individual struggling alone and achieving small successes. Isidore works for a little firm that repairs electronic animals. Luba Luft, the opera singer who admires the paintings of Expressionist Edvard Munch, is the inciting agent causing Rick Deckard to first question the morality of destroying robots.

The fourth theme, and the predominant one in *Do Androids Dream*, explores the response of the individual to the contemporary wasteland universe where he must live. Unable to remain whole, he splits and occupies either the schizoid or the schizophrenic half of his divided self. The schizoid individual is dominated by left brain functions. He denies his emotions and operates as an intelligent, logical machine. The robot, or android, metaphors this schizoid personality. In contrast, the schizophrenic personality is analogous to the right brain function. He still responds emotionally to the world around him, but in doing so, he experiences anxiety and cosmic angst so great that he is driven to madness. In his madness he may descend into the tomb world of death, as did Manfred in [Philip K. Dick's] *Martian Time-Slip* [1964], or ascend into a momentary vision of light

196

where he feels he experiences the true nature of reality. Isidore's life is lived in cycles that lift him up and then plunge him down. As a youth before the holocaust, he had been able to restore animals to life. Then the creative power reversed itself and he descended into the tomb world, from which he later ascended. Another descent and reversal occur during the day portrayed in the novel.

The final theme is the possibility of a messiah, a theme to which Dick has devoted little attention before *Do Androids Dream*. Will someone come to save man from destruction in the entropic wasteland where he finds himself? Traditional religions say yes. Dick discards that answer and explores the question anew. He uses the device of Mercerism and the black empathy box to metaphor metaphysical possibility. His answer to the question of a messiah reminds the reader of that found by French existentialists Camus and Sartre, and makes readily understandable the great popularity Dick's fiction enjoys in France. Like Sisyphus, we must daily push our boulder up the hill of uncertainty, hoping for an answer if the summit is ever achieved.

The messiah in the novel also has a double. Both arrive via electronic media – the screens of the two TV sets. Buster Friendly on the conventional TV set and Wilbur Mercer on the fusion box are complementary opposites who both deal in image making. One acts; one talks. One creates faith; one destroys it. Buster Friendly, the ubiquitous TV commentator, chats endlessly and vacuously with glamorous stars, while Wilbur Mercer eternally toils up his barren hill, dodging rocks. They both turn out to be doubly inauthentic. First, we never encounter them in physical reality but know them only by their images on the screen. In the end, Buster is revealed to be an android, not a man. Mercer turns out to be a drunk from Gary, Indiana, not a savior. And yet for those who believe in them, their images become reality. However, one cannot believe in both since Buster reveals Mercer as a fraud. Or can one? Can a man's actions or his words be true, even though he himself is a fraud? The double-edged contradiction in the Buster Friendly/Wilbur Mercer image is an excellent example of Dick's ability to embody a complex paradox in a dynamic metaphor.

A comparison of Rick's day with Isidore's reveals the parallels between the two narratives. Each man's mind is in motion, but because their starting points are at opposite poles, their motions counter each other. As the novel opens, Isidore is an innocent who accepts and loves all forms, living and electronic. He makes no distinction between authentic and false, android and human. In contrast, Rick is a killer of androids. He dislikes them even though he has difficulty differentiating them from humans. Isidore merges with Mercer through the black empathy box before he sets off to work. Rick has not merged for a long time.

197

Each man returns home in the evening a changed man. Rick, the killer, is transformed by love; Isidore, who loves and nurtures, is altered by violence. Each, prodded by anguish, discovers the answer to the question of how a human is different from an intelligent machine that resembles a human.

The Isidore chapters are interwoven with the Deckard chapters, the action in one echoing the other but reversing it. Deckard destroys; Isidore heals. And although their actions occur simultaneously, in order to understand how they function in the novel, I shall examine each separately.

Analysis is made even more difficult by the fact that each narrative contains sets of Janus-faced metaphors comprised of opposites constantly reversing themselves. Thus each pole of the paradoxical metaphor is both true and not true at the same time. The power comes from their dynamic interaction. One needs to examine the opposites simultaneously, a task easy enough for the mind but not for the printed page.

[. . .]

Rick and Isidore each encounter three androids that are mirrors of but not identical to each other. The only exact duplicates are Rachael, whom Rick loves; and Pris, whom Isidore loves. Rachael, however, is a legal android since she is a model that the Rosen Corporation has kept for experimentation rather than exporting it to Mars. Pris, her double, is an outlaw – one of the eight androids who have killed Martian settlers and escaped to Terra. Android Max Polokov is an aggressive killer; Luba Luft is an artist. In the other plot, Roy Baty is the aggressor; Irmgard the warm, responsive female. Another set of doubles exists in Rick's world: the bounty hunter Phil Resch seems to be an android but turns out to be a man; the police chief Garland poses as a human but turns out to be an android.

Rick metaphors law. He is free from ambiguity. As he begins his day of killing, he is certain of his ability to distinguish android from human. It is not superficial appearance (they look like humans); it is not intelligence (they are as intelligent as humans). It is their lack of emotional response and empathy. They are cold, solitary, indifferent to anyone's survival but their own. They are unable to fuse with others on the empathy box. True, some schizoid humans demonstrate these same symptoms, but the Voigt Empathy Test differentiates the androids in those instances. Rick is certain he has never killed a human and that he is justified in killing androids. After all, they are escaped killers from Mars. But by day's end his encounters with androids have reversed his view about killing and moved it to a kind of anguished and instructed innocence that holds killing to be wrong but an inescapable evil in the world.

In contrast to Rick, Isidore metaphors love.[1] He does not differentiate between good and evil. By nightfall he has lost his naive innocence, schooled by the ruthless android Pris, who holds life valueless and sadistically tears the legs from what may be Earth's last living spider. He learns that Mercer, in whom he believed, is a fraud. And yet, his descent again into the tomb world of death brings about a reversal and the return of his faith even in the face of his shattered illusions. As the novel ends, Mercer appears to him in a vision and the spider comes back to life with its legs restored. Isidore joins Rick – to whom Mercer also appears – in a regained and wise innocence, aware of the existence of death, destruction, and evil, but still able to keep faith with life.

The major narrative dramatizes Rick's encounters with seven mechanical humanoids. As the day begins he is a man of conventional convictions. During the day he completes the assignment his police chief has given him to destroy six escaped killer androids from Mars. Each encounter with an android disorients him further from his certainty that his conventional view of reality and morality is the correct one.

The secondary narrative pictures J. R. Isidore's encounter during the same day with three of the androids that Rick has been assigned to kill. Isidore is unable to recognize the androids as anything but lonely, frightened humans, so he shelters them and feeds them. His later discovery that they are androids does not change his behavior because he loves all creatures regardless of their form and he opposes all destruction.

Outer mirrors inner in the novel. The episodes of the major narrative are carefully structured to represent the inner changes that alter Rick from a killer to a man who abhors violence and finally unite him with his lost second self, Isidore. The most interesting reading of the novel examines the change in Rick's awareness resulting from each of his encounters with an android.

His first encounter with Rachael makes him vividly aware of how difficult it has become to distinguish between a human and an android. He is uncertain whether she is truly an android or merely a schizoid human – one who is cold and unable to respond emotionally. The essential element of an authentic human, Rick believes, is empathy – the ability to respond to the needs of other humans. Rachael's android nature can only be established by the delicate Voigt Empathy Test. Uncertainty and the possibility of error are introduced into Rick's awareness.

Rick's second encounter leads him to realize he cannot trust his perceptions of reality. The android Polokov has so successfully disguised himself as a Russian law officer named Kadalyi that he is almost able to kill Rick before Rick discovers the disguise. When Rick exclaims in surprise, "You're not Polokov, you're Kadalyi," the android replies, "Don't you mean that the other way around? You're a bit confused" [79]. Thus early in the novel Dick gives the reader a clue about the reversals and disguises that are to follow. After killing the android, Rick muses that "the encounter with Kadalyi–Polokov had changed his ideas rather massively" [81]. Now he knows that things may not actually be as they first appear.

His third encounter is with Luba Luft, who performs with the San Francisco Opera. She mirrors to him the feminine, creative part of his nature which he has so totally suppressed. She sings with great beauty an aria from his favorite opera, Mozart's *The Magic Flute*. Thinking of Mozart, who was also young and who died so soon after creating such beautiful music, Rick notes the parallel with Luba. Her fate will be the same as Mozart's when she finishes singing. He is shocked when Luba points out how cold and indifferent he is and suggests he take the Empathy Test to determine if he too is an android.

The fourth encounter is with an android police chief named Garland in a fake police station rigged by the androids to look real. Rick soon discovers that the apparent reality of the police station is merely illusion. This recognition leads to his awareness that any supposed reality is probably only an illusion one's head has been programmed to accept as real.

The episode that follows is a classical recognition scene. Rick looks into the mirror of a character who is his double and discovers his own reflection. In the fake police station he is joined by Phil Resch, the bounty killer who is his twin in inner appearance. They are both men who hunt androids. Or can it be that Phil Resch is really an android who has been programmed to believe he is a man? His cold-blooded killing of Luba Luft makes Rick believe it possible. As he looks at his killer double, Rick recognizes that he may have become what he abhors in Phil Resch. Resch is a man unable to feel empathy. This insight about himself is so shattering that Rick can hardly go on with his assignment of killing androids. Appropriate to this awareness that he has quite wrongly suppressed his feeling self, Rick goes to an animal store and purchases a female goat.

He also impulsively merges with the Mercer box, begging for help as he realizes that he will violate his newly discovered identity if he continues to kill. And yet . . . the androids are killers and must be destroyed. Mercer tells him to carry out his task, saying, "You will be required to do wrong no matter where you go. It is the basic condition of life, to be required to violate your own identity. At some time, every creature which lives must do so. It is the ultimate shadow, the defeat of creation; this is the curse at work, the curse that feeds on all life. Everywhere in the universe" [153]. The view expressed by Mercer is essential Philip Dick philosophy, and we find it in novel after novel. Nothing is easy; nothing is comprehensible. Still, we must go on.

The pair of scenes that next occur are the most powerful in the novel. The two men learn the wrenching pain of loving someone who is unable to respond. Rick makes love to Rachael while at the same moment Isidore has an encounter with Pris, her twin. The scenes are mirror opposites of each other. Each catches the tragic essence of creative power when it has become perverted to destruction. The sexual union of Rick and Rachael is the summa of falsity and mechanical motions. They both yearn for something more than the barren act can possibly produce. She longs to be human and bear a child. She knows she never will. She wonders, "Is it a loss? I don't really know; I have no way to tell. How does it feel to have a child? How does it feel to be born for that matter? We're not born; we don't grow up; instead of dying from old age we wear out like ants. Ants again; that's what we are, Not you; I mean me. Chitinous reflex-machines who aren't really alive. . . . I'm not alive!" [165].

Rick hopes his lovemaking will lead her to be willing to help him destroy her twin, Pris. She promises. But after the act, her promise turns out to have been a mere maneuver to get him in bed so she could vitiate his will to kill, a performance she has successfully carried out with other men on at least nine occasions. She tells him afterward, "Anyway, you know the truth, the brick-hard, irregular, slithery surface of truth. I'm just an observer and I won't intervene to save you; I don't care if Roy Baty nails you or not. I care whether I get nailed" [163].

At the same time Rachael is making love to Rick, we see her double, Pris, mutilating the living spider Isidore has just found with such delight. This is a brilliant metaphorical yoking of meaningless love and death if the reader envisions the scenes simultaneously, as Dick intends he should. The words of Rachael in one scene are echoed by Pris in the parallel scene.

The three brief concluding chapters of the novel bring Isidore and Rick together after each has undergone his destructive experience with a female robot. Again, parallels echo throughout the scene and contradictions abound. The action opens with Isidore's vision of Mercer after Pris has destroyed his spider, and the TV revelation has shattered his faith in Mercer's authenticity. The action closes with Rick's hallucination in the desert where he, too, sees Mercer.

Each man has been schooled by suffering and made ready for an epiphany. Isidore's occurs after he drowns his mutilated spider. Driven by despair, he descends again into the tomb world of death that forever haunts him. Frightened, he calls for help and Mercer seems to answer. Miraculously, the spider returns, alive and with its legs restored. Mercer appears in a vision and tells Isidore that he really is a fraud. The paradox of the imagery is followed immediately by another contradiction. Rick and Isidore meet at last. To Rick's request for help so he can find the androids he must kill, Isidore says no. But Mercer suddenly appears to warn Rick. Just in time Rick saves himself by shooting Pris, who awaits him, gun in hand, on the stairs.

Afterward, when Rick has killed the last two androids, Isidore joins him and the two men mourn over the dead bodies. The contraries of life are united – the logical and the emotional, the masculine and the feminine, the left and the right – brain lobes. The two halves seem contradictory. Rick destroys; Isidore nurtures. And yet they both exist. Rick, finally arriving at a wisdom beyond definition, says, "Everything is true."

The novel appropriately concludes with a final scene containing a contradiction. Rick flees alone into the desert, in anguish because he has been forced to kill. As he plods along, hungry in the desert heat, a "vague and almost hallucinatory pall hazed over his mind." He experiences a vision. Afterward, musing on the experience, he tries to describe it. "It's strange. I had the absolute, utter, completely real illusion that I had become Mercer and people were lobbing rocks at me. But not the way you experience it when you hold the handles of an empathy box. When you use an empathy box you feel you're with Mercer. The difference is that I wasn't with anyone: I was alone" [201].

Maybe reality is a fake. The living toad Rick stumbles upon in the dust after his visions is, he concludes, like life – "Life carefully buried up to its forehead in the carcass of a dead world." He believes his finding of the toad, Mercer's favorite animal, is an omen of regeneration. But upon taking it home, he discovers it is only an electronic construct. What are we to believe? What is false appearance and what is true reality? How can we differentiate illusion from reality? Finally, this is the question which subsumes every other question for Dick in all his fiction. In *Do Androids Dream* the reader is spiraled through so many assertions and negations and negations of negations that at the end of the novel he is uncertain of what Dick would have him believe.

Note

1   John Isidore is reminiscent of Jack Isidore in *Confessions of a Crap Artist*. Comments Dick made during the last years of his life suggest he regarded them as the same character, a character of whom he was very fond. John Isidore is one of Dick's divine fools, one we can easily admire. I find Jack Isidore of *Crap Artist* somewhat less admirable, and wonder if Dick's memory of Jack had not been colored by time. When *Crap Artist* was submitted to publishers after it was written (probably in 1958), Dick used the pseudonym Jack Isidore. When in 1977 he sent me an autographed copy, he signed it with both names, Philip K. Dick and Jack Isidore.

MANUEL PUIG,
KISS OF THE SPIDER WOMAN

39 Michael Dunne, Dialogism in Manuel Puig's *Kiss of the Spider Woman* (1995)

In this article Michael Dunne offers a Bakhtinian analysis of Manuel Puig's *Kiss of the Spider Woman*. He uses Mikhail Bakhtin's ideas about the distinction beween monologic and dialogic texts (the examples explored by Bakhtin are the works of Tolstoy and Dostoevsky), arguing that Puig's novel is dialogic. The erudite footnotes form part of the polyphony of the text and are an important element of its dialogic structure. He goes on to argue that the novel's utterances contain at least two versions of meaning, offering a continual 'double-voiced' discourse. Dunne suggests that any attempt to read the footnotes as authoritative would be to impose a false monologic reading on this playful, postmodern text.

Dunne, M., 'Dialogism in Manuel Puig's *Kiss of the Spider Woman*', *South Atlantic Review*, 60.2, May 1995, pp. 121–36

The lifelong critical project of Mikhail Bakhtin—extending from *Problems of Dostoevsky's Poetics* (1929, trans. 1984) through *Speech Genres and Other Late Essays* (1979, trans. 1986)—was focused on what Bakhtin's most famous English interpreter, Michael Holquist, has called "dialogism." In *Dialogism: Bakhtin and his World*, Holquist provides the following definition:

> Dialogism argues that all meaning is relative in the sense that it comes about only as a result of the relation between two bodies occupying *simultaneous but different* space, where bodies may be thought of as ranging from the immediacy of our physical bodies, to political bodies and to bodies of ideas in general (ideologies). (20–21)

As Holquist explains, these dialogic relations operate on both semantic and ideological levels, which interpenetrate.

In support of Holquist's thesis, we may consult Bakhtin's introduction of the term *polyphony* in *Problems of Dostoevsky's Poetics*:

> *A plurality of independent and unmerged voices and consciousnesses, a genuine polyphony of fully valid voices is in fact the chief characteristic of Dostoevsky's novels*. What unfolds in his works is not a multitude of characters and fates in a single objective world, illuminated by a single authorial consciousness; rather a *plurality of consciousnesses, with equal rights and each with its own world*, combine but are not merged in the unity of the event. (6)

In the essay "The Problem of Speech Genres," collected in his final volume, Bakhtin is still advancing the same idea, even if in different terms:

> Our speech, that is, all our utterances (including creative works), is filled with others' words, varying degrees of otherness or varying degrees of "our-own-ness," varying degrees of awareness and detachment. These words of others carry with them their own expression, their own evaluative tone, which we assimilate, rework, and re-accentuate. (89)

As hundreds of items contained in the *MLA International Bibliography* during the last ten years attest, Bakhtin's ideas apply most immediately to the genre he himself valorized: the novel.

Although Manuel Puig's *Kiss of the Spider Woman* (trans. 1979) is a particularly apt example of Bakhtin's theories, this novel has received surprisingly scant discussion in Bakhtinian terms. This lack of attention is surprising because the basic plot situation is undeniably dialogic. Luis Molina, a homosexual, has been imprisoned for morally corrupting a minor. Valentin Arregui has been arrested and tortured for his political activism against the Argentine government. Locked in the same prison cell in a Latin American political dictatorship, the two men have little else to do but speak to each other. As Valentin says to Molina: "If we're going to be in this cell together like this, we ought to understand one another better, and I know very little about people with your type of inclination" (58–59). The novel consists largely of these two characters' efforts to overcome interpersonal ignorance and to establish authentic communication dialogically.

This philosophical dialogism is represented through a dialogic stylistics, as in Puig's use of what Bakhtin calls "incorporated" or "inserted" genres. In *The Dialogic Imagination*, Bakhtin writes:

The novel permits the incorporation of various genres, both artistic (inserted short stories, lyrical songs, poems, dramatic scenes, etc.) and extra-artistic (everyday, rhetorical, scholarly, religious genres and others). In principle, any genre could be included in the construction of the novel, and in fact it is difficult to find any genres that have not at some point been incorporated into a novel by someone. Such incorporated genres usually preserve within the novel their own structural integrity and independence, as well as their own linguistic and stylistic peculiarities. (320–21)

At one point in the novel, for example, Molina is trying to convince the prison warden that Valentin may be seduced into revealing information about the political underground by means of food delicacies supposedly supplied by Molina's mother. The warden asks to see a list of the required food items, and the dialogue in the text is interrupted by the following: "List of things to go in the package for Molina, please, with everything packed in two brown shopping bags, like my mother carries it." A list of sixteen items follows—beginning with "2 roast chickens" and ending with "jar of mayonnaise and a box of paper napkins"—distinguished from the paragraphing customary in this text by white space, as if it were an "everyday" list (201). This list is immediately followed by a dialogue in which Molina and Valentin discuss and eat these delicacies (201). The contact of these two usually separated modes of discourse clearly demonstrates the kind of discursive polyphony that Bakhtin identifies in his commentary on Dostoevsky.

Another inserted genre is a letter dictated to Molina by Valentin and intended for the latter's lover, Marta. Unlike the grocery list, this letter is not represented directly in the text—like the letters in Nathanael West's *Miss Lonelyhearts*, for example. The letter is heterovoiced even so. This becomes clear when a portion of the dictation is reproduced:

> I'm sorry, Molina, how did I tell her that I'm not going to send her the letter? Read it to me, would you?
> "But I just have to write you a letter, even if I don't send it."
> Would you add, "But I will send it."
> "But I will send it." Go ahead. We were at "If only we could actually talk together, you'd understand what I mean. . . ." (177)

The passage is polyphonic on the typographical level, as signified by the internal quotation marks. But a deeper polyphony is created by Molina's two articulations of the pronoun *we* to signify himself and Valentin as well as Valentin and Marta.

Polyphony also enters the novel through Puig's use of music. Since the term *polyphony* is borrowed metaphorically from music, the absorption of popular songs into this novel would probably fail to surprise Bakhtin. As he observes in the passage from *The Dialogic Imagination* quoted above, "[I]t is difficult to find any genres that have not at some point been incorporated into a novel by someone." Puig's practice validates this assumption and lends further support to the notes Bakhtin collected in 1961, "Toward a Reworking of the Dostoevsky Book." Published in conjunction with the English translation of *Problems of Dostoevsky's Poetics*, these remarks contain the following helpful comment: "Thomas Mann's *Doktor Faustus* as an indirect confirmation of my idea. . . . The complex authorial position. . . . Retellings (verbal transpositions) of musical works: in *Netochka Nezvanova*, but especially in the retelling of Trishatov's opera . . ." (284). Retelling an opera would probably not enhance the dialogism of a novel set in Argentina. Retelling a bolero would.

In chapter 7, Valentin experiences excruciating pain after eating food poisoned by the prison authorities in hopes of driving him into the infirmary, where he can be drugged. Puig locates this very dramatic episode dialogically in a context established by Molina's singing of a bolero entitled "My Letter" and Valentin's receipt of a letter from his lover in the underground. Eventually Valentin says, "There I was laughing at your bolero, but the letter I got today says just what the bolero says" (137). This comes as no surprise to Molina, who later observes, "[B]oleros contain tremendous truths, which is why I like them" (139). Puig likes boleros too, not so much because they contain tremendous truths about the human heart, but because they contain tremendous opportunities to comment on his principal narrative without seeming to do so.

A different bolero appears in chapter 12 while Molina is entertaining Valentin by retelling a romantic movie about an actress and a reporter. In this film, "[t]he guy drinks, and drinks, and starts composing lyrics for the song, while he's thinking about her, and starts singing, because he's actually a singer, the leading man, the reporter." The voice here is clearly Molina's, not Puig's, as is evident in the afterthoughts—"he's actually a singer, the leading man"—typical of spoken rather than written discourse. This illusion is deepened as Molina goes on to recount the lyrics of the bolero:

"Even though you're . . . a prisoner, in your solitude . . . your heart whispers still . . . I love you." And how does the rest go. Let me see, there's something else and then comes, "Your eyes cast a shadow, your smile brings such pain, your lips . . . I remember . . . they once used to lie . . . and I ask my darkest self, if those lips I adore, with their fervent kiss . . . with their fervent kiss . . ." then what else? Something like ". . . could ever lie to me again." And then it goes, "Black flowers . . . of fate, cruelly keep us apart, but the day will come, when you'll be . . . mine forever . . . mine alone . . ." You remember that bolero? (227)

Even apart from the typographical signals provided by the ellipses and quotation marks, the content marks the speech as Molina's. Molina may believe that only fate prevents fervent kisses from creating a world in which lovers can stay happily in love "forever." The rest of Puig's novel treats love and politics with too much sophistication to attribute these sentiments directly to the novelist.

That is to say, Molina's retelling of these boleros involves the polyphony of "double-voiced discourse." In *The Dialogic Imagination* Bakhtin argues that discourse of this sort "serves two speakers at the same time and expresses simultaneously two different intentions: the direct intention of the character who is speaking, and the refracted intention of the author." As a result, "Double-voiced discourse is always internally dialogized," especially in the case of "comic, ironic, and parodic discourse" (324). In the case at hand, Molina's intention is to endorse the romantic sentimentality illustrated by the bolero and by the film in which it appeared. One of Puig's probable intentions is to deepen Molina's characterization by representing his feelings about romantic love. Another likely intention is to interrogate escapist forms of entertainment like boleros and romantic films. Any cultural form equating the term *prisoner* with "prisoner of love" cannot be fully responsive to the social, political, and sexual conditions depicted in Puig's novel. On another polyphonic level, boleros and films must have contributed significantly to the shaping of Puig's consciousness, as well as Molina's, or we would not be reading about them in *Kiss of the Spider Woman*. We must constantly resist the temptation to interpret the polyphony of this novel monologically.

Puig introduces another form of double-voiced discourse into the novel through his representation of "official" police records. The first occasion is used to expand the novel's setting beyond the prison cell of the first seven chapters to include the warden's office. Chapter 8, designated as "Report to the Warden, prepared by Staff Assistants," opens with brief summaries of Molina's and Valentin's criminal records, represented in police jargon (148–49). Being tortured is called "undergoing police interrogation," for example. Molina is economically characterized: "Conduct good." The report on Valentin concludes: "Conduct reprehensible, rebellious, reputed instigator of above hunger strike as well as other incidents supposedly protesting lack of hygienic conditions in Pavilion and violation of personal correspondence" (149). None of the events surrounding the alleged crimes of either character are dramatized in the novel, nor are Valentin's political activities while in prison. Nevertheless, Puig's readers must incorporate these factors poly-phonically into their understandings of the two characters after encountering these police reports.

Chapter 8 continues the official "Report to the Warden" by representing the speech of Molina, a guard, and the warden, accompanied by identifica-tions of the speakers in capital letters, as in: "WARDEN: That will do fine, Sergeant, you may go out now . . . You look thin, Molina, what's the matter?" (149). Again a typographical device representing a polyphonic voice also serves a thematic end. Here the official perspective on Molina's life is allowed to interact dialogically with his own. Puig uses this technique again in chapter 11, before Molina presents his grocery list to the warden, and in chapter 14, when the warden tells Molina that he will be let out on parole.

The most elaborate rendering of this voice constitutes the entire following chapter, designated as "Report on Luis Alberto Molina, prisoner 3.018, paroled on the 9th, placed under surveillance by CISL in conjunction with wiretap unit of TISL" (265). Chapter 15 consists of a series of official reports, identified by time of day and date, reporting on Molina's movements from the moment of his parole to his death by gunfire sixteen days later. Again, the polyphony is more than technical since these reports by undercover police officers reveal the same humorless tunnel-vision that makes the warden susceptible to Molina's manipulations. Thus, a police agent who over-hears Molina saying "camel only" in a conversation about lunch is uncertain whether the phrase is some sort of code or merely "babytalk" (265). It turns out that Molina is asking for "cannelloni," a fact duly entered later into the official report (269). This agent, or another one just as dense, is also puzzled by a conversation between Molina and his friend Lab in which the two gay men "proceeded to address one another by a number of feminine names, this time actresses, or so it seemed: Marilyn, Gina, Greta, Marlene, Merle, Heady (?)" (267).

Obviously, Puig is using the device of official reports to create double-voiced discourse. Here the monologic intentions of the official speaker are clearly signalled by the question mark following the misspelling of "Heddy" and by the pompous officialese of the following remark: "It should be reiter-ated that it did not seem to pertain to any code, but rather a running joke between the two" (267). Several ironies flourish in the gaps created by this double-voiced discourse. The pretensions to monological understanding voiced in the official version conflict with Molina's very different sense of what he is doing on the telephone. Readers must also reject the official version based on their superior grasp of Molina's character and mode of speech. At the same time, readers know—and Molina does not—that Molina's conversations are being bugged and that he is under constant police surveillance. The dialogic exchange is thus highly complex, highly polyphonic.

Puig's most challenging form of polyphony results from his use of footnotes outside his narrative text. A speech by Valentin, quoted earlier, provides an excellent opportunity to begin examining this radical technique: "If we're going to be in this cell together like this, we ought to understand one another better, and I know very little about people with your type of inclination" (58–59). Immediately following the word *inclination*, an asterisk directs the reader's attention to the bottom of the page where a footnote, represented in a different type face, presents a refutation by "The English researcher D.J. West" of "three principal theories with respect to the physical origins of homosexuality." This footnote continues to run at the bottom of several following pages (59–65). Meanwhile, back in the text, Molina responds to Valentin's remark by saying, "I'll tell you how it happened then, quickly though, so as not to bore you" (59). Dialogue between the two central characters continues in the main text above the running footnote.

The rhetorical effect of this first—of nine—footnotes is disconcerting in that it introduces a strikingly alien voice from the discourse of the social sciences into an environment in which the previous chapters have led the reader to expect only representations of fictional dialogue. Puig told Luys A. Diez that "the elitist pedantry of the style of these authors—although not intentional—seemed to me quite reactionary" (qtd. in Rice-Sayre 253). The stylistic contrast to Puig's own prose is, of course, "intentional," and thus polyphonic. The footnote also disrupts the reader's usual mode of reading fiction by distracting attention from the ongoing narrative to the bottom of the page and to a smaller type face.

Despite these rhetorical challenges, the reader's understanding of Puig's characters is deepened by this extended footnote. This understanding extends not only to the homosexual Molina, who is the ostensible object of the footnote, but also to Valentin, whose meager experience of homosexuality does not extend to the three principal theories much less to West's refutation of them. Thus, polyphonic dialogue progresses—between Valentin and Molina, between the reader and Puig's characters, and between the reader and Puig. In David H. Bost's formulation, "Author, narrator, text, and listeners cohere to realize an imaginative literary intention" (105).

Most of Puig's footnotes resemble this first one in presenting information about the social contexts of human sexuality. By referring to the scholarly works of D.J. West, T.C.N. Gibbons, Sigmund Freud, Anna Freud, O. Fenichel, Wilhelm Reich, Herbert Marcuse, Norman O. Brown, Dennis

Altman, Kate Millett, J.C. Unwin, J.C. Flugel, and Anneli Taube, these footnotes create a parallel discourse which interacts polyphonically with the novel's action and dialogue. Read consecutively, moreover, the discourse in the footnotes progresses from the apparently disinterested first report concerning West and the "physical origins of homosexuality" to a highly persuasive argument, based on the work of Millett, Brown, Marcuse, and Taube, concerning the social construction of gender (205–14). The reader's responses to Molina and Valentin must be affected in some way by this carefully constructed argument.

This psychological discourse also progresses toward an interrogation of political power relations, as the final sentence in the final footnote reveals: "The subsequent formation of homosexual liberation fronts is one proof of that" (214). That is to say, the footnotes must also affect the reader's responses to the political forces determining Valentin's imprisonment and torture as well as Molina's social marginalization. As Becky Boling has observed, "Gradually the point of the footnotes becomes clear: To diagnose the causes of homosexuality leads us to a different set of problems, the understanding of repression as a basis for society, the demand to conform on all levels to the ideology of one's society" (80). Further insight emerges in Frances Wyers Weber's perception that "Homosexuality and militant leftist politics violate both Hollywood's moving-picture code of the nineteen thirties and forties and the social code of today's Argentina" (180). Puig's readers thus must engage in political inquiry at some level, however unwillingly or unconsciously. Therefore, discursive polyphony operates within the action of the novel, within the footnotes, and between the footnotes and the main text to suggest that political and sexual repression are two aspects of the same social conditions.

In stating the matter thus, however, I do an injustice to Puig's novel and make it seem too didactic. This book is truly dialogic, not only in its thematic emphases, but also in its stylistics. By refusing to absorb the argument posed by his footnotes into his text, Puig also refuses to dominate his reader rhetorically. The polyphony—visual, semantic, generic—between narrative and footnotes paradoxically increases the opportunities for dialogue between reader and text. This is, of course, perfectly consistent with Bakhtin's principles, as is clear in an extended comment from Holquist's *Dialogism*:

> Dialogically conceived, authorship is a form of governance, for both are implicated in the architectonics of responsibility, each is a way to adjudicate center/non-center relations between subjects. Totalitarian government always seeks the (utopian) condition of absolute monologue: the *Gleichschaltung* which was attempted in Germany

during the 1930s to "Nazify" trade unions, universities, publishing houses, professional associations, and so on had as its aim the suppression of all otherness in the state so that its creator alone might flourish. Dialogism has rightly been perceived by certain thinkers on the left as a useful corrective to Marxism, for it argues that sharing is not only an ethical or economic mandate, but a condition built into the structure of human perception, and thus a condition inherent in the very fact of being human. (34)

In light of Holquist's remarks, the author Puig can be seen to engage with political power dialogically, just as his characters do. Other participants unavoidably implicated in this dialogue are, of course, Puig's readers.

Puig uses his sixth footnote, in chapter 8, to create another thematically productive dialogue with his principal narrative. At this point in the story, Molina is fooling the prison authorities into providing food delicacies for himself and Valentin. The Warden concludes a speech to Molina by saying, "Weigh your words, my friend," and an asterisk directs the reader's attention to the bottom of the page, where a footnote begins: "In Three Essays on the Theory of Sexuality, Freud points out that repression, in general terms, can be traced back to the imposition of domination of one individual over others, the first individual having been none other than the father" (151). In terms of narrative coherence, the remark certainly applies to Molina's subordinate situation vis à vis the Warden.

However, another kind of dialogic coherence develops as the footnote continues to run beneath Molina's requests for sensual refreshments in the narrative. The dialogic encounter here consists of more than the ironic contrast between repression at the bottom of the page and indulgence up above. The discussion in the footnote develops from the concept of sexual repression to an investigation of polymorphous perversity, concluding with a comment about "the essential mutability of human nature" (154). Again, the organic coherence of the remark is notable in the context of Valentin's and Molina's evolving senses of themselves as capable of change. The footnote simultaneously provides ironic commentary on this fictional society's erroneous assumption that human nature is fixed and that political monologism is therefore valid. There is also a larger appropriateness in terms of Bakhtin's overall critical project.

When Valentin and Molina fall joyfully upon these deviously extracted groceries in the next chapter, they are acting out a polymorphous sensuality by recognizing what Bakhtin calls "the grotesque body." The concept is central to Bakhtin's thinking and is especially significant in *Rabelais and his World*, where Bakhtin offers the following definition: "The grotesque body, as we have often stressed, is a body in the act of becoming. It is never finished, never completed; it is continually built, created, and builds and creates another body. Moreover, the body swallows the world and is itself swallowed by the world." Therefore, "the essential role belongs to those parts of the grotesque body in which it outgrows its own self, transgressing its own body, in which it conceives a new, second body: the bowels and the phallus." About the mouth, the bowels, and the sexual organs, Bakhtin concludes: "All these convexities and orifices have a common characteristic; it is within them that the confines between bodies and between the body and the world are overcome: there is an interchange and an interorientation" (317). Even when discussing the graphically physical, Bakhtin's concerns are philosophically dialogical.

Bakhtin thus presents the contrasting view as the monological assumption of "an entirely finished, completed, strictly limited body." This view is characteristic of authoritarian thinking, in which "[a]ll orifices of the body are closed. The basis of the image is the individual, strictly limited mass, the impenetrable facade" (320). In this respect, Bakhtin clearly anticipates Puig, who recognizes the dialogical power of the grotesque body throughout his novel.

Puig's resemblance to Bakhtin is evident not only in the chapters focused on the subversive act of eating delicious food in prison, but also earlier in chapter 7, when poisoned food racks Valentin's body with diarrhea, and later in chapter 11, when Valentin makes love to Molina before the latter's parole. These two affirmations of the grotesque body are also linked stylistically. When Molina offers to clean Valentin's soiled body, Valentin asks, "But it doesn't disgust you?" (142). Molina addresses the same words to Valentin in the later scene: "It doesn't disgust you to have me caress you?" (218). Since the two characters have transcended by this time their formerly monological senses of themselves as "the individual, strictly limited mass, the impenetrable facade," the answer in both cases can be that neither is "disgusted" by the other. Puig's reader is equally implicated in these increasingly dialogic judgments.

Puig's second footnote (82–95) introduces a different form of discursive polyphony into the novel. At this earlier point, Molina has been entertaining Valentin by retelling an old Nazi propaganda film when he breaks off his narrative to go to sleep. The text reproduces Valentin's speech, "Good night," followed by an asterisk. This time the footnote purports to be, not scientific discourse, but the "middle pages" of a "Press-book from Tobis-Berlin Studios" concerning their film *Her Real Glory*. In a sense, this film is the same one Molina has been retelling, with a singer named Leni, a handsome Nazi officer named Werner, and an espionage plot. On the other hand, the press release establishes that Leni is the actress playing the part, as well as the character she plays, and that Werner is an actual Nazi officer, as well as a character in the film. Furthermore, the press release picks up the retelling of the film where Molina left off before going to sleep, including dialogue between Leni and Werner reproduced within quotation marks. Another narrative thus shadows Puig's main plot and unavoidably interacts polyphonically with it.

For convenience, I will borrow some vocabulary from *Figures of Literary Discourse* (128–33) by the French structuralist Gerard Genette to say that Puig's principal diegesis concerning Valentin and Molina contains the latter's metadiegesis about Leni and Werner and that this metadiegesis is continued by Puig's second footnote. Metadiegetic narratives appear frequently in *Kiss of the Spider Woman* and constitute another form of discursive polyphony. In addition to the story of Leni and Werner, Molina retells another film recounting a tragic romance between a singer and a reporter who, as we have seen earlier, turns out also to be a singer; an adventure film with political overtones about a rich, romantic Latin American auto racer and his corrupt mother; a sentimental story about an unattractive, lonely young woman and a scarred war veteran who find true love; a love and horror film about a beautiful woman who turns into a panther; and another about Zombies. Robert Sklar identifies the last two in *Cineaste as Cat People* (1942) and *I Walked with a Zombie* (1943), both directed by Jacques Tourneur. In his *Nomads, Exiles, and Emigres*, Ronald Schwartz traces two more of Molina's plots back to *Paris Underground* and *Holiday in Mexico*. In her "Through the Film Darkly," Stephanie Merrim identifies another source in *The Enchanted Cottage* (1946), directed by John Cromwell. In every case, however, Molina's version differs considerably from the original because, as he admits, "to some extent I have to embroider a little" (18).

In Molina's retelling, the plots and characters of these metadiegetic narratives continually reinflect situations in the "real world" of the diegetic narrative. Thus, Molina identifies with Leni in the Nazi film, and Valentin sees himself as the politically aware auto racer. When the heroine of the Zombie film is warned that voodoo drums often portend death, Molina thinks about his mother—"cardiac arrest, sick old woman, a heart fills up with black seawater and drowns"—and Valentin thinks about the underground: "police patrol, hideout, tear gas, door opens, submachine gun muzzles, black blood of asphyxiation gushing up in the mouth" (158). As a result of this dialogue between two levels of narrative, Puig's readers gain increased insight into the two principal diegetic characters.

Even without such direct identification on the part of the characters, the metadiegetic film narratives interact polyphonically with the diegetic story.

In the love story based on *The Enchanted Cottage*, an unattractive girl, shunned by others, finds love with a hideously scarred veteran who feels equally excluded from "normal" society. When the veteran's parents come to visit the newly married, ecstatic couple, Molina's narrative reports: "[P]arents' bitter disappointment, ferocious scar slashed across the young man's face, his bride a lowly servant with an ugly face and such clumsy manners." The young man wonders, "[H]as it all been nothing but a cruel deception? is it possible that we haven't changed?" His bride "fli[es] to find a mirror, the cruel reality" (110). Filtered through Molina's homosexual sympathies, the feelings of such socially marginalized human beings take on dramatic life. The same may be said concerning Irena, the young woman in *Cat People* forced by an ancient Romanian curse to act in ways she cannot consciously comprehend, and of the dominated souls in *I Walked with a Zombie*. Frances Wyers Weber concludes that Puig's fiction creates a "web that twines the reader's memories into the fabricated lives of Molina and Valentin, a web that seems to stretch out in time and space, linking a prison cell in Buenos Aires and Valasquez and Ovid and Rita Hayworth" (179). In the process, both the parallels and the contrasts between the diegetic and the meta-diegetic narratives deepen the discursive polyphony of Puig's narrative.

One other form of dialogue is pertinent. The plots of popular movies that Molina recounts throughout the novel appeal—as the boleros do—to Molina's sentimentality and his pathetic desire for a world in which lovers live happily ever after. Valentin sees himself as more steely-eyed and real-istic. He scornfully tells Molina that the film about Leni and Werner is "a piece of Nazi junk" (56) and warns that "only thinking about nice things . . . can be dangerous too. . . . It can become a vice, always trying to escape from reality like that, it's like taking drugs or something" (79). Surely there is merit in Valentin's remark. Both the actual and the virtual films that Molina recounts are constructed by Puig so as to bring out their falseness to everyday experience, and even more so their patent irrelevance to the everyday experience of characters in this novel. A political power structure that systematically exploits torture as a matter of policy requires the respon-sible individual to engage in investigation and resistance of some sort rather than in acquiescence and escapism.

Therefore, Valentin says that he prefers the more realistic discourse of political science to escapist "junk." As he explains to Molina, "If you read something, if you study something, you transcend any cell you're inside of, do you understand what I'm saying? That's why I read and why I study every day" (78). In light of the world depicted in Puig's novel, few readers will reject Valentin's proposition out of hand.

Even so, Puig will not endorse Valentin's Marxism as the preferred alternative to Molina's escapism. Thus, Molina plausibly asks in return, "What's the world coming to, with all your politicians?" (78). Also, Valentin dreams of love-ever-after with his bourgeois lover, Marta, rather than with his compatriot in the underground. Finally, when Valentin has been tortured to the point of death and has drifted off into a fantasy from one of Molina's movies, the Marta of his dreams tells him—in the last words of Puig's novel—"[T]his dream is short, but this dream is happy" (281). In other words, Puig will not totally reject escapism, nor will he accord the discourse of political science monologic authority.

This is not to say that since Valentin ends up escaping into fantasy, Puig simply accepts the discourse constructed by popular films instead. The popularity of such films is certainly a factor that Puig cannot ethically ignore. As he admitted to Barbara Mujica: "I decided that I didn't like writing for films. What I liked was going to the movies" (5). Even so, the rest of Puig's novel is too intellectually and emotionally demanding to accept popular escapism as the final solution. If Marxist political analysis is not the answer, however, and if escapist entertainment is not the answer, then what is?

Francine R. Masiello locates the answer in post-modern formalism: "Exploiting the artistic subproducts of mass culture—film, song, soap opera, and common middle-class kitsch—Manuel Puig assembles in his novels a playful pastiche of discursive vanants that emphasize the topographical features of words in print and parody the referential conventions of fiction" (15). Masiello's answer seems inadequate to Laura Rice-Sayre, who accuses her of adopting the strategy of "most critics [who] have taken refuge in a formalist discussion of the plurality of styles, the multiple play of discourses, and the polysemic qualities of the text and have tended to ignore or even deny the political content and form the novel's dialogue embodies" (248). While I would agree with Rice-Sayre's intention to extend Puig's dialogism beyond the formal level, I would also take advantage of her and Masiello's common recognition of Puig's "discourses" to extend the discussion beyond materialist politics.

Puig's novel locates its answer dynamically among a polyphony of voices including popular film, Marxism, literary modernism, psychoanalysis, the social sciences, popular music, third-world nationalism, the search for individual authenticity, and a phenomenological acceptance of the other. In one sense, such a complex answer may seem to be no answer at all because it does not fit into the grooves of aesthetic organicism or polemic coherence worn by the fiction with which we are most comfortable. Once again Bakhtin is pertinent. In the concluding chapter of *Problems of Dostoevsky's Poetics*, he writes: "The polyphonic novel makes new demands on aesthetic thought as well. Raised on monologic forms of artistic visualization, thoroughly steeped in them, aesthetic thought tends to absolutize those forms and not see their boundaries" (271). Overcoming boundaries, socio-political and aesthetic, bridging gaps, meeting the other person as a subjectivity equal to one's own—these are the stylistic strategies as well as the topics of Puig's *Kiss of the Spider Woman*.

Middle Tennessee State University

Works cited

Bakhtin, Mikhail M. *The Dialogic Imagination: Four Essays.* Trans. Caryl Emerson and Michael Holquist. Ed. Holquist. Austin: U of Texas P, 1981.

——. *Problems of Dostoevsky's Poetics.* Ed. and trans. Caryl Emerson. Minneapolis: U of Minnesota P, 1984.

——. *Rabelais and His World.* Trans. Helene Iswolsky. Bloomington: Indiana UP, 1984.

——. *Speech Genres and Other Late Essays.* Trans. Vern W. McGee. Ed. Caryl Emerson and Michael Holquist. Austin: U of Texas P, 1986.

Boling, Becky. 'From *Beso* to *Beso*: Puig's Experiments with Genre.' *Symposium* 44 (1990): 75–87.

Bost, David H. 'Telling Tales in Manuel Puig's *El beso de la mujer arana*.' *South Atlantic Review* 54.2 (1989): 93–106.

Genette, Gerard. *Figures of Literary Discourse.* Trans. Alan Sheridan. Oxford: Basil Blackwell, 1982.

Holquist, Michael. *Dialogism: Bakhtin and his World.* London and New York: Routledge, 1990.

Masiello, Francine R. 'Jail House Flicks: Projections by Manuel Puig.' *Symposium* 32 (1978): 15–24.

Merrim, Stephanie. 'Through the Film Darkly: Grade "B" Movies and Dreamwork in *Tres tristes tigres* and *El beso de la mujer arana*.' *Modern Language Studies* 15 (1985): 300–12.

Mujica, Barbara. 'The Imaginary Worlds of Manuel Puig.' *Americas* (May–June 1986): 2–7.

Puig, Manuel. *Kiss of the Spider Woman.* Trans. Thomas Colchie. New York: Knopf, 1979.

Rice-Sayre, Laura. 'Domination and Desire: A Feminist-Materialist Reading of Manuel Puig's *Kiss of the Spider Woman*.' *Textual Analysis: Some Readers Reading.* Ed. Mary Ann Caws. New York: MLA, 1986: 245–56.

Schwartz, Ronald. *Nomads, Exiles, and Emigres.* Metuchen: Scarecrow, 1980.

Sklar, Robert. Rev, of *Kiss of the Spider Woman.* Dir. Hector Babenco. *Cineaste* 14.3 (1986). Rpt. in *Film Review Annual 1986.* Ed. Jerome S. Ozer. Englewood, NJ: Ozer, 1987: 668–69.

Wyers Weber, Frances. 'Manuel Puig at the Movies.' *Hispanic Review* 49 (1981): 163–81.

40 Stephanie Merrim, Through the Film Darkly: Grade 'B' Movies and Dreamwork in *Tres tristes tigres* and *El beso de la mujer araña* (1985)

In this article Stephanie Merrim explores the relationship between the film narratives interpolated into the text of Manuel Puig's *Kiss of the Spider Woman* and the actual B-movies on which these narratives are based. She points out the many significant differences between the actual films and the character Molina's account of them, going on to offer a detailed Freudian analysis of the zombie film narrative in *Kiss of the Spider Woman* based on the 1943 film *I Walked with a Zombie*. Merrim notes the way in which the distortions reflect both Freudian dream theory and the manipulation of the invisible author, Puig. She draws explicit parallels between Molina's zombie narrative and Hitchcock's *Rebecca*, suggesting that both contain interesting Freudian representations of gender. The article shows how everything in this polyphonic text is subject to several levels of mediation.

Merrim, S., 'Through the Film Darkly: Grade "B" Movies and Dreamwork in *Tres tristes tigres* and *El beso de la mujer araña*', *Modern Language Studies*, 15.4, Fall 1985, pp. 302–12

The use of movies as a language for repressed fears we discover in *Tres tristes tigres* becomes the determining factor in *El beso*, where it forms part of a whole cluster of elements which depend from an analogy between movies and dreams. The six "B" movies narrated in *El beso* reflect Puig's literal and analytical reading of the aphorism which regards Hollywood as a dream machine or, in the author's words, a "fábrica de sueños."[1] [factory of dreams] But of course Puig is not the first person to draw such an analogy and the remarks of critic Michael Wood on movies as a dream language "preview" the shape of our argument: "It seems that entertainment is not, as we often think, a full-scale flight from our problems, not a means of forgetting them completely, but rather a rearrangement of our problems into shapes which tame them, which disperse them to the margins of our attention;"[2] and, "The business of films is the business of dreams, as Nathanial West said, but then dreams are scrambled messages from waking life."[3]

Preliminary to any discussion of the movie-stories' codification of reality in *El beso*, however, we must set the scene; for the structuring situation of the novel simulates that of psychoanalysis. Each evening the homosexual Molina, a self-appointed Scheherazade, retells a portion of a movie to his cellmate, the revolutionary, Valentín, who has agreed to comment on the films ("yo quiero intervenir un poco," 21). [I want to intervene a little]. The movie-stories quickly begin to play the same role as dreams in psychoanalysis and their interpretation occupies not just the analytical Valentín, but both protagonists. At the same time, the movie-stories act as catalysts which, through free association, elicit discussion of the aspects of Molina's and Valentín's past lives suggested by the stories. Molina and Valentín freely exchange roles of analyst and analysand in this ongoing dialogue and auto-biography facilitated by the intermediary of the movies.

It is no accident, however, that the movie-stories touch off discussions of concerns central to the characters, for the emotions and circumstances from their present, as we shall see in detail, provide the scaffolding of the films. But first these elements must pass through something akin to what Freud called the "censor." Similar to press censorship, the dream censor constitutes a barrier which the raw dream thoughts of repressed instincts and emotions must traverse to be either deemed or made acceptable to the dream content: "All elements which find their way into the dream must be withdrawn from the resistance of the censor," wrote Freud.[4] Now, the oppression—or repression—of Argentine society under the military government which imprisoned Molina and Valentín permeates every corner of the cell and comprises the censor which disallows the direct expression of truths.[5] In reaction to this system of oppression, ... Molina and Valentín evolve a counter-system or society apart from cell ("nuestra relación la podemos moldear como queremos," 201) [we can mould our relationship as we wish] in which the movie-stories play a determining role. Valentín adds his particular requirements to this otherwise silent censor by forbidding discussions of eroticism and food ("De veras, te lo pido en serio. Ni de comidas ni de mujeres desnudas," 57). [Honestly, I'm asking you seriously. Nothing about food or naked women]. "Colorín colorado, este cuento se ha terminado," the traditional ending of fairy tales, closes two of the movie-stories produced under this system of censorship: as in a fairy tale, the "message" has been passed through some censor and projected onto an acceptable language, of the frilly and harmless "B" films, in whose unreality lies their essential truth. Their real referents replaced with a neutral set of fictional referents, the concerns of the characters both receive expression and are neutralized in the film-stories. And often, as its crowning achievement, the enchantment proves completely effective, for the movie tales provide a total escape. As Molina says: "Yo me sentía fenómeno, me había olvidado de esta mugre e celda, de todo, contándote la película" (23). [I was feeling fantastic, I'd forgotten about this filthy cell, everything, telling you the movie].

That Molina, unwitting instrument of the censor, so significantly rewrites the movies he tells as to become their author is evident to the reader familiar with the actual films ("Cat People", "The Enchanted Cottage," "I Walked with a Zombie") on which three of the movie-stories are based.[6] In any case, the text of each movie clearly bears the traces of his intervention in the lacunae and resequencing that result from memory failures, as well as in the *modus operandi* chosen by Molina for the telling of the tales: at night, in installments, to heighten the suspense: "me gusta sacarle el dulce en lo mejor, así te gusta más la película" (32). [I like keeping the best bits for last, so that you'll like the film more]. Moreover, each movie is transformed into a showcase for Molina's sensibility, of absolute beauty passed through a romantic kitsch aesthetic. Molina "reads" and rewrites all of the movies through a haze of a Corín Tellado, or Hollywoodesque, rhetoric and optics. The ecstatic attention to material detail, which completely overwhelms the plot of the two movies Molina tells for himself ("Destino" and "The Enchanted Cottage"), or his defense of the Nazi propaganda film: "te creés que no . . . no me doy cuenta que es de propaganda na . . . nazi, pero si a mí me gusta es porque está bien hecha, aparte de eso es una obra de arte" (63) [Believe me I don't take any notice of the fact that it's Nazi propoganda but I like it because it's well made, apart from that it's a work of art], indicate the direction of his narrative acts of *bricolage*.

That Molina actively (if unconsciously) transforms the movies in accordance with his literary and artistic tastes is plain to see. But to understand how Puig, ostensibly through Molina, follows a textual process analogous to dreamwork we should look briefly at the "narrative" aspects of that Freudian construct.

Rather than simply eliminating the offensive material, the censor in dreams functions as something of a translator, who changes the shape of the dream thoughts. The censor's work, known as the dreamwork, consists in a variety of transformations and serves the basic needs of the dream, which are to gather up the repressed recent and infantile material and to present it to the dreamer, providing the fulfillment of a wish. According to Christian Metz, the most interesting aspect of the activities of the censor, then, are how things escape it: "The peculiarity of censorship, and one of its most noticeable characteristics . . . is that things are always managing to get past it, to 'get round' it, you could even go further and say that it consists only of countless swirling movements, twists and turns."[7] Before thus letting the dream thoughts go, as is well known, the censor deforms them, primarily by the techniques of condensation and displacement. Displacement, of the psychic accent onto a more innocuous element, can also perform the very cinematic function of exchanging "a colourless and abstract expression of the dream thought . . . for one that is pictorial and concrete," since "whatever is pictorial is capable of representation in dreams."[8] A final, equally cinematic, transformation, which Freud called "secondary elaboration"[9] molds the assorted dream thoughts into the semblance of a story.

The above description of dreamwork entails so accurate a picture of the process which we shall call "encoding" in *El beso* precisely because, as he admits, Puig has ciphered the novel through a code analogous to the language of dreams: "Allí [in the novel] todo está mediatizado," and "el diálogo trata de no nombrar las cosas. Lo que no se dice, tal vez, va a ser más importante, más sugestivo."[10] [There, everything is mediated . . . the dialogue tries not to name things. What is not said, perhaps, is going to be more important, more suggestive]. Different aspects of the process of encoding, which is the translation of life into art (high or low) and dreams, play a central role in Puig's works, each of which ultimately comprises an essay on the dynamics of exchange between the three elements.[11] Yet only in *El beso* (and *Pubis angelical*) does the code become the novel, whose greatest challenge lies in deciphering, first of all, the information taken from the characters' personal situations which Molina, in rewriting the movies, builds into them.[12]

As in dreams, which are always egotistical, the impetus and apparent substance of *El beso*'s movie-stories derive from the characters' circumstances both inside and outside the cell. We witness the process of encoding most clearly when details from the cell pass directly into the movie-stories: among many such cases, Valentín's philosophy book, mentioned on p. 108, reappears on p. 110 in "The Enchanted Cottage;" Molina's depression, also of p. 108, is passed cathartically on to his alterego (he speaks for her in the first person), the little servant in the same movie. At a further remove, acts of betrayal, betraying in palimpsest Molina's own betrayal of Valentín, compulsively shape the outcome of each movie. Since Molina always identifies with the heroine ("yo siempre con la heroina," 31), the protagonist is invariably the guilty party. In addition to such displacement, circumstances in the cell receive compensatory treatment in the movie-stories: as when Molina, in a fit of pique against Valentín's revolutionary fervor and atheism, portrays Nazism as a specifically anti-Marxist movement, glorifying Hitler as its deity (93–94). On a much larger scale, elements from the characters' previous lives actually determine the choice and plot of the movies. The rosy "Enchanted Cottage" (the counter fable to "Cat People"), with its tale of a miraculous transformation through love, reflects and writes a happy ending onto Molina's relationship with the waiter Gabriel, whose love for Molina might transform him into a homosexual. A transparent act of wish fulfillment, the movie signals the connection with Gabriel by applying a Freudian double entendre, "un muchacho buena mozo," to the film's protagonist (113 and *passim*). Finally, a curiously dense act of encoding takes place when Molina, as a penance for his betrayal, creates an adventure movie for Valentín which obliquely exposes the latter's conflict between his bourgeois origins and revolutionary ideals. Halfway through the movie-story, we are shown how Valentín's dream or delirium thoughts, the passages in italics, personalize the movie: appropriating it as a means of telling his, own, most intimate, autobiography, Valentín plots or re-encodes himself back into the movie.

The most striking feature, however, of the movie-webs is the degree to which their elements, like the images which reach the dream content, are *overdetermined*, forming nodal points in which coincide various dream thoughts:[13] they not only radiate laterally from the characters' concurrent lives, but also vertically, onto an "allegorical" plane. Analogous to dreams, which draw their material from both recent events and infantile—often sexual—neuroses, when submitted to a close reading these film-stories emerge as psychosexual moral tales, the locus of personal and supra-personal forces. While the characters themselves supposedly encode the films with their personal circumstances, the author has built an extra dimension into each film which addresses matters of homosexuality, sex roles, repression, and so on.

Our first indication of this extra dimension, as well as the first of a series of scholia to the films, comes with Valentín's Freudian reading of Jacques Toumeur's "Cat People."[14] Valentín, who identifies with the analyst in the film, sets the path for similar readings of the other films with his interpretation of "Cat People" as an allegory of sexual fears: "¿Pero sabes qué me gusta?, que es como una alegoría, muy clara además, del miedo de la mujer a entregarse al hombre, porque al entregarse al sexo se vuelve un poco animal . . ." (36). [But you know what I like? That it's like an allegory, a very clear one too, of a woman's fear when she submits to a man, because in giving herself sexually, she becomes slightly animal-like again]. The importance of the somewhat distracting footnotes detailing theories of homosexuality, which begin with the second movie and assume the same function of gloss, for this reason cannot be underestimated: as Puig has said in their defense, ". . . a esta novela no se puede realmente *acceder* sin esa información—siempre, te insisto, tan represivamente escamoteada—, de manera que había que darla."[15] [You can't really *accede* to this novel without that information—always, I must stress, so repressively covered up—so that it was necessary to give it]. Though the notes seem to turn up at odd moments in the text, they invariably suggest a psychological reading—a psychoanalytical interpretation—of those or subsequent pages. At times the connection is patent: a note on repression accompanies Molina's first meeting with the prison director; or, the peripatetic heroics of the adventure movie, with the son betraying first his father then his mother, only make sense in light of the Oedipal and Electra complexes described in the footnotes. Often, the more oblique the dialogue between the text and notes, the more telling: while they seem to refer only to Molina and Gabriel, the theories of the physical origins of homosexuality cut in between two installments of the Nazi propaganda film also constitute a subtle comment on the Nazis' racial theories. As this last remark attests, the footnotes and films may bear political implications: taken together, the footnotes (which also treat bisexuality), narration (with its "feminine" sensibility) and dialogue (establishing the popularity of Nazi films during Perón's reign) surrounding "Destino" draw a trenchant, if clearly ironic, equation between homosexuality, Peronism and Nazism.

Sexual shades into political liberation as the footnotes progressively widen their scope at the same time as they enter into a more polemical relationship with the movie narrations. To do justice to the full dynamics of the allegorical, as well as other dreamwork that we have described, let us undertake a close reading, beginning with the original story, of the fifth and most elaborate film-story in *El beso*. Puig tells us that his "La vuelta de la mujer zombie" is based, with "importantes variaciones,"[16] on a film also alluded to in *Tres tristes tigres*, "I Walked with a Zombie" (1943), produced by Val Lewton and directed by Jacques Tourneur. Both Cabrera Infante and Puig undoubtedly find appealing the manner in which the Tourneur horror films portray fleshed-out characters reacting with human emotions to terrifying events.[17] "I Walked with a Zombie," which Val Lewton intended to be a West Indian version of the romantic *Jane Eyre* in the guise of a zombie chiller,[18] offers the full gamut of heightened emotions, as this synopsis of the film (borrowed from *Val Lewton: The Reality of Terror*) indicates:

> Betsy, a Canadian nurse, comes to St. Sebastian in the West Indies to care for Jessica Holland, an invalid who seems to be suffering from a rare form of mental paralysis. She falls in love with Paul, Jessica's husband, although she is courted by Wesley Rand, his half-brother. Believing Paul to be still in love with his wife, Betsy selflessly takes Jessica to a voodoo ceremony in the hope of restoring her to him. Her effort fails but forces Mrs. Rand, a missionary's widow and mother of Paul and Wesley, to reveal that she had employed voodoo to turn Jessica into a zombie when she announced that she was going to leave St. Sebastian with Wesley. Wesley kills Jessica in order to free her from the curse of death-in-life, and then dies in the sea himself.[19]

All of this takes place in a town called Ti-Misery, a name which alludes to the inhuman conditions under which the island's natives live and work.

Certain aspects of Puig's radical translation of "I Walked with a Zombie" will prove crucial to the two kinds of encoding present in the novel. Attracted by the zombie motif, and particularly its political connotations (the peasants really *are* zombies in his version), Puig retains the background of the original while grossly rearranging the plot and characters to achieve a symbolic configuration. The extra-marital complications of the original fall away and the erstwhile nurse becomes a second wife so that the new version can focus on the triangle of a husband and his first and second wives. In essence, then, Puig reverts to *Jane Eyre* itself, a story of passion and repression. Or, even better, to another "B" movie (which Cabrera considers a paen to "la soledad del amor perdido"),[20] Hitchcock's "Rebecca," whose nameless, ever-adoring and submissive protagonist, living in the shadow of the first wife, could well have served as the prototype for the heroine of Puig's movie-story. Further, as hinted by the change in emphasis from the title "I Walked with a Zombie" to "La vuelta de la *mujer* zombie," [The return of the zombie *woman*] the spotlight in Puig's movie shifts to the heroic actions of the two women, which stand in stark contrast to those of the husband: a far cry from the male authority figures of *Jane Eyre* and "Rebecca," the weak man pines after (and perhaps even rapes, p. 193) his zombied first wife, drinking himself into oblivion each night. His misery drives the second wife to the witch doctor in order to save her husband's (rather than the first wife's) soul. And Puig's movie culminates with the zombie killing her husband (rather than being killed herself) and setting fire to the house, thereby ending the oppression of the islanders.

In making these changes, Puig deforms "I Walked with a Zombie" to fit the other "B" films of *El beso*, to the end that the invariant features of the films display as faithful a blueprint of Molina's preoccupations as do the many details from his immediate situation encoded in the movie-stories. Due to these changes, the gothic turned love story with a tragic ending, "La vuelta de la mujer zombie," now enacts the same drama of the transition to marriage, a reflection of Molina's questioning of his own sublimated sexuality, as "Cat People" and "The Enchanted Cottage." Molina's romantic inclinations also determine the rewriting of the heroine into a long-suffering figure, a *mujer sufrida*, and the hero into a weak anti-authority figure.[21] The debility of the hero, which figures so prominently in the movie narration, at the same time condenses into one figure several situations from Molina and Valentín's lives. At the deepest level, both the weak male and the love triangle transcribe Molina's impressions of Valentín's physical and spiritual weakening. Temporarily turned into something of a zombie by the poisoned

223

food, Valentín exposes his bourgeois family origins, hidden emotions and tastes. Even more important, he confesses that he loves, not his comrade in revolution, but the middle class Marta, thereby framing a love triangle between a 'healthy' woman and a political 'zombie,' who nonetheless (as did the first wife) retains his affections. As in the adventure movie, here, too, the male protagonist embarks upon a revolutionary course (to end the oppression of the slaves) but proves unfit, too weak and too bourgeois, for the task. The woman, as we have noted, then achieves the victory. It is at this point that Molina—"yo siempre con la heroina"—[I'm always with the heroine] enters the dense fabric of condensation through a dual identification with the two female protagonists. The fact that Molina, in his role of nurse to Valentín, identifies with the oppressed second wife in the film, who attempts to cure her alcoholic husband, explains as displacement (of psychic charge) the demotion of the second wife to a minor role in the film as well as her seemingly inexplicable farewell at the end as the island's liberator. And, through this identification, Molina subtly inserts himself in the love triangle with the role both of caretaker and victor, auguring the sexual "liberation" of Valentín which will allow him to become Molina's lover.

Two of the situations encoded through condensation and displacement into the coherent movie narration reappear, now incoherent and barely recognizable, in the mysterious italics interspersed throughout the zombie story. Since the italicized images divide themselves into two series, they would appear to represent Molina's thoughts as he narrates the zombie story, and Valentín's as he listens to it. Molina's series begins with the heart attack (similar to that of his mother) of an old woman and moves into a hospital setting where a good nurse, a bad nurse and a "sonámbula traidora" (167) [treacherous] who blurts out the truth, all fade into one figure, illustrating Molina's duplicitous role as both cause and cure of Valentín's illness. As does Molina, the nurses care for, and eventually cure, the contagious (i.e. contaminated) young patient. A police shoot-out leads off Valentín's series, which quickly disintegrates into a surrealistic flow of images revolving around empty heads and bodies like those of the zombies. Using the somewhat obscure image of a girl going to the movies as a transition, the series ends happily, with the political motif of the rich donating their wealth to the poor, a fulfillment of Valentín's Marxist dreams (217). Now, much as this synopsis seems to render the italicized comments intelligible, they actually consist of both transparent and opaque images and thus represent something of a literary *tour de force* on the part of Puig.[22] For with these oblique and opaque images Puig pretends to depict, as he will in *Pubis angelical*, the actual dream-thinking, the otherness of the language of the unconscious. He implicitly sets this level of encoding over and against that of the film-narrations: both the italic and movie-narrations, as we now know, translate or encode the same circumstances through the dreamwork of condensation and displacement, but the extraordinary degree of secondary elaboration of the movie-stories sets them apart from the less polished dreams and make of them an intermediate language between the conscious and the unconscious.

Valentín's hallucinations associating the police, and thus the state, with the zombie theme bring us, finally, to the "allegorical" dimension of the movie. With the death-in-life of the zombies described in the following manner: "el muerto ya no tiene voluntad y obedece todas las órdenes que le dan y los brujos los usan para que hagan lo que a ellos se les de la gana" (172), [the dead person no longer has a will and obeys all orders given and the witch-doctors use them so that they do whatever they want them to] the reader can easily imagine several symbolic identities for the zombies and their masters (Cabrera, we remember, related the political *desaparecidos* with zombies). The abundance of footnotes immediately preceding and during the film channel these speculations, drawing an unmistakeable equation between the culpability of the state—*patria*, patriarch, *pater*—and the family unit. "Estoy convencido de que la escuela de la explotación está en la pareja, en la primera célula y que de allí se traslada al campo del trabajo," [I am convinced that the school of exploitation is in the couple, in the first cell and that from there it translates into the field of work], Puig has stated.[23] Women, the footnotes tell us (209–211), fall victim to a system of oppression in which men, both at home and in society, are the oppressors. Yet men are also the oppressed, cast in an authoritarian role which squelches the "female" in them (168–171). Society's rejection of the homosexual who has refused the authoritarian masculine role only confirms the oppression of the male, his need for liberation (199; 209). Sexual liberation thus inevitably joins forces with social liberation, but the question remains of whether society can survive without repression and sublimation (209–211). While Freud would probably respond in the negative, the zombie movie thinks otherwise. Dramatizing these issues on a transparent symbolic plane, "La vuelta de la mujer zombie" insinuates that it is marriage which turns the woman, not into a panther this time, but into man's zombie: auguring the woman's loss of self, the voodoo doll which curses the new wife wears a replica of her wedding dress. Due to the influence of the *brujo* [witch-doctor, magician] (the state?), both wives (the first literally, the second figuratively) as well as the plantation workers of the young husband, have been transformed into zombies. According to this allegorical reading, the young husband, his attempts at rebellion against the *brujo* having failed, takes to drink. Liberation eventually issues from the women, the zombied first and second wives. And the songs of thanks and love of the islanders, while the house of the oppressors burns in the background, intimate a future free of repression.

The chorus of now-liberated natives should not, however, obscure the true reason for celebration at the end of the story: the second wife has, happily, escaped the zombiedom of love. The "allegorical" strata of the story, which emerges from the interplay of text and footnotes, proffers the startling equation between the silken net of love and the fatal web of repression and exploitation. This "allegory," further developed in the final movie-story, will, in turn, determine a subversive reading of the *dénouement* of the entire novel: Puig's works, always divided into two parts, often feature a baroque design of *engaño* and *desengaño* [illusion and disillusion]; it is no accident that the zombie movie opens the second part.

By virtue of its doubly-encoded nature, the final film-story holds the key to both Molina and Valentín's love affair and to the larger message of the book. On the surface, the Mexican picture recounts an act of liberation as a young woman frees herself from the tyranny of the magnate to pursue her true love. In reality, she has only entered into another bondage: a slave of love, she sacrifices career, comfort and dignity, ultimately prostituting herself to save her gravely ill lover. Her guilded zombiedom reaches its peak when her lover dies, leaving her to gaze (as in the zombie movie) into the water, still transported by the joys of having truly loved someone. Both Molina and Valentín consider this "enigmatic" ending the best part of the movie— and well they might, because it is their story, in code, the movie has told. Liberated from the tyranny of social prohibitions, in sexually consummating their relationship Molina and Valentín accede to a space beyond personal and social repression. As they themselves remark ("Es como si estuviéramos en una isla desierta . . . Porque, sí, fuera de la celda están nuestros opresores, pero adentro, no. Aquí nadie oprime a nadie . . .", 206), [It's as if we were on a desert island . . . Because, yes, our oppressors are outside the cell, not inside. Here no-one oppresses anyone], the two men believe they have escaped the system of oppression.

There is, unfortunately, much evidence to the contrary. The day after their first sexual encounter, Molina and Valentín assume stereotypical male-female attitudes towards each other, with Molina waiting on Valentín and Valentín insistent upon maintaining a romantic atmosphere at all costs ("¡Carajo! te he dicho que hoy acá no entra la tristeza, ¡y no va a entrar!," 235). [Hell, I've told you that today sadness won't come in, and it won't!]. Throughout, Molina refuses to abandon the stereotyped concepts about the ideal man of "una señora burguesa" (50), even when Valentín, in his stance as the 'superior' and wiser man, tries to disabuse Molina of his 'feminine' notions. Nothing, though, is as telling as the two characters' fates. Molina, not a revolutionary but a slave of love, as Valentín realizes, dies (just like the chorus girl in "Destino") trying to live out his grade "B" movie fantasies: "¿por una causa buena? Uhmm ... yo creo que se dejó matar porque así se moría como la heroína de una película, y nada de eso de una causa buena" (285). [for a good cause? Um ... I believe that he let himself be killed because that's how he could die like a film heroine, and not at all because of a good cause]. And from Valentín's delirious thoughts in the "Epilogue," we gather that the greatest effect this process has wrought in him is the acceptance, not of homosexuality, but of his own bourgeois nature:[24] he reveals his repugnance for the spider woman ("la telaraña le crece del cuerpo de ella misma ... unos hilos peludos como sogas que me dan mucho asco ...", 285) [the web grows from her own body ... some hairy threads like ropes which disgust me very much] and the novel ends with his first declaration of love to the middle-class Marta. Valentín, it would appear, has trapped Molina in a web of his own, a web of exploitation.

As *this* "final enigmático" (285) [enigmatic ending] indicates, there may well have been no conversion: the characters remain unwitting victims of oppression, of the web which only the footnotes, and hence the "allegorical" dimension of the last movie, elucidate. The final set of footnotes in the zombie film call for the liberation of homosexuals, with heterosexuals to follow their lead. At the same time, they note the great difficulty of finding a "third way," that is, for homosexuals to break away from the oppressor-oppressed model of sex roles. Viewed in relation to these footnotes—for the Mexican movie has none of its own—the anachronistic romantic *cursilería* of the last film seems to constitute an ironic and definitively negative response to the call for a new way. The heroine's attempted liberation, only to be shackled by a conventional notion of love, therefore corresponds to the characters' inability to escape established sex roles.

Why are Puig's characters unable to escape the spider woman's web? What holds them prisoners and makes them zombies of sorts? The personal and "allegorical" messages encoded in the last film, as the reader will have noticed, almost coincide precisely because the same force is responsible for both, parallel, phenomena. And part of that force, sadly, are the movies which so mold our thinking. Particularly the romantic, convention-ridden "B" films with their strong silent heroes and wilting heroines. Here the theme of betrayal attains its final definition for, as Puig has stated, "los personajes no son totalmente reponsables de su conducta. Son productos de su medio. Lo que oprime es la imposibilidad de pensar por sí mismos, de ser originales."[25] [the characters are not totally responsible for their behaviour. They are products of their milieu. What oppresses is the impossibility of thinking for themselves, of being original]. Thus viewed as a weapon of cultural brain-washing, Puig's movies prove to operate under the same double sign as those of Cabrera: bitter and sweet, repository of the unspeakable, vehicle for what would otherwise remain unsaid.

Notes

1 Manuel Puig, *Pubis angelical* (Barcelona: Seix Barral, 1979), p. 132. Also, Manuel Puig, *El beso de la mujer araña* (Barcelona: Seix Barral, 1976). All further references to this text are incorporated into the body of the study. We will be referring to the six films narrated in *El beso*, three of which are based on real films, three of which are composites of several films: (in order of their appearance in the novel) 'Cat People,' dir. Jacques Tourneur (1942); the invented Nazi propaganda film called 'Destino;' 'The Enchanted Cottage,' dir. John Cromwell (1946); what we call the 'Adventure' film; 'I Walked with a Zombie,' dir. Jacques Tourneur (1943); what we will call the 'Mexican' film.

2 Michael Wood, *America in the Dark* (New York: Basic Books, 1975), p. 18.

3 *Ibid.*, p. 16.

4 Sigmund Freud, *The Interpretation of Dreams* in *The Basic Writings of Sigmund Freud*, ed. A. A. Brill (New York: Random House, 1938), p. 339.

5 I refer the reader to Alicia Borinsky's excellent discussion of *El beso* in Chapter 2 of her *Ver y ser visto* (Barcelona: Antonio Bosch, 1978) where she argues that everything in the novel is determined by the system of oppression.

6 In her 'Manuel Puig at the Movies' (*Hispanic Review* 49 [1981] particularly pp. 167–70), Frances Wyers details Molina's interventions in the telling of the movie stories. Molina's retellings, according to Professor Wyers, 'almost always contain extratextual explanations that make us aware of two simultaneous series, the story and the intervention of the story-teller' (p. 168).

7 Christian Metz, *The Imaginary Signifier: Psychoanalysis and the Cinema*, trans. Celia Britton *et al* (Bloomington: Indiana Univ. Press, 1982), p. 254.

8 Freud, *Interpretation*, p. 361.

9 *Ibid.*, p. 445 ff.

10 Danubio Torres Fierro, 'Conversación con Manuel Puig: la redención de la cursilería', *Eco*, 28, no. 173 (March 1975), p. 507.

11 As I show elsewhere, *La traición de Rita Hayworth* (1968) and *Boquitas pintadas* (1969) examine the impact of culture on the individual's consciousness while the dreams, stream of consciousness and clinical narration of *The Buenos Aires Affair* (1973) attempt a psychosexual case history of its protagonists. Like *El beso*, *Pubis angelical* (1979), the ultimate psychological novel, gives us a graphic illustration of the way the unconscious encodes the real data presented to it. See my 'For a New (Psychological) Novel in the Works of Manuel Puig,' *Novel* 17, 2 (Winter 1984): 141–57.

12 José Miguel Oviedo, 'La doble expresión de Manuel Puig,' *Eco*, 31, no. 192 (Oct. 1977), p. 675 also describes the mediated signifying system: 'El texto no habla de lo que parece . . . habla de *otra cosa*, remite a otro sistema oculto y conectado con él. O dicho de otro modo: el plano expresivo de la novela es, él mismo, un sistema significativo en el que hay que desentrañar una forma y un contenido y

una relación entre ambos.' Oviedo also lists certain of the characters' personal circumstances which enter into the movie-stories.

13 As Freud wrote, using a case study to illustrate a general point, [certain elements] 'were taken up into the dream content because they were able to offer the most numerous points of contact with the greatest number of dream-thoughts and thus represented nodal points at which a great number of the dream-thoughts met together . . .' *Interpretation*, p. 323.

14 The original 'Cat People,' which featured quotations from Freud and Donne as its epigraphs, certainly lends itself to such a reading. It has been described by Joel E. Siegel, in his *Val Lewton: The Reality of Terror* (New York: Viking Press, 1973), p. 102, as a movie containing 'suggestions of sexual anxiety, antagonism, the identification of physical passion with destruction, and overtones of lesbianism.'

15 Marcelo Coddou, 'Seis preguntas,' pp. 12–13. Let us suggest that it is not altogether inconceivable that these footnotes represent Valentín's readings, as he takes down information relevant to the situations in the cell and in the movie-stories. Valentín's laughter (the only time in the novel) and comment on p. 225, 'ay, qué buen psicólogo resulté,' referring to Molina's childhood pastimes and following upon a note about childhood role models (p. 211), seem to plant the seeds for such an interpretation.

16 Coddou, 'Seis preguntas,' p. 5.

17 Segal, *Val Lewton*, p. 29.

18 *Ibid.*, p. 41.

19 *Ibid.*, p. 107.

20 Guillermo Cabrera Infante, *Arcadia todas las noches* (Barcelona: Seix Barral, 1978), p. 78.

21 Puig has often remarked on his dislike of the authoritarian male role, as in his *Partisan Review* interview by Ronald Christ (XLIV, no. 1 [1977], p. 62): '. . . I myself have always rejected the role of the authoritarian male . . . I consider the rejection of authority which has cost me so much trouble throughout my life, an unconscious rebellion, but a healthy one.'

22 The parallel between the function of these italics and those of the epilogue of *Tres tristes tigres* is striking. *TTT*'s epilogue; the broken images of a madwoman's discourse, also represents a translation onto another level of the concerns and the unique language of the nightworld.

23 Coddou, 'Seis preguntas,' p. 12.

24 I again refer the reader to Alicia Borinsky's discussion of the novel, and particularly, pp. 59 ff. Professor Borinsky sees Molina and Valentín as, 'la misma persona en relación de dobles' (p. 60), and their relationship as a web which 'ha anulado la diferencia entre amantes' (p. 60). The two men, she writes, 'han reconstituido— en una cárcel fascista—la sexualidad de una sociedad que los ha encarcelado' (p. 62).

25 Danubio, 'Conversación,' p. 509.

Part IV

JUDGING
LITERATURE

SAMUEL BECKETT,
WAITING FOR GODOT

41 Samuel Beckett, Three Dialogues
(1949)

It is possible that Samuel Beckett's (1906–89) 'Three Dialogues with Georges Duthuit' (first published in *Transition*, 49, December 1949) are based on actual conversations he had with Georges Duthuit (1891–1973), art critic and editor of the journal *Transition* after the Second World War (to which Beckett contributed frequently in the 1940s), but they are clearly crafted as a sort of short play. The extract here is the first of the dialogues, ostensibly regarding the paintings of French artist Pierre Tal Coat (1905–85). It however says little about these paintings, and the dialogue (all the three dialogues actually) is usually understood to reveal more about Beckett's own post-war attitude to art: here Beckett appears to deny art not only the possibility of representation (of any sort of external or internal reality, or ideological position) but even of expression. 'The expression that there is nothing to express, nothing with which to express . . . together with the obligation to express' could be (and often has been) thought of as an apt description of Beckett's own post-war writing; it can also be regarded (and again, often has) as a general expression of post-war and post-modern resignation. Worth noting also is the ponderous manner in which Beckett expresses his opinions here, and in which the dialogue proceeds – a deliberate stylistic ploy, no doubt, which distances the reader from the ideas that are being developed (or that fail to develop) even as they unravel. The sentiments of the first dialogue are repeated in different ways in the other two, very briefly with reference to paintings by French artist André Masson (1896–1987), and rather more verbosely with regard to the work of Beckett's friend, the Dutch artist Bram van Velde (1895–1981).

Beckett, S., 'Three Dialogues', in *Disjeda: Miscellaneous Writing and a Dramatic Fragment*, London: John Calder, 1983, pp. 138–9

I Tal Coat

B. — Total object, complete with missing parts, instead of partial object. Question of degree.

D. — More. The tyranny of the discreet overthrown. The world a flux of movements partaking of living time, that of effort, creation, liberation, the painting, the painter. The fleeting instant of sensation given back, given forth, with context of the continuum it nourished.

B. — In any case a thrusting towards a more adequate expression of natural experience, as revealed to the vigilant coenaesthesia. Whether achieved through submission or through mastery, the result is a gain in nature.

D. — But that which this painter discovers, orders, transmits, is not in nature. What relation between one of these paintings and a landscape seen at a certain age, a certain season, a certain hour? Are we not on a quite different plane?

B. — By nature I mean here, like the naivest realist, a composite of perceiver and perceived, not a datum, an experience. All I wish to suggest is that the tendency and accomplishment of this painting are fundamentally those of previous painting, straining to enlarge the statement of a compromise.

D. — You neglect the immense difference between the significance of perception for Tal Coat and its significance for the great majority of his predecessors, apprehending as artists with the same utilitarian servility as in a traffic jam and improving the result with a lick of Euclidian geometry. The global perception of Tal Coat is disinterested, committed neither to truth nor to beauty, twin tyrannies of nature. I can see the compromise of past painting, but not that which you deplore in the Matisse of a certain period and in the Tal Coat of today.

B. — I do not deplore. I agree that the Matisse in question, as well as the Franciscan orgies of Tal Coat, have prodigious value, but a value cognate with those already accumulated. What we have to consider in the case of Italian painters is not that they surveyed the world with the eyes of building contractors, a mere means like any other, but that they never stirred from the field of the possible, however much they may have enlarged it. The only thing disturbed by the revolutionaries Matisse and Tal Coat is a certain order on the plane of the feasible.

D. — What other plane can there be for the maker?

B. — Logically none. Yet I speak of an art turning from it in disgust, weary of its puny exploits, weary of pretending to be able, of being able, of doing a little better the same old thing, of going a little further along a dreary road.

D. — And preferring what?

B. — The expression that there is nothing to express, nothing with which to express, nothing from which to express, no power to express, no desire to express, together with the obligation to express.

D. — But that is a violently extreme and personal point of view, of no help to us in the matter of Tal Coat.

B. —

D. — Perhaps that is enough for today.

42 Hans Bertens, *The Idea of the Postmodern* (1995)

'Postmodernism' is, in Bertens's words, 'an exasperating term' that seems to encompass a variety of connotations in a range of disciplinary and chronological contexts, and which is impossible for students of twentieth-century literature to avoid. One of the first to use the term (Bertens doesn't mention this) was the historian Arnold Toynbee – at least it appears in D. C. Somervell's summation of the first six volumes of Toynbee's *A Study of History* (1947), and is thereafter used by Toynbee himself in volumes 8 and 9 (1954). For Toynbee, the postmodern period starts after 1875, and is characterised by the collapse of Enlightenment rationality and social turmoil (the modern period, in this scheme, is 1475–1875). This origin is only remotely connected to the complex set of associations and theorisations – to do as much with literature, architecture and art, as with critical theory, sociology, philosophy and politics – that Bertens does introduce briefly but succinctly in this extract without immediately taking an ideological position, and elaborates in the remainder of the book.

Bertens, H., 'Introduction', in *The Idea of the Postmodern: A History*, London: Routledge, 1995, pp. 3–11

Postmodernism is an exasperating term, and so are postmodern, postmodernist, postmodernity, and whatever else one might come across in the way of derivation. In the avalanche of articles and books that have made use of the term since the late 1950s, postmodernism has been applied at different levels of conceptual abstraction to a wide range of objects and phenomena in what we used to call reality. Postmodernism, then, is several things at once. It refers, first of all, to a complex of anti-modernist artistic strategies which emerged in the 1950s and developed momentum in the course of the 1960s. However, because it was used for diametrically opposed practices in different artistic disciplines, the term was deeply problematical almost right from the start.

Let me offer an example. Clement Greenberg, for more than thirty years easily the most influential art critic on the American scene, defined modernism in terms of a wholly autonomous aesthetic, of a radically anti-representational self-reflexivity. For Greenberg, modernism implied first of all that each artistic discipline sought to free itself from all extraneous influence. Modernist painting had thus purged itself of narrative – the presentation of biblical, classical, historical, and other such scenes – which belonged to the literary sphere, and had turned to a necessarily self-reflexive exploration of that which could be said to be specific to painting alone: its formal possibilities. From this anti-representational, formalist point of view, postmodernism gives up on this project of self-discovery and is a (cowardly) return to pictorial narrative, to representational practices. Architectural post-modernism has clear affinities with this. For Robert Venturi, Denise Scott Brown, Charles Jencks and other theorists, modernist architecture is the purist self-referential architecture of the Bauhaus – Mies van der Rohe, Gropius, and others – and of the corporate architecture of the postwar International Style. Postmodern architecture turns away from this self-absorbed and technocratic purism and turns to the vernacular and to history, thus reintroducing the humanizing narrative element that had been banned by the Bauhaus group and its corporate offshoots.

However, for many of the American literary critics that bring the term postmodernism into circulation in the 1960s and early 1970s, postmod-ernism is the move *away* from narrative, from representation. For them, postmodernism is the turn towards self-reflexiveness in the so-called meta-fiction of the period, as practiced, for instance, by Samuel Beckett, Vladimir Nabokov, John Barth, Donald Barthelme, the Surfictionists, the *nouveau romanciers*, and a host of other writers. For them this particular form of post-modernism rediscovers and radicalizes the self-reflexive moment in an otherwise representational modernism (the self-reflexivity of the later Joyce, especially of *Finnegans Wake*, of the experiments of Raymond Roussel and others). Seen from this perspective, postmodernism is a move towards radical aesthetic autonomy, towards pure formalism.

The other arts further complicate the picture. Sally Banes tells us that in dance criticism the term postmodern has been applied both to an early movement toward functionality, purity, and self-reflexivity ('analytic post-modern dance') and to a later 'rekindling of interest in narrative structures' (91). Film presents its own specific problems – of periodization, for instance. Maureen Turim's persuasive periodization of the early history of film – prim-itive (1895–1906), early classical (1906–25), and classical (1925–55) – coincides largely with literary modernism, whereas her modernist (1955–75) and 'potentially' postmodernist (1975-present) periods coincide with the postmodern period in most of the other arts (Turim 1991). There is, moreover, the intermittent presence of avant-gardist film which in its 'anti-structural' manifestations of the later 1970s and 1980s – which reintroduce 'cultural content' – is Noël Carroll's 'likeliest nominee for the title postmodern film'.

In photography, however, 'content' is associated with realism and modernism, and the pendulum swings the other way again. For Douglas Crimp, Abigail Solomon-Godeau and other theorists, writing in the late 1970s and early 1980s, it is the fiercely anti-representational, anti-narrative, deconstructionist photography of Cindy Sherman, Sherry Levine, and Richard Prince that is postmodern, to the exclusion of everything else. Depending on the artistic discipline, then, postmodernism is either a radicalization of the self-reflexive moment within modernism, a turning away from narrative and representation, or an explicit return to narrative and representation. And sometimes it is both. Moreover, to make things worse, there are, as we will see, postmodernisms that do not fit this neat binary bill. Yet, there is a common denominator. In their own way, they all seek to transcend what they see as the self-imposed limitations of modernism, which in its search for autonomy and purity or for timeless, representational, truth has subjected experience to unacceptable intellectualizations and reductions. But at this level we again find complications. The attempt to transcend modernism follows two main strategies, which unfortunately do not coincide with the distinction that I have just made between a self-reflexive postmodernism and a postmodernism that reintroduces (some kind of) representation. Those who opt for the first strategy are content to question modernism's premises and its procedures from within the realm of art. Those who wish to break more radically with modernism do not only attack modernist art, but seek to undermine the idea of art itself. For them the idea of art, that is, art-as-institution, is a typically modernist creation, built upon the principle of art's self-sufficiency, its special – and separate – status within the larger world. But such an autonomy, these artists argue, is really a self-imposed exile; it means that art willingly accepts its impotence, that it accedes to its own neutralization and depoliticization.

At a second level of conceptualization we find similar confusions. Here postmodernism has been defined as the 'attitude' of the 1960s counterculture, or, somewhat more restrictively, as the 'new sensibility' of the 1960s social and artistic avant-garde. This new sensibility is eclectic, it is radically democratic, and it rejects what it sees as the exclusivist and repressive character of liberal humanism and the institutions with which it identifies that humanism. Here the avant-garde attack on art-as-institution is broadened and raised to a socio-political level. Such an early politicized form of postmodernism was first identified in the mid-sixties by Leslie Fiedler and other critics who monitored the contemporary American scene.

In the course of the 1970s, postmodernism was gradually drawn into a poststructuralist orbit. In a first phase, it was primarily associated with the deconstructionist practices that took their inspiration from the poststructuralism of the later Roland Barthes and, more in particular, of Jacques Derrida. In its later stages, it drew on Michel Foucault, on Jacques Lacan's revisions of Freud, and, occasionally, on the work of Gilles Deleuze and Félix Guattari. The translation of Jean-François Lyotard's *La Condition postmoderne* (1984; original edition 1979), in which a prominent poststructuralist adopted the term postmodern, seemed to many to signal a fully-fledged merger between an originally American postmodernism and French poststructuralism. Like poststructuralism, this postmodernism rejects the empirical idea that language can represent reality, that the world is accessible to us through language because its objects are mirrored in the language that we use. From this empirical point of view, language is transparent, a window on the world, and knowledge arises out of our direct experience of reality, undistorted and not contaminated by language. Accepting Derrida's exposure, and rejection, of the metaphysical premises – the transcendent signifier – upon which such empiricism is built, postmodernism gives up on language's representational function and follows poststructuralism in the idea that language constitutes, rather than reflects, the world, and that knowledge is therefore always distorted by language, that is, by the historical circumstances and the specific environment in which it arises. Under the pressure of Derrida's arguments, and of Lacan's psychoanalysis, which sees the subject as constructed in language, the autonomous subject of modernity, objectively rational and self-determined, likewise gives way to a postmodern subject which is largely other-determined, that is, determined within and constituted by language.

One can, as I have suggested, distinguish two moments within this poststructuralist postmodernism. The first, which belongs to the later 1970s and the early 1980s, derives from Barthes and Derrida and is linguistic, that is, textual, in its orientation. The attack on foundationalist notions of language, representation, and the subject is combined with a strong emphasis on what in Derrida's 'Structure, sign, and play in the discourse of the human sciences' (1970) had been called 'freeplay' – the extension *ad infinitum* of the 'interplay of signification' in the absence of transcendent signifiers, of metaphysical meaning – and on intertextuality. This deconstructionist postmodernism saw the text, in the terms made famous by Roland Barthes's 'The death of the author' of 1968, as 'a metadimensional space in which a variety of writings, none of them original, blend and clash'; as 'a tissue of quotations drawn from the innumerable centres of culture'. Intent upon exposing the workings of language – and especially its failure to represent anything outside itself, in other words, its self-reflexivity – this Derridean postmodernism largely limited itself to texts and intertexts. In its firm belief that the attack on representation was in itself an important political act, it was content to celebrate the so-called death of the subject – and thus of the author – without realizing that the end of representation had paradoxically made questions of subjectivity and authorship (redefined in postmodern terms, that is, in terms of agency) all the more relevant. If representations do not and cannot represent the world, then inevitably all representations are political, in that they cannot help reflecting the ideological frameworks within which they arise. The end of representation thus leads us back to the question of authorship, to such political questions as 'Whose history gets told? In whose name? For what purpose?'. In the absence of transcendent truth it matters, more than ever, who is speaking (or writing), and why, and to whom. Deconstructionist postmodernism largely ignored these and other political questions that the demise of representation had given prominence to. As a result, with the increasing politicization of the debate on postmodernism in the early 1980s, its textual, self-reflexive, orientation rapidly lost its attraction.

The other moment within poststructuralist postmodernism derives from Foucault and, to a much lesser extent, Lacan. It belongs to the 1980s rather than to the 1970s, although it is difficult to pinpoint its appearance. Foucault's influence materializes almost imperceptibly until it is suddenly very much there, like a fine drizzle that to your surprise has managed to get you thoroughly wet after an hour's walk. Like the earlier deconstructionist postmodernism, this later poststructuralist postmodernism assumes a reality of textuality and signs, of representations that do not represent. Here, however, the emphasis is on the workings of power, and the constitution of the subject. From the perspective of this postmodernism, knowledge, which had once seemed neutral and objective to the positivists and politically emancipatory to the left, is inevitably bound up with power and thus suspect. Although it does not necessarily follow Foucault in his extreme epistemological skepticism, which virtually equates knowledge with power and thus reduces it to the effect of a social relation or structure, it fully accepts that knowledge, and language *tout court*, have become inseparable from power. This postmodernism interrogates the power that is inherent in the discourses that surround us – and that is continually reproduced by them – and interrogates the institutions that support those discourses and are, in turn, supported by them. It attempts to expose the politics that are at work in representations and to undo institutionalized hierarchies, and it works against the hegemony of any single discursive system – which would inevitably victimize other discourses – in its advocacy of difference, pluri-formity, and multiplicity. Especially important are its interest in those who from the point of view of the liberal humanist subject (white, male, hetero-sexual, and rational) constitute the 'Other' – the collective of those excluded from the privileges accorded by that subject to itself (women, people of color, non-heterosexuals, children) and its interest in the role of representa-tions in the constitution of 'Otherness'. Drawing on the later Foucault's interest in the subject, it more generally investigates the ways in which human beings are constituted – and reconstituted – by discourses, that is, by language, and recognize themselves as subjects. Some, especially British, theorists sought to supplement this with Louis Althusser's analysis of ideology and its effects upon the subject. In the course of the 1980s this mostly Foucauldian postmodernism had a far-reaching democratizing influ-ence within cultural institutions – and on the relations between them – and in the humanities at large (even if a new dogmatism followed on its heels). It is this 1980s redefinition of the postmodern that enabled the close links with feminism and multiculturalism that are now, generally associated with postmodernism.

On this second level of conceptualization – postmodernism as a *Weltan-schauung* – the term is also not without its problems. On the political left some commentators distinguish between a 'good' deconstructionism, which they refuse to call postmodern, and a 'bad' version, which they then con-temptuously label 'postmodern'. Christopher Norris, for instance, obviously convinced of the political correctness of Paul de Man, Derrida, and those deconstructionists who work in their spirit, chooses to see their work within a politically constructive framework, as engaged in the necessary process of erasing the old, harmful intellectual structures of liberal humanism in order to make room for new ones that will admit the light and fresh air of a revamped Enlightenment. Others, the postmodernists, from his point of view, are merely engaged in the wanton destruction of intellectual property without the ultimate aim of rebuilding on the scorched earth they leave in their wake. For Norris and a good many others on the left, postmodernism, rather idiosyncratically defined, is thus merely intellectual vandalism. There are, as I will argue below, good reasons to make a distinction between deconstructionism proper and postmodernism, but not along such evaluative lines.

In any case, no matter how one would want to draw such lines, in the later 1970s a broad complex of deconstructionist/poststructuralist practices became firmly associated with postmodernism. In some artistic disciplines, the new theoretical interest more or less absorbed the departures from modernism that had characterized the 1960s, leading to works of art in which artistic practice and theoretical argument became indistinguishable. On the theoretical level, these practices made themselves felt all over the humanities, first in the field of literary criticism, which had, after all, brought French theory to the US, and then in adjacent fields. Nowadays often called 'theory' – although it goes against all theory in a more traditional, say Popperian, sense – it has in the course of the 1980s filtered into and affected a large number of disciplines, in which its intellectual premises are usually simply called postmodern or postmodernist. It is this recent wide proliferation of the postmodern, in ethnology, sociology, social geography, urban planning, economics, law, and so on, that is responsible for the ever more frequent use of its terminology outside its original core area, the humanities, and that has increasingly led people to speak of the postmodern world that we inhabit. But that merely adds to the confusion. It's not the world that is postmodern, here, it is the perspective from which that world is seen that is postmodern. We are dealing here with a set of intellectual propositions that to some people make a lot more sense than they do to others. Although the omnipresence of the postmodern and its advocates would seem to suggest otherwise, not everybody subscribes to the view that language constitutes, rather than represents, reality; that the autonomous and stable subject of modernity has been replaced by a postmodern agent whose identity is largely other-determined and always in process; that meaning has become social and provisional; or that knowledge only counts as such within a given discursive formation, that is, a given power structure – to mention only some of the more familiar postmodern tenets.

I emphasize this because at again another conceptual level one can indeed speak of the postmodern world, or at least argue that the world as such has become postmodern, that is, entered a new historical era, that of postmodernity. Such arguments restrict themselves in practice to developments in the US, Western Europe, and some less prominent bulwarks of western capitalism such as Canada and Australia, and tacitly assume that the rest of the world will have to follow suit. To some critics postmodernity is still limited to certain areas of contemporary culture – usually to mass culture as mediated by television or to the more elitist yuppie life style promoted by designer magazines – or to certain sociologically definable groups within the western world. Others, casting a wider net, see postmodernism, both as a complex of artistic strategies and as a loosely coherent set of theoretical assumptions, as a sign of the times, as emblematic of a cultural shift of epistemic proportions. That new 'cultural logic' (Fredric Jameson's term) may then in turn be seen as a corollary of the changed nature of western capitalism. A key factor in this interpretation of postmodernism as the superstructure of the current socio-economic order is the ever-increasing penetration of capitalism into our day-to-day existence, or, to put it differently, the ever-increasing commodification of both the public and the private. The onslaught of commodification that is characteristic of late capitalism has, in the view of theorists such as Jameson and Jean Baudrillard, even managed to obliterate the classically Marxist distinction between the economic and the cultural. The causal relationship between base and superstructure that obtained in capitalism's earlier stages has given way to an indeterminate situation in which the economic and the cultural – representations, signs – create and feed each other. Industrial production has given way to Baudrillard's 'semiurgy': the sinister production of signs.

Postmodernism, then, means and has meant different things to different people at different conceptual levels, rising from humble literary-critical origins in the 1950s to a level of global conceptualization in the 1980s. The result was, and still is, a massive but also exhilarating confusion that has given important new impulses to and opened new territories for intellectual exploration. If there is a common denominator to all these postmodernisms, it is that of a crisis in representation: a deeply felt loss of faith in our ability to represent the real, in the widest sense. No matter whether they are aesthetic, epistemological, moral, or political in nature, the representations that we used to rely on can no longer be taken for granted. Whatever its origins, which are diagnosed in different ways by Daniel Bell, Lyotard, Jameson, and other theorists, this crisis in representation has far-reaching consequences. Some would seem to be debilitating. For example, now that transcendent truth seems forever out of reach, hermeneutics must replace our former aspirations to objectivity. Not surprisingly, Marxists like Jameson find this particularly hard to accept because it undermines the conceptual basis of Marxist politics. Other consequences are positively enabling. If all representations are constructs that ultimately are politically informed, then it should be possible, for instance, to break away from our current ones and really confront the Other. Still other effects have changed the map of the humanities: postmodernism has for instance led to a spectacular upgrading of cultural studies. Since the awareness that representations create rather than reflect reality has taken hold of contemporary criticism, representations have been endowed with an almost material status. Culture, long seen by many as determined, either directly or indirectly, by a more fundamental mode of production, has now become a major constitutive power in its own right. In fact, for many theorists signs (a term which of course includes all forms of representation) are the most important constitutive element in the contemporary world, if not, indeed, the only one, as for instance in the later work of Baudrillard. Inevitably, this revaluation of culture has led to an interest in the origins and history of specific representations and has thus stimulated historical projects that to the deconstructionist, self-reflexive, postmodernism of the late 1970s and early 1980s seemed pointless exercises in reigning in the play of textuality. In the wake of Foucault, postmodernism has with increasing frequency visited the past in order to illuminate the present.

43 James F. English, Winning the Culture Game: Prizes, Awards, and the Rules of Art (2002)

The amount of media space that literary prizes occupy, and the degree to which literary prizes tie in with the marketing and distribution of books, and appear to influence reading practices and critical evaluations, can hardly be under-estimated. This is particularly so for the latter part of the twentieth century, and indeed continues to be so. James English's essay 'Winning the Culture Game' (2002) argues that the significance of such literary prizes derives not so much from the evaluative criteria and processes on the basis of which they are given, as through the controversies (even apparently damaging ones) that often surround such awards and are carefully nurtured and even generated. English brings a great deal of useful information to bear on this argument, with particular attention being given to controversies surrounding the Booker Prize and the Nobel Prize for Literature. Changing attitudes to literary prizes are also commented on.

English, J. F., 'Winning the Culture Game: Prizes, Awards, and the Rules of Art', *New Literary History*, 33.1, 2002, pp. 113–35. http://muse.jhu.edu/journals/new_literary_history/v033/33.1 english.html

What I want to discuss here is the postmodern form of this constitutive threat, the gradual shift of prize commentary in recent years onto a register of *mock-scandal*, whereby the prize can continue to occupy, discursively, the place of the illegitimate, the embarrassing, the scandalously middling insti-tution of culture—a place with which no "serious" critic or artist wants to be too firmly associated—while securing in fact an even greater symbolic efficacy not only among the mass consumers of art but among the most specialized producers, the serious (academic) critics and artists themselves.

In describing this change in the commentary on prizes, I will focus initially on Britain's Booker Prize for Fiction. It is no secret that the success of the Booker Prize—its seemingly magical power to attract the attention both of the broad book-reading public and of the most critically respected British novelists—is bound up with the annual flurry of scandal that attends it in the dailies and in the literary press. Founded in 1968 as the brainchild of Tom Maschler, a rising young celebrity-editor at Jonathan Cape, under the sponsorship of Booker Brothers (today Booker PLC), then a postcolonial agribusiness company seeking to diversify domestically and to improve its public profile, the prize was not in fact well positioned to succeed.[1] It lacked, for one thing, the important symbolic distinction of being the oldest book prize in Britain. Not only were there continuous prizes dating back half a century (the James Tait Black and the Hawthornden), but there were already other newcomers, such as the *Guardian* Fiction Prize, which had been founded in 1965, and the Silver Pen fiction prize, which had been announced earlier in 1968. While the Booker's cash value (£5000) was somewhat higher than others initially, this has not remained the case and was never a very significant differentiating marker.[2] Nor was the Booker on any account remarkable for its professed criteria or aims: it was a Novel-of-the-Year award of the most generic sort, one more would-be *Prix Goncourt*.[3] Though the Booker organization would deny this today, the whole venture was very close to folding within just a couple of years of its launch. The private correspondence and the minutes from committee meetings of 1970 and 1971 read like the blackbox transcript of a crashed plane: publishers were threatening to stop nominating books; people invited to serve as judges were routinely declining to do so; Maschler insisted on acting like the chair of the management committee, . . . while the actual chair resigned; the Book Trust was abruptly brought in to assume administrative responsibility (though they had never administered a prize); and the sponsor, though committed to an initial seven years of funding, was already making sounds of an early exit.[4]

But what happened instead is that the Booker began, in 1971, to deliver a series of annual scandals, the best known of which is that of John Berger's rude acceptance speech in 1972, when Berger, enjoying the celebrity attendant on his *Ways of Seeing* series for the BBC, stood before assembled Booker executives, denounced their corporation as a colonialist enterprise built on the backs of black plantation workers in Guyana, and declared that half his prize money would be donated to the London branch of the Black Panthers.[5] This incident alone gave an enormous boost to the Booker's public profile, but it had been prepared for by the intemperate behavior of another (in this case *right*-wing) television celebrity, Malcolm Muggeridge, the year before, and it was reinforced by another politicized, anti-Booker acceptance speech by J. G. Farrell the following year. By early 1974, after these three successive scandals, two of them powerfully leveraged by the cross-over with television and the third virtually guaranteeing that the other two would be revisited and the whole sequence retraced in all the arts pages, the tone of frustration had entirely disappeared from the committee's minutes. They were congratulating themselves on "very satisfactory" results, and particularly on the fact that "publicity for the prize has now gained its own momentum."[6] Press coverage, which had risen to about fifty stories in 1971 and two hundred in 1972, had risen again in 1973;[7] publishers had stopped complaining about the entry fees, prestigious judges had become easier to find, and Booker PLC happily renewed the seven-year sponsorship agreement. Within two more years, the BBC had decided to televise the award ceremony, a development which in turn led the Organizing Committee to revise its procedures along more Oscar-like lines, such that the judges' decision could be kept absolutely secret and the shortlisted authors could be assembled, under conditions of maximum anxiety and close public scrutiny, to endure the announcement. This "celebrity sadism," as one commentator called it, ensured that incidents of scandalous misbehavior (Rushdie pounding his fists on the table, saying the judges know "fuck all" about literature, and so on) would be even more regular, and could be even more eagerly anticipated; journalists covering the Booker would always have "cultural" material of just the sort they require.[8] Just a decade after its near collapse, the Booker outstripped all other British literary prizes combined in terms of the sheer volume of publicity, renown, and book sales it could generate for its winner. Even to be shortlisted for the Booker was distinction of greater value—symbolic as well as monetary—than any . . . other prize could muster. To win it, as Thomas Keneally's editor said when Keneally received the 1982 prize for *Schindler's Ark*, was "like an avalanche hitting you all at once."[9]

It is well known that the postwar decades have seen a general reshaping of the relationship between journalistic and cultural capital, between celebrity and canonicity.[10] Starting in the early 1970s, prize sponsors and administrators—particularly in fields that enjoy programming time on television, as literature does in England, France, and to a lesser degree the U.S.—became adept exploiters and manipulators of this relationship. The Booker's chief administrator, Martin Goff, who should be regarded as a major figure in the history of prizes, was fully and actively complicit in exploiting the association of the Booker with scandal, wagering that the prize stood to reap the greatest symbolic profit precisely from its status as a kind of cultural embarrassment. Goff could see that each new scandal provoked objection not just to a particular jury decision or management policy but to the very existence of the prize. The Booker's critics do not simply weigh in on one side or the other of a given evaluative controversy, but use each controversy to rehearse the more fundamental dispute over the Booker Prize itself.[11] In the *Times*, the Booker has been dismissed as "rubbish,"[12] mere "razzmatazz, . . .

a laughing stock," "an annual rusty nail . . . hammered in the coffin of fiction."[13] The *Daily Telegraph* has called it "an embarrassment to the entire book trade."[14] And the *Economist* has pronounced it "a sad and shoddy farce," adding that it is high time "for the backers to call it a day."[15] Such wholesale denunciations, appearing in the most powerful journals, are clearly not an unhappy side effect of the promoters' publicity strategy, but a central aim. It is the charge of fundamental, irremediable illegitimacy that keeps the prize a focus of attention, increasing its journalistic capital, *and* speeds its accumulation of symbolic capital, or cultural prestige. Far from posing a threat to the prize's efficacy as an instrument of the cultural economy, scandal is its lifeblood; far from constituting a critique, indignant commentary about the prize is an index of its normal and proper functioning.

Until quite recently, however, there has not been much room in the game to acknowledge this simple fact of complicity or convergence of interests between the more or less lofty and disdainful cultural commentators and those who have a direct stake in promoting the prize and enlarging its cultural role. Instead, commentators tended, misleadingly if not disingenuously, to describe the relationship between the Booker's increasingly privileged cultural position and its perceived scandalousness as a paradoxical one, the prize having miraculously succeeded "in spite of" all the outraged and scandalized book critics.[16] The tendency of commentators automatically to describe the situation in this way, as a . . . strange deviation from the proper and expected course of things, has depended on their misapprehension of the economy of cultural prestige and of their own place in that economy. Arts editors, book reviewers, and academics who write for the newspapers or do book-chat on TV are by no means perfectly opposed to the sponsors and administrators of prizes, nor, where the two sets of interests do diverge, would the writers stand to gain by driving prizes off of the cultural field altogether. Prizes are as useful to them as to the sponsoring corporations and societies, of which in many cases they are members or proxies. Apart from being a means of derivative consecration for journalist-critics themselves (since members of this fraction often receive the symbolically subsidiary but structurally primary honor of being asked to serve as nominators or judges), prizes have traditionally been useful in providing regular occasions for journalist-critics to rehearse Enlightenment pieties about "pure" art and "authentic" forms of greatness or genius, and thereby to align themselves with "higher" values, or more symbolically potent forms of capital, than those which dominate the (scandalously impure) prize economy as well as the journalistic field itself. Such rehearsals, I should add, do nothing to discredit the cultural prize, and in fact serve as a crucial support for it in as much as they help to keep aloft the collective belief or make-belief in artistic value as such, in the disinterested judgment of taste, the hierarchy of value or prestige that is not a homology of social hierarchies, not a euphemized form of social violence. Like the magazine profiles of "great writers on vacation" memorably described by Roland Barthes in *Mythologies*, journalistic coverage of prizes serves by its very emphasis on the banal, the social, the petty side of cultural life to reinforce belief in the higher, "intrinsically different" nature of artists and artistic value.[17] The prize depends on this collective belief since its own currency, however tainted or debased, is understood to derive from this other and purer form, which stands in relation to the economy of cultural prestige as gold did to the cash economy in the days of the gold standard: a perfectly magical guarantor of an imperfectly magical system.

In any event, the longstanding fiction that scandalized commentators stand outside of and in opposition to the cultural-prize game—in a stance of independent critique rather than "dependent independency"—has finally begun in recent years to give way. Increasingly one finds these writers, journalists and academic critics alike, acknowledging a prize's dependency on denunciation by "independent" writers such as themselves, its need to be represented by them as a scandalous and degrading instrument of cultural manipulation. Mark Lawson, a book-review editor at the *Independent* who has himself served as a Booker judge and been involved in more than one Booker scandal, observed in 1994 that the . . . function of the Booker Prize is not simply "to promote the cause of serious fiction . . . [but], to provoke rows and scandals, which may, in due course, promote the cause of serious fiction."[18] Richard Todd, an academic who in 1996 published an entire book on the Booker Prize, dismisses as "fatuous" the kind of "highbrow literary" denunciations that have been directed at the prize, and he takes it as "surely evident" by now that the prize's loftiest critics are its best allies, that the Booker thrives "precisely by 'getting it wrong'" (as it cannot fail to do) in the eyes of so many established experts (*CF* 64).

Alongside this new readiness to acknowledge the smooth working relationship between cultural prizes and their critics, we find more and more a kind of playful or reflexive prize commentary in which "scandal" seems to circulate in scare quotes, with winks and nudges passing between the ostensibly scandalous artist or jury member, the ostensibly scandalized critic, and the reader. The whole event is seen as being pinned on what a chair of judges at the NCR Non-Fiction Prize called "the hope that there might be a row in inverted commas."[19] Doubtless a certain conscious duplicity or jocularity has always been observable in coverage of the Booker (and in British cultural journalism generally), but it has become far more conspicuous over the past decade, with fewer critics sounding the note of sincere outrage and more of them openly playing around with "scandals" that are at least partly of their own invention. Geraldine Brooks, in an account of the 1992 award dinner, recalls the feeling of disappointment as things wound down without an embarrassment or a controversy. The judges that year failed even to choose an outright winner, dividing the prize between Barry Unsworth and Michael Ondaatje; the evening seemed flat, anticlimactic, given over to timidity, compromise, and decorum. But soon after the two winners made their acceptance speeches, Ian McEwan, a shortlisted also-ran for the second time, took his publishing entourage and left the Guildhall. Brooks seized eagerly on this gesture. "Is it possible?" she wrote. "Yes! He's walking out! Before the closing speech and the toast to Poor Salman, Who Can't Be With Us! . . . What a relief. The Booker Prize for 1992 will have its scandal after all."[20]

This new rhetoric of amused complicity in the manufacture of scandal is an instance of what Bourdieu calls a "strategy of condescension," a strategy that enables one to enjoy both the rewards of the game and the rewards due to those who are seen as standing above the game.[21] It does not permit of outright denunciation or implacable opposition, except as a kind of put-on, a form of trash-talk, ritual insults within the bounds of a game; it does not allow one to say explicitly and in all seriousness that, as a "literary critic" or "intellectual," one is above such stakes as are at issue in the prize economy. It does still enable one to gesture toward that . . . imaginary separate space on which the ideology and institution of modern art have been predicated, the space outside of all economies, where artistic genius is a gift rather than a form of capital and where the greatness of great art is beyond all measure or manipulation except by the sure determinations of (homogeneous, empty) Time.[22] But the gesture, which is in any case no longer obligatory, seems more and more often to be oblique, apologetic, ironized. It has come to involve a certain acknowledgment, though always a partial and incomplete acknowledgment, that this "world apart" is a matter of collective make-believe. What used to be describable as the "sincere fiction" informing commentary on prizes, and indeed underpinning the entire economy of cultural prestige—the fiction of socially unmediated aesthetic value—does remain in place as a kind of necessary predicate. But this new (or rather, newly dominant) rhetoric suggests new difficulties in the very problematic of *sincerity* as it applies in such instances. What Bourdieu calls the "illusio" of literature—the fundamental belief in the literary game and in the value of its stakes—has been complicated or compromised by something that is neither a perfect lucidity regarding "the objective truth of literature as a fiction founded on collective belief" nor a radical disillusionment from which literary practice can only seem a form of "cynical mystification or conscious trickery" (*RA* 274).[23] We are, rather, dealing with a kind of suspension between belief and disbelief, between the impulse to see art as a kind of ponzi scheme and the impulse to preserve it as a place for our most trusting investments. Under these circumstances, cultural prizes can be, at one and the same time, both more dubious—more of a joke—than they used to be, and more symbolically effectual, more powerfully and intimately intertwined with processes of canonization.

II Strategies of condescension, styles of play

While the Booker is possibly the most talked-about of high-cultural prizes, its relationships to criticism, scandal, and the field of journalism are largely unexceptional. Even in fields of culture to which the press pays far less attention than it does to literature, when a prize makes the news it is generally due to some "scandal" which takes the same basic form—the increasingly (though never perfectly) parodic or insincere form—as those connected with the Booker. Indeed, we find other prizes more and more often being compared to the Booker, usually in order to suggest the "Bookerization" of the whole cultural-prize phenomenon.[24] So that when a "scandal" or "row" breaks out in connection with some literary or arts prize these days, those who attack and denigrate or . . . embarrass the prize are less likely to be perceived as acting within the long tradition of sincere animosity between artists and bourgeois consecrations—artistic freedom fighters on the old model of art versus money—and more likely to be seen as players in a newer cultural game whose "rules" and "sides" are rather more obscure and of which the Booker happens to be the best known, and hence the most generic, instance.

Let's consider, for example, the scandals of refusal that periodically, and memorably, interrupt the regular ceremonies at which prizes are awarded and received. Award ceremonies are rituals of symbolic exchange, requiring of all participants acknowledgement of and respect for the conventions attendant upon the giving and receiving of gifts. Any display of indifference or ingratitude on the part of the honored recipient must be calculated with great care or it will provoke the indignation not only of the presenters of the prize, but of the entire participating community (including, for example, the other nominees as well as all past recipients). For this reason it has always been difficult to profit, in symbolic terms, by refusing a prize outright. Traditionally, in order to do so, one had to have already accumulated a wealth of symbolic capital of the sort that would be regarded as virtually non-fungible with prizes, awards, and trophies: the sort, that is, which accrues not to just any recognized aesthetic innovator but only to those who are also resolute social oppositionists or heretics, "old-style intellectuals" in Bourdieu's sense (FE 52). These are artists who have deployed the prestige, or symbolic capital, granted them in their particular and more or less discrete fields of production in a broader "mission of prophetic subversion," a political mission in which the existing social order has been consistently denounced, and the rewards it places within reach consistently rejected, in the name of autonomy (*RA* 129–31). And even for these symbolically powerful figures, refusing a prize was always a delicate and risky maneuver. Sartre's exemplary refusal of the Nobel in 1964 was seen by him as an unfortunate entanglement, which he had tried to ward off in advance by asking the Swedish Academy to remove his name from the list of candidates. Had the Academy's Secretary not misplaced Sartre's letter, in which it was tactfully explained that a lifetime of refusing all such awards (Soviet as well as Western) would be compromised by any special exemption for the Nobel, the entire affair would have been averted. In the event, Sartre was as low-key and apologetic as possible about refusing the prize. Nevertheless, his refusal was widely regarded as an act of tremendous symbolic violence— and rightly so.[25] After all, Sartre could have taken the route of George Bernard Shaw, accepting the prize reluctantly, tactically, keeping none of the substantial monetary award for himself; he might have exploited . . . the high-profile occasion of the acceptance speech to focus attention on those to whom he would be redistributing the money. By refusing even this much contact with the Nobel, Sartre was maximizing the barriers of exchange, the "trade barriers" of the symbolic economy, between his cultural capital— his specific importance and value as an artist and intellectual—and the capital that the Academy held out to him. In his view, such an exchange transaction would be so catastrophically to his disadvantage, so ruinous of his symbolic wealth, that the Academy's proffered "gift" was in effect a Trojan one.

In 1964, it was still possible to occupy a position on the cultural field from which such a sincere and implacable refusal made symbolic sense. The field was still understood to conform in a broad way to what we habitually think of as the high-culture/mass culture opposition, or what in Bourdieu's terminology is the "dualist structure" that has prevailed since the nineteenth century. It was characterized, that is to say, by its two subfields of cultural production: the restricted field, in which avant-garde artists produced art for one another and for university intellectuals ("a field that is its own market, allied with an educational system which legitimizes it"), and the extended field, in which artists of more conventional habitus produced for a wider public of bourgeois art-lovers and, later, for a mass-entertainment audience ("a field of production organized as a function of external demand, normally seen as socially and culturally inferior").[26] And a field structured in this way was still capable of producing prophetic-subversive intellectuals more or less on the model of Zola, who could put their symbolic capital, initially hard won on the restricted field, to work politically by linking autonomy with truth. Even in the early 1970s, there was clearly some measure of symbolic efficacy in such refusals if the artist declining the award was sufficiently admired by others in the field: the Academy Award refusals of George C. Scott, Marlon Brando, and Luis Buñuel come to mind. These figures could rely on their peers approvingly to recognize the maneuver as, in Scott's terms, the best means of sustaining one's "real commitment to the legitimate theater," that is, to the or most autonomous subfields of art, in the face of a relentlessly expanding general field on which all events and activities of production were made to accord with the logic of commerce, were "contrived," as Scott put it, "for economic reasons."[27] (But by the time Thomas Bernhard writes, in a 1982 memoir, of his own decision in the 1970s not to accept any more literary awards, on the grounds that for the serious artist, "receiving a prize is nothing other than having one's head pissed upon,' this Flaubertian posture seems already a self-consciously dated and curmudgeonly one, Bernhard's novelistic representation of a traditional artist-intellectual who finds himself out of place and strategically at a loss ... on the contemporary field.[28] Bernhard himself had in fact resumed accepting awards by then, just as George C. Scott had taken to attending the Academy Awards ceremony. For either to have done otherwise, to have maintained the position of incorruptible refusenik or prophetic subversive, would likely have made him appear not more authentic or serious as an artist but more out-of-date, more plainly part of an earlier generation of artists whose positions had been voided and tactics superseded.

One can still refuse a prize, of course, but the refusal can no longer be counted upon to reinforce one's artistic legitimacy by underscoring the specificity or the properly autonomous character of one's cultural prestige, its difference from mere visibility or "success." On the contrary, the scandal of refusal has become a recognized device for raising visibility and leveraging success. When Julie Andrews refused a nomination for a 1996 Tony Award, no one even considered taking the gesture seriously as an attack on the Tonys, much less as a defense of the integrity or autonomy of the "legitimate theater." Instead, it was seen as a media event carefully "staged" by Andrews, "the biggest star on Broadway, playing in one of its biggest-grossing hits," and intended "to help [her] show" attract even more paying customers. The media "scandal" surrounding her refusal, despite its involving many disparaging observations about the commercialism of the Tonys, was widely recognized as doing those awards far more good than harm in terms of their future capacity to produce visibility and put it into cultural circulation. As Peter Marks expressed it in *The New York Times*, Andrews's action succeeded in "doing what Broadway publicity agents thought was the impossible ...

turn[ing] the Tony Awards into a tabloid story"—an outcome that "did not displease some involved with the promotion of the Tonys."[29] Indeed, the televised Tony Awards ceremony that year opened with Julie Andrews jokes and seemed to have been consciously and happily orchestrated around the mock-scandalous fact of her absence.

Being already a recognized move in a game characterized by insincere or duplicitous the refusal of a prize can no longer register as a refusal to play. Nor can the reluctant player make appeal to some proper home on the cultural field where such games are unknown and where the symbolic money that prizes represent is no good. The artists, writers, and intellectuals who today are major holders of symbolic capital, those whom the culturally esteemed themselves esteem, have for the most part left the task of denouncing prizes to journalists and old-guard humanities professors while taking the game up themselves more tactically. A transitional moment, perhaps, was Thomas Pynchon's famous acceptance of the National Book Award for *Gravity's Rainbow* in . . . 1974. At that time, Pynchon was certainly still capable of refusing a major prize outright, as he did in a deliberately "rude" letter declining the 1975 Dean Howells Medal of the American Academy of Arts and Letters ("I don't want it. Please don't impose on me something I don't want").[30] And, more recently, he has shown himself willing to accept such an award with no display of reluctance, as he did the MacArthur "Genius" Award in 1989. An ambiguity of position between these two extremes was nicely captured by his handling of the National Book Award, for which he sent the professional comic Irwin Corey to accept on his behalf. Corey, in character as "Professor Irwin Corey," offered by way of an acceptance speech an incomprehensible amalgam of academic jargon and nonsense, bewildering most of those in attendance at the award ceremony and annoying many. This was not exactly a way to renounce the symbolic and material profits associated with the prize. The event increased Pynchon's specific visibility as an "invisible" recluse writer, thereby augmenting both his celebrity and his special symbolic position as an artist who shuns celebrity (a position he shares with Salinger).[31] The event also increased the sales of his (academically acclaimed but commercially resistant) novel, enabling an imposition of specifically academic preferences on the broader book market. Professor Corey's appearance also brought visibility and symbolic stature to the prize itself, which by selecting Pynchon as its winner and securing his acceptance (even on comic terms) gained some ground in its originary and ongoing struggle to unseat the Pulitzer as America's most legitimate book prize—that is, as the prize most closely aligned with the academically legitimated hierarchy of literary value. (The Pulitzer jury had proposed *Gravity's Rainbow* as its sole nominee that year, but, in a "scandalous," though amply precedented, imposition of its heteronomous constraints, the Pulitzer's governing board had rejected the jury's choice, calling the novel "obscene" and "unreadable," and voting not to award a prize at all.)[32] At the same time, however, Pynchon clearly made of the award ceremony a kind of parodic version of itself, a false or pretended exchange, a simulation of a consecration, an event which, however well it succeeded in accomplishing its purposes, could not quite be taken seriously. His tactics thus suited the postmodern circumstances of the prize—its paradoxically increasing effectivity and decreasing seriousness—as well as prefiguring the whole range of mock-prizes, antiprizes, and flippant pseudoprizes which have symptomatically come to shadow and even to merge with the prize industry proper.

In connection with this latter point, we might briefly consider the two Scottish conceptual artists Bill Drummond and Jimmy Cauty, who, as the pop music duo KLF, had a string of hit records in the early 1990s, but then, in 1993, refashioned themselves the K Foundation and announced . . . their sponsorship of a new £40,000 prize for the artist who had produced the year's worst work of art. Their award announcement was timed to follow immediately after the presentation of the (merely £20,000) Turner Prize, the so-called "Booker Prize of British art," and they named as their winner the very artist who had just been awarded the Turner, the sculptor Rachel Whiteread. Whiteread even felt compelled to accept the Worst Artist prize so that she could donate the money to charities rather than give Drummond and Cauty the opportunity to make good on their threat to burn the unclaimed cash on the spot. The whole affair clearly mocked the Turner Prize and its sponsors at the Tate Gallery, on whose steps the K Foundation Award was presented. (Drummond and Cauty had hoped to implicate the Tate even more directly, by offering the museum their own work *Nailed to the Wall*— 1 million of KLF pop-music proceeds nailed to a wall—while threatening to burn the entire million if the Tate refused to accept and exhibit this "gift." But, on advice of their solicitor, they rejected this plan in favor of simply burning the work unexhibited in 1994, documenting the act in an hour-long silent film called *Watch the K Foundation Burn a Million Quid*, which they later screened before various nontraditional audiences, such as rival football team supporters, at venues ranging from jails to pubs to art center canteens.[33]

But this was a curious kind of mockery, quite different from a simple denunciation or an act of straightforward antagonism. Part of what the Foundation succeeded in demonstrating was that their own Worst Artist prize wasn't really much different from the Tate's Best Artist prize, that best and worst, most serious and most frivolous, most legitimate and most commercial, were no longer readily mappable binaries, that the presumed dualist

structure of the cultural field, while still alive discursively, had been fundamentally scrambled. The artists themselves, after all, were *both* ultracom-
mercial pop stars, named Best British Band at the previous year's industry-
sponsored Brit Music Awards (the equivalent of America's Grammys), *and*
fringe avant-gardistes of the conceptual art world, producing, out of the
"material" of their own pop stardom, works which had no apparent commercial value at all. Their antics suggested that the Turner Prize was already
a mock prize, a booby prize, a joke; but also, just as significantly, that their
mock prize was for real, imperfectly distinguishable from economic instruments such as the Turner: it, too, was an instrument for converting "heteronomous capital" (money from the mass market) into specific symbolic
capital (stature in the legitimate art world) by way of journalistic capital
(visibility, celebrity, scandal).

Indeed, there has been as much comical play, or playing around, with the
different forms of capital and their intraconvertability by recipients of the
Turner Prize as by the K Foundation. Two years after Whiteread . . . won
the Turner, the award went to Damien Hirst for his now famous work of
mutilated, formaldehyde-immersed cow and calf carcasses, "Mother and
Child, Divided." Hirst played his win for all it was worth, giving the press
some scandalous sound bytes: "it's amazing what you can do with an E grade
in A-level art, a twisted imagination, and a chainsaw."[34] And the press duti-
fully mounted a great show of outrage, calling the award "an odious and dis-
gusting scandal" and (in reference to the ongoing beef panic) a case of
"mad-judges disease."[35] Much of this was certainly play-acting. Hirst's win
was among the least surprising, least newsworthy events of the year: he'd
been short-listed twice already, and was rated a prohibitive 4–5 favorite by
the bookmakers at William Hill (which offers odds on all the major prizes
as part of its "culture file"). The arts editors who wrote of the event in tones
of shock and horror were simply advancing their interests in an ongoing fac-
tional struggle between the so-called "New" British art and the defenders of
tradition. The sheer hyperbole of the rhetoric (Hirst's work was said to have
"the aesthetic value of a bucketfull of spittle"[36]) suggests again that the "scandal of the middlebrow" in which modern cultural prizes have always been
implicated has become a highly self-conscious game of positions, journalist-
critics seizing on the prize as a way to reanimate flaccid oppositions between
art and money, culture and society, fortifying their own positions with reference to an inadequate but still habitual binaristic scheme. In these journalistic *games* of scandal, the defense of art for art's sake is mounted not by
a determined avant-garde willing to make longterm investments (that is,
willing to labor penniless and in obscurity for decades toward the goal of
ultimately prevailing on the field of production), but by the most comfort-

ably established artists and the most risk-averse journalist-critics—even and especially those who are underwritten by, and whose habitus brings them into accordance with, the increasingly active cultural wing of the corporate right. (We find, for example, Hilton Kramer, chief art-lackey of the Olin Foundation, among the anti-Turnerites.[37])

Without disappearing, the modern discourse of autonomy has become a tactical fiction, or at least an imperfectly sincere one, most often and most effectively deployed in the interests of reaction. It is thus a treacherous if not a hopeless tool for the young or avant-garde or minority artist seeking specific legitimacy. What we see in the most recent awards scandals is that these latter artists have been forced, not to relinquish their interest in autonomy properly understood—that by definition cannot happen—but to pursue it by means of strategies of differentiation, styles of play, which defy a simple dualistic, two-axis/four-quadrant geography of cultural positions— a geography in which autonomy can only appear as a kind of safe corner and sanctuary for . . . artists as such. To take an example closer to home, Toni Morrison has over the last decade been perhaps the most active and enthusiastic collector of literary awards, lobbying for them and openly embracing them as a form of "redemption."[38] Even by contemporary standards, she seems to have abandoned too completely the protocols of condescension. But it would be a political error to join with those who have condemned this behavior as a scandal and an embarrassment, or to imagine that by chasing prizes Morrison has abandoned the pursuit of autonomy. In fact this is precisely the pursuit she is carrying out, by means of a strategy within which an extravagant overvaluation of prizes (positioning them as "the keystones to the canon," for example, or the supreme form of literary "validation") has a tactical function.[39] By virtue of her Pulitzer and her Nobel, Morrison has gained considerable symbolic leverage against the organized cultural right, which has not only done everything in its power to resist the rising prestige of African-American literature in general, and its expanding place within the university curriculum in particular, but has since the mid-80s launched campaigns specifically against Morrison.[40] Those who have thundered against Morrison's strategy as an embarrassment to literary culture, a scandalous capitulation, are playing the culture game according to rules that no longer apply, misconstruing the nature of the contemporary struggle for autonomy—a multivalent struggle of positive engagements— and hence blundering into a position from which they can only assist their cultural and political antagonists.[41] They are ill-equipped to recognize or appraise the tactical dimension of Morrison's relationship to prizes—its deployment as "strategic misappropriation"—and therefore ill-equipped to develop winning strategies of their own.

Notes

1 For the financial details of Booker's sponsorship of the prize, which grew out of their so-called 'Artists' Services' division, see John Sutherland, 'The Bumpy Ride to the Booker, 1981,' *Times Higher Education Supplement*, 30 October 1981, 11, and Richard Todd, *Consuming Fictions: The Booker Prize and Fiction in Britain Today* (London, 1996), pp. 62–4; hereafter cited in text as *CF*.

2 The relationship between a cultural prize's monetary and symbolic values is by no means perfectly inverse, but neither is it direct. (Witness the flop of the Turner Tomorrow Award, a $500,000 prize for 'visionary fiction' launched by Ted Turner in 1995 and almost universally ignored.) If there is some symbolic advantage to being the prize with the highest cash value on a given field, the Booker forfeited this advantage in the 1980s. The NCR, founded in 1988, has always been worth a bit more than the Booker, as has the Orange Prize for Fiction by Women, founded in 1996—and the IMPAC Dublin literary prize, founded in 1995, carries a cash award of £100,000. It is true that none of these is in direct competition with the Booker, since the former is a non-fiction prize and the latter two are open to non-British novelists. But even among the British-only fiction prizes, the Trask, the Whitbread, and the *Sunday Express* have all offered more cash than the Booker in recent years.

3 In fact, Maschler has said quite explicitly that he modeled the Booker on the Goncourt; see Maschler's recollections of the prize's genesis, 'How It All Began' in *Booker 30: A Celebration of Thirty Years of the Booker Prize for Fiction, 1969–1999*, ed. Booker PLC (London, 1998), pp. 15–16. There is no space here to trace out the special logic of imitation and differentiation at work in the history of cultural prizes and the seemingly insupportable redundancies it has produced. I will simply note that, just as the most successful of the Goncourt's domestic imitators has been the feminist *Prix Femina*, so the most successful domestic imitator of the Goncourt's most successful foreign imitator (that is, the most successful of the so-called 'Baby Bookers' within Britain) has been the Orange Prize for Fiction by Women: a kind of double-imitation of an imitation.

4 Documents pertaining to the administration of the prize in these years are housed in the uncatalogued Booker archive of the Book Trust in London. I am grateful to Sandra Vince and Russell Pritchard of the Book Trust, as well as to Martin Goff, for granting me access to this archive and assisting me in my research.

5 The full text of Berger's speech was printed in the *Guardian*, 24 November 1972, 12.

6 Minutes of the Organizing Committee meeting, 8 January 1974, Booker archive, Book Trust.

7 These counts are based on the clipping files in the Booker archive.

8 Bryan Appleyard, 'Glittering Prizes and a Game Called Celebrity Sadism,' *Sunday Times*, 21 October 1990. Christopher Hope, a South African writer shortlisted in 1992, vividly described the ethos of the award banquet from the vantage of the also-ran: 'the TV cameras get into your earhole and watch you push food around your plate while you get slagged off' (quoted by Geraldine Brooks, 'No Civility, Please, We're English,' *Gentleman's Quarterly* [February 1993], 58).

9 Patricia Miller, 'Booker Triumph "Like Avalanche Smothering You,"' *Sunday Times*, 24 October 1982.

10 The classic denunciation of these tendencies is Daniel J. Boorstin, *The Image: A Guide to Pseudo-Events in America* (New York, 1964), pp. 45–76, 118–80. A more ambitious and less tendentious study of contemporary celebrity culture and its place in the long history of fame is Leo Braudy, *The Frenzy of Renown: Fame and its History* (New York, 1986). A recent study of the specifically literary dimension of celebrity culture is Joe Moran, *Star Authors: Literary Celebrity in America* (London, 1999); hereafter cited as *SA*.

11 I do not mean to suggest that the individual scandals are of no interest in themselves or that they perform no significant cultural work apart from that of supporting through pseudo-critique the institution of the cultural prize. On the contrary, through the annual convulsions around the Booker, critics have pursued the most urgent struggles animating the scene of British literature. Some of these disputes have been convincingly read by Graham Huggan, for example, as expressions of a tension between two competing systems of postcolonial value in contemporary Britain: the symbolic system of 'postcolonialism' within which long-marginalized literatures are finally achieving significant consecration, and the commercial system of 'postcoloniality' within which this very consecration functions as a device to assure that such literatures are kept available for further imperial appropriation. (See Huggan, 'Prizing "Otherness": A Short History of the Booker,' *Studies in the Novel*, 29 [Fall 1997], 412–33; and 'The Postcolonial Exotic: Rushdie's "Booker of Bookers,"' *Transition*, 64 [1994], 22–9.) My own aim, though, is to consider the effects of these sorts of controversies in aggregate, in relation to the broader cultural logic that assures their continued production irrespective of any specific content.

12 Philip Howard, 'Curling Up With all the Bookers,' *Times* (London), 19 October 1982, 12.

13 E. J. Craddock, 'Why the Booker Prize is Bad News for Books,' *Times* (London), 7 October 1985, 15.

14 Susannah Herbert, 'The Night Booker Became a Dirty Word,' *Daily Telegraph*, 13 October '1994. Herbert is here quoting Bing Taylor, general marketing manager of W. H. Smith's book department—but as the headline suggests, she takes essentially the same view as he.

15 'Who Needs the Booker? The Sorry State of a Literary Prize,' *The Economist* (21 October 1989), 101.

16 Anthony Thwaite, 'Booker 1986,' *Encounter* (February 1987), 32: 'In spite of the jibes about 'hype' and 'ballyhoo,' etc., that go with the Booker Prize . . . [it is] internationally recognized as the world's top fiction prize.'

17 Roland Barthes, 'The Writer on Holiday,' *Mythologies*, tr. Annette Layers (New York, 1973), p. 30.

18 Mark Lawson, 'Never Mind the Plot, Enjoy the Argument,' *Independent*, 6 September 1994, 12.

19 This was the Tory minister Alan Clark, who chaired the (scandalously) fractious jury for the 1995 NCR prize. 'They didn't put me in for my taste and discernment in this field,' Clark observed in a post-ceremony interview. 'I was put on the committee in the hope that there might be a row, in inverted commas, and that I might be controversial and this would attract publicity to the whole affair.' See Julia Llewellyn Smith, 'They Invited Me Hoping For Controversy,' *Times* (London), 6 May 1995, Features Section.

20 Brooks, 'No Civility, Please,' 62. Rachel Kerr, publicity director for Cape, later issued a statement denying any scandalous intention on the part of McEwan or his entourage, saying that they had simply gotten mixed up about the order of events and had gone off to a post-Booker gathering at the house of Tom Maschler. This explanation was received skeptically. See the 'Times Diary,' *Times* (London), 15 October 1992.

21 Bourdieu, 'Price Formation and the Anticipation of Profits,' *Language and Symbolic Power*, ed. John B. Thompson, tr. Gino Raymond and Matthew Adamson (Cambridge, Mass., 1991), pp. 67–72.

22 The phrase 'homogeneous empty time' is of course Walter Benjamin's, from the thirteenth of the 'Theses on the Philosophy of History,' in *Illuminations*, tr. Hannah Arendt (New York, 1969), p. 261. Appeals to Time as an arbiter magically disconnected from history and society are everywhere in the commentary on literature and arts prizes. A typical example is Phillip Howard, 'And Thundering in to the Final Page . . . ,' *Times* (London), 19 October 1982, 12: 'The only objective judge of literature is Time. . . . Let us not pretend that [winning a prize] means anything about [a book's] literary value in the long eye of history.' From the obvious, and often triumphantly catalogued, gaps between the rosters of past prize-winners and the contemporary canon, critics erroneously infer that prizes have nothing to do with the patterns of canonicity that emerge later than other hierarchies of value, such as those that obtain in higher-educational curricula, have tended to be more accurate predictors of later symbolic success than prizes are; and, above all, that the long-term process of literary valuation operates independently of the interests and flows of social, economic, and political capital.

23 For Bourdieu, this persistence of belief in disbelief is scarcely imaginable, appearing only as a special complication or nuance in the habitus of the most refined and reflexive authors: his example is Mallarmé. But in fact this seems to be an increasingly general circumstance of the illusio, and if such terms as naivete and cynicism were ever adequate to describe the relationships between cultural agents and the cultural field, they certainly are not so today.

24 Even in America the charge of Bookerization is a familiar one; see, for example, David Lehman's account of the Bookerization of the National Book Awards, 'May the Best Author Win – Fat Chance' (cited above). According to Lehman, Barbara Prete, who was in charge of these prizes back in the mid-1980s when they were struggling along under the name American Book Awards, made a number of trips to London to study the way Martin Goff and the Book Trust administered the Booker Prize. One result of these visits was Prete's decision to begin announcing a shortlist of nominees some weeks prior to the announcement of a winner. If this adoption of a Booker practice was intended to produce Booker-style publicity, as Lehman suggests, it succeeded. In 1986, the first year of the new system (and the last year the awards were called the American Book Awards), one nominee, Peter Taylor, angrily withdrew when the name of the winner (E. L. Doctorow, for *World's Fair*) was leaked prematurely. Though Taylor would presumably have accepted the prize if he had won, he said it was too demeaning to be put publicly in the position of an also-ran. The next year saw the even larger scandal, mentioned below, involving open lobbying for Toni Morrison's *Beloved*; Morrison's partisans challenged the NBA jury for overlooking her masterpiece in favor of *Paco's Story*, a war novel by a little-known white male author named Larry Heinemann.

Rather than defending their selection, the National Book Foundation conceded problems in the way the NBA was judged, and promptly overhauled the jury format, increasing the number of judges from three to five. See 'NBA Names Judges for 1988, Increases Fiction Jury to Five,' *Publishers Weekly*, 234 (August 12 1988), 320.

25 A good, brief account of the affair can be found in Annie Cohen-Solal, *Sartre: A Life* (New York, 1985), pp. 444–49.

26 Bourdieu, 'The Market of Symbolic Goods,' tr. R. Sawyer, *The Field of Cultural Production: Essays on Art and Literature* (New York, 1983), p. 130. Since this essay's original appearance in 1971, Bourdieu's analysis of the logic of relation between the field of restricted production and the field of general production has undergone some refinements, particularly as regards the differing temporalities ('modes of ageing') of the two fields. For the most recent version, see 'The Market for Symbolic Goods,' *Rules of Art*, pp. 141–73.

27 Mason Wiley and Damien Bona, *Inside Oscar: The Unofficial History of the Academy Awards*, 4th ed. (New York, 1993), p. 447.

28 Thomas Bernhard, *Wittgenstein's Nephew: A Friendship*, tr. Ewald Osers (London, 1986), p. 78.

29 Peter Marks, 'Adding Drama to Musical, Andrews Spurns a Tony,' *New York Times*, 9 May 1996, A1, B6.

30 A section of the letter appears on the San Narciso Community College *Thomas Pynchon Homepage* at http://www.pynchon.pomona.edu/bio/facts.html (July 2000).

31 The cases of Salinger and Pynchon, and, more generally, the capacity of the literary star system to translate absence or refusal into stardom, recognizing silence as a sign or even a device of celebrity, are discussed by Moran, *Star Authors*, pp. 54, 64–6.

32 'Pulitzer Jurors Dismayed on Pynchon,' *New York Times*, 8 May 1974.

33 Lynn Cochrane, 'Fans to Watch £1m Go Up In Smoke for Glaswegian Football Fans,' *The Scotsman*, 4 November 1995; Robert Sandall, 'Money to Burn,' *Sunday Times*, 5 November 1995. The whole sequence of events is documented in *K Foundation Burn a Million Quid*, ed. Chris (London, 1998), pp. 5–30.

34 'Damien Hirst is Unanimous Winner of the Turner Prize,' *Daily Telegraph*, 29 November 1995.

35 'Prize Idiots: The Turner Prize Award,' *Daily Mirror*, 30 November 1995.

36 'A Turner for the Worse,' *Daily Telegraph*, 29 November 1995.

37 Founded in 1982, *The New Criterion* has been consistently supported by six-figure donations from the John M. Olin Foundation, along with contributions from some of the other major right-wing corporate foundations. Indeed, Kramer, who has been the journal's editor since its inception, initially had his editorial office in the Olin Corporation headquarters. Haacke and Bourdieu discuss Kramer's cultural role in *Free Exchange*, pp. 52–4.

38 'Morrison, duCille, Baquet, Pulitzer Prizewinners,' *Jet*, 74 (18 April 1988), 14.

39 These extravagant terms were integral to the lobbying effort for Morrison's 1988 Pulitzer, which was launched soon after she was passed over for both the NBA and the NBCCA. A paid advertisement appearing as an open letter in the *New York Times Book Review*, signed by June Jordan, Houston Baker, and forty-six other black writers and academics, referred to the Pulitzer and the NBA as the 'keystones to the canon of American literature' ('Black Writers in Praise of Toni Morrison,'

The New York Times Book Review, 24 January 1988, 36). Jordan, who had first met with Morrison to discuss the possibility of undertaking this sort of preemptive media campaign, was quoted as saying that Morrison was wounded by her failure to win the NBA and 'was having doubts about her work,' since 'the awards are the only kind of validation that makes sense in the literary world' (Elizabeth Kastor, '"Beloved" and the Protest,' *Washington Post*, 21 January 1988, B1).

40 There is little doubt that the journals of the cultural right were attempting to prevent Morrison from winning the Pulitzer for *Beloved*. *The New Criterion* ran a Morrison-bashing piece perfectly timed to coincide with the decision-making of the NBCC and Pulitzer judges: Martha Bayles, 'Special Effects, Special Pleading' (January 1988), 34–40; and so did *Commentary*: Carol Iannone, 'Toni Morrison's Career' (December 1987), 59–63. Indeed, Iannone, who would go on to be George Bush's alarmingly underqualified nominee for the top post at the National Council on Humanities, devoted a good share of her literary journalism to attacks on Morrison, Alice Walker, and other prize-winning minority authors. In 1991, when she was positioning herself for the NCH nomination, she published a full-scale denunciation of book prizes called 'Literature by Quota' (*Commentary*, 91 [March 1991]), in which Morrison's Pulitzer served as a prime example of judges' willingness to assuage their white guilt by 'sacrificing the demands of excellence to the "democratic dictatorship of mediocrity"' (53).

41 Examples include George Christian, who said the lobbying had made Morrison 'a figure of fun' ('Literature Needs a Triple Crown,' *Houston Chronicle*, 7 February 1988, 20) and Chistopher Hitchens, ('Those Glittering Prizes'), who characterized Morrison as a writer who, for the sake of a book prize, would 'jump through hoops that ought to embarrass even a hardened Oscar seeker."

THE POETRY
OF SEAMUS HEANEY

44 Seamus Heaney, Crediting Poetry
(1995)

This extract comes from the beginning of Heaney's Nobel lecture. Moving from an account of his first contact with the name 'Stockholm' as a child in the 1940s, Heaney clarifies his sense of the value and importance of poetry.

Heaney, S., 'Crediting Poetry', in *Opened Ground: Poems 1966–1996*, London: Faber & Faber, 1998, pp. 447–50

When I first encountered the name of the city of Stockholm, I little thought that I would ever visit it, never mind end up being welcomed to it as a guest of the Swedish Academy and the Nobel Foundation. At that particular time, such an outcome was not just beyond expectation: it was simply beyond conception. In the nineteen-forties, when I was the eldest child of an ever-growing family in rural Co. Derry, we crowded together in the three rooms of a traditional thatched farmstead and lived a kind of den-life which was more or less emotionally and intellectually proofed against the outside world. It was an intimate, physical, creaturely existence in which the night sounds of the horse in the stable beyond one bedroom wall mingled with the sounds of adult conversation from the kitchen beyond the other. We took in everything that was going on, of course – rain in the trees, mice on the ceiling, a steam train rumbling along the railway line one field back from the house – but we took it in as if we were in the doze of hibernation. Ahistorical, presexual, in suspension between the archaic and the modern, we were as susceptible and impressionable as the drinking water that stood in a bucket in our scullery: every time a passing train made the earth shake, the surface of that water used to ripple delicately, concentrically, and in utter silence.

But it was not only the earth that shook for us: the air around and above us was alive and signalling also. When a wind stirred in the beeches, it also stirred an aerial wire attached to the topmost branch of the chestnut tree. Down it swept, in through a hole bored in the corner of the kitchen window, right on into the innards of our wireless set where a little pandemonium of burbles and squeaks would suddenly give way to the voice of a BBC news-reader speaking out of the unexpected like a *deus ex machina*. And that voice too we could hear in our bedroom, transmitting from beyond and behind the voices of the adults in the kitchen; just as we could often hear, behind and beyond every voice, the frantic, piercing signalling of Morse code.

We could pick up the names of neighbours being spoken in the local accents of our parents, and in the resonant English tones of the newsreader the names of bombers and of cities bombed, of war fronts and army divisions, the numbers of planes lost and of prisoners taken, of casualties suffered and advances made; and always, of course, we would pick up too those other, solemn and oddly bracing words, 'the enemy' and 'the allies'. But even so, none of the news of these world-spasms entered me as terror. If there was something ominous in the newscaster's tones, there, was something torpid about our understanding of what was at stake; and if there was something culpable about such political ignorance in that time and place, there was something positive about the security I inhabited as a result of it.

The wartime, in other words, was pre-reflective time for me. Pre-literate too. Pre-historical in its way. Then as the years went on and my listening became more deliberate, I would climb up on an arm of our big sofa to get my ear closer to the wireless speaker. But it was still not the news that interested me; what I was after was the thrill of story, such as a detective serial about a British special agent called Dick Barton or perhaps a radio adaptation of one of Capt. W. E. Johns's adventure tales about RAF flying ace called Biggles. Now that the other children were older and there was so much going on in the kitchen, I had to get close to the actual radio set in order to concentrate my hearing, and in that intent proximity to the dial I grew familiar with the names of foreign stations, with Leipzig and Oslo and Stuttgart and Warsaw and, of course, with Stockholm.

I also got used to hearing short bursts of foreign languages as the dial hand swept round from the BBC to Radio Eireann, from the intonations of London to those of Dublin, and even though I did not understand what was being said in those first encounters with the gutturals and sibilants of European speech, I had already begun a journey into the wideness of the world. This in turn became a journey into the wideness of language, a journey where each point of arrival – whether in one's poetry or ones life – turned out to be a stepping stone rather than a destination, and it is that journey which has brought me now to this honoured spot. And yet the platform here feels more like a space station than a stepping stone, so that is why, for once in my life, I am permitting myself the luxury of walking on air.

I credit poetry for making this space-walk possible. I credit it immediately because of a line I wrote fairly recently encouraging myself (and whoever else might be listening) to 'walk on air against your better judgement'. But I credit it ultimately because poetry can make an order as true to the impact of external reality and as sensitive to the inner laws of the poet's being as the ripples that rippled in and rippled out across the water in that scullery bucket fifty years ago. An order where we can at last grow up to that which we stored up as we grew. An order which satisfies all that is appetitive in the intelligence and prehensile in the affections. I credit poetry, in other words, both for being itself and for being a help, for making possible a fluid and restorative relationship between the mind's centre and its circumference, between the child gazing at the word 'Stockholm' on the face of the radio dial and the man facing the faces that he meets in Stockholm at this most privileged moment. I credit it because credit is due to it, in our time and in all time, for its truth to life, in every sense of that phrase.

45 Conor Cruise O'Brien, A Slow North-East Wind (1975)

In this review (first published in the now defunct BBC journal *The Listener*), the politician and historian Conor Cruise O'Brien identifies Heaney's *North* (1975) as a volume which verbally encapsulates 'the tragedy of ... the Catholics of Northern Ireland'. Note also O'Brien's comparison of Heaney with Yeats (an earlier Irish Nobel laureate) and his rejection of simplistic analogies between the two poets.

O'Brien, C. C., 'A Slow North-East Wind', review of Seamus Heaney's *North* in *The Listener*, 25 September, 1975, pp. 404–5

> The pigskin's scourged until his knuckles bleed.
> The air is pounding like a stethoscope.
>   ('Orange Drums, Tyrone, 1966')

I had the uncanny feeling, reading these poems, of listening to the thing itself, the actual substance of historical agony and dissolution, the tragedy of a people in a place: the Catholics of Northern Ireland. Yes, the Catholics: there is no equivalent Protestant voice. Poetry is as unfair as history, though in a different way. Seamus Heaney takes his distances—archaeology, Berkeley, love-hate of the English language, Spain, County Wicklow (not the least distant)—but his Derry is always with him, the ash, somehow, now standing out even more on the forehead.

A prehistoric body, dug out of a bog 'bruised like a forceps baby', leads to and merges with the image of a girl chained to a railing, shaved and tarred, with the poet as silent witness:

> My poor scapegoat,
> I almost love you
> but would have cast, I know,
> the stones of silence . . .
>
> I who have stood dumb
> when your betraying sisters,
> cauled in tar, wept by the railings,
>
> who would connive
> in civilised outrage
> yet understand the exact
> and tribal, intimate revenge.
> ('Punishment')

'Betraying' . . . 'exact' . . . 'revenge' . . . The poet here appears as part of his peoples assumption that, since the girl has been punished by the IRA, she must indeed be guilty: a double assumption—that she did, in fact, inform on the IRA and that informing on the IRA is a crime. The IRA—nowhere directly referred to—are Furies with an 'understood' role and place in the tribe. It is the word 'exact' that hurts most: Seamus Heaney has so greatly earned the right to use this word that to see him use it as he does here opens up a sort of chasm. But then, of course, that is what he is about. The word 'exact' fits the situation as it is felt to be: and it is because it fits, and because other situations, among the rival population, turn on similarly oiled pivots, that hope succumbs. I have read many pessimistic analyses of 'Northern Ireland', but none that has the bleak conclusiveness of these poems.

In a poem with the finely ironic title, 'Act of Union', Heaney has 'the man' addressing a woman pregnant by him, with the metaphor of England addressing Ireland:

Conquest is a lie. I grow older
Conceding your half-independent shore
Within those borders now my legacy
Culminates inexorably.

And I am still imperially
Male, leaving you with the pain.
The rending process in the colony,
The battering rain, the boom burst from within.
The act sprouted an obstinate fifth column
Whose stance is growing unilateral.
His heart beneath your heart is a wardrum
Mustering force. His parasitical
And ignorant little fists already
Beat at your borders and I know they're cocked
At me across the water. No treaty
I foresee will salve completely your tracked
And stretchmarked body, the big pain
That leaves you raw, like opened ground, again.

The terms of the metaphor are surprising. After all, it is not just the 'obstinate fifth column' engendered by England—the Ulster Protestants—who wield parasitical and ignorant little fists; and most Ulster Protestants would be genuinely bewildered at the thought that it was they, rather than their enemies, who were beating at borders, or threatening England.

It is true that the act of impregnation can be thought of as producing the total situation in Northern Ireland, a fifth column relative to both England and Ireland: the poem is rich enough. (Elsewhere, Seamus Heaney writes of the *Catholics* as 'in a wooden horse', 'besieged within the siege'.) In a sense, the poet here is deliberately envisaging the matter mainly as 'the man' feels the woman (Ireland, the Catholics of Ireland within the metaphor) feels it to be; and in relation to these feelings he is never likely to be wrong. In any case, there is a kind of balance at which Seamus Heaney is not aiming. He mocks at one of the protective Ulster clichés in 'Whatever You Say Say Nothing': '"One side's as bad as the other," never worse.' His upbringing and experience have given him some cogent reasons to feel that one side *is* worse than the other, and his poems have to reflect this.

Many people in Northern Ireland are in the habit of arguing that they 'have nothing against Catholics as such' (or 'Protestants as such', as the case may be). The trouble, is that neither lot, in practice, can remain just 'such', they have to be the much more and much less that it means to be *Irish*

265

Catholics and *Ulster* Protestants: such-plus and seen as such-plus, inherently hostile and frightening. In these poems of Seamus Heaney's, Protestants are seen as such-plus: a matter of muzzles, masks and eyes. About his own such-plusses he is neither sentimental nor apologetic. This, on their mood in (I think) the winter of 1971–2:

> As the man said when Celtic won, 'The Pope of Rome
> 's a happy man this night'. His flock suspect
>
> In their deepest heart of hearts the heretic
> Has come at last to heel and to the stake.
> We tremble near the flames but want no truck
> With the actual firing. We're on the make
>
> As ever. Long sucking the hind tit
> Cold as a witch's and as hard to swallow
> Still leaves us fork-tongued on the border bit:
> The liberal papist note sounds hollow
>
> When amplified and mixed in with the bangs
> That shake all hearts and windows day and night.
> ('Whatever You Say Say Nothing')

Seamus Heaney is being compared with Yeats, and this is unavoidable, since his unmistakable emergence as the most important Irish poet since Yeats. Yet to call them both 'Irish poets' would be more misleading than illuminating, unless the Protean nature of 'Irishness' is remembered. It would be wrong to say that 'Southern Protestant' and 'Northern Catholic' have nothing in common, but to state what they do have in common, which they *do not* have in common with the British, would be an enterprise requiring delicate discriminations within the concept of 'Irishness'. One such common characteristic is an uneasy but fruitful relation to the English language, a tendency to use the language in surprising ways, yet without individualist eccentricity.

Seamus Heaney's writing is modest, often conversational, apparently easy, low-pitched, companionably ironic, ominous, alert, accurate and surprising. An Irish reader is not automatically reminded of cats by this cluster of characteristics, yet an English reader may perhaps see resemblances that are there but overlooked by the Irish—resemblances coming, perhaps, from certain common rhythms and hesitations of Irish speech and non-speech. One may, of course, be reminded, by the subject-matter, of Yeats's 1916 poems and of 'Nineteen Hundred and Nineteen' and 'Meditation in Time of Civil War'.

Again, I am more struck with the differences than the resemblances. Yeats was free to try, and did splendidly try, or try on, different relations to the tragedy: Heaney's relation to a deeper tragedy is fixed and pre-ordained; the poet is on intimate terms with doom and speaks its language wryly and succinctly:

> I am neither internee nor
> informer;
> An inner émigré, grown
> long-haired
> And thoughtful: a wood-kerne
> Escaped from the massacre . . .

As I read and re-read *North*, I was reminded, not so much of any other Irish poet, as of one of Rudyard Kipling's most chilling fairystories, 'Cold Iron'. It is a story in which bright and tender hopes are snuffed out by ineluctable destiny, the hand of Thor. And the way in which Thor makes his presence felt is always 'a slow north-east wind'.

46 Ciaran Carson, Escaped from the Massacre? (1975)

Carson's review (first published in the Northern Irish poetry magazine *The Honest Ulsterman*) takes a different approach to *North*. Carson is arguably the first to articulate misgivings about the 'bog' poems, suggesting that Heaney aestheticises violence in poems like 'Punishment'. 'Bord na Mona' in Carson's penultimate paragraph is the Gaelic name of the Irish Peat Commission.

Carson, C., 'Escaped from the Massacre? *North* by Seamus Heaney', *The Honest Ulsterman*, 50, 1975, pp. 183–6

Badly reproduced on the literary pages, beside the reviews, Edward McGuire's portrait of Seamus Heaney is blurred and ambivalent; it appears both as an advertisement and as a record of literary achievement. Idealized almost to the point of caricature the foreshortened legs, the hen-toed boots, the squat fingers resting on the table, the open book) – it seems to forestall criticism; the poet seems to have acquired the status of myth, of institution. One can hardly resist the suspicion that *North* itself, as a work of art, has succumbed to this notion; Heaney seems to have moved – unwillingly, perhaps – from being a writer with the gift of precision, to become the laureate of violence – a mythmaker, an anthrpologist of ritual killing, an apologist for "the situation", in the last resort, a mystifier. It makes *North* a curiously uneven book. Its division into two parts seems to reflect some basic dilemma, between the need to be precise, and the desire to abstract, to create a superstructure of myth and symbol.

The first few lines of section III of 'Kinship' for example, can hardly be faulted for their accuracy and sense of reality:

> I found a turf-spade
> hidden under bracken,
> laid flat, and overgrown
> with a green fog.
>
> As I raised it
> the soft lips of the growth
> muttered and split,
> a tawny rut
>
> opening at my feet
> like a shed skin. . . .

But then something goes wrong. Not content to leave well enough alone, Heaney finds it necessary to explain, to justify the lines in terms of his myth. The spade is no longer a spade; it becomes elevated to the status of a deity:

> And now they have twinned
> that obelisk:
>
> among the stones,
> under a bearded cairn
> a love-nest is disturbed,
> catkin and bog-cotton tremble
>
> as they raise up
> the cloven oak-limb.
> I stand at the edge of centuries
> facing a goddess.

The two methods are not compatible. One gains its poetry by embodiment of a specific, personal situation; the other has degenerated into a messy historical and religious surmise – a kind of Golden Bough activity, in which the real difference between our society and that of Jutland in some vague past are glossed over for the sake of the parallels of ritual. Being killed for adultery (for example) is one thing; being tarred and feathered is another, and the comparison sometimes leads Heaney to some rather odd historical and emotional conclusions. In 'Punishment' he seems to be offering his "understanding" of the situation almost as a consolation:

> I who have stood dumb
> when your betraying sisters,
> cauled in tar,
> wept by the railings,
>
> who would connive
> in civilized outrage
> yet understand the exact
> and tribal, intimate revenge.

It is as if he is saying, suffering like this is natural; these things have always happened; they happened then, they happen now, and that is sufficient ground for understanding and absolution. It is as if there never were and never will be any political consequences of such acts; they have been removed to the realm of sex, death and inevitablity. So, when he writes 'Act of Union' Ireland's relationship with England is sentimentalized into something as natural as a good fuck – being something that has always happened, everywhere, there is no longer any need to explain; it is like a mystery of the Catholic Church, ritualized and mystified into a willing ignorance.

For all that, some of the bog poems do succeed – 'Strange Fruit' for example, refuses to fall into the glib analyses which characterize too many of the poems. It does not posture in its own "understanding" of death; Heaney says quite honestly that he doesn't know:

> Murdered, forgotten, nameless, terrible
> beheaded girl, outstaring axe
> And beatification, outstaring
> What had begun to feel like reverence.

The same honesty of observation comes across again in – for instance – Part 1 of 'Funeral Rites.' This time it is a visual honesty: this, we feel, is what a corpse looks like:

> They had been laid out
> in tainted rooms,

their eyelids glistening,
their dough-white hands
shackled in rosary beads.

Their puffed knuckles
had unwrinkled,
the nails were darkened,
the wrists obediently sloped.

Yet, the rest of the poem seems to suggest that Heaney doubts the worth of his own simplicity; all too soon, we are back in the world of megalithic doorways and charming, noble barbarity. The poem ends with Gunnar looking beautiful and dead, chanting – inevitably – verses about honour, and staring at the moon.

Gunnar seems to be a sort of relative to Shakespeare, Hercules and Raleigh (to name but a few who figure in the Madame Tussaud's Gallery of Greats), and there is at times a temptation to think that Heaney is trying to emulate Eliot, or Yeats, or both, in a quest for importance. Certainly, the references are sometimes verbal Cornflakes; sometimes, as in 'The Seed-Cutters', the apostrophe works perfectly; we realise how Breughel's realism, his faithfulness to minutiae, are akin to Heaney's, and what could have been portentousness takes on a kind of humility. I think this is one of the best poems in the book.

They seem hundreds of years away. Breughel,
You'll know them if I can get them true.
They kneel under the hedge in a half-circle;
Behind a windbreak wind is breaking through.
They are the seedcutters. The tuck and frill
of leaf-sprout is on the seed potatoes
Buried under that straw. With time to kill
They are taking their time. Each sharp knife goes.
Lazily halving each root that falls apart
In the palm of the hand: a milky gleam,
And, at the centre, a dark watermark.
O calendar customs! Under the broom
Yellowing over them, compose the frieze
With all of us there, our anonymities.

The second half of *North* is a kind of Pyrrhic victory: it doesn't quite hang together, either by itself, or as the other side of the mythical coin. Poems like 'Whatever you say, say nothing' are not improved by age or by their inclusion in the Great Work, and the good bits in 'Singing School' are almost but not quite – obscured by the bad bits. And yet, in an odd way, there is more humanity and honesty in this section than in the acres of bogland in Part I; one gets the impression of someone involved in writing, of trying to come to terms with himself, instead of churning it out like Bord na Mona. 'Singing School', for all its faults, has an air of going somewhere; in its tentative precision, it continues where *Wintering Out* left off, and 'Exposure', the last poem in the book rates with 'Mossbawn' as one of the real successes of *North*.

No-one really escapes from the massacre, of course – the only way you can do that is by falsifying issues, by applying wrong notions of history instead of seeing what's before your eyes, or by taking blurbs at their face value (as many reviewers seem to have done). Everyone was anxious that *North* should be a great book; when it turned out that it wasn't, it was treated as one anyway, and made into an Ulster '75 Exhibition of the Good that can come out of Troubled Times. Heaney is too good and too sensible a poet to turn into Faber's answer to Georgie Best.

ABDULRAZAK GURNAH,
PARADISE

47 Pico Iyer, The Empire Writes Back
(1993)

When Salman Rushdie won the Booker Prize for his novel *Midnight's Children* in 1981, it was argued by many that Rushdie had put a 'depth charge' into the world of 'British fiction'. These two extracts from essays by Pico Iyer and Graham Huggan raise important questions about literary judgement and posit different perspectives on how and why the prize has been seen to have transformed the face of contemporary writing in Britain. Whereas Iyer takes up the now familiar argument of the empire writing back to the centre and celebrates the ways in which such writers have transformed the nature of the English tongue, Huggan is more sceptical about the cultural politics behind the fashionable valorisation of 'the postcolonial exotic', a debate that still continues today amongst critics assessing the work of many other shortlisted writers and winners.

Iyer, P., 'The Empire Writes Back', *Time*, 8 February, 1993, pp. 46–52

In 1981 the Booker went to Salman Rushdie's tumultous, many-headed myth of modern India, *Midnight's Children*. In the eleven years since, it has been given to two Australians, a part Maori, a South African, a woman of Polish descent, a Nigerian and an exile from Japan. Runners-up have featured such redoubtably English names as Mo and Mistry and Achebe; when a traditional English name takes the prize – A.S. Byatt, say, or Kingsley Amis – it seems almost anomalous.

[. . .]

There could hardly have been a more vivid illustration of how the Empire has struck back, as Britain's former colonies have begun to capture the heart of English literature, while transforming the language with bright colors and strange cadences and foreign eyes. As Vikram Seth, a leading Indian novelist, whose books have been set in Tibet and San Francisco says, "The English language has been taken over, or taken to heart, or taken to tongue, by people whose language historically it was not".

[. . .]

The centers of this new frontierless kind of writing are the growing capitals of multicultural life, such as London, Toronto and, to a lesser extent New York, but the form is rising up wherever cultures jangle. All these places are witnessing a transformation of the very canon of English literature, where not long ago a student of modern literature would probably have been weaned on Graham Greene, Evelyn Waugh and Aldous Huxley, now he will more likely be taught Rushdie and Okri – which is fitting in an England where many students first language is Cantonese or Urdu. . . . None of this is entirely new of course: four in every five English words are already foreign born, and writers like V.S. Naipaul, Wole Soyinka and C.L.R. James have long staked distinguished claims beside the English writers they studied at school. . . . The fact of writers moving from a foreign tongue to English is as familiar as Joseph Conrad and Vladimir Nabokov, and that of bilingual writers as extraordinary as Samuel Beckett and Isaac Bashevis Singer.

[. . .]

But the new transcultural writers are something different. For one, they are the products not so much of colonial division as of the international culture that has grown up since the war, and they are addressing an audience as mixed up and eclectic and uprooted as themselves. They are the creators, and creations, of a new postimperial order in which English is the lingua franca, just about everywhere is a suburb of the same international youth culture, and all countries are part of a unified CNN and MTV circuit, with a common frame of reference in McDonald's, Madonna and Magic Johnson.

[. . .]

Most of all they make a virtue of their hyphenated status. Instead of failing through the cracks, they hope, through their Janus-faced perspective, to straddle different worlds, and pick and choose from all traditions. . . . They use their liminal position not just as a theme but as an instrument.

[. . .]

What all of them are saying, in a sense, is that we are living in a decentred world, and the publishing business has not been slow to make capital of what investors call the "borderless economy".

48 Graham Huggan, The Postcolonial Exotic (1994)

Huggan, G., 'The Postcolonial Exotic', *Transition*, 64, 1994, pp. 22–9

Last year's suspiciously self-congratulatory decision to award Salman Rushdie the 25-year commemorative 'Booker of Bookers' for his 1981 novel *Midnight's Children* affords a useful opportunity to reflect upon the glamorous world of literary prizes.

[. . .]

The Booker's pomp and circumstance might seem peculiarly British: the Anglo literati's "superior" answer to the Academy Awards. Yet despite the smugness of the ceremony, with its complacent inside jokes and specious literary camaraderie, the Booker stakes a powerful claim to being an international award. Writers from across the British Commonwealth (Ireland and Pakistan currently enjoy honorary membership) are eligible to compete for the prize. In the Booker's 26-year history, writers from outside Britain or with non-British cultural backgrounds, have been by far the most successful. As Pico Iyer quips in a 1993 article in *Time*, the prize since Rushdie won it has gone to

> two Australians, a part Maori, a South African, a woman of Polish descent, a Nigerian and an exile from Japan. Runners-up have featured such redoubtably English names as Mo and Mistry and Achebe; when a traditional English name takes the prize—A. S. Byatt, say, or Kingsley Amis—it seems almost anomalous.

Iyer attributes this eclecticism to the internationalization of English literature. A new "frontierless" writing has emerged "wherever cultures jangle." "Postcolonial" has become the codeword for these transnational productions. The Booker McConnell company has evolved into a postcolonial patron: through its sponsorship it celebrates the hybrid status of an increasingly global culture. English literature is no longer English: it speaks in many tongues, from many different points of view. The Booker Prize acknowledges and embraces this plurality it rewards its far-flung writers for "writing back" to the former Empire.

The problem with Iyer's argument—a problem of which he, a successful writer, is surely well aware—is that it overlooks the commercial basis of the multicultural vitality it applauds. The pliability of the term "postcolonial" —its ready availability as a market strategy—suggests that it functions not merely as a marker of anti-imperial resistance, but as a sales tag for the international commodity culture of late (twentieth-century) capitalism. Postcoloniality, says Anthony Appiah is best understood as a condition. It is the condition, first and foremost, of a "comprador intelligentsia": "of a relatively small, Western-style, Western-trained group of writers and thinkers who mediate the trade in cultural commodities of world capitalism at the periphery." (Needless to say, these writers and thinkers need not be stationed at the "'periphery": some of them, like Rushdie, are very much at the "center.") In negotiating their condition, and turning it to their own advantage, postcolonial writers are adept at manipulating the commercial codes of the international open market. They recognize that the value of their writing as an international commodity depends, to a large extent, on the exotic appeal it holds to an unfamiliar metropolitan audience. They thus risk becoming complicit with the cultural imperialism they denounce. Contradictions inevitably emerge: writers wish to strike back against the center, yet they also write and are marketed for it; they wish to speak from the margins, yet they are assimilated into the mainstream; they wish to undo the opposition between a European Self and its designated Others, yet they are pressed into the service of manufacturing cultural Otherness (Appiah).

This is not to accuse the writers of bad faith or of blatant opportunism; it is merely to insist that postcolonial writing be seen in its requisite material context, as part of a wider process in which the writers' anti-imperial sentiments must contend with imperial market forces. Postcolonial writing beguiles the line between resistance and collusion; the best-known writers are those like Rushdie—or, from a different perspective, Naipaul—who understand how to manage the *realpolitik* of metropolitan dominance. It is no surprise to find, then, that both writers are former Booker winners. (Naipaul won in 1973 with his novella sequence *In a Free State*.) For Naipaul, the Booker confirmed an already well-established reputation; for Rushdie, it was instrumental in bringing him to the public eye, where he has remained ever since, acquiring the dubious status of a "canonical" postcolonial writer. The Booker helped both writers; did it also compromise them?

[. . .]

The ambivalence of the situation is instructive. The Booker Prize may reward its writers for speaking out against the Empire, but this doesn't stop it from affiliating itself with the British Commonwealth, that aging guardian of unshared values whose ward, Commonwealth Literature, has been memorably dismissed by Rushdie as a figment of the imperial imagination, and, more memorably still, by Aijaz Ahmad as "a British Council construct, limited largely to its clients." The Commonwealth's paternalistic rhetoric smacks of colonial condescension; so too does Booker's promotional push, which arrogates to itself the rights of patronage. In early Commonwealth literary criticism, amid much empty talk of happy families, there was an implicit assumption of Britain's arbitrational cultural role; the "filial" literatures of the former colonies were urged to refer for guidance to the "parent stock." This mantle is now assumed by the Booker and its panel of "disinterested" (white male) judges: these mostly establishment figures are to determine what carries "intrinsic" literary value. They are to confer legitimacy, from the "center," on the literature of the "periphery."

If the Booker, in this sense, continues to be stolidly unregenerate, in another it has proved itself to be very much up-to-date. Commonwealth Literature, like the Commonwealth itself, is a diplomatic dodo; it represents, as Ahmad says, a "cultural hangover from the Empire." Yet the Empire, if not the Commonwealth, is obviously in vogue. The recent Raj revival, fueled by Thatcherite nostalgia, is showing few signs of waning; books and films on Africa and other former tropical colonies pour out; and travel writing, that ever-reliable vehicle of outdated imperial heroism, continues to stock booksellers shelves with its vicarious thrills and spills.

[. . .]

The critical agendas of the writers need not coincide, of course, with the way their books are marketed. The mismatch is often striking. Exoticist myths and stereotypes, apparently dismantled by the writers, reappear with a vengeance in the commercial packaging of their books. Take the "Booker of Bookers," Rushdie's novel *Midnight's Children*. The 1981 Picador edition is largely unexceptionable—except, that is, for the blurb emblazoned across the book's front covers "At last a literary continent has found its voice," proclaims an undoubtedly enthusiastic, if suspiciously anonymous, reviewer. One can imagine the wry amusement with which Rushdie must have greeted this astonishing news—just elide several thousand years of Indian literary history and presto, the "representative" Indian voice! A sleight of hand well worthy of Rushdie's "magic-realist" novel.

Various exoticist maneuvers—the construction of the representative foreign writer, the appeal to local color, the search for, or assertion of, an "authenticity" not normally ascribed to one's own culture—can be traced in the metropolitan marketing of postcolonial literature. What say do postcolonial writers have in the commercial packaging of their books? Is it possible to speak of a "postcolonial exotic," and if so, to what extent do postcolonial writers collaborate in these exoticist productions? Clearly, individual cases vary; one constant, however, is the impact of metropolitan mediation. (Booker's involvement, though important, is arguably indirect. More significant are the publishers: Heinemann, for example, whose popular African Writers Series, now running to several hundred titles with excellent worldwide distribution, has its marketing control room in the heart of darkest Oxford.) Though publishers' agendas differ widely, they all know exoticism sells. African or Indian writing offers a window onto a different, exciting world. This world produces wonder: it rejuvenates the sensibilities of a readership tired of provincial navel-gazing; tired also of a literature that reflects the realities of a society from which they badly need release. Not that postcolonial literature offers harmless escapism: on the contrary, it repoliticizes the act of reading, providing an opportunity for focused rage or an outlet for indefinite liberal guilt. The discourse of exoticism allows for multicultural celebration; it also provides a basis for considered self-critique.

Exoticism relieves its practitioners, however, from the burdensome task of actually learning about "other" cultures. As Tzvetan Todorov says,

> The best candidates for the exotic label are the peoples and cultures that are most remote from us and least known to us. . . . Knowledge is incompatible with exoticism, but lack of knowledge is in turn irreconcilable with praise of others; yet praise without knowledge is precisely what exoticism aspires to be. This is its constitutive paradox.

Exoticists, adds Tododrov, "cherish the remote because of its remoteness." There is a further paradox here; for in the "global" cultural environment of the late twentieth century, exoticism becomes a function not of remoteness but, on the contrary, of proximity. Exotic artifacts from other cultures circulate as commodities within the global economy—it is precisely their availability that renders them exotic.

Postcolonial literature participates despite itself in this mediating process. "Other" cultures are made available for consumption by a metropolitan readership. Books by African and Indian writers acquire an almost totemic value: they are wrapped in the exotic aura of the cultural commodity fetish. In the imperialistic logic of the universal market, the distinction between the global economy and global culture can be conveniently collapsed. Cultural differences devolve into the stuff of tourist spectacle; "otherness emerges everywhere"; the world becomes a theme-park. The ubiquity of exoticism doesn't make it less exotic—but it does help to convey the illusion of cross-cultural reciprocity. Multiculturalism is the latest of these exoticist panaceas. The appeal to cultural diversity disguises a reluctance for social change: pre-existing hierarchies can be maintained through commodified gestures toward bilateral convergence.) The blatant hypocrisies of exoticism—complacency masked as appreciation; novelty mediated through cliché; the creation of a cultural distance that the discourse claims to be narrow—are inimical to the objectives of anticolonial writers such as Rushdie. Exoticism remains integral, nonetheless, to the reading and writing of postcolonial literature: it reflects the writing's market value as a cultural commodity. (Exoticism is arguably central, also, to the teaching and study of postcolonial writing. The obsession of many postcolonial critics with theories of "otherness" is by no means incompatible with exoticist predilections. Smorgasbord university courses on postcolonial literatures run the risk of encouraging a kind of licensed intellectual tourism. Meanwhile, in scholarly books and journals, postcolonial writing is co-opted into self-marginalizing discussions on the function of "minority discourse," or grafted onto totalizing paradigms of transcultural resistance. The institutionalization of postcolonial studies is another effect of "post coloniality": the "postcolonial" is as much an intellectual as a cultural commodity.)

What options are open to writers of, say, African or Indian background who wish to translate their complex cultural realities for an unaccustomed metropolitan audience? The task is made more difficult when those realities have been shaped, for centuries, according to others' dictates: tailored to the requirements of a European exoticist imaginary. Clearly, the writers' choice is not to discover a language—an alternative kind of English—that is somehow uncontaminated by exoticist mythologies. A viable option instead is to lay bare the process by which those mythologies are constructed. The commercial success of *Midnight's Children* owes much to the canniness with which its author displays this seductive process.

49 Abdulrazuk Gurnah, Imagining the Postcolonial Writer (2000)

Abdulrazak Gurnah's fourth novel *Paradise* was shortlisted for the Booker Prize in 1994. As both a critic of 'African' literature as well as a writer of fiction, Gurnah has frequently commented in his non-fictional essays on how the post-colonial writer has come to be imagined in the West. In the first essay, Gurnah maps the historical background to a number of current theoretical and literary debates; he also provides a number of illuminating insights into the construction of his own fictional world in *Paradise*. 'An Idea of the Past' expands further on these questions. Beginning with the vision of Nobel-winning Caribbean poet Derek Walcott that 'The truly tough aesthetic of the New World' is 'one that neither explains nor forgives history', he argues that the canon of literature should not be locked into fixed hierarchies but remain open. In urging for a revisioning of the ways in which historical narratives are constructed, he not only reveals his own story as a writer who grew up in Zanzibar before Independence but asks for a wider reassessment of how the histories of such nations come to be constructed.

Gurnah, A., 'Imagining the Postcolonial Writer', in S. Nasta (ed.), *Reading the 'New' Literatures in a Postcolonial Era*, Leicester: The English Association, Essays and Studies, 2000, pp. 73–86

It is the discussion of the 'literary', of writing, which has turned out to be the most amenable form for the exercise of postcolonial methods in institutions in the West and elsewhere, and this is no doubt due to its links to 'literary theory'. It would not be contentious to say that 'theory' is characterised by its challenge to constitutive narratives of origin and cultural hierarchies. And in its institutional dimension, 'theory' has generated its sternest challenge to the arts and the humanities, even though its beginning was in linguistics. For despite privileging the humane in the name of a universal moral instinct, it is the humanities that have clung tenaciously to cultural hierarchies when other institutional practices have abandoned them for interdisciplinarity in the interests of use and legitimacy. It is in this locale that the post-structuralist challenge to the universal, to narratives of truth and knowledge, proved so devastating. And it is out of this that post-modernity emerges, if we agree with Lyotard that postmodernity is the recognition that reason cannot validate itself but only appears to acquire legitimacy through a fragmented set of discursive practices. So the narrative of postmodernity is characteristically de-centred, denying the universal its privileged space and de-legitimising the narrative of mythic origins. This is the fragmented space that is claimed by postcolonial theory and which energises arguments for postcolonial identity. . . .

But if the liberating potential of ascendant postmodernism allows the emergence of postcolonial conceptions of identity in difference, these conceptions find only a muted echo, or worse, in African and Caribbean critical discourses. Kwarne Anthony Appiah scrutinises the connection between postcolonial and postmodern in his eloquent article 'Is the Post- in Postmodernism the Post- in Postcolonial?',[1] and in the process arrives at a distinction of the possibilities of the category:

> Postcoloniality is the condition of what we might ungenerously call a comprador intelligentsia . . . In the West they are known through the Africa they offer; their compatriots know them both through the West they present to Africa and through an Africa they have invented for the world.
>
> (Appiah, 1991, 348)

Whether ungenerous or not, this description certainly gives the postcolonial intellectual undeserved powers of agency, seeming to set aside briefly the preceding narratives of difference that prompt the contesting position of postcolonial discourse. Appiah establishes the different senses of the post in postcolonial, between that sense understood by the postcolonial theorist as a rejection and transcending of the coloniser's discourse of otherness, what Aijaz Ahmad had called 'a monstrous machinery of descriptions'[2] and that other sense which does not acknowledge or seek to refuse, which seems insensitive to, the 'claim to exclusivity of vision' (Appiah 1991, 348) seen as characteristic of cultural imperialism. Appiah makes the particular point that the latter sense is true of contemporary *popular* African cultural life, and that it is a characteristic of popular culture to be insensitive to the politics of its borrowings, and this is precisely the argument of postmodern theory as it concerns the international commodification of culture. While this might seem to suggest that theories of postmodernism are relevant here, this would only be misleadingly so, argues Appiah, for despite appearances, 'these artworks are not understood by their producers or their consumers in terms of a postmodernism', in terms of a rejection of or a challenge to a dominant antecedent narrative or practice.

[. . .]

Appiah worries, then, that the imprecision of the connection between postcolonial and postmodern, and the sense in which they reflect different historical and cultural experiences, is an expression of expedient but misplaced parasitism. And if in his own account Appiah is, to a large degree, imprecise about *Africa*, and its history of suffering, and how its ethical universal is any different from anyone else's, including for that matter the postmodern theorist's and the postcolonial critic's, who apparently deny its legitimacy, his analysis serves to disentangle important issues and clarify the theoretical debate. Other responses have been less tolerant than this. From some critics and writers, postcolonial conceptions have impelled outright and outraged resistance: because they are held to distort and homogenise, and are held to be dependent on a formulaic jargon that allows the critic to pronounce without having any detailed knowledge of the context. Postcolonial critical discourse, in this account, intellectually appropriates the object of its analysis, colonising that object into a homogenised Other, and perpetuating an institutional hegemony of the West. In an editorial to a special issue of *Research in African Literatures* focused on 'the place of theory in the apprehension of meaning' in African writing, Abiola Irele expresses sympathy with these concerns and invites a debate on the issue:

The dissatisfaction that attended the introduction of the term. ['postcolonial'], which seeks to designate a whole category of non-

Western literary texts and to inaugurate a new mode of interpreting them, has not hindered its widespread adoption as one of the key terms of contemporary critical discourse. At the same time, its very success seems to have inspired a debate as to its appropriate terms of reference. At issue is the fact that, in its use . . . the term's very generality tends to obscure the fundamental problem it is concerned with, that of the deliberate marginalization of an ongoing discourse on history in the literatures of the so-called Third World.

(Irele 1995, 1)

His editorial makes clear his own doubts about postcolonial conceptions and methods, especially, as the above quotation demonstrates, with the marginalisation of history and the specific, detailed experience of postcolonial reality which is adjacent and contiguous with it.

[. . .]

But it is Karin Barber's powerful article, 'African-Language Literature and Post-Colonial Criticism' (1995), that Irele nominates as a 'valuable' and 'extremely thoughtful' contribution to 'the role of theory' in African writing, and in part this is because Barber lucidly develops the objections Osundare refers to above. This is how she opens her discussion:

The 'postcolonial' criticism of the 1980s and 90s . . . has promoted a binarized, generalized model of the world which has had the effect of eliminating African-language expression from view. This model has produced an impoverished and distorted picture of 'the colonial experience' and the place of language in that experience. It has maintained a centre-periphery polarity which both exaggerates and simplifies the effects of the colonial imposition of European languages. It turns the colonizing countries into unchanging mono-liths, and the colonised subject into a homogenized token . . . an Other whose experience is determined so overwhelmingly by his or her relation to the metropolitan centre that class, gender, and other local and historical and social pressures are elided.

(Barber 1995, 3)

Barber distinguishes two forms of 'postcolonial'. The first one, exemplified by Said, Spivak and Bhabha, is concerned with the production of a counter-narrative to colonial discourse. This 'style of postcolonial criticism' only obliquely invokes what Barber calls 'indigenous discourses', and largely as a point of vantage from which to demonstrate both the invention of the colonial Other and the limits of the authority of that invention.

The emphasis of this form of 'postcolonial', in other words, is on the deconstruction of the imperial narrative rather than on recuperating its Other. The latter procedure, in fact, is to be carefully avoided for its implication of 'nativism'.

The second form of 'postcolonial', which Barber refers to less respectfully as 'buoyant-type postcolonial criticism', is exemplified by Ashcroft et al. It is to this second form that Barber devotes her attention. She presents this second 'postcolonial' as a position which turns on the argument that post-colonial writing is the expression of suppressed voices of those cultures silenced by colonial experience. The most potent form of this silencing is the privileging of colonial language, to the point that indigenous languages became unusable for 'expressive purposes'. So the discovery of an articulacy in an appropriated form of the colonial language, in a new and refashioned English, for example, is also a refusal of otherness and a reconstitution of the self. It is this breaking of the silence which links 'all postcolonial texts'[3] and which defines the moment of subjectivity and identity. In her article, Barber demonstrates unanswerably how the 'finding a voice' argument assumes that until that moment of recognition that colonial languages could be fashioned to contest the imperial ethos, native cultures had been mute about their experience of colonialism. She shows how this argument, therefore, 're-enacts the very erasure of indigenous languages and cultures that it takes as its initial problematic' (Barber 1995, 7). In the 'finding a voice' argument, 'indigenous' languages are a medium for articulating the pre-colonial world, an authenticating register for evoking the integrity of what preceded rupture. Paradoxically, writing in native languages is also the ambition of the future, when the postcolonial subject would, presumably, have gone beyond the indeterminacies of the present and learnt to speak without angst. Barber then demonstrates how partial and ill-informed such a position is by a discussion of writing in Yoruba, its historical sources and its promotion by colonial policy, its contemporary viability as a popular cultural form, and its intertextual complexity. She demonstrates, in other words, how in this example and in others she refers to (Kiswahili and Hausa, among others), the silence imagined by the postcolonial argument was nowhere widespread and complete, and that, just as importantly:

Contemporary African-language written literature, gaining additional resonance and extension from its location in huge, heterogeneous, popular cultures, is fully as capable of confronting contemporary 'postcolonial' experience as European-language literature.

(Barber, 1995, 12)

Focusing so exclusively on writing in English, Barber argues, to the point of making the use of colonial language the qualifying criterion of post-colonial writing, is to offer a misguided and even false representation of postcolonial cultures and their cultural productions.

[...]

I would now like to turn briefly to why postcolonial methods appeared such an attractive, or even indispensable, way forward for the literary discourse of non-Western writing. As a way of speaking about a category of writing, this term was preceded (though not necessarily in that order) by the post-imperial Commonwealth literature, the truly clumsy emergent literatures, the apparently innocent new literatures, and the sociopolitical thematisations of Third World literature – which all had their heyday and still have a currency. This is not the place to enter into a discussion of the history of these terms and why it was they seemed right or bearable at the time they were in institutional vogue, but their currency and supersession demonstrate, at the very least, their provisional usefulness. It also expresses the tentativeness with which liberal institutional discourse has groped towards describing and naming cultural difference in the aftermath of an empire which was constructed by wide-ranging and aggressive narratives of hierarchy and power. This institutional tentativeness derived from uncertainty about how to revise a way of speaking of cultures bluntly constructed as lesser by inflated narratives of self-description.... The uncertainty about how to speak of non-European cultures afflicted not so much these progressive optimists but the institutions themselves. For how to speak of non-European culture was also part of the self-description within which unequal difference was so critical. To imagine this, we might consider the institutional discomfort of offering a course on Charles Dickens alongside one on Chinua Achebe or R.K. Narayan. To offer such courses alongside each other was to give up their hierarchical relationship, whereas to contain them in a distancing term that was unambiguously othering was to sustain difference. In addition, the process of finding a way of speaking about the cultural products of the colonised, was also (progressively) to allow space in the developing discourse for the Othered who was aspiring to become a Self.

Within the institution, this uncertainty about terms derives partly from a desire to avoid the more blatant cultural supremacist accents which are an aspect of dominance. The failure to fulfil this desire, which I believe is evident in the hectic substitution of categories to contain non-European cultures, and in particular their writing, reveals the difficulty of disentangling the affiliated signifiers that make up the transcendental narrative of the world in the Western era. That is to give more credit than is perhaps deserved, because this failure may also be to do with bad faith, a refusal to let go of the sustaining myths of narratives of knowledge, their genealogies and transmissions, and the hierarchies which inform their ordering. Hence implied in such terms as new literatures, Third World literature and Commonwealth literature – to say nothing of emergent literatures – is a trope of such smug magnitude, on the one hand, and such an ardent liberal reaching for something lukewarm and inoffensive, on the other, that the result is contradiction and logical discomfort. In one way or another, these terms and their contexts, signify difference and an arriviste transparency, and a congenitally knowable lack of complexity which makes the writing accessible from within a reading practice informed by complex and sophisticated textual provenance. That certainly would be true of 'new' and 'emergent', and in a more sinister way, it would also be true of 'Third World'. There is something of the clang of the compound gates in that phrase, distancing the pathologically different. 'Third World' is where there is famine and casual and grotesque violence, and whose writing can be taken uncritically to be the wails of the oppressed to be applauded without putting too fine a point on the flourishes of the text. As for 'Commonwealth', it makes perfect sense that the term should exclude British writing, otherwise it would make for a grotesquely over-balanced object – but it does make the category historically appealing and something of an indulgent euphemism for boogie writing, for *their* writing.

If that describes the uncertainties of Western liberal institutions in speaking of non-European cultures, in producing knowledge of those cultures, how might we describe the uncertainties in this context of the historically Othered. I am still thinking of writing and the categories to contain it and its subject, and I am still thinking of institutions that are part of this discourse. I suspect the discomforts for those I call 'historically othered' are even more acute in this context. Not only are these categories clumsy and partial in the way I have described, but they contain within them implicit seductions. In whatever limited form, such descriptions are inclusive, they appear to endorse the cultures of the Other, and they give unprecedented authority to the non-Western intellectual.

In this sense, postcolonial seems to be an advance as a way of speaking of non-European cultures, though non-European in the use of this term appears to include, quite problematically, European settler cultures. I say quite problematically, because the settler was, and probably still largely is, the visible beneficiary and token of European colonialism. In any case, 'postcolonial' enables a discussion of culture that is not based on insider authority, whether this authority is that of the orientalist scholar or of the native claiming an essentialist proprietorship on visceral grounds. Both appear to be superseded by the larger analytic structure derived from the common experience of colonisation. Such an analytic structure, which I have argued is post-structuralist in conception, inevitably involves a challenge to ideas of truth, authenticity or even a cultural identity that is located in *place*. But because postcolonial sites its readings of non-European texts at the encounter of Europe and the native, it fails to avoid the seductions implicit in such a generalised synthesis, precisely the argument put forward so effectively by Karin Barber. The emphasis then falls on incommensurable difference between the European and the native, and in the process the fragmentations of the colonised culture recede into unimportance, into a kind of necessary detail to the larger issue. The critical literary discourse of non-European cultures as it is institutionalised in Western institutions by such terms as postcolonial, is also a way of avoiding having detailed knowledge of those cultures, and ultimately to seem to be suggesting that those cultures do not have a particularity.

The objection to such a conception of culture is that it is a colonised one, one derived from colonial mapping of the world as the West and the Rest. Let me give an example. One of the myths of colonial construction is the homogeneity of the colonised territory and its natives, simultaneously with their complex unknowability except by the initiated coloniser, who can only seek to know their difference disparagingly and instrumentally. By accepting this myth of homogeneity . . . the colonised writer implicitly, where it suits other agendas, observes the same homogeneity. So Nigerian writing in English says little or nothing of the North of Nigeria, except to endorse colonial tropes of semi-oriental vapidity and despotism. For example, in Soyinka's *Season of Anomy*, the North is there only to figure as the Underworld of violence and bizarre sexual indulgence into which his Orpheus-like hero will descend to rescue his Eurydice. Also, Ngugi's account of Kenyan history is the dispossession of the Gikuyu, and their eternal contest with the land-grabbing European settler. Present in both these accounts are structures which originate in the historical accounts which were constructed by an imperial discourse. On the one hand, in the case of Nigeria, it was imperial construction that saw the Muslim North as an oriental despotism, although not without a kind of back-handed admiration of one stern administrator for another though less efficient one. On the other hand, in the case of Kenya, imperial concerns could only focus on the consequences of European settlement in Kenya. These accounts, then, as they are taken up and elaborated on by Soyinka and Ngugi to their contrasting agendas, do not contradict the regional integrity given to them by colonising discourse.

I come from Zanzibar, and the history of the colonisation of East Africa in the 1890s sees European intervention as a benign deliverance of Africans from Arab slavers. As a result, the decline of the coast is seen as a 'national' response of the now liberated nation – the expulsion of alien invaders. This is now the authoritative account, despite the impossible construction of nation in retrospect, an impossibility tolerated in other colonial-constructed territories and their nominal histories and cultures. In the case of Zanzibar, this account has now been internalised or naturalised into history, but it was not one which ever even felt complete.

Let me develop this notion with an example. In Kiswahili, the word for culture or cultural accomplishment used to be *ustaarabu*, the way of the Arabs. It is a dramatic expression of a consciousness of culture as something that can be represented by a principal authority. It reflects the hegemony of Arab Islam over the hierarchy of values which had been internalised into and then represented in language. Its agents were not, of course, Arabs them-selves. If they were, *ustaarabu* would be a term to express crude cultural domination and self-valorisation, and no doubt it had utility in this sense in a parochial and rigid understanding of the historical relations between Arabia and the east coast of Africa. For first-language speakers of Kiswahili, especially in the period before independence, the slippages in what the term signifies would not have been problematic, on the whole, but would have been a dimension of its plenitude, in the sense of its capacity to evade precise definition. Even such a permissive sense of plenitude still implies an originary and coherent and infinite myth of reference, but it is precisely because of this diffusion that a term like *ustaarabu* refuses a concrete reading, and as with similar words, is liable to capture in order to endorse cultural hierarchies. It had certainly exceeded its literal sense by the time I refer to here, though this is not to say that 'the way of the Arabs' did not signify the highest forms of refinement and accomplishment in someone's cultural vocabulary. For example, *mstaarabu*, which is the personal form of the abstract term, might have referred to someone who spoke with a certain flourish and command of language, to someone who observed social etiquette with punctiliousness, just as much as it might have referred to someone who demonstrated a concern for the welfare of others or who had a reputation for honesty and reliability. It is clear then that *ustaarabu* was a privileged term comparable to *civilised* in English, and equally as flexible in its capacity for extension.

This is not to suggest that either of these two terms are innocent and open-ended, as the examples above no doubt demonstrate. The very use of these terms to refer to cultural practice implies the opposite, that there exists a consensus, at times rational at others visceral, about what constitutes them in application. My interest in these terms here is not in their capacity to describe representations of such practices accurately, but in the sense that they are expressions of self-perception, or what in a loose and popular sense is sometimes described as identity. I shall stay with 'identity' for the time being, despite the obvious problems with the implication of essence and uniqueness which the abstraction implies, a limitation which is a familiar hazard when we talk about culture.

I have spoken of *ustaarabu* as the Kiswahili word for culture in the past tense, as if it is no longer used to mean that. So what has changed? In varying degrees, the campaign for independence in East Africa polarised on arguments of ancestral ownership and alien usurpation of rights to the land. By *rights*, I mean the right *to*: to make the laws, police the citizens, plan strategies of change, admit and expel and so on. I distinguish here between anti-colonial resistance movements, which in retrospect seem desperate and vain attempts to prevent the inevitable, and the campaign for *rights* which largely characterised independence movements in Africa. Clearly, in a context where culture is already valorised as suppressed identity, as the denial of the expression of the full self, to cite it as 'the way' of the oppressing alien is inconceivable, despite the ambivalences I mentioned earlier. When it came to the campaign for independence in the 1950s, the politics of Zanzibar polarised along 'racial' lines. One of the parties, the Afro-Shirazi Party, saw itself as representing the oppressed and dispossessed natives against aliens and Arabs. Since this party triumphed with its *coup-d'etat* in 1964, the expulsion of *ustaarabu* was both a linguistic as well a general priority. In this context, the ambivalent dimensions of the term were secondary to the larger symbolism of expelling emblems of alien domination. To some extent, then, by independence or soon after, *ustaarabu* had become implicated in a reinterpretation of history and identity, and its deliberate obsolescence was a refusal of the principal authority it apparently proposes.

What has all this to do with postcolonial theory? Apparently nothing. The inattentiveness of postcolonial analysis to particularities of the fragmentations within colonised cultures is to do with its emphasis on their encounter with European colonialism above all. The inattention to the fragmentations within these cultures, which are of profound consequence in any understanding of their cultural products, and most of them far more spectacular than the example I gave of little Zanzibar, are most clearly evidenced in the complete lack of interest in writing in native languages. The very detail with which such writing would speak of the competing relations within the cultural hotch-potch of colonised territories, would complicate the otherwise coherent and homogenous narrative of postcolonialism. In this respect, postcolonial theory is a triumph of the imagination over a more problematic reality, and the postcolonial writer, shed of her or his complicating difference, comes into being.

If the encounter with European colonialism is the defining category for speaking about culture, as it would be if we were to take postcolonial to derive from a common historical experience of colonisation, then the particularities of this encounter are critical in order to evade the homogenising and ahistorical narratives of difference which brought the colonised into being. That the critical category postcolonial falls far short of this, and is inclined in the opposite direction, is inclined towards the production of homogenised ahistorical narratives, means that as method it falls far short of theory, however determinate its mode of pronouncement. It still seems to me a method worth having, for the reasons I discussed earlier and because of the way postcoional analysis has opened up texts in a way that the more culturally contextualised accounts are not interested in doing, especially since so much contemporary writing thematises dislocation and estrangement. But it is a method we can make best use of if we remain clear about its provisionality and the limitations of its scope as a mode of enquiry.

Notes

1 Appiah 1991, 336–57.
2 'It was by assembling a monstrous machinery of description – of our bodies, our speech acts, our habitats, our conflicts and desires, our politics, our socialities and sexualities, in fields as various as ethnology, fiction, photography, linguistics, political science – that those discourses were able to classify and ideologically master colonial subjects, enabling the transformation of descriptively verifiable multiplicity and difference into the ideologically felt hierarchy of value' (Ahmad 1992, 182). Ahmad is on his way to offering yet another ferocious critique of the postcolonial intellectual at this point, but as the quotation indicates, he is just as aware of the totalising nature of the discourse of imperialism and is just as keen to reject it.
3 Ashcroft et al. 1989, 187 (quoted in Barber 1995, 6).

Works cited

Ahmad, Aijaz 1992. In Theory, London: Verso.
Appiah, Kwame 1991. 'Is the Post- in Postmodernism the Post- in Postcolonial?', Critical Inquiry, Vol. 17, No. 2 (Winter), 336–57.
Ashcroft, B., Griffiths, Gareth and Tiffin, Helen eds 1989. The Empire Writes Back: Theory and Practice in Post-colonial Literatures, London: Routledge.
—— eds 1995. The Post-Colonial Studies Reader, London: Routledge.
Barber, Karin 1995. 'African Language Literature and Postcolonial Criticism', Research in African Literatures, Vol. 26, No. 4 (Winter), 3–30.
Bhabha, Homi 1994. The Location of Culture, London: Routledge.
Irele, Abiola 1995. 'Editor's Comments', Research in African Literatures, Vol. 26, No. 4 (Winter), 1–2.
Ngugi wa Thiong'o, 1987, Matagari, Oxford: Heinemann International.
Soyinka, Wole 1973. Season of Anomy, London: Rex Collings.

50 Abdulrazak Gurnah, An Idea of the Past (2002)

Gurnah, A., 'An Idea of the Past', *Moving Worlds*, 2.2, 2002, pp. 6, 13–17

For many people in Africa, European colonialism and its aftermath are urgent contemporary events. I want to put the emphasis here not so much on colonialism but on the contemporaneity of its consequences. I don't have to detail these consequences ... as I am sure you are aware of them in their complex manifestations. For many African states, though not for all, colonialism is the constitutive past and its significant present. What I mean is this: the states came into being as colonial administrative units and continued in an unchanged territorial form into independent states, often with the administrative machinery and its coercive instruments intact. Whereas it is possible, and even preferable, to administer a territory with a fragmented population, it is a nightmare to do so with the assumption that such a population constitutes a nation. The instruments of colonial rule were blunt and appropriate for keeping subject peoples politically disorganized and rivalrous; but, as the means of formulating an idea of nation, especially when resources, social infrastructure and expertise were limited, they could only lead to disaster.

We can anticipate that ideas of the past in such a context will be even more fiercely contested than they are ordinarily, because of the way they give legitimacy to claims of priority. [Let me give you an] example which I will ... expand on briefly. For sixty-seven years, until December 1963, Zanzibar was administered by the British. For a hundred years before that, it was an Omani colony, ruled at first from Oman and then by resident sultans of the same dynasty; the al Busaids. Before that it was briefly under the influence of the Portuguese medieval empire. And before that it was organized in small communities which ruled themselves, but which nonetheless were open to influence by others, both near and far. I grew up with these several narratives simultaneously. The primacy of British intervention in Zanzibar, and in Africa as a whole, and its beneficial effects was given to us in our colonial education. I remember my first History lesson in secondary school, which was taken by a Rhodesian of Danish descent, who for some reason was teaching school in Zanzibar. On the first page of our history books was a map of Africa in outline, with a dotted line separating North Africa from the rest. I can't remember the rubric that accompanied this map, but I remember the first question the teacher asked the class. He wanted us to explain why it was that Africa below this dotted line was uncivilized throughout the centuries until the arrival of the Europeans. I can't remember (again) the answer he provided us in the end. I think it had something to do with the Sahara, and impenetrable forests, and forbidding mountains. Perhaps the reason I don't remember his answer was that we did not believe we were uncivilized, and his question struck us as being quarrelsome merely.

Islam had been the dominant religion on the coast of East Africa for centuries before the arrival of the Europeans, and that and Omani rule had inserted us into another narrative, that of belonging to the great house of Islam, and its great achievements were also ours. This narrative and other popular narratives of trade and travel connected us to the great world. Yet another narrative, the founding myth of the original inhabitants of the coast from Lamu to Kilwa, has in it somewhere the arrival of a ship from Persia. In the way of myths, this event is always made more ancient in the telling, which is intended to add greater potency to the myth. People who describe themselves as the original indigenes of Zanzibar call themselves Shirazis, people of Shiraz. And in fact, when Karume formed the party which, he had intended, would contest for African rights, he called it the Afro-Shirazi Party, where Afro stood for people of migrant origin from the African mainland and Shirazi for the original inhabitants of the island.

The uprising in January 1964 was driven by a desire to remove Omani rule; and, successful as it was, it banished these competing but not contradictory narratives of the past, and inaugurated another of Omani colonialism and the primacy of African power. The latter was an idea impossible to establish without the use of extreme cruelty and oppression in such a hybrid society as Zanzibar then was, and still is. Nonetheless, the authorities understand that their ability to govern, in whatever slapdash fashion, depends on legitimizing its rule by possession of the past, and the reiteration of a mendacious narrative of unrelieved oppression under Omani rule. It is as if British colonialism did not happen.

When I first read Chinua Achebe's *Things Fall Apart* (1958) as a schoolboy, it was a million miles away from my experience, but I understood that I was to read it as if it was part of my experience. It is still very often read that way, particularly by schoolchildren, as a narrative about first encounter and its consequences. Similarly, when I read Ngugi at about the same time, I was required, and did not resist, to see the rural environment of those early novels as familiar and 'natural', when it was not. I remember we were encouraged to enter for a regional short story competition, and several of us wrote stories about village life and stealing chickens when our reality was as urban as could be imagined. Decolonization had heightened our idea of solidarity with 'Africa', and we understood that the appropriate way of reading such texts was as Africans who had that sense of progressive solidarity. Of course the texts invited such a reading because of the way they figured the past that was their subject. I can't believe that there is anybody left in the world who has not read *Things Fall Apart*, but in case anybody here hasn't, the events of that novel take place in the 1890s. The present time of Ngugi's *Weep Not, Child* (1964) is the approach of the Mau Mau uprising in the early 1950s, but its mythic time, which is crucial to the legitimacy of the uprising, is the early 1900s. So both these texts occupy, in an important sense, the same period of colonial encounter and in their narrative strategies, and their later, exegesis, offer this encounter as normative. In what ways did these texts invite a reading as archetypal African experiences? Not in the particular narrative drama, perhaps, but in the foregrounding of the encounter with Europe. There is little or no sign of African rivalries to obscure this encounter, and there is no possibility in these texts of confusion as to where our sympathies should lie. Ngugi's idea of the past, for example, is a celebration of oppression, and that celebration in itself is to be seen as a liberation. And his texts, especially later ones, allow no room for demur or reservation. What makes *A Grain of Wheat* (1967) his most interesting novel, I think, is that it allows room for ambivalence and doubt about the meaning of resistance and freedom. At least this was so until Ngugi revised the novel in 1987 to reflect the historical triumph of the oppressed.

When I started to write, and I think probably long before then, but writing made a resolution imperative, I understood that the idea of the past which had become the legitimate African narrative of our times, would require the silencing of other narratives that were necessary to my understanding of history and reality. These narratives, which were familiar to me and which allowed room for negotiation, what Walcott called 'the miracle of possibilities', were not available to me in texts such as *Things Fall Apart* and *Weep Not, Child*, even though it might be said that it was not their intention to provide them for me. I understood also that history, far from being a rational discourse, is successively rewritten and fought over to support a particular argument, and that, in order to write, you had to find a way through this competing babble. Writing operates in terms of its own procedures, not in terms of the procedures of history; and arrives at conclusions which it would be inappropriate to check by history. Writing can challenge history's idea of itself and reveal it as discourse, just as in its turn writing reveals itself as discursive. Why then argue with Armah's historical metaphor of Africa's past, and with Soyinka's championing of it as a prescription for self-knowledge? Because it deludes with an originary fantasy of order and tolerance that also requires compliance, and the only miracle it promises is an authoritarian one. And because it silences rather than gives room to other voices.

Controlling the past is a precondition of power. Power forgets the past and constructs a new one. This was as true of the colonizing project as it is of the new imperialism which we are now being told about as a way of rescuing Africa's 'pre-modern states' from themselves. And of course those states and their polity also construct new pasts. As Walter Benjamin said in his 'Theses on the Philosophy of History' (1955), warning us to be alert: 'Only that historian will have the gift of fanning the spark of hope in the past who is firmly convinced that *even the dead* will not be safe from the enemy if he wins.'[1] Ultimately we have to be resigned to the notion that the past will always be beyond our grasp, that in reading the past we are reading back from the present, and that at best we should resist the possibility of capture and paralysis.

Note

1 Walter Benjamin, 'Theses on the Philosophy of History', in *Illuminations*, trans. H. Zohn (London: Fontana Collins, 1977), p. 257.

PAT BARKER,
THE GHOST ROAD

These two reviews of *The Ghost Road* appeared in British broadsheet news-papers, before the judges' choice of novels for the Booker Prize shortlist was announced on 28 September 1995. Candice Rodd's review in the *Independent on Sunday* appeared on 10 September, on the eve of the novel's publication, and Harriet Patterson's appeared in the daily *Independent* on 23 September. Although both reviewers offer a positive response to Barker's novel, there are notable differences in the features they select for comment and in their overall judgements.

51.1 Candice Rodd, Spirits in Waiting (1995)

Rodd, C., 'Spirits in Waiting/Booker Nomination; *The Ghost Road* by Pat Barker', *Independent on Sunday*, 10 September, 1995

For a book of such dark brilliance, this third and final novel in Pat Barker's superb exploration of the First World War is conspicuously full of sunlight. Sometimes the sun is a bloody disc, pregnant with apocalyptic threat, but more often it's just the sun, twinkling with democratic indifference on the dead and soon-to-be-dead in the battlefields of France and on pink-skinned non-combatants at the English seaside. Nothing could better suit Barker's incisively ironical vision than that this mad, savage war should climax to the accompaniment of so much delightful weather.

The Ghost Road belongs to William Rivers and Billy Prior, two of the most complex and engaging figures from the earlier novels. Rivers was the real-life neurologist who spent the war treating shell-shocked and wounded British soldiers, when possible rendering them fit enough to have another opportunity to die for England. In *Regeneration* his star patient was the poet

Siegfried Sassoon. Prior is the (wholly fictional) young working-class officer – clever, enthusiastically bisexual – whose battle trauma Rivers tried to cure in *The Eye in the Door*. In that novel their edgy encounters led to a cautious and ambiguous mutual affection. Now, in the summer of 1918, a patched-up Prior is about to leave for his fourth tour of duty in the trenches.

The novel chiefly alternates between the diaries Prior writes while preparing for one of the last, most self-evidently suicidal British offensives of the campaign, and Rivers's recollections of a pre-war anthropological expeditions to Melanesia. Either of these extended meditations would alone be powerful stuff. In tandem, they echo and illuminate each other in ways that both wrench your heart and make the hairs on the back of your neck stand up. Barker has never tackled her themes – the nature of courage, kindness, cruelty and hypocrisy, what happens to minds at the lonely extremities of experience, what it means to be a man – with more rigour or cogency.

For Prior there is a brief, bucolic interlude in the ruined French countryside before he resumes his dual duties of mothering and brutality at the Front. (One of your men needs a new boot? Take one from a corpse, remembering to scrape out all remnants of the former owner.) Among the seasoned officers, most of them perfectly aware that the war is out of control, there's a terrible weary fatalism. Only the innocent new recruits and the top brass can afford to be sentimental. At a patriotic sing-song, fat mawkish tears roll down the cheeks of the fearsomely brave and bullish Colonel Marshall-of-the-Ten-Wounds, while Prior's new batman, an actor in civilian life, is much given to 'once-moring unto the breach at Agincourt during bayonet practice'.

The bitter realism of Prior and his peers in no way precludes heroism in battle, or pity either, though the fallen are soon out of mind. When even the living are only 'ghosts in the making' you have to 'economise on grief'.

In London, Rivers tends the other wreckage of the war: the officer whose guilt and horror make him smell putrefaction on his own body, the one whose hysteria – a term the victims resent for it implication of 'female' weakness – has paralysed his legs. Briefly feverish with Spanish flu (one of the book's few transparent formal devices), Rivers starts reliving his bizarre, revelatory Eddystone Island experiences.

Frightened but fascinated among people patently itching to get back to their now-banned favourite pastime of head-hunting (it was such fun), Rivers, his protective inhibitions for once peeled away, was privy to the awesome rituals by which the bloodthirsty islanders displayed their paradoxical reverence for life and their easy acceptance of the power of ghosts. They also had a matter-of-fact word for the condition of approaching death, of being beyond help. It's a condition that applies equally to the ghosts-in-waiting in Prior's French dugout and to Hallet, the so-recently idealistic boy now lying in Rivers's hospital with half his head shot away, gargling out a final bleak verdict – on war? on life? while his doubly uncomprehending family (they are civilians, they can never know) look on appalled.

If this is an uncompromising work, it's far from spare. As in the two earlier books, there is an unwavering commitment to vividly concrete (though never incidental) narrative detail, a lot of sly humour and an inspired and seamless welding of the real and imagined. Wilfred Owen appears memorably and so, in Rivers's recollections of childhood, does Lewis Carroll, a family friend. This famous admirer of little girls adored Rivers's sisters but disliked William and his brother, prompting the offended future student of human nature to stammer out one of the questions that haunts this book: What's wrong with boys?

The Ghost Road is a marvellous novel, not least for its tough, unself-important prose which nevertheless flexes effortlessly to encompass the narrative's many moods and voices. Here for instance is Prior, squaring up to catastrophe not long before the book's quietly stunning end: 'Patriotism honour courage vomit vomit vomit . . . I look around this cellar with the candles burning on the tables and our linked shadows leaping on the walls, and I realise there's another group of words that still mean something. Little words that trip through sentences unregarded: us, them, we, they, here, there. These are the words of power, and long after we're gone, they'll lie about in the language, like the unexploded grenades in these fields, and any one of them'll take your hand off.'

51.2 Harriet Patterson, Trench Trauma and Jungle Ghosts (1995)

Patterson, H., 'Trench Trauma and Jungle Ghosts: The Final Part of Pat Barker's War Trilogy Explores a Society with the Lid Off', *The Independent*, 23 September, 1995

This is the third part of Pat Barker's trilogy about the psychological effects of war, based on the experiences of the neurologist William Rivers who treated Siegfried Sassoon during the First World War. Sassoon doesn't appear in this book, although Wilfred Owen is shipped in for a cameo role; Barker returns instead to Rivers's fictional patient, Billy Prior.

The mental and emotional duress that war has inflicted on Prior move one stage further than events in the last book, *The Eye in the Door*: having coped with wounds, trench fever and a dual personality brought on by shell-shock, Prior now has to go back and fight. As an example of war trauma, he is a living lab experiment, a test-case for Rivers, who now watches to see how his therapy will hold up.

Prior is here to demonstrate widespread symptoms as well as individual problems: although homesick, he feels hopelessly alienated among civilians and returns to France with relief. He also has typical lost-youth syndrome – three tours to the front mean he has seen it all, done it all; he is ancient in comparison with the new recruits: 'A generation lasted six months, less than that on the Somme, barely twelve weeks. He was this boy's great-grandfather.'

So far this is familiar ground, but variation is provided by Rivers's other patients back at the hospital, who range right across the spectrum of nervous disorders. There's Moffet, who lost all movement in his legs at the first sound of the guns, and Wansbeck, who murdered a German prisoner and is now visited by his ghost together with the stench of decomposing flesh. To complicate Rivers's job, most of his patients also suffer form acute stiff upper lip with regard to the efficacy of psychotherapy – this is, after all, 80 years ago.

This is a potentially fascinating area, and one could read plenty more about these early theories and treatments; instead, Pat Barker spends a lot of time flashing back to Rivers's pre-war experience as an anthropologist living among headhunters. The fact that Rivers really did this does not automatically make these sequences congruous with the rest of the book, apart from the obvious parallel between Rivers and the local healer-witch-doctor. It all calls for a lot of emotional advance-and-retreat: once you are focused on the realities of trench-trauma it is difficult to find yourself suddenly in the middle of the bush inspecting tribal courtship rituals.

This said, Barker uses the primitive world as a comparison with what happens to a more 'civilised' society once war has blown the lid off. The tribal people are better equipped to deal with instinctive forces, being quite at home with the ghosts which cause Rivers's patients so much distress. Prior, hardly the loveable hero, does his level best to reverse the civilising process, breaking one sexual taboo after another as extreme conditions push his sadism to the fore, but he remains too much of a Western man to stick a bayonet in without feeling squeamish.

The Ghost Road is refreshingly free from bogus 'period' flavour, from farthing buns and cheery war songs. Facts and figures are kept at the minimum necessary to remind us that women under 30 can't vote or that homosexuality is punishable by imprisonment. Through the streetwise eyes of Billy Prior, the author presents a surprisingly unsentimental view of war.

The sensationalist possibilities for violence are not over-exploited, yet there are harrowing moments. One may feel that the suffering of the First World War is well-known by now; Pat Barker's startling evocation of what it did to people shows why books on the subject still need to be written.

52 Lorna Sage, Both Sides (1995)

Lorna Sage (1943–2001) was a literary critic and author. She taught at the University of East Anglia, where from 1994 she was Professor of English Literature, but also made time for a great deal of literary journalism. She had a special interest in women's writing, and in 1999 edited the *Cambridge Guide to Women's Writing in English*. Her review of *The Ghost Road* in the fortnightly *London Review of Books* is based on a thorough-going appreciation of Barker's work before and including the *Regeneration* trilogy. The essay-length format of *LRB* reviews allows her to explore the novel's themes and techniques in considerable depth.

Sage, L., 'Both Sides: The Ghost Road by Pat Barker', *London Review of Books*, 5 October, 1995, p. 9

The present novel completes Pat Barker's First World War trilogy. It ends just before the war itself ends, with the attempted crossing of the Sambre-Oise canal in which Wilfred Owen was killed. You can read it without having read *Regeneration* or *The Eye in the Door*, because these are novels that cover the same ground again, and again, like the battles their characters replay in memory and nightmares. This produces a powerfully ironic sense of imprisonment in the moment. Barker's strategy is pointedly different from that of most historical novels exploring the processes of change. Sequence and progress and narrative line have largely given way here to a palimpsest history. You cut rapidly from document to dream to memory to dialogue. Historical figures – Owen, Graves, Sassoon, the psychologist Rivers – mingle with invented ones like Prior, the working-class officer who is a kind of exemplary figure, with what one might call a palimpsest personality. The effect is of spread, not sequence. Nonetheless, revisiting the same material from book to book is a compulsive experience. In *The Ghost Road* the return to the front line gathers intensity from the fact that we've been here so often before in Rivers's patients' recovered memories of its horrors.

Rivers's methods as a psychologist, probing the memory, bringing the past back, have an obvious affinity with Barker's methods as a novelist – which is doubtless why she picked him out for a central role. It's Rivers who speculates that the reason the war has produced in men the hysterical

symptoms thought to belong to women is the enforced passivity of mecha-
nised, trench warfare. Barker also sees Rivers, with his stammer and his own
damaged memory, as someone who can turn the doctor-patient hierarchy
back on itself, turn the tables. Rivers was himself changed and divided by
the 'neurasthenic' men he set out to make whole. In this novel, helped out
by fever and Spanish flu, he is recovering his own memories of his pre-war
expedition to the Solomon Islands – when he realised for a dizzy moment,
then promptly forgot, that cultural standards were all relative. He saw
Europe and European assumptions from the 'wrong' side. In *Regeneration* he
recaptured that insight for the first time – 'a moment of the most *amazing*
freedom . . . we weren't the measure of all things . . . there was no measure.'
And in this novel it's replayed: 'the whole frame of social and moral rules
that keeps individuals imprisoned – and sane – collapsed, and for a moment
he was in the same position as these drifting, dispossessed people. A condition of absolute free fall.' This is how the palimpsest effect works, recalling
and repeating such 'moments', bringing far-flung and scattered materials
into a level present-tense focus.

In *The Ghost Road* Barker, a note tells us, is using material from Rivers's
unpublished notebooks on the Solomons – case-histories from the other side
of the world. Rivers's mental homelessness is, it turns out, what makes him
such a good therapist – 'his power over people, the power to heal, if you
like, springs directly from some wound or deformity in him.' These words
come from an invented document – Billy Prior's journal of his return to the
Front which is intercut and juxtaposed with the accounts of the doomed
Solomon Islanders. Fact and fiction collude with one another. Prior, indeed,
has now openly become what he quietly was all along, the author's surro-
gate. Sassoon, Graves, Owen, can't say for her what she wants, by definition,
since what she wants is the point of view of those whose words didn't get
into print. Prior is on both sides of nearly everything: working-class but an
officer, bisexual, and sick-but-well, since living such divisions is the most
honest option. Wilfred Owen is glimpsed out of the corner of Prior's eye.
Sassoon and Graves, who can live to tell the tale, have been left behind.
Solomon islanders and unhistoric soldiers acquire a borrowed reality by
existing in the same plane of vision as those 'real' people. Barker has often
written, and does again here, about class conflict. But it's her assault on the
class distinction between real and unreal that's most striking and disconcerting. Superficially, the effect is 'realistic'. Actually, though, there's a more
insidious suggestion of creeping unreality which is almost gothic, certainly
uncanny. Prior is distrusted by both his brother officers and his old radical
friends, one of whom, in *The Eye in the Door*, accuses him (probably rightly,
we never quite know) of betraying him to the authorities: 'It strikes me

you'd be a bloody good recruit, *for them* ... Officers' mess one night, back streets of Salford the next. Equally at home or ... equally *not* at home, in both.' Prior is a kind of class-traitor, but he's also from another angle, in his element, a native of no man's land:

> One of the ways in which he felt different from his brother officers, one of the many, was that *their* England was a pastoral place: fields, streams, wooded valleys ... They couldn't grasp that for him, and for the vast majority of the men, the Front, with its mechanisation, its reduction of the individual to a cog in the machine, its blasted landscape, was not a contrast with the life they'd known at home in Birmingham or Manchester ... but a nightmarish culmination. Equally at home in either.

Prior's ability to step outside himself this way sometimes slips over into full-blown alienation, Jekyll-and-Hyde style. But that doubleness is not Barker's point. It wasn't really Robert Louis Stevenson's either, perhaps – for poor old Jekyll speculates that the real horror he's discovered is not that he is two, but that he is legion, many, the anonymous masses are living inside him. Ugh! This is what Barker wants Prior to be, the one *and* the many.

In other words, she makes use of his equivocal status – a fictional character rubbing shoulders with real, historical people – to rub in a bitter message about the invisibility of most people's lives and deaths. Rivers's Solomon Islanders were perfectly real, but nothing more is known of them than what he chose to record (and never got around to publishing). His Melanesian opposite number, the witch doctor and shaman Njiru, who foresees the death of his beliefs, tells Rivers his secrets so that they can be carried off in words, and survive. The first-person written account that Prior is given in *The Ghost Road* had to be invented, because none of the natives of no man's land wrote about it in this spirit. Prior is her go-between, bridging fiction and non-fiction, the individual and the masses, the living and the dead. Like Jekyll he secretes multitudes, he is forever decomposing as a character, and that is why he is at the last only 'at home' at the Front.

Another officer, Manning, describes him as 'neither fish nor fowl nor good red herring. *Socially*. Sexually too.' Manning should know – he is one of Prior's pick-ups, a middle-class paterfamilias who just happens to have this masochistic thing about working-class men on the side. Prior lives with many more of his selves than men such as Manning can manage, and this means (again echoes of Stevenson) that he presages the death of a certain kind of solid individual. Not that he writes in a stream of consciousness, or psychobabble, or anything like that; his manner is rather stoic and 'factual'. But we're meant, I think, to understand that this sanity in the midst of the war's insanity is a sign of Prior's disintegration. Helms left behind him the other story that might have put him back together: his love for Sarah, the prospect of children. Instead in this novel his sexual encounters – just as graphically and exactly and lovingly described as those with Sarah – are casual and anonymous. There's an odd and telling thread of sexual imagery that captures the effect. Sarah's mother in a fit of folk wisdom early on warned her that she should be harder to get, because promiscuity in women disgusts men. 'No man likes to think he's sliding in on another's leavings.' But this, it turns out, is just what Prior does like to think. In Scarborough, waiting to embark, he goes home with a prostitute, and finds himself lying in a wet patch on the bed:

> Dotted here and there on the sheet were tiny coils of pubic hair. He wondered whose spunk he was lying in, whether he knew him, how carefully she'd washed afterwards. He groped in his mind for the appropriate feeling of disgust, and found excitement instead, no, more than that, the sober certainty of power.
>
> All the men who'd passed through, passed through Scarborough, through her, on their way to the Front . . . And how many of them dead?

This gives an additional frisson of suggestion to the title. The ghost road of wartime sex doesn't – as Prior's relation with Sarah might have done, in another world – enhance and fix your sense of who you are, instead it is yet another route to dissolution. Later on Prior sodomises an available youth in recaptured territory, and savours the sense that German soldiers have been there before.

Prior's bisexuality is, he's come to realise, his family heritage, the result in part of his identification with his mother's ambitions for him, and his rejection of his violent father. His father lives on in him, too, though, and it's tempting to imagine that somehow he has reconciled them in himself. But that is not what Barker thinks happens.

> Obviously his present attempt to understand his parents' marriage was more mature, more adult, more perceptive . . . it was also a lie: a way of claiming to be 'above the cattle'. And he was not above it, he was its product. *He* and *She* – elemental forces, almost devoid of personal characteristics – clawed each other in every cell of his body, and would do so until he died.

300

Putting yourself together ('more mature, more adult') is in this context a kind of offence against the others. Rivers's doubts about his own work in 'curing' neurasthenic casualties of the war run along the same lines. In persuading the mute to speak he's really silencing their protests. This seems to connect, for Barker, with the need to invent the disintegrated character of Prior: to have a figure who speaks in fiction, but didn't in fact, the kind of character born of the war, and largely lost and denied at its end. Speaking through Prior you call up ghosts, rather than exorcising them as psychiatry tried to do.

Death isn't final in the way it's usually made out to be. The novels dwell in memorably terrible detail on bodily mutilation (there's a chilling continuity between the tone in which sexual encounters are described, and that employed for bodies blown apart). In one flashback there's a bizarre and telling scene in which soldiers inured to death, and to the company of the dead, find themselves in a churchyard that's been shelled, so that bodies in the vaults are exposed. They find these bodies eerily fascinating – 'as if these people were *really* dead, and the corpses by the road weren't. Any more than we were really alive.' Those reborn in the war feel, it's suggested, unable ever to return home – whether because they expect to be killed in the next battle, or because to go back will mean erasing what they knew. 'We've all been home on leave and found home so foreign that we couldn't fit in.' The last and most strange permutation of Prior as fiction is Prior as ghost, the voice of the dead. The Solomon Islanders, Rivers recalls, were familiar with ghosts, they thought of the moribund as already dead, and of the dead as still in some ways living – and this is very much the territory this concluding book of the trilogy covers, eroding the boundary between death and life.

Indeed there's a real haunting to prove it. You realise how very misleading Barker's documentary strategy can be. She looks as though she's modestly immersing herself in the sources, whereas actually she is using them as a point of departure, to mark the boundaries she'll transgress. Though she hides her own narrative voice, the use of echoes and repetitions is ruthless and savagely consistent. She is one of fiction's most dedicated levellers – not the one but the many, and the many in one. (This is why – though you can indeed read each novel separately – you need all three to get the full effect.) There is a kind of horror or obscenity lurking in the way she breeds facts with fictions, rather like the scene in *The Ghost Road* where Prior, watching his men undress to bathe, is reminded of one of his favourite fantasies, 'being fully dressed with a naked lover': 'what I feel (apart from the obvious) is a great tenderness – the sort of tenderness that depends on being more powerful, and that is really, I suppose, just the acceptable face of sadism.'

Barker suggests that what makes Rivers a healer is his own deformity; his Solomon Islands opposite number actually has a hump. Prior is qualified for his role precisely by his lack of moral coherence. He's a way of displacing the power of hindsight, and the authorial power of the overview – a way of dissolving the one of the writer into the many of the written-about, in the end. But it's nothing to do with passivity, or reverence for the traditional real.

53 A. S. Byatt, Fathers (2001)

A(ntonia) S. Byatt (b.1936) is a writer and critic with an international reputation. She taught for some years in the Extra-Mural Department at the University of London and later became a full-time Lecturer in English and American Literature at University College, London. She travels widely overseas, often lecturing for the British Council, and the extracts below are from an essay based on a lecture originally given in the USA in 1999. She has a high public profile in British literary culture, having been at various times Chairman of the Society of Authors, a member of the British Council's Literature Advisory Panel, and judge for several literary prizes, including the Booker Prize. She won the Booker Prize herself in 1990 with *Possession: A Romance*. Her essay 'Fathers' takes the idea of literary prizes as its starting-point before going on to explore the theme of war in a range of twentieth-century novels, including Barker's trilogy.

Byatt, A. S., 'Fathers', in *On Histories and Stories: Selected Essays*, London: Vintage, 2001, pp. 9–13; 26–32

During my working life as a writer, the historical novel has been frowned on, and disapproved of, both by academic critics and by reviewers. In the 1950s the word 'escapism' was enough to dismiss it, and the idea conjured up cloaks, daggers, crinolined ladies, ripped bodices, sailing ships in bloody battles. It can also be dismissed as 'pastoral'. My sister, Margaret Drabble, in an address to the American Academy of Arts and Letters, spoke out against the 'nostalgia/heritage/fancy dress/costume drama industry'. She believes passionately that it is the novelist's duty to write about the present, to confront an age which is 'ugly, incomprehensible, and subject to rapid mutations'. This is largely the position of reviewers of shortlists for literary prizes, who ask disapprovingly, 'Where are the serious depictions of the contemporary life?' These essays are not an answer to those reasonable questions, though I think it can be argued that the 'historical' novel has proved more durable, in my lifetime, than many urgent fictive confrontations of immediate contemporary reality. I think it is worth looking at the sudden flowering of the historical novel in Britain, the variety of its forms and subjects, the literary energy and real inventiveness that has gone into it. I want to ask, why has history become imaginable and important again? Why are these books *not* costume drama or nostalgia?

The renaissance of the historical novel has coincided with a complex self-consciousness about the writing of history itself. Hayden White begins his book about history and narrative with a quotation from Roland Barthes, who said that 'narrative is simply there, like life itself . . . international, trans-historical, transcultural'. White is interested in the refusal of narrative by contemporary historians, who are sensitive to the selective, ideological shapes produced by the narrator, the narrator's designs and beliefs. Historians like Simon Schama have recently made very deliberate attempts to restore narration, and a visible narrator, to history. Schama's *Dead Certainties (Unwarranted Speculations)* appeared after his best-selling histories of the Dutch Golden Age and the French Revolution. It was characterised as a 'novel' and was in fact a patchwork of interrelated histories – the death of James Wolfe at the battle of Quebec in 1759 and the 1849 murder in Boston of George Parkman, the historian, whose nephew was to write Wolfe's biography. In this factual fiction, which made many readers very uneasy and unsettled, Schama mixed his own inventions and speculations into the historical facts. Other writers, particularly biographers, have taken up such hybrid and selfconscious narrative devices. Peter Ackroyd, in his biography of Dickens, and D.J. Taylor in his biography of Thackeray, have inserted imaginary dialogues between subject and biographer. Richard Holmes invents a new form for each of his life-stories, beginning with the wonderful *Footsteps*, which connects Mary Wollstonecraft, Stevenson, the Shelleys and de Nerval, with tantalising and oblique revelations of Holmes's own autobiographical reasons for choosing these particular subjects to follow and imagine. My own short novel, *The Biographer's Tale*, is about these riddling links between autobiography, biography, fact and fiction (and lies). It follows a poststructuralist critic who decides to give up, and write a coherent life-story of one man, a great biographer. But all he finds are fragments of other random lives Linnaeus, Galton, Ibsen – overlapping human stories which make up the only available tale of the biographer. It is a tale of the lives of the dead which make up the imagined worlds of the living. It is a study of the aesthetics of inventing, or re-inventing, or combining real and imaginary human beings.

Beyond the serious, aesthetic and philosophical study of the forms of history in the last decade, lay a series of cultural prohibitions derived from intellectual beliefs about life as a cultural product. We cannot know the past, we are told – what we think we know is only our own projection of our own needs and preoccupations onto what we read and reconstruct. Ideology blinds. All interpretations are provisional, therefore any interpretation is as good as any other – truth is a meaningless concept, and all narratives select and distort. Hayden White is wise about the narrative energy Fredric Jameson's Marxist analysis of history derives from the narrative nature of the Marxist account of reality itself. 'The history of all hitherto existing society is the history of class struggle . . .' Jameson says. Marxism is a master narrative whose amplitude allows us to 'unite all the individual stories of societies, groups and cultures into a single great story', White comments. He quotes Jameson on modern life as 'a single great collective story . . . the collective struggle to wrest a realm of Freedom from a realm of Necessity . . . vital episodes in a single vast unfinished *plot* . . .'

I think the fact that we have in some sense been forbidden to think about history is one reason why so many novelists have taken to it. The sense of a new possibility of narrative energy, as I said, is another. Recent historical novels cover almost every time, from the Neanderthal to the Second World War, from mediaeval monks to nineteenth-century scientists, from Restoration beaux to French revolutionaries. It could be argued that the novelists are trying to find historical paradigms for contemporary situations – Rose Tremain has said that she sees the England of the restoration of Charles II as an analogy for Thatcher's Britain, and novels about the French Revolution, may have something to say about the revolutionary atmosphere of the 1960s. It may be argued that we cannot understand the present if we do not understand the past that preceded and produced it. This is certainly true of the war novels I shall discuss in this essay. But there are other, less solid reasons, amongst them the aesthetic need to write coloured and metaphorical language, to keep past literatures alive and singing, connecting the pleasure of writing to the pleasure of reading.

One very powerful impulse towards the writing of historical novels has been the political desire to write the histories of the marginalised, the forgotten, the unrecorded. In Britain this has included the histories of blacks and women, and the whole flourishing and brilliant culture of the post-colonial novel, from Rushdie's India and Pakistan, through Caryl Phillips's novel of slavery, *Cambridge*, and Timothy Mo's account of Hong Kong and opium, *An Insular Possession*. I am not going to discuss these novels, because they are already the subject of much scholarship, and also because I want to complicate the impression everyone has, that the main energies of modern British writing come from what the South African Christopher Hope calls 'writers from elsewhere'. I think the existence of these often polemical revisionist tales has given other British writers the impulse to range further historically and geographically than the immediately post-war social realists. But I also think that exciting things were going on anyway, in the work of Anthony Burgess, William Golding, and others, who were neither moribund nor insular.

This first essay is about narratives of war, or about war. I became interested in this subject partly because I became interested in the slippage between personal histories and social or national histories. I began to write a novel called *The Virgin in the Garden* in the 1960s. Part of the impulse behind it was that I felt that I had now lived long enough to have lived in something I experienced as 'history', and this was a great relief to me, as I didn't want to write personal novels about the constitution of the Self, and yet as a beginning novelist I had no other subject-matter I could claim. I was born in 1936, and lived through the war and its aftermath, though hardly conscious of much of it. My novel was about what was called the new Elizabethan Age, and carried with it the ghost of the first Elizabethan Age, with its English literature of the Golden Age. Part III of the projected quartet of which that novel, with its images of history was the first, appeared only in 1996 although it was set in 1968, which meant that I was doing historical research on things I had in some sense lived through. And this sense of the edge between lived and imagined history made me in turn interested in a group of novels by young men – Graham Swift, Julian Barnes, Ian McEwan, Martin Amis – about the war they were too young to have experienced, their fathers' war. I was interested in images they had fabricated that didn't quite ring true in my experience (but I was a small child, then). I was interested in how their selection of subject-matter did and didn't coincide with that of the older generation who had lived and fought in the war, my own father's generation, Henry Green, Evelyn Waugh, Burgess, Golding. I was interested in narratives written during that historical cataclysm when its end was not known, histories without hindsight or foresight.

[. . .]

Much more interesting is Graham Swift's bleak and schematic little book, *Shuttlecock*, whose subtitle is 'a psychological thriller'. The hero of this is employed in a government department that investigates and deals with the records of past crimes. His office is reminiscent of those inhabited by the heroes of le Carré and Deighton, crossed with a Kafkaesque aimlessness. He begins his narration by telling how he was driven to torture his hamster; it later turns out that his sex-life consists of ever more ingenious and tortuous painful scenes. His father was dropped behind enemy lines in France as an agent, was captured and tortured and escaped. The father wrote a best-selling account of his heroism, under the title of *Shuttlecock*, which was his code-name, a figure for a man on the end of a parachute. The narrator is now obsessively reading and rereading the book. The father is speechless and motionless in a mental hospital. His breakdown may have something to do with the fact that his son's superior is investigating his files. It is possible that he did not remain heroically silent – that he betrayed his friends and collaborators. It is possible that his autobiography is a fiction, designed to impress his son. The narrator tortures, beats up, terrifies his sons, whom he accuses of stealing his father's book. Salvation comes when he decides to cast off the whole tangle, not to visit his father, to make innocent love to his wife and take his sons for a walk on the common, as an ordinary pater-familias. The story analyses the guilt of those born too late for heroism, and also the obsession with the images of the immediate past.

Julian Barnes's *Staring at the Sun* has the same deliberately restricted world. It tells the tale of Jean Serjeant, a very ordinary girl, who is born before the war, gets married, has a son, and is an old woman in 2020. The novel, in which little happens, is a meditation on life, death, and the impossibility of immortality. Its central image is that of the opening pages, in which a Spitfire pilot called Prosser, in 1941, comes back from the French coast and dives so steeply that he sees the sun rise twice

> the same sun coming up from the same place across the same sea. Once more, Prosser put aside caution and just watched: the orange globe, the yellow bar, the horizon's shelf, the serene air, and the smooth weightless lift of the sun as it rose from the waves for the second time that morning. It was an ordinary miracle he would never forget.

The idea that Barnes relates to this 'ordinary miracle' is that of La Rochefoucauld, 'Le soleil ni la mort ne se peuvent regarder fixement.' The sun rising is simply life; the Spitfire is in a sense death, or at least mortality. Prosser has lost his nerve in fire. Jean's son, Gregory makes balsa-wood aeroplanes. Jean, watching him, makes images in her head of his future, of the relations of the generations.

> They stand on our shoulders, she thought, and with the added height, they can see farther. They can also, from up there, look back at the path we have taken, and avoid making the mistakes we did. We are handing something on to them – a torch, a relay baton, a burden. As we weaken, they grow strong: the young man carries the ancestor on his back and leads his own child by the hand.
>
> But she had also seen enough to doubt all this. These images appeared strong, but they were made only of balsa-wood and tissue-paper. As often as not the parent stands on the child's shoulders,

crushing it into the soft soil . . . And so Jean also wished for her son the negative things, the avoidances. May you avoid poverty, misery, disease. May you be unremarkable. May you do the best you can but not chase impossibilities . . . May you not get burnt, even once.

In later years she wondered if these wan ambitions had communicated themselves to Gregory.

The tone is sober, deliberately banal. Gregory's model planes are built to look at, not to fly. He is afraid of them crashing. He paints them in bright colours – 'a scarlet Hurricane, a purple Spitfire, an orange Messerschmitt and an emerald Zero' – 'with its joke colouring and silly yellow wheels it had ended up as no more than a child's toy'. But finally he makes a gold Vampire, which flies and crashes. Jean finds its engine in a hedge, and Gregory makes a metaphor of it as the soul, which 'might be superior to the body without being different from it as some people imagined. The soul might be made of a more durable material – aluminium as against balsa wood, say – but one which would eventually prove just as susceptible to time and space and gravity . . .'

Gregory goes into Life Insurance, and in the futuristic end of the novel, just before the aged Jean goes up to look twice at the sun herself, interrogates a computer about God and Immortality. We are now in a world of humane euthanasia and the possibility of needing to choose death. Gregory receives from the computer, amongst a lot of odd fragments of pseudo-wisdom, the remark of Kierkegaard's that is the epigraph to Part III of the novel – 'Immortality is no learned question.' This takes us back to the epigraph to the first part, a quotation from a letter of Olga Knipper to Chekhov – 'You ask me what life is? It is like asking what a carrot is. A carrot is a carrot, and nothing more is known.'

[. . .]

Related to *Shuttlecock* and to *Staring at the Sun* is a brief novel by Pat Barker, *The Man Who Wasn't There*. This is the story of twelve-year-old Colin whose mother is a waitress who dresses up as a fawn, and who does not know who his father is or was. Colin lives increasingly in a fantasy-world, constructed from films, of secret agents and torture and betrayal behind enemy lines in France. Like Gregory he spends his time constructing miniature bombers and fighters out of fragile balsawood. He creeps into cinemas, without paying, and recognises his mother's emotional account of his father's departure as part of the crew of a bomber that never came back, as simply the plot of the last film he saw. He is followed by a sinister man in black, who may be his father, or a child molester, or a phantasm. When he finally comes face to face with this figure late in the book – having had a fright when he discovered he was psychic at a séance – it is another version of the projected future, and he realises that the man is his future self, who has been unable to let go of the past, or the pain of the uncertainty of his father's identity. (He slowly comes to see that his mother *simply doesn't know* who his father was.) This novel, like the others, is about the necessity to let go of the past, including the heady fantasies of its violence and urgency. Cohn's war-daydreams are both a resource and a danger to him, like the father's book in *Shuttlecock*. They are also a formal exploration of the structure of his consciousness and anxieties – funny and sharp.

In this context I should like to look briefly at Barker's much more substantial war novels, the *Regeneration* trilogy, which go much further back in time, and recreate the world and the language of the First World War. I believe Barker's trilogy is much the best, and formally much the most interesting, of the flourishing and increasing number of novels about the First World War in Britain. In 1981 D.M. Thomas published *The White Hotel*, a phantasmagoric novel in many voices which recreated a Freudian analysis of a lost trauma, and also retold the horrors of Babi Yar, in words so derivative that – despite our sophistication, even then, about faction, postmodern quotation, 'framing' truth with fiction, or interweaving the two in the way I admire immensely in Peter Everett – it was accused of plagiarism, and felt to gain its chief shock from someone else's purloined text. But Thomas's bravura, and only partly successful use of the Freudian vision of the concealed and suppressed narratives of past shocks, made me see just how startling and formally inventive was Barker's decision to use the real army psychologist, W.H.R. Rivers as her central character – along with Siegfried Sassoon, the real poet, and Billy Prior, an invented officer risen from the northern working-class. Freud wrote *Beyond the Pleasure Principle* because he could not understand why shell-shocked soldiers dreamed repeatedly the horrors they had lived through – dreams for Freud, until then, had been wish-fulfilment. Dreams, re-presentations, either paralysed the patient, or made it possible for him to live through the repetitions and into a future self. Rivers cures the shell-shocked by taking them through their traumas until they can live with them – and then he sends them back to the Front, and the death many of them desire, with their men, as the only possible conclusion of the horror. Barker uses Prior to explore the enormous shifts and rifts in the structure of society, sexuality, and the psyche brought about by the war. She shows women empowered and rejuvenated by work, however dreadful. She shows men becoming bisexual, or revealing homosexuality they might have suppressed or hidden. She shows the inadequacy, of art with a quick description of a performance of Oscar Wilde's *Salome*, where the soldiers see the severed head of the Baptist not tragic or terrible, but simply grotesque and ludicrous – though Wilde's epicene Salome is much to the point in the lives of their world. I have not time to show the local precision of Barker's understanding of both people and larger issues – her story is told simply, and realistically, and the difficult sanity and responsibility of her adult men is a greater achievement than Thomas's erotic spillage of risky description. A German professor said to me that he had been told that the novels were 'simply about the ideology of the feminisation of society brought about by the war'. Barker can recognise ideology when she meets it, but it is not what she is doing – she has a true novelist's curiosity about whole people, thinking, feeling, and acting, with complex constraints of background, personal history and language. Indeed, I think that she found her great subject partly because she was a woman avoiding the constraints of prescribed feminist subject-matter. She is interested in men, she cares for and about men, and her book is about maleness, combativeness, the values of courage and the dangers of cruelty and violence. Rivers puts together the selves, the frail identities, of his soldiers, with love and respect, and then they die. The novel is haunted, not as the Second World War ones, including Barker's, are, by projections of the far future, but by the presence of returning ghosts, most of whom were sons who would not be fathers.

Freud's work, and Rivers's, is about the constitution of the Self, which was the great theme of the modernist novel. I believe that postmodern writers are returning to historical fiction because the idea of writing about the Self is felt to be worked out, or precarious, or because these writers are attracted by the idea that perhaps we have no such thing as an organic, discoverable, single Self. We are perhaps no more than a series of disjunct sense-impressions, remembered Incidents, shifting bits of knowledge, opinion, ideology and stock responses We like historical persons because they are unknowable, only partly available to the imagination, and we find this occluded quality attractive. After the disappearance of the Immortal Soul, the disappearance of the developed and coherent Self. Proust, Joyce and Mann were disintegrating their immense consciousnesses as fast as they, integrated them. We think we are like Olga Knipper's carrot. The joking, self-deprecating plainness of *Shuttlecock* and *Staring at the Sun* is to do with a sense of the diminished importance of the Self, which is no longer the battleground of cosmic forces of good and evil, honour, and betrayal, but a school for minor virtues – a little courage, a lost delicacy of human kindness.

INDEX